HAVE MERCY BABY

American Made Music Series

ADVISORY BOARD

David Evans, General Editor
Barry Jean Ancelet
Edward A. Berlin
Joyce J. Bolden
Rob Bowman
Curtis Ellison
William Ferris
John Edward Hasse
Kip Lornell
Bill Malone
Eddie S. Meadows
Manuel H. Peña
Wayne D. Shirley
Robert Walser

HAVE MERCY BABY

THE LIFE OF CLYDE MCPHATTER

STEVE BERGSMAN
FOREWORD BY RONALD ISLEY

UNIVERSITY PRESS OF MISSISSIPPI / JACKSON

The University Press of Mississippi is the scholarly publishing agency of
the Mississippi Institutions of Higher Learning: Alcorn State University,
Delta State University, Jackson State University, Mississippi State University,
Mississippi University for Women, Mississippi Valley State University,
University of Mississippi, and University of Southern Mississippi.

www.upress.state.ms.us

The University Press of Mississippi is a member
of the Association of University Presses.

Copyright © 2026 by University Press of Mississippi
All rights reserved
Manufactured in the United States of America

∞

Publisher: University Press of Mississippi, Jackson, USA
Authorised GPSR Safety Representative: Easy Access System Europe - Mustamäe tee 50, 10621 Tallinn, Estonia, gpsr.requests@easproject.com

Library of Congress Cataloging-in-Publication Data

Names: Bergsman, Steve author | Isley, Ronald author
Title: Have mercy baby : the life of Clyde McPhatter / Steve Bergsman, Ronald Isley.
Other titles: American made music series
Description: Jackson : University Press of Mississippi, 2026. |
Series: American made music series | Includes bibliographical references and index.
Identifiers: LCCN 2025045128 (print) | LCCN 2025045129 (ebook) |
ISBN 9781496854780 hardback | ISBN 9781496861283 trade paperback |
ISBN 9781496861290 epub | ISBN 9781496861306 epub |
ISBN 9781496861313 pdf | ISBN 9781496861320 pdf
Subjects: LCSH: McPhatter, Clyde | Drifters (Musical group) |
Singers—United States—Biography | Rhythm and blues music—History and criticism |
Doo-wop (Music)—History and criticism | LCGFT: Biographies.
Classification: LCC ML420.M341845 B47 2026 (print) |
LCC ML420.M341845 (ebook) | DDC 782.42164092 [B]—dc23/eng/20251125
LC record available at https://lccn.loc.gov/2025045128
LC ebook record available at https://lccn.loc.gov/2025045129

British Library Cataloging-in-Publication Data available

TO ADAM MOSS

CONTENTS

Foreword ix

CHAPTER ONE: Sixty Minute Man 3
CHAPTER TWO: I'd Be Satisfied 23
CHAPTER THREE: What'cha Gonna Do 30
CHAPTER FOUR: These Foolish Things (Remind Me of You) 38
CHAPTER FIVE: Money Honey 54
CHAPTER SIX: Such a Night 70
CHAPTER SEVEN: Bip Bam 83
CHAPTER EIGHT: Treasure of Love 95
CHAPTER NINE: Without Love (There Is Nothing) 111
CHAPTER TEN: A Lover's Question 137
CHAPTER ELEVEN: Lovey Dovey 148
CHAPTER TWELVE: There You Go 161
CHAPTER THIRTEEN: Lover Please 172
CHAPTER FOURTEEN: Crying Won't Help You Now 185
CHAPTER FIFTEEN: Deep In the Heart of Harlem 202

Honors and Awards 221
Selected Discography 223
Research and Acknowledgments 227
Notes 229
Index 247

FOREWORD

RONALD ISLEY

"You know you make me wanna SHOUT; kick my heels up and SHOUT; throw my hands up and SHOUT; throw my head back and SHOUT; come on now SHOUT."

If you were at a wedding or bar mitzvah party anytime over the last three or four decades, the deejay probably played the song "Shout." Not just the parents but even the teenagers would get up and yell, scream and whisper to the simple lyrics. Not bad for a song that came out in 1959 and although I remember it as big hit for my group, the Isley Brothers, in truth, it was a Top Ten hit for a different pack of singers, Joey Dee and the Starlighters. They, as the industry used to say, "covered" our record. The "our" in this case being the songwriters O'Kelly Isley Jr., Rudolph Isley, and me, Ronald Isley.

What was actually the first major hit for the Isley Brothers occurred in 1962 with a song called "Twist and Shout," but once again another band did better with the tune. The other group was called the Beatles; you may have heard of them.

All that was at the beginning of the Isley Brothers' career. By the time we scored with hits such as "This Old Heart of Mine" in 1966, "It's Your Thing" in 1969, "That Lady (Part 1)" in 1973 and "Fight the Power (Part 1) in 1975, we were frequent visitors to the pop charts.

The reason we got to the top of the record listings was due to one thing. The oldest Isley brothers, O'Kelly and Rudolph, who were young teenagers at the turn of the new decade 1950, had an infatuation with Clyde McPhatter, who was the lead singer of the Dominoes. I was born in 1941, so I was on the cusp of teenagerhood, but where my brothers went, so did I, and I was as much in adoration of Clyde McPhatter as they were. One might say the Isley Brothers traveled the road to success in the spit-shined, glossy black shoes of Clyde McPhatter.

There was an entertainment gene in our bodies. My father O'Kelly Isley Sr. had been a vaudeville performer and my mother was a music instructor at our church in the suburbs of Cincinnati, Ohio. I began singing with mother at two years of age. Everyone in the family could sing, so our parents organized O'Kelly Jr., Rudolph, and me as a gospel group called the Isley Brothers. We sang with many famous gospel singers including Clara Ward and The Ward Singers, but when we got older, we leaned more into the rhythm and blues that we heard on local radio stations. Our father saw the future for us, but he wanted us to be more like the Mills Brothers and Ink Spots, which were innovative, small vocal groups popular in the 1940s. They were by 1950 "old school" and the pioneers of a totally new sound were the Dominoes, with their fantastic lead singer Clyde McPhatter. The group had a major hit in 1951 with the innuendo-laden "Sixty Minute Man," but the real revolution began with "Have Mercy Baby," which was rock 'n' roll years before there was rock 'n' roll. My brothers and I knew every Dominoes' song, and we could mimic the Dominoes sound as well as anyone or any group in Cincinnati. Since my father always made my brothers take me along wherever they went, when the Dominoes came to Cincinnati, they had to take me to the show with them. Oh boy, we were even more impressed seeing them in person.

When Clyde left the Dominoes, we were literally broken-hearted. He was our hero. Over and over, we churned the question, "What's he going to do now?" Then he formed the Drifters, and the group's first record, "Money Honey," was a monster hit. We were saved, and the Isley Brothers kept going in Clyde's direction. I mean we would walk in every footprint that Clyde left behind. In later years, when we started turning out hits, we structured our career at that time to do what Clyde was doing, where he recorded, where he lived, and the people he talked to.

After Clyde McPhatter got drafted in 1952, the Drifters came to town. They heard about the local group called the Isley Brothers, and since I was the tenor, they asked me to sing for them. I mean, I patterned myself after Clyde, and they were intrigued, but I was too young at that time to perform in clubs. I also sang for Dinah Washington.

Eventually the next youngest brother after me, Vernon, joined the group, and we became a quartet. I was thirteen and he was eleven when he died in an automobile accident. My brothers and I decided to continue as a trio. By that time, we had conquered Cincinnati, winning all the contests and appearing on local television stations. When I turned fifteen, my brothers O'Kelly and Rudolph, Rudolph's wife Elaine, and I moved to New York. Since Clyde sang for Atlantic Records, that was our target, and we managed to wangle a tryout with the heads of the company, Ahmet Ertegun and Jerry Wexler. Then we proceeded to do everything wrong. Instead of doing a Clyde McPhatter song—and we knew them all inside and out—we opted for Nat King Cole's "Mona Lisa." We were so nervous we managed to sing the tune with each one of us in a different key. Ertegun and Wexler were kind about it but basically said, "Why don't you come back when you all get it together."

Our father passed away and we had to return to Cincinnati, but before leaving New York, the Isley Brothers recorded a couple of songs, "Angels Cried" and "The Cow Jumped Over the Moon," which became regional hits in the Cincinnati area.

We got a new, big-time agent who decided to hook us up with a woman singer, Arlene Harris; the grand idea was that we would mimic the very successful Platters, who sang with one female, Zola Taylor. We were called the Cousins. After gigs at the Howard Theater in Washington, DC, and Palace Theater in New York, we found ourselves at the Uptown Theater in Philadelphia. At that point, we decided to split from the woman singer and just be the Isley Brothers again. One of the songs we chose to sing was Jackie Wilson's big hit from 1958, "Lonely Teardrops." The audience was really engaged with the song, dancing and shouting along. I started yelling encouragement, "C'mon on, shout now," and the crowd went crazy. When we came back to New York, we told our producers Hugo (Peretti) and Luigi (Creatore), who were major players (producing or writing such songs as "Twistin' the Night Away" for Sam Cooke, "The Lion Sleeps Tonight" for the Tokens, and "Can't Help Falling in Love" for Elvis Presley) about the Philadelphia show, and they said, "Why don't you all get some of your friends to come into the studio and create the same thing." We did, and the song was "Shout, Part 1," which was released in August 1959.

The song did so well, we were invited to join one of the big tours at the time, The Biggest Show of Stars for 1960. The headliner was Frankie Avalon, but for us the real star of that show was Clyde McPhatter, our childhood hero. (Other stars on the tour were Bobby Rydell, Johnny and the Hurricanes, the Crests, Freddy Cannon, Sammy Turner, Linda Laurie, Isley Brothers, Clovers, and Cliff Richard.) We all rode the bus on this monthlong tour, but Clyde had his own vehicle, a big ol' Chrysler. For the Black audience, Clyde McPhatter was the king, and the women went crazy over him. He didn't know it, but we, the Isley Brothers, were protective of him. If anything was going to happen to him, we would have jumped in front of the bus. Of course, we introduced ourselves to him and even sang along with him during the journey. He was amazed that we knew all his songs going back to the Dominoes years. He saw how much we admired him, and when the tour was all over, he invited us to visit him at his house in Englewood, New Jersey.

The Isley Brothers didn't drink or carouse. We saved our money from the tour, and when we did go visit Clyde, he said to us, "I'm going to introduce you to my real estate person who I bought this house from." We called that guy and ended up buying a house in Englewood on Liberty Road. Then when I got married, I got a house in Teaneck. We eventually bought a house for our mother, who lived with our two younger brothers, Ernest and Marvin. And, we purchased another house for my brother Rudolph and his wife. Now we were real neighbors. Sylvia Robinson of Micky and Sylvia fame lived right across the street from us. We knew her husband in Harlem before we knew her.

We were so enamored with Clyde we did whatever he did. He had this couch that went this way and that way. We found out where he bought it and acquired the same type of furniture. What he had, we wanted to have because we thought it would make us feel famous. Where he had his clothes made, we would have our clothes made. When it was time to get publicity photos taken, we used the same photographer, James Kriegsmann, as Clyde did.

Eventually, our career paths crisscrossed as we moved in opposite directions. In the 1960s, Clyde, who had been in the business for more than a decade, was no longer a hitmaker, while the Isley Brothers were just hitting their stride. By 1971, our younger brothers Ernie and Marvin officially joined the Isley Brothers, along with our brother-in-law Chris Jasper. We were now a sextet. Although Clyde said he admired us because we had our own band, he was feeling alienated from the music world. Late one night, one of my brothers was driving some friends through Englewood and passed Clyde's house. From the shadows, he hears Clyde's voice. My brother stops and Clyde, feeling aggrieved, yells to him, "Hey, you ain't comin' around to see me no more." There was really no call for that, so we just assumed he had been drinking, which had become a crutch for him.

We would never have turned our back on Clyde McPhatter. Early on, he was the one who said to us, "You guys are going to make it. You guys will be bigger than me."

How intertwined were our lives? The history of the Isley Brothers and Clyde McPhatter has remained interlaced even in death. Clyde McPhatter was buried in George Washington Memorial Park, Bergen County, New Jersey. My brothers O'Kelly, Rudolph, and Marvin are buried there as well, as is my mother.

Clyde McPhatter, we loved him more than anyone in the music business. To the Isley Brothers, he was our mentor.

Ronald Isley is the lead singer and founding member of the Isley Brothers, who were inducted into the Rock and Roll Hall of Fame in 1992. Ronald Isley was inducted into the Songwriters Hall of Fame in 2022, and the group received a Grammy Lifetime Achievement Award in 2014. The Isley Brothers are the only artist to have been listed on the *Billboard* pop charts in every decade since the 1950s. *Make Me Say It Again, Girl*, the most recent Isley Brothers album from 2022, is also the same name of the single from that album and features Beyoncé. It reached Top Ten and stayed on the charts for 8½ months. He continues to tour with his Brother Ernest Isley.

HAVE MERCY BABY

CHAPTER ONE

SIXTY MINUTE MAN

It's September, late summer, and the Orioles, naively and simply referred to as a "popular singing group" by the *Detroit Tribune*,[1] had been on the road throughout America before finally arriving at the Lyric Theater in Lexington, Kentucky. The five-person singing group led by Sonny Til (Earlington Tilghman) espoused the softest, most romantic side of rhythm and blues. Indeed, the Orioles first big hit, "It's Too Soon to Know," two years before in 1948, was a slow-crawl of romantic insecurity. "Does he love me, it's too soon to know; Can I believe him, when he tells me so."

The lush, dilatory train, from engine to caboose, was driven by the group's engineer, lead singer, and resident heartthrob, Sonny Til. Not the classic skinny boy, teen idol, Til was burly with a wide, engaging smile. He sported a thin, straight mustache, which looked good on his paunchy face. Like any good Black singer in the later 1940s, he kept his hair trimmed at the side and piled in curled waves at the top. The follicle tide atop may have given the appearance of ebb and flow but it would always stay in place. It was a look that would easily slide into the famed pompadour of the early 1950s. Indeed, one or two of the Orioles were already heading in that direction. All of them, as an individual or even together as the group, could melt ice cream in a January snowstorm.

As the lead singer, most affection was directed at Til, who drove Black female teenagers into a hot frenzy of expectation in the same way Frank Sinatra did with white teenagers a few years before and Elvis Presley would in the new decade. As writer Larry Birnbaum wrote, "Til's slightly tilted crooning drove young female fans to screaming, crying, fainting, hysteria"—or worse. Rowdy, raunchy crowds of young women would scream, "Ride my alley, Sonny! Ride my alley."[2]

Whew, it was hot in the Lyric Theater and the humidity hung in the air like stale cigarette smoke. It was a full crowd of teen boys and girls—lots of girls, all dressed to the nines with stiff dresses. If their shoulders weren't bare, dark stains moved out from under their arms. The boys grumbled nervously. The girls, many at their first concert, all jittery with expectation, grabbed at each other for support. The Orioles, who set their vulnerable hearts palpitating every time the young teens listened to the song, "It's Too Soon to Know," were here in Louisville, to appear on the stage right before them. Except for Sonny Til, the names were still unknown: Alexander Sharp, George Nelson, Johnny Reed, and Lloyd "Tommy" Gaither.

Then the dream-vision congealed; Gaither with his guitar and Reed with bass flanked the singers Til, Sharp, and Nelson. Nattily dressed in matching suits, white shirts, and wide ties, they were like cotton candy to the young ladies. The two musicians quickly readied as did the singers, bunched into two groups behind two microphones. Til led the group into their beautiful, unified sound. It was all too much for one antsy young lady—oh, those gorgeous guys right there in front of her. My goodness, she thought she could step out and touch them. And she did. Barely seconds into song, the young woman rushed onto the stage and embraced one of the singers before anyone knew what happened. There was an unexpected moment of shock not just on stage but in the audience as well. It didn't last long as a sudden, rising tide of ardent females swelled up like a tsunami and engulfed the stage. Suddenly, as the press reported, pandemonium reigned. Somehow the Orioles managed to tear themselves loose from their "female attackers," save the instruments, and rush to the safety of their backstage dressing rooms. Eventually security managed to clear the stage of pulsating, sweating females. About thirty minutes later, the young men of song deemed it was safe to sing once again, and the show resumed. The local press called it a near riot.[3]

Read any book about the history of popular music and the phenomenon of teenagers going gaga over a handsome, talented singer, especially from the 1940s into the 1960s, and it is all about the racial divide in Jim Crow America. Stories, press reports, legendary tales of teen idols, from Frank Sinatra to Johnnie Ray and Eddie Fisher to Elvis Presley, are all about white singers and white teenagers. However, music didn't stop at the color line. Black musicians in that segregated world had their own concert halls, juke joints, nightclubs, and increasingly independent music companies where they could record, and expanding time slots on radio stations where that music could be heard.

Jack Schiffman, whose family owned the Apollo Theater in Harlem, the most important "Negro entertainment" venue in America, once explained the Sonny Til joy ride: that he affected girls like an aphrodisiac and when he bent over the mic and leaned to one side, "sensuously gyrating his shoulders and caressing the air with his hands, girls would shriek."[4]

Black teens had their own idols and unbridled emotional attachments to singers. Teen hysteria happened in this other world as well, but if the mainstream press didn't report these happenings, then it was as if it never occurred—and history books made it so.

As America settled down after five years of World War II, teenagers, both Black and white, found they had more time to listen to music, and with the advent of universal television still a couple of years away, the most important deliverer of culture to even the poorest household was the radio.

If one listened closely in those years after World War II, the white world of music had opened the door slightly to a unique sound that was made popular by African American singers. The musical purveyance was performed by a combo of four or five singers. The musicianship was sparse, maybe one or two instruments. Replacing the massive swing orchestra hubbub was a unified vocal sound. This was neither jazz nor rhythm and blues, just popular music delivered simply. The stars of this sound were two groups, the Mills Brothers and Ink Spots, who skipped the old "race" record charts and traveled straight to the mainstream pop charts. While organizationally they were different, even with the swing orchestras removed, musically they offered a group harmony version of what the white singers were doing in the pop music world.

Teenagers have little patience, and even in the late 1940s music trends changed quickly. That Mills Brothers sound evolved from the barbershop quartet style to a lead singer with the other singers humming chords or occasionally singing along.

The real revolutionaries, or creators of a proto-doo-wop tonality, were led by two "bird" groups, the Ravens and the Orioles, both of which hit big in 1948. The Ravens' celebrated tune was "Ol' Man River," a bouncy, lively version of the old chestnut from Jerome Kern and Oscar Hammerstein III. This jazzy, not quite R&B version featured a bass singer, Jimmy "Ricky" Ricks, at forefront and a trio of background singers filling the space normally inhabited by instruments. The bass voice, popularized by Ricks, would become a standard in the doo-wop world to come.

Then there was the Orioles group with "It's Too Soon to Know." Both songs crossed over to the pop charts. In December 1948, *Billboard* magazine listed the "Records Most Played by Disk Jockeys," essentially the most popular songs on the radio. Amidst the stars of the day, including Benny Goodman, Kay Starr, Gene Autry, Bing Crosby, Frankie Laine, and Margaret Whiting, are the Orioles with "It's Too Soon to Know."[5]

As was the practice then and through the 1950s, when a song began to become popular, other record companies would rush out a different version of the same tune by one of its own stable of recording stars. This wasn't just a case of white performers covering a song initially recorded by a Black singer. Everyone came in on "It's Too Soon to Know," including the Ravens and Black songstresses Ella Fitzgerald and Dinah Washington.[6] The competition for a song that was originally recorded five years before was intense, and when it came to record reviews in the important trade publications, even *Billboard* tried not to play favorites. On September 4, 1948, its selection of songs that would most likely become hit records, included a joint review of Ella Fitzgerald's and the Orioles' offerings of "It's Too Soon to Know." The initial commentary, written in partial hipster talk, read: "The Orioles platter, first disk effort of small Natural label, serves to intro the quintet as well—a fine group of chanters [singers] with a strong tenor lead [Sonny Til]. Ditty [song], a pretty slow ballad, has also been waxed [recorded] by Ella Fitzgerald . . ."[7]

Ella was good, but the Orioles had the sound that was au courant, selling 750,000 records in the first three months, which is what could happen when a song by Black performers crossed over to the popular music stations.[8]

By the time of the Louisville concert, the Orioles, who before their hit record were singing for $125 a week, were earning $5,000 for a week's engagement at Baltimore's Royal Theater, one of the top venues on the chitlin circuit.[9] The group was at the top of its game, but unknown to it, the Orioles would suffer a steep decline in popularity as the group sound would evolve once more into a genre that would come to be called doo-wop. (In 1953, the Orioles would come back from the dead like Lazarus to perform its hallmark song, "Crying in the Chapel.")

The Ravens and the Orioles influenced the stream of popular music in two ways. The individual Orioles chose the name for its group to honor their hometown heroes, the baseball team Baltimore Orioles. Why Jimmy Ricks and gang decided on "Ravens" is unknown, although it has been speculated that Ricks's group was doing a bit of racial homage, as a raven's color is black. For many up-and-coming groups trying to emulate the success of the Orioles and Ravens it was only natural that some would choose other bird names, so when doo-wop began to dominate R&B in the 1950s, top groups, for example, included the Crows, Swallows, Robins, Flamingos, and Penguins.

More importantly, the Ravens and Orioles moved the needle away from the crooning style of singing still popular on white radio stations and more toward R&B. As author Arnold Shaw observed, the two groups produced a "blacker sound than their predecessors (Ink Spots and Mills Brothers)."[10]

As a 1976 *Rolling Stone* publication on the history of rock 'n' roll noted, by the end of the 1940s, the Ravens and Orioles had gained national stardom, at least among Black radio listeners; Jimmy Ricks (Ravens) virtually created the role of Mr. Bassman; the two groups added a slightly bluesier vocal tone and more prominent background parts; and Sonny Til, who carried on in the groove of the Ink Spots, added the wordless falsetto, "doing a kind of obbligato to the lead vocal." The magazine concluded that the pioneering groups like the Ravens and Orioles recorded many fast numbers and jive tunes done with a restrained, delicate touch, but by the early 1950s it all "sounded like pussyfeet." The review added, "The emerging boppers may have been as sentimental as their older sisters and brothers, when it came to the slow stuff at evening's end, but when they wanted to get it on, the Ravens' 'Ol' Man River' didn't quite fit the bill."[11]

What about the great Sonny Til, who set young African American girls' hearts aflutter? Time marches on, and so do teen idols. There was a new, much sexier star on the horizon—a young man named Clyde McPhatter, who was lead singer of a new group called the Dominoes. Musicologist Larry Birnbaum put it very bluntly: "One reason for the decline in the Orioles popularity was the rise of the Dominoes and their stratospherically pitched lead singer, Clyde McPhatter, who replaced Sonny Til as the foremost Black teen idol."[12]

In 1950, a quartet in Detroit called the Royals started making some noise, but the group didn't take off until Lawson Smith got drafted and was replaced by Hank Ballard. In 1951, they won amateur night at Detroit's Paradise Theater, which caught of the attention of Johnny Otis, who was a bandleader, songwriter, and even a roving talent scout for King Records, which, along with Atlantic and Chess, produced many of the country's R&B hit records.

"During that time (early 1950s) all the groups were sounding like Sonny Til and the Orioles," said Hank Ballard. "All this sweet, pretty stuff. I told my group, we needed to change the style if we wanted to get a hit. Then Johnny Otis came to town looking for a group to sing a slow ballad called "Every Beat of My Heart" (a 1961 hit for Gladys Knight and the Pips). He liked the way that we did it; Johnny Otis got us our contract with King Records."

The Royals changed their name to the Midnighters because there was already a popular group called the 5 Royales.

King boasted a number of good solo singers such as Little Willie John and Roy Brown, but after the Dominoes hit with "Sixty Minute Man," King realized it needed a group on the label that could pick up the pace. Ballard explained, "Billy Ward with Clyde McPhatter sang 'Have Mercy Baby' and 'Sixty Minute Man,' and that changed the tempo (of music). That's where I came in. Clyde McPhatter was my last idol."

The rapid glide by Clyde into the hearts and wallets of American teens can be attributed to a couple of factors, the most important being Clyde's range as a singer. While he is accurately labelled as a tenor, that doesn't quite explain his versatility, because he could stretch those top notes across a span, which is referred to as melismatic singing. Think of it this way. Commonly, in music each syllable of a lyric is matched to a single note. In melisma, the singer can hit that syllable while moving between more than one note in succession. The technique was often used in traditional gospel music.

Secondly, the enthusiastic Clyde, unlike the mostly stationary Sonny Til, could really push a tune, whether ballad or early rock 'n' roll. He was the embodiment of song, which, in itself, was very sexy. Again, to quote *Rolling Stone*, "few could sell a sexy song with the verve of . . . Clyde McPhatter."[13]

Or as *Jet* magazine recalled, when Clyde was lead tenor of the Dominoes, "teenagers used to go into hysterics."[14]

How popular was Clyde McPhatter? In 1965, as a solo performer and long after his teen idol years, Clyde issued an album called *Clyde McPhatter Live at the Apollo*. The album notes read, "The fact that Clyde McPhatter has hit it big with teenagers (hear them scream here) is, of course, of considerable consequence . . . when he pushes it through his rhythm and blues style, the kids dig and in digging they sometimes scream in delight or agony."

When Elvis was drafted, there were a lot of well-publicized tears and hand-wringing on the part of his female fans. When Clyde was drafted in 1954, before anyone even heard of Elvis, he hired two of his GI buddies to help him answer the more than 500 letters he received weekly from his female fans. The one thing PFC McPhatter didn't do while in the service was get engaged to the daughter of an air force officer.[15]

This didn't mean that the overtly sensual McPhatter abstained from the usual liaisons; he was just more coy about it. He had to be careful because some of those one-nighters may not have been with women. As singer Ruth Brown, who spent a weekend with Clyde, observed, "like everyone else, I heard rumors of his bisexuality."[16]

That was all music business gossip. To the outside world, to his fans, to his admirers, he was matinee idol handsome, heterosexual, and the center of attention in the hottest singing group, the Dominoes, at the turn of new decade, the 1950s.

The story of the Dominoes begins with the independent record companies Savoy and King, and a man who worked for both, Ralph Bass.

Born in the Bronx, New York, in 1911, Bass ended up toiling for Black and White Records, which was founded in 1943. Two years later, the company moved to Los Angeles and hired Ralph as recording director. With a sharp eye for talent, Bass grabbed Jack McVea, who headed the company's studio band, and convinced him to record the song "Open the Door, Richard." It was a huge hit, as was a tune by another talent he found, T-Bone Walker. The song was "Call It Stormy Monday," and it was a ray of sunshine. In 1948, Bass went over to Savoy Records, which was back on the East Coast in Newark, New Jersey. It was run by Herman Lubinsky, who had one of the worst reputations in the music industry for being tyrannical, parsimonious, and exploitive. Nevertheless, in the 1940s, he recorded Charlie Parker, Dexter Gordon, and Miles Davis. Non-mainstream Black artists found a home at Savoy—at least until that moment when they realized better contracts could be found at almost any other label.

Ralph Bass wasn't so much a jazz aficionado. His specialty was R&B and he recorded Brownie McGhee and Johnny Otis on the label. Bass hated Lubinsky, calling him "the cheapest motherfucker in the world," but that was not the reason he decided to leave Savoy. Lubinsky, in Ralph's telling, did him dirty and got him in trouble with his wife. What happened was, Bass was recording a couple of blues acts in Harlem when he got a call from his boss. Lubinsky told him there was party at the Baby Grand next to the Apollo that night which would be attended by the company's New York distributor and he would have to be there. Since the party wasn't going to start until midnight, Ralph told his wife not to expect him home until the wee, wee hours of the morning.

Ralph finally arrives back at his apartment about five or six in the morning and his wife is waiting for him. "Where were you," she wants to know. Ralph calmly explained that he had already gone through all this, that he was at a late party at the Baby Grand. His wife says, "No, you weren't. My brothers came to my house and I called Herman [Lubinsky] asking where you were and he said, 'I don't know where he is.'" So, his boss sent him to a late-night party and then told his wife that he didn't know where he was. Ralph was furious and decided to quit. He just didn't tell Lubinsky right away. After a couple of days, Lubinsky calls up Ralph, who was not at home. Instead, Ralph's wife answered the call. "Why isn't Ralph coming in?" he asked. She didn't know, so Lubinsky said to tell him he's fired.

The trouble was, Ralph was Lubinsky's R&B man and Lubinsky didn't have a backup. When Ralph finally showed up to get his last paycheck, Lubinsky grabbed him and said, "Aren't you coming in tomorrow?" Ralph got the last laugh, saying to Lubinsky, "No, you fired me."

Ralph could be insolent because he had another record company, Mercury, interested in him. Mercury was big and Bass asked for a written contract and production deal. The company's attorney met with Bass and told him, "I'm going to Europe, but everything looks good, so don't do anything for three weeks until I come back and we'll have contracts made."

Ralph didn't have deep savings and was a little worried about finances, so after a couple of weeks he hears that Syd Nathan was in town and wanted to meet with him.[17]

Syd Nathan, born in Cincinnati in 1903, opened his first record shop on West Fifth Street in his home town. Due to an off-handed business deal, he ended up with hundreds of non-pop music records, including hillbilly (country), western, and race (rhythm and blues) records. They sold well, but Nathan closed his shop and in 1939 opened a new store on Central Avenue in the city's Black neighborhood, where the rent was cheap. His mainstay offerings were blues, gospel, and to a lesser extent jazz records. Then once again, he swung a deal and ended up with a cartons of "hillbilly" (country and western) records, which also sold well because Cincinnati was right across the river from Kentucky, and that was popular music in that region.[18] According to the local Jewish newspaper, the *American Israelite*, Nathan's King Records was "the nation's largest country and western recording firm, with annual production of six million records."[19]

Nathan succeeded by staying out of the competitive pop record markets, focusing on "race" and "hillbilly" music. As an outgrowth of his retail business, he began recording musicians, first the country-western singers and then, after World War II, rhythm and blues, which was a genre of music that was beginning to steamroll across America. In 1947, Nathan issued his first rhythm and blues (still called "race") records, with such singers as Bullmoose Jackson and Wynonie Harris. He was successful so quickly that by the end of 1948, Nathan's King Records was the top-selling R&B label of the year.[20]

The R&B side of King had the potential to be even bigger, but, based in Cincinnati Nathan didn't have the opportunities to hear or meet up-and-coming singers and musicians. "Syd Nathan was a visionary," said singer, songwriter, and author Billy Vera. He was out there in Cincinnati so he was off the beaten path. He always lamented that after people tried the New York, Chicago or Los Angeles companies, they came to Cincinnati. "What did we get when they finally made it to my city," he whined, "we got the crap." But, in truth, he signed a lot of great acts.

In 1947, Nathan swung a deal to buy 51 percent of Deluxe Records, based in New Jersey. That partnership didn't work out so he acquired the 49 percent of the company he didn't own. That only made King's limitations more dire. Nathan needed someone with experience who could be his rhythm and blues czar. When he heard that Ralph Bass was free from Savoy Records, he made his move.

Nathan and Bass talked. Nathan, who would prove as unlikeable as Lubinsky, was at that moment hot to sign Ralph Bass, and Nathan gave him everything he was asking for including a production deal, the ability to establish a publishing firm under Bass's stewardship, and Nathan would create a new label for him called Federal, which would be focused on rhythm and blues. "In order to entice Ralph, Nathan said to him, 'I'll give you your own label and we will split ownership. I'll also give you your own publishing company that will also be owned by you and me,'" explained Vera. "The publishing company became Amro. It was a good deal for Ralph."[21]

Writer Jon Hartley Fox, who wrote a history of King Records, maintained that the Federal label had already been established a couple of months prior to Bass getting hired. Near the end of 1950, Nathan created Federal to record both hillbilly (country and western) and a "Rhythm, Blues and Spirituals Series."[22]

Billboard magazine clears up the confusion. A story from November 4, 1950, headlines "King Sets New Tag, 'Federal.'" The news article buried at the bottom of an interior page read, "Sid [Syd] Nathan, King Records prexy [president], at press time confirmed reports that he would put out a new label, probably to be named Federal. Nathan also stated he had signed a deal with Ralph Bass, whereby the latter would become artists and repertoire [A&R] executive for Federal. Bass, who has severed his connection with Herman Lubinsky's Savoy diskery [record company] . . . Federal will emphasize rhythm and blues material initially . . ."[23]

Once Ralph was on board with King, he got to work immediately. Already in his sights was a New York–based singing group called the Dominoes. Before the ink was dry on his own contract with Nathan, Bass signed the Dominoes to the company's new label, Federal Records. The Dominoes thus became the first act for Nathan's newest enterprise. There was no celebration because everyone seemed to be in a great hurry. Before November rolled into December, Bass had his new group in the recording studio.

Nick Tosches, one of the great writers about pop music in the late twentieth century, was a big fan of the Dominoes, who he called "brilliant" and the "classiest of the rock 'n' roll vocal groups." When Tosches decided to write about the group in his book *Unsung Heroes of Rock 'n' Roll: The Birth of Rock in the Wild Years Before Elvis*, he scribbled that the group was founded and managed by Billy Ward, who was born in Los Angeles in 1921.[24] Musicologists are not sure where Tosches got that information, because it is generally accepted that Ward (Robert Williams) was born September 19, 1921 (musicologist Marv Goldberg claims September 15, 1921), in Savannah, Georgia, and then grew up in Philadelphia.[25] His father was a preacher, mother a singer in the church choir, and he was set on a path to music at early age, eventually joining the family business, also singing in the choir and becoming the church organist. According to most stories on Ward, he was classically trained on the piano, was something of a prodigy, and at the age of fourteen won an award from famed composer Walter Damrosch for a piano piece he wrote.[26]

In 1942, at the age of twenty-one, with the United States in the world conflict, he was drafted into the army and rose to the rank of second lieutenant. It's here the mythology gets murky, as it is often reported he was Golden Gloves boxing champion, a notation that has appeared on many a curriculum vitae of African American singers in the 1950s, including Screamin' Jay Hawkins, although there is no proof such a thing ever happened. The name Robert Williams (the name change to Billy Ward happened in the later 1940s) does not appear on any list of Golden Gloves champions.

After the war, Ward was in New York to attend the Juilliard School of Music. He also became a voice coach. Early in his New York sojourn he met Rose

Marks, who ran either a Broadway advertising firm, talent agency, or both, but also had musical skills of her own. They began composing together, and Marv Goldberg reported the first copyrighted song by them was in 1946.[27] Like Mick Jagger and Keith Richards, Ward and Marks would jointly be listed as songwriters on all compositions they created together or singularly, starting with tunes sung by the Dominoes.

With the sudden rise of the Ravens and Orioles, Marks encouraged Ward to form his own group, so in 1948 Ward (under the sobriquet E. William Ward) began to advertise for young male singers to make up a quartette. It wasn't until two years later that the now renamed Billy Ward organized a racially mixed singing group, which, perhaps, because of the racial makeup of his singers, was called the Dominoes. The group fell apart quickly, so Ward formed an all-Black group, which he called the Ques. Ward was a strict disciplinarian and teenagers will be teenagers, so that group didn't work out either. Ward didn't let go of the idea. One night, he went to amateur night at the Apollo Theater and saw a performer called Clyde McPhatter take first place. Ward invited an unsure McPhatter to an audition, which took a little doing because McPhatter had been singing gospel, and, as Tosches noted, persuading him to join Billy Ward's worldly enterprise was not an easy task.[28]

Nevertheless, Ward was persuasive and fixated. Ward liked the high tenor voice of Bill Kenny of the Ink Spots, and his grand idea was to create a more modern version of that group structure. To do that he had to find a tenor that he could build a group around, and when he heard Clyde McPhatter, he knew he had found the right person. Ward resurrected the Ques, adding Joe Lamont as baritone, Bill Brown as bass, and Charlie White as second tenor (some musicologists list James Van Loan as the second tenor). What was unique about the formation of the Ques was that Ward was not officially part of the group, instead continuing his role as a co-manager with Marks, songwriter, and sometimes pianist for live appearances. Also, all the singers had come out of the gospel world and were inclined to sing in that style even when addressing popular or rhythm and blues music.

The new Ques first appeared in public at another Apollo Theater amateur night, where they took first prize. (Writer Arnold Shaw claims when the group to be eventually known as the Dominoes first appeared at the Apollo they sang opposite the Orioles, and their program embodied "raucous gospel/jubilee-styled material.")[29]

With the victory at the Apollo's amateur night, Rose Marks was able to get the Ques a slot on *Arthur Godfrey's Talent Scouts*. On October 23, 1950, the Ques won first prize singing a more spiritual-stylized version of the popular song "Goodnight Irene." After the win, Ward changed the name of the group to the Dominoes, an appellation he had used before.

Things get a little confusing at this point. According to Marv Goldberg, René Joseph Hall, an African American arranger working as a talent scout for King Records, saw the Ques perform on the Arthur Godfrey show and told Syd Nathan about them. Ralph Bass waved his finger back and forth at that assertion, claiming he discovered the Ques, soon to be the Dominoes, and that's how they came to be the first group signed to the Federal label. Billy Vera, who knew Clyde McPhatter in the 1960s, backs up Bass's averment.

René Joseph Hall, who became one of the most famous West Coast studio guitarists from the 1950s to the 1970s, was born in Morgan City, Louisiana, in 1912, and by the time he was in his twenties, he was working in New Orleans as a banjo player. In the early 1950s, he was passing time as a session musician in New York. Hall had heard the Dominoes on the Arthur Godfrey show and told Ralph about the singing group. Ralph trusted Hall's judgment and musicianship, and brought them around. He liked what he heard and quickly signed the Dominoes to his new label. According to Vera, Hall became the group's guitar player, which was really beneficial to what Billy Ward was trying to accomplish. "Hall played through his amp with a vibrato," said Vera. "On the Dominoes' records, you can hear the tremolo, which was Hall's signature sound."[30]

In later interviews, Ralph expounded on the signing of the Dominoes. Hall sent him a "dub" of the group. Bass listened listlessly. He initially told René Hall he couldn't use them because "they were singing some pop song. Billy Ward was writing pop music, not R&B. They didn't sound like a black group to me." Hall was persistent, so Bass told him to bring them around to the King Records office in New York.

Ward and Marks accompanied the group to see Bass. He listened to them. "The lead singer was legitimate," Bass recalled for an interviewer. "But I pointed to another cat in the group and said, 'Let me hear you sing lead.' When I heard him, Clyde McPhatter, I said, 'My God, there's your lead singer.' And when I heard the bass singer, Bill Brown, I said, 'There's your other lead singer.'"[31]

What happened next is a tale refined by time. In one interview, Bass said he told Ward to buy some R&B records and listen to them, adding, "You write songs like that and I'll sign you." Ward responded, "That's what you want? You got a deal."

Here's another version of the same tale. Ralph listened to Ward lead his group through the existing pop song universe. Ralph shook his head wearily and said to Billy Ward, "I need blues songs" and then proceeded to play him records as an example of what he was seeking. Ward responded, "I could write that shit all day."[32]

As it turned out, he could.

Ward's initial idea was to create a modern version of the Ink Spots. It didn't work out that way. What he ended up with was what author Charlie Gillett, back in 1970, said of the Dominoes, that they were "the first deliberate use of gospel-trained singers in 'secular music.'" To buttress his argument, Gillett quotes a prior interview with Clyde, who said, "We had patterned ourselves after the Ink Spots because I had such a high voice, but I just didn't believe in trying to sound like Bill Kenney (lead singer of Ink Spots) and that's how we started the gospel stuff."[33]

"Clyde couldn't sing a song straight," explained Vera. "He sang it the way he felt it, with that churchy feeling."

Ward, who was a toe-the-line guy, was smart enough to let the group determine the style of singing. When Ward was still dreaming of the Ink Spots in the first recording session, McPhatter said to him, "Well, I don't feel it that way," and Ward basically said to him, "OK, we'll try it your way."[34]

The experiment began right away because Ralph Bass ushered the Dominoes into the studio before the blink of an eye.

By mid-November, the singing group had recorded four songs: "Weeping Willow Blues," "No! Says My Heart," and for the group's first single, "Chicken Blues" and "Do Something for Me." The A-side was "Chicken Blues," a rollicking, double-entendre song fronted by bassman Bill Brown. It begins with a boogie piano followed by the other three Dominoes on chorus. Brown sings, "If you don't like chicken, leave that hen alone / she'll give you so much chicken you cannot do a thing but moan." About midway into the song, the structure loosens and Clyde screams in the background. Although it was a fun song, when the single was released in late December, and after all the holiday tunes faded away, the disc jockeys took to the B-side, "Do Something for Me."

They recognized something different was going on here. The lead singer, Clyde McPhatter, with his natural melismatic singing, bordered on the ecstatic. By mid-song, the other Dominoes filled with something close to a gospel-tinged chorus. Radio listeners and record buyers slowly began to realize the song was tight. It climbed to #6 on the R&B charts—a good start for the Dominoes, which was also the opinion of *Cash Box* magazine's unknown Los Angeles correspondent, who led off his January 20, 1951, column with these remarks: "Looks as if Syd Nathan picked a winner in Ralph Bass to handle the blues and rhythm A&R on the new Federal label . . . or so it would seem by the quick success won by the first Federal release, 'Do Something for Me' by the Dominoes."[35]

Ralph Bass had been in a hurry since he brought the Dominoes onto the Federal label so he induced the group to come back for two more quick-to-the-draw recording sessions including one on December 30, 1950. He liked the formula he used for the "Chicken Blues"/"Do Something for Me" record, where a bawdy fun tune was matched to a strong ballad. Before the year closed, the Dominoes recorded another Bill Brown–fronted ditty called "Sixty Minute

Man" along with Clyde McPhatter's deep dive into the 1937 standard, "Harbor Lights." Bass probably realized Clyde's "Harbor Lights," although a bit over-the-top, had hit potential, as did "Sixty Minute Man," so the two songs were released as separate singles in 1951.

At the start of the new decade, it was becoming obvious that one geographic node of R&B talent was not on the East Coast, but in South-Central Los Angeles. When he was still with Savoy, Bass decided to mine that location for talent. One of the acts he stumbled across was a thirteen-year-old singer who had won a bunch of talent contests at a movie theater on 103rd Street in Watts. He was doing a recording session with the Robins (members Carl Gardner and Bobby Nunn would form the Coasters in 1955) when he brought the girl, who would be known as Little Esther or Little Esther Phillips or Esther Phillips, in for an audition. One song Bass had Little Esther sing was "Double Crossing Blues" with the Robins backing her. Initially, Bass signed her to Savoy, but there were omissions in her contract, and when he went to Federal one of the first items on his agenda was to steal her away from Savoy for his new label.[36] This was big news for *Cash Box*, which on January 20, 1951, exclaimed: "Bursting into the jazz and blues picture with a spurt, officials of Federal Records, this week disclosed that they had signed Little Esther to a recording contract . . . Little Esther is due to arrive in Cincinnati sometime next week to make her first waxings [recordings] on the new label. The session will be under the direction of Ralph Bass."[37]

According to Marv Goldberg, in February 1951, Federal released a Dominoes song called "The Deacon Moves In," which is backed by Little Esther.[38] It went nowhere in the marketplace, which was odd for Little Esther, who could brag three #1 R&B hits the year before. As for the Dominoes, they were about to unleash "Sixty Minute Man," which would end up as the #1 R&B hit in 1951. It would stay atop the R&B charts for an astounding fourteen weeks. The song even jumped to the pop charts, rising as high as #17, which was a bit of a music miracle because most pop stations rarely played pure R&B and certainly not this tune, which was considered too salacious for mainstream radio listeners. The song was not so much the usual double-entendre blues cut because the lyrics were humorous and conspicuously sexual. Bill Brown, the group's bassman, took the lead on this number and he was smooth as a glass tabletop.

The song was all about Lovin' Dan, whose modus operandi was: "There'll be fifteen minutes of kissin', then you'll holler, 'Please don't stop!' / There'll be fifteen minutes of teasin' and fifteen minutes of squeezin' and fifteen minutes of blowin' my top." In 1951, one couldn't get more erotic on a record and still be heard on radio.

It's generally considered that Billy Ward wrote "Sixty Minute Man," although officially (probably contractually) he and Rose Marks are given credit for the song. Nevertheless, as with most blues numbers, the end song is usually a result of an evolution of tune-making. Musicologist Lary Birnbaum tracked down the origins of Lovin' Dan, the stud in the song who promised to "rock 'em, roll 'em, all night long." As Birnbaum discovered "Dan" had always been a busy dude in blues records from "Dapper Dan the Ladies Man from Dixie Land" in 1921 to "Dancin' Dan" in 1923 to "Hustlin' Dan" in 1930 to "Dan the Back Door Man" in 1936.[39]

"Sixty Minute Man" was released in March 1951. In September it was still the #1 R&B record played on jukeboxes around the country, which would be the equivalent of being the #1 streaming song in 2020s vernacular. It's not as if 1951 was a weak year for R&B. Among the classics from that year: "Teardrops from My Eyes" by Ruth Brown, "The Glory of Love" by the Five Keys, "Rocket 88" by Jackie Brenston, "Please Send Me Someone to Love" by Percy Mayfield, and "I Got Loaded" by Peppermint Harris.[40]

When 1951 came to an end, the Dominoes not only boasted the #1 R&B song of the year with "Sixty Minute Man," but also the #20 tune with "Do Something for Me." Federal also released "I Am with You" with "Weeping Willow Blues" on the B-side. It climbed as high as #8 on the R&B charts.

Around the third quarter of 1951, it suddenly occurred to the writers who followed R&B for *Billboard* magazine that the music world, as if in an earthquake, was shifting ground right under their feet. In a late September issue of the magazine, the "Rhythm and Blues Notes" column began with this declaration: "Vocal groups have taken command in the R&B field." The column went on to explain that never before in the industry, in regard to this particular genre, have so many groups taken such a deep hold both on recordings and in personal appearances. After giving a nod to the pioneering efforts of the Orioles and Ravens, the article observed almost a dozen other groups had sprung up, "most of them in the past six months." The first of the new groups mentioned was the Dominoes, followed by the Swallows, the Clovers, the Five Keys, the Cardinals, and the Four Buddies. The article concluded, "These vocal groups have taken the play in the R&B field away from the small instrumental groups and intimate solo blues singers, which held sway for some time."[41]

The music by these new groups would come to be called doo-wop and it was coming on strong, but the American music world was still segregated. In the dominant pop market, solo singers such as Tony Bennett, Mario Lanza, Perry Como, Frankie Laine, Tony Martin, and Guy Mitchell all boasted good years. Even the jazzy, African American soloists Nat King Cole and Billy Eckstine had big hits in the pop market.

Bass and Nathan made a couple of other corporate moves in 1951. Since they were doing so well outside of the pop music field with R&B, King Records decided to also go all in on another outlier genre, what it called folk and western (country and western). The other strategic change was to move Ralph Bass to Los Angeles so as to be able to tap into the talent goldmine of that city.[42]

By the end of 1951, Bass had released four records by the Dominoes: "Do Something for Me," "Sixty Minute Man," "I Am with You," and "Harbor Lights." Only the latter song sank without a trace.

"Sixty Minute Man," with its ribald lyrics, was an unusual song in many regards. To some critics it was a stereotypical minstrel song about a sexually obsessed Black man, while others, including musicologist Birnbaum, consider it a song ahead of its time. "Due to its beat, its bold sexuality, and its use of the words rock 'n' roll, 'Sixty Minute Man' was a signal smash that helped light the fuse for the rock 'n' roll explosion soon to come," wrote Birnbaum.[43]

The influential disc jockey Alan Freed began playing R&B on WJW in Cleveland in the summer of 1951. "Sixty Minute Man" would have been in heavy rotation on his show, which is why on January 23, 1952, the Dominoes were to appear at the Palace Theater in Ohio. A promotional ad, which appeared two days earlier in the *Daily Express* out of Dayton, screamed "The Dominoes" with a sub-header that read "Those Sixty Minute Men."[44] Even better, on March 21, 1952, in what is considered the first rock 'n' roll concert, Freed unleashed the Moondog Coronation Ball at the Cleveland Arena with Paul Williams and his Huckchbuckers, Tiny Grimes and His Rockin' Highlanders, Danny Cobb, Varetta Dillard, and the Dominoes. Tickets for this big show were $1.50. At some point before the concert 6,000 (perhaps as many as 20,000) teens crowded in front of the venue. When it looked like they were going to storm through the front doors, the Cleveland police panicked and shut down the concert.

What most people missed on the "Sixty Minute Man" record was the B-side tune, "I Can't Escape from You," a fine bluesy ballad with Clyde on the lead, that was closer to the real sound of the Dominoes. Billy Ward was a master talent at songwriting; he could easily shift from the novelty, humorous composition to pre–rock 'n' roll, but in his heart of hearts he adored a slow, romantic tune. "I Can't Escape from You" was straight-up a Dominoes standard.

In May 1952, the *Miami Times*, a newspaper for the local Black community, decided it would take a peek into the future with a list of new records that it expected to be hits. Among the notable selections was "Chloe-E" by the Ravens. Its review highlighted the use of the bass singer, which was once again important after "Sixty Minute Man." Another pick was Earl Bostic's "Linger Awhile." Bostic was a well-regarded saxman, who recorded for Syd Nathan's primary label, King. His most popular recording was "Flamingo" from 1951. The newspaper's final pick was "I Only Have Eyes for You" by the Swallows. Another standard, this one from 1934, got an interesting treatment here, but would become a big hit when another doo-wop group, the Flamingos, redid it in 1958. The *Miami Times* commentary said, "The Swallows have had several fine recordings but for some reason or another never have clicked. They might do it this time with their smooth rendition of 'Eyes.' Notice the similarity between them and the Dominoes."[45]

In 1952, if you intended to ape the sound of another group, then the optimum choice was definitely the Dominoes, who were peaking in popularity and recording excellence that year.

Working for an independent label such as King/Federal, Ralph Bass recognized he had limitations as to what he could or could not do. The big labels could flood a market with a half dozen records from one of their top stars, but Bass didn't have that option. Although the Dominoes were as big as could be in the R&B world, Bass could push out only four releases (or three according to some sources) and they were all good ones. "That's What You're Doing to Me" went to #7 on the R&B charts while "I'd Be Satisfied" pushed all the way to #4 on the same listing.

The real standout platter for the Dominoes in 1952 and probably the best record in the group's history was "Have Mercy Baby," which was on the R&B charts for twenty weeks, half that time sitting at #1. It's an important song because it was rock 'n' roll before there was rock 'n' roll. Musically, "Sixty Minute Man" wasn't rock 'n' roll, writer Robert Palmer explains: "It had a light, bouncy, jazz-related groove, and the only electric instrument was a trebly, discreetly amplified guitar. 'Rocket 88' (which came out in 1951 and is often called the first rock 'n' roll record) had a furious drive, heavily amplified guitar, and screaming saxophone solo . . . rocked out."

"Have Mercy Baby" begins with a honking saxophone and then Clyde quickly jumps in singing "Have mercy, mercy baby," with the rest of the Dominoes subtly in chorus. It's a song about a man seeking forgiveness for his dalliances. "Have mercy, mercy baby, I know I've done you wrong / . . . my heart is full of sorrow, take me back where I belong." The lively cut, which put teenagers on the dance floor, is attributed to Billy Ward and Rose Marks, although as a kind of call-and-response gospel shout, it's doubtful that Marks, a white Jewish lady, had much to contribute here. Shaw called the record "a highly-charged disk, with a torn-up tenor sax solo, handclapping and raucous shouting. It ends with McPhatter wailing and crying in a manner suggestive of the uncontrolled emotionalism of the sanctified churches."[46]

"Have Mercy Baby" was the third most popular R&B song of 1952, according to a poll by *Cash Box* magazine. Number two was "My Song," by Johnny Ace, another African American teen heartthrob that left the young ladies panting. The top song was Lloyd Price's "Lawdy Miss Clawdy." The Dominoes got a measure of revenge because they were chosen as the "Best Rhythm and Blues Artist of 1952," outpacing both Lloyd Price and Johnny Ace.[47]

By November, there were still some places in the country such as in Harlem, the most important Black record market in the United States, where "Have Mercy Baby" was still on the charts and the group, exciting performers, was making the most of it with a heavy touring schedule. On November 1, 1952, the *Cash Box* column "Rhythm & Blues Ramblings" noted, "Billy Ward and his Dominoes continue to tear old house records to shreds as they travel through Ohio, Kentucky, Tennessee, Pennsylvania and New Orleans. Letters come in from managers of every theater the boys played attesting to the tremendous drawing power of the group."[48]

A story about the Dominoes, going back to 1951, has Dinah Washington, the Queen of the Jukeboxes, headlining a weeklong gig at the Paradise Theater in Detroit. Whoever arranged the shows secured the Dominoes for one of the opening acts. That was the good news. The bad news was the group was to perform just ahead of Washington, the star of the show. According to Yusuf Lamont, the son of Joe Lamont, one of the original Dominoes, by the time the Dominoes left the stage, they had whipped the crowd into such a frenzy that the audience wasn't terribly appreciative of Dinah Washington's quiet, sophisticated act. She was furious and demanded promoters never again put her on stage after a group like the Dominoes.[49]

The responses of the few professional writers who covered R&B at the time were malleable and sometimes strange. For example, the unknown columnist of *Cash Box*'s "Rhythm & Blues Ramblings" was such an unabashed fan of the Dominoes, he (or she) wrote this strange observation: "Rose Marks, manager, has made it a fetish to put on only clean shows and has proven to everyone's satisfaction that you don't need smut to sell a show. If you have talent you don't have to employ gimmicks to put yourself over. The dollars rolling in prove that the Dominoes have the formula."[50]

For a group that had a huge hit with "Sixty Minute Man," this was, indeed, an odd endorsement and sat at the other end of the critical continuum, at least in comparison to comments from another veteran columnist, whose beat was the "Negro" entertainment world.

Larry Douglas wrote a syndicated column called "Theatrically Yours," for the African American press. So, if you lived in Phoenix, for example, and on November 14, 1952, perused the *Arizona Sun*, you could have read Douglas's column, which seriously cribbed "Rhythm & Blues Ramblings." Douglas wrote, "Billy Ward and his Dominoes continue to tear old house records to shreds as they travel through Ohio, Pennsylvania, Kentucky, Tennessee and Louisiana." That lift from elsewhere helped Douglas fill his column inches, although as a very conservative African American writer, he was beginning to have misgivings about the Dominoes and the havoc they generally caused at concerts. It all came to a boil in Douglas's head about a year later. Lucky Millinder, who had been fronting bands since the late 1930s, had appeared at the Apollo Theater in New York around the end of September 1953 and Douglas was a big fan. Appearing on the same show was the Dominoes, who got top billing and that threw Douglas into a tizzy.

Douglas heatedly scribbled, "As for the Dominoes, it is difficult to see how such a group can satisfy paying customers, especially after hearing such fine groups as the Mills Brothers." Then he went on to list other tepid performers including the Four Lads, a white quartet that sang weak but popular pap such as "Moments to Remember."

Lucky Millinder, Douglas continued to condescendingly write, does a fine job educating the Apollo audiences in a newer and finer type of music but he seems to be having a difficult time educating die-hard managers that the time of "Uncle Tom music" such as anything by the Dominoes has passed. For a guy who covered the entertainment waterfront, one wonders what world Douglas was living in. He concluded with this remark: "We [African Americans] are supposed to have grown beyond this lower type of entertainment and we hope those musicians who have a finer quality of music to offer will be able to sell the managers on it." Douglas wrote this in a year (1953) that produced some of the best R&B of the early 1950s: "Shake a Hand" by Faye Adams, "Hound Dog" by Big Mama Thornton, "Crying in the Chapel" by the Orioles, "One Scotch, One Bourbon, One Beer" by Amos Milburn, and "Money Honey" by the Drifters with Clyde McPhatter.[51]

In 1953, Douglas need not have worried about such a base group as the Dominoes because things had already gone off the rails for the guys.

After "Have Mercy Baby," the Dominoes became Billy Ward and His Dominoes and one could say the quality of his group's recordings declined although new issues were almost as popular as "Have Mercy Baby" and "Sixty Minute Man." So, who's to say what is a bad song if everyone on the street wants to buy the record? Such is the conundrum when addressing "The Bells," perhaps the most bizarre song the Dominoes recorded. Undoubtedly Screamin' Jay Hawkins listened to this tune before he and friends got drunk and babbled, moaned, and screeched while recording "I Put a Spell on You." G. Houston Byrd, another syndicated columnist for the African American press in the 1950s, made this observation about the Dominoes new effort: "'The Bells' maybe the saddest or sorriest [song] that has been waxed in quite some time."[52]

"The Bells" begins with a haunting voice: "Brothers and sisters, we are gathered here," Clyde screams, a brief moment of doo-wop chorus, and then a lachrymose Clyde sings a bluesy tune. Lots of bells ringing, lots of Clyde crying, lots of woeful sax, lots of disparate Clyde, and lots more of Clyde sobbing. When he's singing, Clyde is in good form, but there is so much going on with this record that it ends up as a swirl of B-movie ingredients.

"The Bells" is not without its fans. When Dave Marsh compiled songs for his book *The Heart of Rock and Soul: The 1001 Greatest Singles Ever Made*, he chose "The Bells" at number 379, one ahead of "Crying in the Chapel" by the Orioles. Marsh wrote: "They call the kind of . . . lead singing that men like Clyde McPhatter did in harmony groups like the Dominoes 'crying,' but nobody else ever took it as literally as Clyde did in this bizarre variation on the Huck Finn theme of attending your own funeral. The record consists entirely of a histrionic Clyde weeping and shrieking . . ."[53]

The song broke in December 1952, and with the Dominoes hotter than New Orleans in August, both industry trade magazines jumped on the offering and highlighted it out of a sea of new releases.

Billboard was succinct: "The group, led by Billy Ward, comes through with a sock performance on unusual material. Stacks up as an item, which will continue the group's disk strength."[54] In comparison, *Cash Box* was verbose: "The most unusual recording yet attempted by Billy Ward and His Dominoes. . . . The unusual story of a funeral, complete with sobs, bells and opening remarks by the attending preacher is told with telling force by the group and since the entire aspect of the tune is so entirely different this side will be played again and again. The lead voice [Clyde McPhatter] carries the major share of the burden with the rest of the boys supporting in subdued style and good taste. . . ."[55]

Among the songs passed over at the time were Sydney Hogg's "Do It No More," also on the Federal label; Earl Bostic's "You Go to My Head," on Syd Nathan's other label, King; and "Wedding Boogie" by Johnny Otis, on Ralph Bass's earlier employer, Savoy.

Sugar Ray Robinson, both a welterweight and middleweight title holder, boasted a professional record of 129 wins, one loss, and two draws. *Ring* magazine ranked him as the top fighter of all time. He began his pro career in 1940, and in 1952 he retired for the first time. (Sugar Ray returned to boxing in 1955 and regained the middleweight title.) In 1952, when it looked like his boxing career was in the past, Robinson went into show business, singing and tap dancing. In February 1953, Sugar Ray headlined a show in Detroit, and like Dinah Washington a few years before, made the mistake of putting the Dominoes on the undercard.

Detroit's Fox Theatre booked Robinson, Louis Armstrong, and the Dominoes for three shows on a Sunday. At the early 3:30 show, the Dominoes ran on stage to sing their funereal hit song "The Bells," but had to stop when the capacity crowd of over 7,000 responded with what the *Detroit Tribune* called hysterical screaming and cries.

Crowd enthusiasm was even worse at the 5:45 performance when the show was stopped cold after the Dominoes finished their set and ran off stage so that Louis Armstrong could follow. The audience demanded the Orioles come back and went into such a dangerous frenzy that Armstrong could only watch from the wings as the stagehands frantically wheeled back onstage Billy Ward's piano so the Dominoes could return to sing.

For the much-in-demand encore, the Dominoes launched into "Have Mercy Baby." Big mistake. The fast-paced song whipped the audience into deeper delirium. The frightened Dominoes retreated. The mood in the auditorium was precarious until the operator of the theater bravely stepped to the microphone and pleaded with the audience to allow the show to continue.

After the Fox debacle, a *Detroit Tribune* reporter managed to corral Joe Glaser, president of the Associated Booking Corporation, which put together the $25,000-a-week Robinson-Armstrong tour package. He told the press, "This is something which happens to an act only once in a lifetime."[56] Obviously, Glaser hadn't been following the teen market for R&B. This was not the Dominoes' initiatory running for their lives. However, it might have been one of the last times because Clyde McPhatter and Billy Ward would end up scooting in opposite directions, or as their mid-tier hit of 1953 declared, "Don't Leave Me This Way."

CHAPTER TWO

I'D BE SATISFIED

Here's a quick story about a musician named Thomas Norwood. One day in the late 1950s, Ike and Tina Turner had entered his world. The famous singers were playing a gig in his community of Hayti (pronounced HAY-tie), a Black neighborhood in Durham, North Carolina.

Hayti was a popular spot on the chitlin' circuit, loosely defined as juke joints, honky-tonks, and other more established urban venues that African American audiences patronized. While Durham boasted hot chitlin' circuit locales such as the Stallion Club, Your Thing Theater, and Baby Grand Club, the premier venue was Hayti's Regal Theatre adjacent to the Biltmore Hotel, an "upscale" accommodation that catered solely to African Americans because this was the Jim Crow South and Blacks could neither stay at hotels nor play at music venues where white people were the patrons.

Ike and Tina Turner were staying at the Biltmore Hotel and playing the Regal. The Ike and Tina Turner revue arrived in town without a drummer, so Ike called Doug Clark from nearby Chapel Hill. Doug, who would form a popular frat band called Doug Clark and his Hot Nuts, knew all the local musicians and recommended a high school kid named Thomas Norwood, who did get the gig. Ike and Tina liked his performance so well that they asked Thomas to tour with them. Since he was underage, permission had to be granted by Thomas's parents. So, the next day Ike and Tina traveled the short distance to the Norwood house to have tea with Thomas's parents. Permission was granted and for many years Thomas continued to play drums for the singers.[1]

Although it was not necessarily a hothouse of talent, a number of more famous singers and entertainers came out of Hayti, including seminal blues musician Blind Boy Fuller, gospel singer Shirley Caesar, comedian Pigmeat Markham, and the most famous of all, Clyde McPhatter.

He was born Clyde Lensey McPhatter on November 15, 1932, and grew up in Hayti. His life was dominated by the local Baptist church where his father was a minister. According to the *Carolina Times* newspaper, the father preached at Mt. Calvary Holiness Church. Writer Arnold Shaw claims it was the Mount Calvary Baptist Church. (The nearest Mount Calvary Holiness Church is about a half hour drive away in Wake Forest. In Northern Durham, African American worshippers constructed the Mount Calvary Missionary Baptist Church in 1938.) Blessed with a beautiful voice, Clyde became a boy soprano in the church choir, as did his brothers and sisters.[2] The 1940 census lists the McPhatter siblings in order of age: Bertha, 14; Ethel, 13; Thomas, 11; Gladys, 9; Clyde, 7, Lorene, 3; and Joseph, 1.[3] An eighth child, George Jr., arrived not long after Joseph.

When Clyde turned ten years old, he became the soprano soloist for the choir. Even as a young sprout, Clyde was also singing outside of church. The hard-working boy earned extra income for his family by shining shoes at a local barbershop. He was a popular stop not just for his ability to put a spit shine on loafers but also because he would entertain patrons with song. In September 1956, when a Clyde McPhatter tour rolled through North Carolina, the local paper played up his youthful endeavors, writing: "Just a few years ago, a Durhamite in need of a shoe shine might be lucky enough to wander into a parlor where he not only got a shine but also an earful of tuneful melodies in four-part harmony. And unless he was possessed by an unusually insensitive ear, he could not fail to notice the clear, high pitch tone of a young bootblack, who was soon to give up the harmony of shoe shine parlors and barber shops for the lights of the stage."[4]

Despite Clyde's endeavors to a make a dime, his youth wasn't a hardship. His neighborhood of Hayti was a long-established African American community with a deep entrepreneurial infrastructure.

After the Civil War, former slaves began settling on the southwest of edge of Durham. The community came to be known as Hayti, which was common vernacular for any independent Black settlement (based on a reference to Haiti, the first independent, predominantly Black country in the western hemisphere). Originally, the influx of people to Hayti was due to freedmen looking for work in the vast tobacco warehouses of the Durham area. By 1880, Black-run businesses began to prosper. The community boasted its own schools, a library, theater, hotel and hospital. After 1909, Hayti found itself adjacent to the new North Carolina College for Negroes, which became North Carolina Central University. In 1911, when Booker T. Washington visited Hayti, he called it "a city of Negro enterprises," adding it was a "shining example of what a colored man may become." By the 1940s, Hayti could boast hotels, churches, attorney offices and it was even where Durham's Black Wall Street was located.

One of the most important structures was the Biltmore Hotel, built in 1923. A 1930 postcard pictured a gleaming, three-story, red-brick hotel adorned with striped awnings. Additional printed copy read: "The Biltmore Hotel, Durham NC, half block from Union Station. America's Finest Colored Hotel. All out side [sic] rooms. Running hot and cold water in each room. The last word in comfort. 'Do It the Biltmore Way.' Atlas Barbee, Manager."

An old photo of the hotel, probably from the 1940s, shows the adjoining Regal Theatre with posters pasted to the side wall advertising the coming of Count Basie to town. Indeed, most performers on the southern chitlin' circuit stopped in Hayti, from jazz musicians such as Louis Armstrong and Cab Calloway to rock 'n' rollers and soul singers.[5]

A young Clyde McPhatter could only absorb from a distance the excitement of a famous musician coming to town, as his father was a serious Baptist and there was a defined line of acceptable music, gospel, and unacceptable, just about anything else.

A young Thomas Norwood could benefit from the town's predominant entertainment venue, but not a young Clyde McPhatter. By the time Ike and Tina Turner came to town, Clyde and his family were long gone from Hayti—and Clyde was way more famous than the Turners.

After World War II, it became apparent to Clyde's father, Rev. George McPhatter, that the oppressive segregation of the South was not going to improve in the immediate future and better jobs than tobacco warehouse work could be found elsewhere. Already tens of thousands of African Americans had made the decision to move north, and Rev. McPhatter decided it was time for his family to do the same. In 1945, when Clyde was twelve years of age, the family moved out of the South. Across the state of North Carolina and two years later, the family of Benjamin Earl Nelson, age nine, moved from Henderson to Harlem. Benjamin, known as Ben E. King, would take over as lead singer of the Drifters in 1958 before launching a successful solo career.

The effect on the music industry from the great migration, or the period from 1910 to 1970 when six million African Americans left the South for the Northeast, Midwest, and West, often focuses on Chicago, the last stop for many blues singers heading north from the Mississippi Delta. Chess Records, founded by Leonard and Phil Chess, recorded many of these singers such as Muddy Waters and Howlin' Wolf. Aspirations and ultimately direction were different for other musicians in the South. Texas and Oklahoma African Americans often headed west to Los Angeles, where they jump started the West Coast doo-wop era, and from the East Coast states of Virginia to Georgia, many headed to the mid-Atlantic states.

Rev. McPhatter had good instincts, because if there was ever a peak of Hayti community *esprit de corps* and prosperity, it was the mid-1940s. Economically and socially, things would slowly turn downhill for Hayti until the late 1950s when the community was, for all practical considerations, eviscerated.

Hayti's fortunes began to fade over the course of the 1950s, as it did in other solidly African American urban neighborhoods. According to Open Durham, a digital archive: "The progressive end of segregation meant less exclusive patronage of Hayti stores and businesses, and visitors from out of town could stay at hotels outside of Hayti." The archive added, the general economic flight of the 1960s "affected the African-American community as well as the white community. Those with the means to do so began to move to suburban areas."[6]

The last nail in the coffin for Hayti arrived at the end of 1950s; the construction of North Carolina Highway 147, a freeway that ran right through the center of the community. Since Blacks were still absent from almost any North Carolina political entity, they had no say in the decision to destroy the neighborhood.

Howard Burchette, who owns a local real estate company and is the announcer for the radio program *The Funk Show* on WNCU-FM, affirmed, "When they built the Durham Freeway, they put it directly through Hayti. It was racism. Even today people are angry that the government put a highway through a Black neighborhood. On one side of the highway is downtown Durham, which is more developed. Almost nothing on the other side has the remnants of the original Hayti."[7]

In 1940, the McPhatter family lived at 321 Gray Street in Durham, North Carolina. (On his registration card for military service, George McPhatter originally wrote Grace Street, but crossed out "Grace" and wrote "Gray." On the same card, his wife Beulah was still listed on Grace Street.) Deborah McPhatter, the daughter of Clyde McPhatter, recently located the house where Clyde lived as a boy. It still stands. She observed, "The houses are still the same but very run-down. Back when my father lived there this was a very nice section of Durham for Blacks to live, now it is a disadvantaged neighborhood."[8]

Years later, while touring Canada, Clyde was playing a venue at Exhibition Point in Vancouver. Robert "Red" Robinson, who was the first deejay to play rock 'n' roll music in that city, corralled Clyde for a brief interview. When asked where he came from, Clyde first uttered New York City. Then, for a brief moment, he reconsidered his statement and decided to correct himself, saying, "I was born in a small city; I'm used to small city life."[9]

As to why the McPhatter family moved north, Deborah McPhatter said, "I always thought it was for the same reason many Black families left the South during that time; for a better life." Burchette added, "Clyde McPhatter and future Drifters lead singer Ben. E. King had similar histories. King was born in Henderson, North Carolina, but his family moved where it was perceived there was more opportunity and less oppression. It's where the work was."[10]

There is still a bit of controversy over where the McPhatter family moved after leaving North Carolina. Writer Arnold Shaw and others claim the family moved first to Teaneck, New Jersey, and Clyde attended Chelsior High School, where he formed his first gospel quartet. That information was taken as gospel, but it was incorrect. According to Deborah McPhatter, Chelsior High was in New York and that when the family left North Carolina, they moved directly to 145th Street in Harlem. The New Jersey family residency came later. She explained, "Teaneck and Englewood, New Jersey, were towns of professional Black entertainers, doctors, lawyers, and radio disc-jockeys. One did not leave your Durham, North Carolina, American Tobacco Company job and move to Teaneck with eight kids. When my father started making money, he purchased a house in Teaneck for his parents and then bought a home for himself not far away in Englewood, New Jersey. Singer Chuck Jackson lived right behind my dad."[11]

Winfred "Brother" Tolor, Clyde's nephew, who was very close to his Uncle Clyde when growing up, added that when Clyde was flush in his career, "he bought a house for his mother and father at 142 Garden Street in Teaneck. Where Clyde bought the house there was a hill and another uncle, Thomas, bought his mother a car so she wouldn't have to walk up the hill."[12]

There is more credibility to family lore about where the McPhatters ended up after coming north, because, as a teenager, Clyde began singing with a gospel group called the Mount Lebanon Singers. According to Marv Goldberg, who interviewed a number of the original Drifters back in 2001, the name derived from an association with a Mount Lebanon Church on 132nd Street in Harlem, which no longer exists.[13] Yusuf Lamont concurs that the group was named after a Harlem church.[14] Many accounts of Clyde's life suggest he founded the Mount Lebanon Singers when he was a teenager. The *Carolina Times* in 1959 reported, "At the age of 13, he [Clyde] had already organized his own gospel singing quartet, which was much in demand for after-school appearances in New York City."[15]

Nevertheless, Marv Goldberg maintains that the group already existed as a quintet when Clyde came to them. Two of the singers in the group, Wilmer and David Baldwin, were brothers of famed author James Baldwin. Of the many iterations of Drifters over the years, only one of the Mount Lebanon Singers, besides Clyde, became a member of the Drifters, and that was Charlie White.[16]

Through the first part of the twentieth century, pop music was not exactly overwhelmed by small male groups. In the 1930s, the Boswell Sisters, out of New Orleans, paved the way for the female group phenomenon. However, until the success of the Mills Brothers and Ink Spots, male groups were more popular in the hillbilly (country), jazz, and gospel genres. In the late 1940s, when R&B and the blues were dominated by the individual performer, many young Black men seeking a collective harmony experience opted to form small gospel groups such as the Mount Lebanon Singers or the Thrasher Wonders.

"Black Youngsters listening to the Mills Brothers or Ink Spots would find the gospel stream models for careers that would soon bridge the road to 'rock-nroll,'" concluded writer Philip Ennis.[17]

Take the experience of original Drifters member Bill Pinkney. He was raised in the tiny South Carolina population-dot called Dalzell. He sang in his junior high school glee club but broke away to form a gospel group called the Singing Cousins. In an interview from the mid-1980s, Pinkney claimed the Singing Cousins competed against other gospel groups throughout the Carolinas, including bumping up against a gospel group led by Clyde McPhatter. Bill said he had known Clyde "since he was 14 years old."

After high school, Bill was drafted. Instead of returning to South Carlina, upon leaving the military service in 1949, he decided to come to New York to follow his dreams." Shortly after arriving in the North, he met fellow South Carolinian Benjamin Peay, who as a popular singer and songwriter would change his name to Brook Benton. At the time, though, Benjamin Peay was an occasional singer with the Jerusalem Stars gospel group. Bill joined the group in 1950 before moving over to the Southern Knights. Benjamin switched to Bill Landford and the Landfordaires. All these groups were competitive (like a battle of the bands but with no instruments) and complementary. As Pinkney noted, "The Southern Knights would get together with other gospel groups for quartet singing in churches in New York City."[18]

Gospel was the perfect farm team for future group singers. It was primarily vocal music; as writer Philip Ennis observed: "The human voice, solo and in choir, carried the heart, the heat and the message. The skills of the vocal craft are the core of gospel; the piano, organ, guitar and occasionally other instruments are but augmentation."[19]

Clyde McPhatter made his first public appearance at the age of five, singing in his father's church choir, according to liner notes from a 1965 album, which added, "And there it is again—the root word, 'church.' It keeps turning up in the backgrounds of so many of today's better singers. The cradle. The source of what is real in what they sing and how."[20]

Atlantic Records' Ahmet Ertegun, who was Turkish and had a skin tone darker than most white Americans, suggesting an affinity with Black Americans, said he understood what Black life was like in America: "I knew what Black music was in America. I felt I knew what Black roots were—gospel music and blues from the Delta. In loving America, I felt I knew more about America than the average American knew."[21]

Before establishing Atlantic Records, Ahmet and Herb Abramson meandered into musical blind alleys with two other labels, Quality and Jubilee. Thet latter label was supposed to be only for gospel music. According to Ertegun, Jubilee only created one record, for Sister Ernestine Washington, accompanied by Bunk Johnson and his orchestra. It didn't sell, nor did anything they recorded on Quality. Dismayed, financial backer Max Silverman of the Waxie Maxie record store in Washington, DC, bailed on Ahmet and Herb and they then started all over again with Atlantic. Gospel may have been a good place to start for African American singers with popular music aspirations, but it didn't have wide enough appeal to be profitable for record companies.

The record producers adjusted. In 1953, when Ahmet asked Clyde to form a singing group, the first bunch of singers he brought in to record were, as expected, from the gospel world. They recorded four songs—all rejected by Ahmet and producer Jerry Wexler. Clyde quickly understood what Ahmet was seeking and found new singers. At least one of the first four tunes, "Lucille," written by Clyde, was considered by Ahmet and Wexler as too gospel. It, however, was brought back to life the next year as a "B-side" song.[22]

As one reviewer observed, "Flip [B-side] is a slow blues which sports overtones of gospel music, entitled 'Lucille' and is a McPhatter original."[23]

Tom Bialoglow sang with the 1960s doo-wop group the Duprees, which shared the stage with Clyde McPhatter for one show in the Midwest back in 1962. The Duprees were riding high with their biggest hit, "You Belong to Me," but for Bialoglow, the real excitement was Clyde McPhatter. "I was a fan of Clyde. He had a beautiful tenor voice. Although the Duprees sang doo-wop, I couldn't come near a voice like that. My favorite song of his was 'Lucille,' where Clyde sings in that high-pitch falsetto. 'I'm staring into space, haven't got a word to say.'"[24]

With the rise of the Orioles and the Ravens, many other secular groups began to form, most of them recruiting out of the gospel world. When Billy Ward formed the Dominoes, Clyde and Charlie White came from the Mount Lebanon Singers while Bill Brown and Joe Lamont arrived courtesy of the International Gospel Singers of South Carolina.

After the Southern Knights finished one of its gospel programs, Bill Pinkney walked over to a small storefront church in Harlem to hear the Mount Lebanon Gospel Singers, where he was very impressed by the lead singer, who had "unique, clear and beautiful tenor voice." After the performance, Bill introduced himself to the singer, Clyde McPhatter. Bill didn't know it, but Clyde would follow his career in the Harlem gospel scene.[25]

When Canadian deejay Red Robinson interviewed Clyde before a concert in Vancouver, he asked, "How did you get started?" Clyde, who was responding almost monosyllabically answered, "I was a choir singer," further explaining that this man called Billy Ward, who was starting a group, heard of his performances as a local gospel singer and asked him to audition. Said Clyde, "I was accepted as a lead singer and that was the beginning of it."[26]

CHAPTER THREE

WHAT'CHA GONNA DO

Outside of gospel, in the early 1950s, another popular place to recruit singers in New York was at the Apollo Theater, which had the most famous amateur night for burgeoning talent.

Amateur nights at auditoriums for African American patrons first became very popular in the 1930s, because a winning performance earned a singer, dancer, or musician a few dollars' award, which was important during the Depression years when so many people were out of work and even a handful of dollar bills could make a difference. Many parents would enroll their talented little ones for an amateur contest (also very popular on radio shows), which smacked a little of exploitation, but everyone in the family had to contribute something to the welfare of the household. Youngsters still participate in amateur nights. Louise Harris Murray, a singer for the Hearts ("Lonely Nights") in the 1950s and Jaynetts ("Sally Go Round the Roses") in the 1960s, first participated in an amateur night in the 1940s, when she was eight years old. According to Louise, she won that night, earning twenty-five dollars. Since she liked to sing and wasn't at all nervous in front of an audience, she continued to compete at amateur nights into the 1950s, warbling songs such as "I Will Wait" by the Four Buddies and "Heavenly Father" by Edna McGriff. She remembers winning first place a second time. Around late 1953 or early 1954, an entrepreneurial Harlem woman named Zell Hicks decided to put together an all-girl doo-wop group. She heard three young, local singers (Joyce West, Forestine Barnes, and Hazel Crutchfield) at Apollo's amateur night and teamed them up with Louise to form the Hearts, which in 1955 was the second female doo-wop group to score a record on the R&B bestseller charts.[1]

Two of the most successful amateur night contests were in Memphis and New York. They both were started in the 1930s. In Memphis, the venue was the

Palace Theater, which was the preeminent entertainment showcase for African Americans in the mid-South. During its peak years of the 1940s, '50s, and '60s, the Palace's amateur night winners include B.B. King, Al Hibbler, Johnny Ace, Rufus Thomas, and Isaac Hayes.[2]

In Harlem, the Apollo boasted its first amateur night in 1934, when Ralph Cooper created a live version of his radio show *Amateur Nite Hour*. The alumni of Apollo's amateur night shows could fill many auditoriums: Jimi Hendrix, James Brown, the Jackson Five, Stevie Wonder, Billie Holiday, Lauryn Hill, and even Machine Gun Kelly, to name a few. Talent scouts and record producers would haunt the Apollo during the 1930s, '40s, and '50s. The Apollo's first great success story was Ella Fitzgerald, who after winning amateur night, joined the Chick Webb orchestra. Some of the top female singers of the early 1950s, including Ruth Brown, Varetta Dillard, and Faye Adams, were discovered at the Apollo's amateur night.[3]

Bill Pinkney moved to New York in 1949, but didn't work up the courage to face amateur night until 1952, when he climbed onto the Apollo stage to sing Willie Mabon's big hit of that year, "I Don't Know." He didn't win, but came back again. It's a tradition for Apollo amateur night contestants to rub the Tree of Hope, which is the remains of a chestnut tree that stood outside the old Lafayette Theater in Harlem. Unemployed performers once gathered there in hopes of finding jobs, and rubbing the tree stump is said to bring good luck to performers. When Bill came back to the Apollo, the headliner for the night was the Lucky Millinder Band. Bill was looking for a little luck of his own. "I went on stage and touched the Tree of Hope. I told the emcee my name and where I was from, and you would have thought the whole theater was from South Carolina." This time around, Bill sang "It's Too Soon to Know," the 1948 hit record by the Orioles. Bill, indeed, caught a bit of luck and came in second place that night.[4]

Bill wasn't the only member of the Drifters to test his voice and performance craft at an amateur night. Two years before, Clyde McPhatter made his first appearance at the Apollo. Clyde always said he won first prize that night, which Deborah McPhatter confirmed. More importantly, he caught the attention of Billy Ward.

Clyde was seventeen at the time of his Apollo amateur night performance, and he would have invited his family and neighbors. Louise Murray always remembers many of her neighbors showing up for her spot and giving boisterous support (the audience votes by cheering or booing). Clyde was still living at his parents' house in Harlem, so it would have been a long walk or short cab ride to the Apollo. His mother, who he adored, would have definitely been there. As for his father, that was a contentious bond and Clyde couldn't always be sure he would be there when performing. To put it succinctly, Clyde and his father did not have a good relationship.

Clyde had a small scar on one of his hands, and one day when Deborah McPhatter was talking with her cousin who she called "Brother," he told her that Clyde's father stabbed him there with a knife. Apparently, Clyde and his father were having an argument about religion and Clyde questioned him about his relationship with God and how religious he really was. That discussion didn't sit well with the father. Brother downplayed the episode, "They had an argument and Clyde got stabbed on his hand. I often saw them having words. One would raise his voice and then the other would raise his voice louder."[5]

Religion is a good place to start when discussing Clyde's father. Born on March 18, 1903,[6] he is often referred to as Rev. McPhatter (even his granddaughter Deborah called him Rev. McPhatter), denoting a leadership association with a church. That may or may not be true. On his 1940 military service card, he listed his place of employment as the American Tobacco Company in Durham. Still, he seemed to have had a close association with a Baptist church in Durham, so the term "reverend" would have been honorary. Once the family moved north, he became more of a lay minister as he continued to work secular jobs to feed his family. Brother suspects the reason why the family left North Carolina was economic. "I never saw or heard that he was ordained. My thinking is the family moved probably for better work opportunities for my grandfather," he said.[7]

The one person in the family with definite minister credentials is not Clyde's father, but his mother. In 1949, the Bethel Bible Institute in Jamaica, New York, awarded Beulah McPhatter a diploma for having "completed the studies and satisfied the requirements prescribed for the course in Evangelism."[8] When Beulah McPhatter died in 1972, the memorial service listed her name as Rev. Beulah McPhatter.

"I was under the impression for many years that Clyde's father, while in Durham, was a deacon at the family church. It was much later I was told he was a reverend," Deborah McPhatter ruminated. "I'm not sure if he gave himself that title due to the fact Beulah was indeed a minister. As we know, jealousy ran deep within him."

Brother's age was nearer to Deborah McPhatter's than to Clyde's. His mother was Clyde's sister Ethel and he had a close relationship to his grandparents. When Brother knew well the McPhatter family, Clyde's father worked at a New Jersey department store called Packard's, which was originally Packard-Bambergers. It closed in 1991.. "Grandfather worked there for many years," said Brother. "He didn't make a living as a minister. He had a nine-to-five job."[9]

The Rev. George McPhatter was a trim, generally well-dressed man. In later years, he wore eyeglasses. With a thinner face, he didn't resemble his son much, especially as Clyde aged and his features became more rounded. George McPhatter had a hard look, his son a soft countenance. The one feature they had in common was a receding hairline. In later years, Clyde would take to wearing a toupee when performing.

What was the Rev. George McPhatter like? Brother called him a "one-way man," meaning it was his way or the highway. Brother also used the terms "difficult" and "very controlling" when referring to his grandfather. He probably wasn't far off in his estimation because Clyde, as a successful son, was always stuck in the weird psychological position of financially supporting his father and mother and looking for father figures elsewhere, first with Billy Ward and later on with his agent, Irvin Feld.

On the other hand, Clyde was something of a mama's boy. Said Brother, "He loved his mother and was always buying her expensive gifts [besides purchasing a home in New Jersey for his parents]."

Both Brother and Deborah McPhatter proffered that their grandfather was envious of his son's success and the wealth that came with it. "Father was jealous of the son because of what Clyde would do for his mother," Brother claimed. "He was doing things for her that my grandfather couldn't do, such as buying his mother a mink coat. Grandfather didn't like that. It was his whole thing against Clyde."

Jealousy ran rampant in the McPhatter family. Clyde paid for his two younger brothers to attend a prep school. One of the brothers, Joseph, also called Leroy, thought he was a better singer than Clyde and he should have been the star of the family.[10]

"My dad's final years were hell," suggested Deb McPhatter. "I think he was beat down not only by the music industry, but by his family and those he thought were close friends. Someone told me this story a few years ago when they heard me mention the crush I had on Lloyd Price. They asked, 'Why would you like him? He and another guy [Price's business partner Harold Logan] beat your father up at his New York nightclub [Lloyd Price's Turntable on Broadway].' I was shocked. I still don't know how true it is. I'm not making excuses for my dad, but the issues with his last wife Lena Rackley and his two brothers, honestly, it is enough to make one drink. Those three were a handful."

Clyde was married three times: the first to Nora Thompson; the second to Mary Peake; and then Lena Rackley, who was the ex-girlfriend of baseball Hall of Famer Willie Mays. He was faithful to none of them. Bill Curtis, who was the drummer for Clyde for ten years during his solo career, said he knew Nora and Mary, and that wearing a ring meant little to Clyde because he had a girlfriend in every city.[11]

Curtis wasn't exaggerating.

The "New York Beat" gossip column in the July 23, 1953, issue of *Jet* magazine, announced "Clyde McPhatter, who formed his own quartet after leaving the Dominoes, will legally share his name next week with Nora Thompson."[12] Two years later, he initiated an affair with popular R&B singer Ruth Brown, who was also an Atlantic Records artist. They recorded as a duet singing "Love Has Joined Us Together," which was a Top Ten R&B hit. After a promotion in New York, Clyde, who had been drafted in 1954, was on leave and asked Ruth to join him in Buffalo, where he had borrowed a friend's house. As Ruth recalled, they had no illusions that they were embarking on anything but an affair. Ruth wrote, "When we got ready for bed that first night I watched as he took off his battle dress, slipped off his tie and began to unbutton his shirt. As I caught sight of his chocolate chest under the khaki, he looked up and smiled his dazzling smile. 'Ever unwrapped a soldier boy before,' he asked before beckoning me over."

The affair lasted several more weeks, although Ruth said she knew the rumors already swirling about Clyde's bisexuality.[13]

The trouble with all this is, Ruth Brown is not always a reliable witness, even to her own history. At various times, she claimed three different men were the father to her son.

At the time of her affair with Clyde, Ruth was still married to the musician Willis "Gator Tail" Jackson. Deborah McPhatter was born in April 1953 and Ruth Brown's son, who now calls himself Ronn David McPhatter, was born in January 1955. In her book, Ruth Brown wrote, "As he grew up there was never any reason to say anyone other than Willis was his daddy." Before Ruth died, she confessed to her son that Clyde McPhatter was his father. However, she also wrote after the birth of Ronald David, "four weeks later in February 1955, I felt able to go back to work." If Clyde was Ronald David's father, then her affair with Clyde had to be earlier than 1954 and she became pregnant immediately. That's one theory. Ruth also wrote that the affair with Clyde began six months after she split with Willis in 1955. So, did Clyde and Ruth have an earlier tryst than the one she wrote about? In her memoir, Ruth forthrightly said the father of her baby was Drew Brown, known as "The Great Bundini," who she had a brief affair with. However, there was also the rumor that when Clyde McPhatter and Ruth Brown were on a tour bus together in the early 1950s, the other musicians bet her she could not get Clyde into her bed and she proved them wrong.

While Clyde and Nora continued as a married couple far longer than anyone expected, it was never a love-match. According to Deborah McPhatter, "if they stayed married more than two years, it was only on paper as they didn't live under the same roof." At the time he said his wedding vows, Clyde was more in love with Lorraine Lowe, the mother of his child, Deborah. Lorraine was from Bermuda, came to the United States either in 1948 or 1949, and attended a boarding school in New Jersey. In 1950, hearing that the Dominoes were going to play Atlantic City, Lorraine and friends snuck off campus and made their way to the show. A strikingly beautiful young woman, she caught the attention of Clyde and they struck up a romance.[14]

An inveterate letter-writer, with exactingly clear and clean penmanship (which declined with age), Clyde wrote beautiful love notes to Lorraine over the course of a lifetime. In August 1952, he wrote: "I know it's rather surprising, me writing so soon, but being away from you for two days leaves me with no other alternative but to write and you know I miss you terrible. I miss what I think is the most beautiful eyes ever to exist, not only eyes, but the most charming and lovable person I've ever known."[15]

Just a few months before the press reported he would marry a woman named Nora, Clyde was writing Lorraine: "Before I met you, I was all mixed up and my only escape was drinking and running wild with any girl that looked nice, but now everything has changed, you've inspired me to really make something of myself." The letter was signed "Love, now and forever, Clyde."[16]

Clyde would often splurge on telegrams. In January 1953, just about three months before he announced he was getting married, he wired Lorraine from Denver: "Will send for you on the fifteenth bring a heavy coat with love Clyde."[17]

Clyde was so detached from the concept of monogamy he could operate in three worlds of women at the same time. While married to Nora, he met Ruth Brown in Buffalo, and wired this note to his daughter Deborah, a child he had with Lorraine Lowe: "With a thousand words I couldn't say more or mean more than this. Happy Birthday."[18]

As noted, Clyde would remain a dependent friend to Lorraine for his entire life, even after she married someone else. As to why he didn't marry Lorraine, that was mostly due to his parents' opposition. Apparently, his father and mother felt Clyde should marry someone from the South who was a god-fearing woman. "My mother was very pretty, but she didn't look like a woman from North Carolina," said Deborah McPhatter. "They wanted Clyde to marry Nora Thompson, who wasn't even from the South, but from Long Island, New York. They were like, 'I don't care who you like or who you love, this is going to be your wife.' He married her."[19]

While married, Clyde and Nora lived in New Rochelle, New York. He opened a record store there, which was initially run by Nora, but eventually Ethel McPhatter, one of his sisters, took over.

Having a grandchild by another woman didn't help things either. Clyde's parents were not happy that Clyde continued to have a relationship with Lorraine. Beulah McPhatter refused to see her granddaughter. The grandfather would visit but not tell Beulah. Needless to say, Deborah McPhatter, over the years, did not see her grandparents very often. "I remember one time I was at my dad's house in Englewood and we walked over to his parents' house. My grandmother was having tea with women from her church. She gave me tea in a broken cup. My family on my mother's side was from Bermuda and very British about tea. My mother would never serve tea in a broken cup. I told my grandmother, 'I'm not drinking out of that cup, there's 10 cracks in it.' That didn't go over well."

Things weren't much better with the other grandparents. Lorraine's mom was not a fan of rhythm and blues, so when Lorraine got pregnant by an R&B singer, this was not a good thing, and Clyde didn't handle it well. He went to Lorraine's mother's house, knocked on the door, and said, "Hi, my name is Clyde McPhatter. I love Lorraine and she is pregnant." Grandmother nearly fainted. That relationship never got any better. Clyde and Lorraine's mother fought constantly.[20]

The oddity was that Clyde couldn't let go of Lorraine, because he had no one else to confide in. He would contact her all the time. In 1968, he was still writing letters to her with the opening, "Dearest Darling" while she was happily married to someone else. Sometimes Lorraine would just get fed up with him, especially when he was on the booze. She would exclaim, "I don't know what else to do to help him."[21] Deborah McPhatter recalls seeing her mother and stepdad put Clyde in the car and drive him to the hospital to get help for his drinking. When Clyde died, there was no money left, so Lorraine's husband paid for the funeral.

As can be expected, after Clyde's death, the old wives club got revived, except for the second wife, Mary. That marriage came and went so quickly, no one except Clyde's drummer Bill Curtis even remembered her. Said Curtis, "she was a young lady out of Greensboro, North Carolina," and that was it.[22]

First wife Nora was eventually stricken with loss of eyesight. Long after Clyde was dead, she filed a lawsuit saying she went blind because he mistreated her, that he beat her and hit her in the head with a golf club forty years before. There were a couple of problems with that story. First, Clyde was generally a very nice person. He could be acerbic when drunk, but never violent. Second, as Deborah McPhatter testified, Clyde didn't play golf and never had golf clubs in his house.

Then there was Lena Rackley McPhatter, the third wife. "As soon as he would pack a bag to get out of town to go to a gig, she called everyone she knew to come to house for a pool party," Deborah said. "She partied, partied, screwed and screwed (but not her husband). That wasn't my father. He was a quiet guy and when he came home, he wanted a quiet house."[23]

Around 1967, Lena was gone from Clyde's house in Englewood, New Jersey, and surprisingly Lorraine and Deborah went on tour with him. This odd shift occurred because Clyde had a fight with Lena about her affair with a jazz musician who lived nearby. Lena moved back to her apartment on West 90th

Street in Manhattan. As Deborah McPhatter recalled, "I never saw Lena again until my father's funeral."

Sometime after Clyde came back from England in 1970, he was served with divorce papers. He signed them while on the phone with Lorraine.

When Clyde died in June 1972, Lena claimed she and Clyde were still married. Lorraine and Deborah said they weren't because Clyde signed divorce papers. It wasn't until the 1990s that a copy of the divorce papers, which Lena said she knew nothing about, was found. In the meantime, Lena took control of Clyde's estate including royalties going back to his Atlantic Records days.

After Beulah McPhatter died, which was soon after Clyde's death, Clyde's father found himself another girlfriend. George McPhatter worked out a deal with Lena, where he sold her the house that Clyde had bought for his parents. As noted, when Clyde died everything had gone to Lena—except that house.

One day Brother was sitting in a local bar when his grandfather (Clyde's father) came in. He said to Brother, "I need you to take me to the Port Authority Terminal as I need to catch a bus." Taped to his body was all the cash Lena had paid him for the house Clyde had given his parents. Brother said this was ridiculous and told his grandfather he needed to go to a bank and open an account. The Rev. McPhatter waved that off and repeated his request to be driven to the Port Authority, so Brother did. For his efforts, Rev. McPhatter gave him five dollars.

Brother laughed when recalling the incident because the Rev. McPhatter went south to live with his new girlfriend, who was no youngster and had adult offspring. The story is, said Brother, "The girlfriend's kids beat him up and took all his money. Whatever goes around, comes around."[24]

CHAPTER FOUR

THESE FOOLISH THINGS (REMIND ME OF YOU)

It was somewhere in Virginia and the Dominoes were headlining a show in front of an integrated crowd—the word "integrated" used very, very broadly. Unlike in some states such as Louisiana, where it was illegal for white folks to be in venues that catered to African Americans, and vice versa, Virginia allowed both races in one venue if they were separated. On this particular night, Black teenagers were in the balcony while the ground floor was reserved for the white teenagers. This was around 1951 or 1952 and the Dominoes on stage were either the original line-up with Clyde McPhatter, Bill Brown, Joe Lamont, and Charlie White or the one with David McNeil taking the place of White. (Joe Lamont, who told this story, couldn't remember the specifics, although he related this tale more than once.) It wasn't a large venue and the stage came right up to where the audience was standing. As noted, the Dominoes generated quite a bit of heat among female, teenage fans, and this wasn't just among the African American population, but, to fearful parents and segregationists everywhere in the country, among white girls as well.

The Dominoes eventually incorporated some dance steps into their performance. Nothing as complex as, for example, the Temptations in the 1960s, but a few coordinated steps and standard shoulder dipping. On this particular night, the Dominoes brought their performance right to the lip of the stage, where crowded to the front, even in this Southern state, was a phalanx of girls. There were a number of close calls as the young ladies would reach up to touch the performers. Joe Lamont in the thick of melody and movement forgot himself for a moment and dipped his shoulder way down. A white girl in front of him reached up and grabbed the lapel of his tuxedo. Joe was a little surprised and his first thought was to get back into the routine. The slight tug as he uprighted would cause the young lady's grip to relent, or so he expected. However. the girl, also caught up in the melody and the group's movement, didn't let go; she just held on. In a nanosecond, Joe considered the show and the state of his tuxedo and blurted out something akin to "what the fuck are you doing?" And everything stopped. Joe Lamont had publicly sassed a white girl in the state of Virginia, and fun and joy departed as quickly as a storm blowing in from the Atlantic. Heavy clouds of hate billowed, and like rain in a strong wind, objects began to fly across the stage. The Dominoes backed away and then ran. The Black teenagers in the balcony didn't necessarily hear what Lamont had exclaimed, but knew what was going to happen next and in panic fled the theater as fast as they could get out the doors and down the street. At the time, the Dominoes traveled in what was essentially an extended Cadillac. It looked like a hearse. They, too, busted out of the theater and jumped into the car, heading out of town with the local police and a string of cars coming after. The Cadillac didn't stop until they were in the next county and the pursuers had long since stopped coming.[1]

This was one of the hazards of the road. One had to be careful how the audience might react, especially in those houses with segregated seating. A Black performer could not only get brutalized with impunity, especially in the South, if local mores were transgressed, but perception could ruin a career, which was what happened to the talented pop-chart-visitor Billy Eckstine.

In the late 1940s and early 1950s, two Black singers, Billy Eckstine and Nat King Cole, with their urban, jazzy-pop style, easily crossed over to the mainstream markets, on radio, in record sales, and eventually with listings on the *Billboard* pop charts. Eckstine, with a deeper singing voice than Cole, caught the wave of bass and baritone popularity that arose from the rhythm and blues side of the market. For the most part, he eschewed the jocular, and his most popular songs were serious ballads. Some would herald him as the first romantic Black male in popular music, or as one writer scribed, "Eckstine's sex appeal and suave singing made him one of the earliest black stars to be loved by white female fans, despite the racial tension of the 1950s."[2] His career peaked at the turn of the bright new decade. In 1950, his song "My Foolish Heart" was a Top Thirty pop song for the year, coming in at #28. Eckstine was not the only Black performer that year to break into the Top Thirty annual listing created by *Billboard*. He was joined by Nat King Cole, whose "Mona Lisa" was the #2 song of the year. In 1951, Eckstine would again crash the Top Thirty listing of the best-selling pop songs of the year with "I Apologize," at #25. Again, he would be joined by Nat King Cole, who had the #1 song of the year, "Too Young."

Eckstine was so popular *LIFE* magazine decided to feature him and on April 25, 1950, the popular, photo-based news magazine ran a three-page profile of the singer. Martha Holmes, the photographer for the feature, caught on camera a candid moment when Eckstine, after performing at the club Bop City in Manhattan, is swarmed by adoring fans, who are all white females. One admirer, a laughing young woman with a wedding band on her left hand, has that hand on his shoulder as she rests her head against his chest. Everyone close by is laughing, including Eckstine. Not laughing were the racists.[3]

As Kerrie Mitchell wrote for the New York Historical Society, "More than a few white readers were appalled. *LIFE*'s internal report on letters to the editor noted that 59 complaints were received about the Eckstine story, expressing vicious, hysterically racist sentiments like, 'That picture of Billy Eckstine with a white girl clinging to him after a performance just turns my stomach.' Other readers described the photo as 'the most nauseating picture of the year' and 'the most indecent picture ever published by *LIFE*.'"[4]

Eckstine's career peaked soon after, and a lot of his contemporaries laid blame to that photo. Even if they didn't write letters, as Tony Bennett recalled, the picture "just offended the white community."[5]

"That picture almost ended his career," said Yusuf Lamont. "My father, Joe Lamont, always talked about that photo because, as a black performer, he said you always had to be careful. It was not necessarily something you did; it was how it looked."[6]

Joe Lamont understood that because he had his own photo moment. On October 3, 1953, *Cash Box* ran a photo of Lamont coming back to the Dominoes after being ill. The cutline reads: "Joseph Lamont, baritone of Billy Ward's Dominoes, who was taken ill 11 months ago and has been convalescing ever since, is welcomed back by Billy Ward and his Dominoes at the Michigan State Fair while autograph-seeking bobbysoxers look on." The photo shows Lamont running a gauntlet of well-wishers. Closest to him are Billy Ward and the rest of the Dominoes. Standing next to them are young white girls, the "autograph-seeking bobbysoxers" of the cutline.[7] While, thematically, outside the entertainment world the photo was a caution, it does represent the then existing economics of the music business. Although the Dominoes were Black R&B singers, it was the young white girls who could afford autograph books and had the yearning and disposable income to buy records and record players. Young white girls would purchase a Tony Martin, Rosemary Clooney, or Ames Brothers record, but increasingly they were also purchasing platters by the Dominoes and other R&B performers.

If young white girls wanted to hear rock 'n' roll live, well, that was a dicey business in the Jim Crow South. For example, in 1957, Clyde McPhatter was coming back to North Carolina for two shows at the Durham City Armory and the Raleigh Memorial Auditorium. An advertisement in the *Carolina*

Times read "2 Big Rock and Roll Shows and Dances" with this additional note: "White Spectators Invited."

Allowing white spectators to attend rock 'n' roll shows by Black performers and vice versa was generally against state, city, or county codes in much of the Jim Crow South, but economically it made sense. Nevertheless, when allowed, everyone, even white performers, had to be careful.

Charlie Thomas, who became a Drifter in 1958, told this story. The Drifters were on one those long bus tours filled with myriad performers, this one under the auspices of Dick Clark. In Mississippi, the crowd in the bus got rambunctious and bet him one thousand dollars that he and white singer Jackie DeShannon wouldn't hold hands and walk down the main street of the town they were currently in. When Dick Clark, who took care of his performers, heard about the bet, he was so unnerved about the potential for violence not only to Charlie and Jackie but all the performers that he warned the two directly, "If either one of you gets off this bus, you won't ever have to worry about working with me anymore." Thomas added, "We would probably have gotten killed."

Johnnie Ray was the next pop performer after Frank Sinatra to attract screaming crowds of teenagers. His most extraordinary year was 1950, the first of the new decade, when he sent "Cry" to #1 on the record charts and "The Little White Cloud that Cried," to #2. Perhaps, because of his unusual emotive singing style as compared to the bland performances of his contemporaries such as Vaughn Monroe, Guy Mitchell, and Perry Como, he was popular with African American teenagers. "Cry" was also #1 on the R&B charts and "The Little White Cloud that Cried" rose to #6 on the same listing.

On tour in 1952, Johnnie Ray landed in Mobile, Alabama, where they converted a local baseball field into an outdoor venue for his concert. Ray arrived at the field in the afternoon to watch the city set up, and he noticed a separate section of seats being unfolded near the first base line. Curious, he asked what those were for. He was told "that's where the n-----s sit." Ray quickly realized that was not going to work, because whoever sat along the first base line would be looking at his back the whole concert. So, he suggested that maybe a part of the main bleachers could be sectioned off for his Black fans. The city agreed only because the workers were able to rope off what was considered the worst seats. Johnnie Ray was an active performer and would rush around the stage instead of stiffly standing next to a microphone. The Black fans actually ended up with good seats and no one else was happy about that. Every time, Johnnie Ray moved toward the African American audience, anger rose with the white audience. The longer the show went on, the more palpable the hostility became. The tension was so great that as soon as his set ended Ray's handlers whisked him off the stage as quickly as possible. As Ray recalled, "After I finished the jubilee number at the end of my act, it was all a blur. I was not even allowed to take a curtain call. They rushed me into a waiting limousine—I was not even allowed to stay in the city of Mobile. I nearly ignited a race riot."[8]

Tennessee wasn't any better for Black performers or white teenagers attending rock 'n' roll concerts. In late April 1959, Sulphur Dell Park in Nashville hosted a big rock 'n' roll show of African American performers including Clyde McPhatter, LaVern Baker, Lloyd Price, the Coasters, and Frankie Lymon. The event was segregated, with white people on one side of the park, Black people on the other. At some point, police waded into the crowd of five thousand teenagers to arrest "two Negroes," a husband and wife, for fighting, and then they went after white teenagers who stepped over a perceived line of decorum. A white couple was arrested for dancing suggestively in public, and for good measure, the police also took into custody a second white couple who were seated next to the dancers. Maybe they had too much of the rock 'n' roll spirit.

After his difficult tour in 1952, Johnnie Ray's team did not book any more stadium shows in the South. In the north, Ray instead did shows with Black groups. He 1952, he appeared with the Dominoes at the (Chicago) Oriental Theatre. The show was so successful, he wanted to tour with the group. The problem was the Dominoes were in high demand and already booked out. *Jet* magazine's gossipy "Talking About" column on June 19, 1952, elucidated: "Johnnie Ray's explosive reaction upon finding the record-rave Dominoes, the singing quintet, had a long string of commitments and could not appear with him on other dates. . . . He had now taken an option to book for his own show when they run out of dates already contracted."[9]

Ray remained on good terms with Billy Ward. A year later, *Ebony* magazine ran a four-page spread on Johnnie Ray, titled "Negroes Taught Me to Sing." One of the highlights for the story was a double-spread photo of Ray and Ward "crying" together backstage at the Oriental.[10]

While Ray and Ward could compare experiences with racist crowds from the opposite side of the race divide, Joe Lamont's sudden, angry reaction to a fan ripping his tuxedo wasn't just because he stirred up a hornet's nest of hostility from the audience. He knew the torn lapel would cause him other problems and probably additional expenses. The Dominoes escaped a tough situation by driving like hell to another county. However, there was no escaping the wrath of Billy Ward.

Ward was angry at Lamont from the start, yelling at him, "why did you let them get that close?" That was only the beginning of Lamont-targeted criticism because Ward, an ex-soldier, was an absolute martinet and fanatical about the appearance of the Dominoes. No facial hair was allowed, and having spent years spit-shining shoes while in the service, any Dominoes with scuffed shoes meant the levying of a fine on the unpolished perpetrator. According to Yusuf Lamont, Ward would inspect shoes and if one was more highly polished than the other, both had to be redone. The Dominoes performed in tuxedos, which had to be perfect. The tuxedos were a uniform and the singers had a different tux for different nights—all of which they had to buy on their own.

"My father's tux was wrecked and they were 450 miles from New York where they could get it fixed," recalled Yusuf Lamont. "Next to what is now the Ed Sullivan Theater in Manhattan there used to be the Academy Cleaners, where the Dominoes had their tuxedos made and altered. The Academy would do spot cleaning and tailoring if you had a gig that night. Ward was from the military and it was all about the look of things. If a singer showed up at a gig and there was a spot on the "uniform" or it didn't fit right, Ward would dock his remuneration."[11]

It wasn't just his performers' clothes that worried Ward. He wanted control over their whole being, as a school does with a student or the military with a soldier. Ward created rules upon rules, each associated with a fine. As former Dominoes member David McNeil told musicologist Marv Goldberg: singers couldn't talk to members of the band, couldn't talk to the chauffeur, weren't allowed to leave their hotel room at night (and if you knew one of the other band members left the room and didn't tell Ward, it was a fine), couldn't stay at a hotel with other performers, not even in New York, and made them drink a warm glass of milk at night.[12]

Why would the individual Dominoes put up with such nonsense? The answer was simple; as with many groups at the time, formation was top-down. A manager or management group would create a singing group as they would employ people at a random company. Think of the singing group as a business entity and the singers as employees. Indeed, the Dominoes were salaried employees, as were other groups at the time. If you were the lead singer, you might get paid a little more, otherwise all singers got paid the same amount. Royalties went to management, which even owned the rights to the name of the group.

With the Dominoes, Billy Ward shared management and songwriting with his partner Rose Marks, who was a white Jewish woman. They met around 1945. At the time, Marv Goldberg reports, she owned a Broadway advertising agency although most other music historians say she ran a talent agency. The latter claim makes a little more sense because she became the manager of the ambitious ex-serviceman, who she immediately saw was a real talent and (unlike the people that worked with him) an amiably attractive young man. The two worked well together and tried their hand at cowriting songs, although not successful at first. Their better idea was for Ward to form a singing group, like the successful Mills Brothers and Ink Spots. They started working on that concept as early as 1948, and at this point it appears they officially teamed up as a management company because the two flirted with the idea of an all-female singing group, and in a classified ad looking for talent, the contact was Rose A. Marks, executive director. Later, when the two started successfully writing together for the Dominoes, they also formed the Ward-Marks Music Publishing Company.

Eventually, the two focused on getting a male group of singers formed. After a couple of false starts, in 1950, Ward formed the original lineup of the Dominoes. The name was initially chosen for an integrated group Ward put together and then disbanded. Goldberg speculated he resurrected the name in 1950 because of the white Rose Marks and Black Billy Ward team—domino tiles are black and white.[13]

Ward handled the talent and Marks, because of her history in the entertainment industry, worked the rest of the business, including getting the new Dominoes booked. When the group, then known as the Ques, won amateur night at the Apollo, according to Billy Vera, she was able to leverage that success to get the renamed Dominoes on the *Arthur Godfrey Show*.[14] Marks was aggressive. "She knocked down a lot of barriers for the Dominoes," said Yusuf Lamont. "Whatever the agreement was between Billy and Rose Marks, it was in return for getting them into new venues and not having the wrong people bothering them." Joe Lamont once said, "Rose always went to bat for us. She went out her way to not let people mistreat us. Rose didn't let anyone mistreat the group."

Although Yusuf claimed Rose was not a songwriter, per se, her name alongside Billy Ward appeared on almost all the Dominoes' songs, from "Weeping Willow Blues" to "Sixty Minute Man," from "Have Mercy Baby," to "I'd Be Satisfied," and from "The Bells" to "Pedal Pushin' Papa."[15]

Apparently, some people reacted badly to the close relationship between a white woman and a successful Black man—and that wasn't the white crowd. The unknown writer of another gossip column in *Jet* magazine went after Marks. For the June 25, 1953, issue, the "New York Beat" columnist wrote: "Woomance is rumored to have struck Billy Ward, leader of the Dominoes quartet, and his ofay personal manager, Rose Marks, who is his constant companion." The slang expression "ofay" was a derogatory term for white people used by African Americans.[16]

Of all the Dominoes, Joe Lamont was especially close with Rose Marks and there were rumors that he and Marks had a relationship, although Yusuf Lamont never bought into that gossip: "As far as I know they did not have a romantic relationship. They were good friends and sympatico. For that matter, I don't think Billy [Ward] did either."[17]

Rose was older than Billy and Joe Lamont, but that wasn't the issue. The tenor of the times was still segregation, legally and psychologically. Both Black people and white people did not like any commingling of the races.

Two years later, the columnist was still at it even when the news was tragic. For the July 14, 1955, issue of *Jet*, the scribe wrote: "Rose Marks, ofay manager and part owner of the Dominoes quartet, died after a long illness."[18]

The magazine finally dropped the offensive "ofay" adjective when the news was positive for Ward. On October 13, 1955, "New York Beat," reported, "The family of the late Rose Marks, ex-manager of the Dominoes quartet, is rumored to be quite unhappy because she willed most of her possessions to quartet leader Billy Ward."[19]

"I don't think she had any children," said Yusuf Lamont. "My dad was sad about Rose's passing. The group was her legacy; it was her children." Rose and Billy split the duties, with Billy as group leader and Rose as manager. After she died, Billy assumed both roles.[20]

Rose Marks's and Billy Ward's personal and professional relationships gripped like interlocking fingers. Together they were wonderfully creative, productive, and maybe—at least according to rumors—a little amorous. Obviously, Rose enjoyed working with Billy. She might have been the only one. Ward's management style with all the rules and fines, did not play well with the Dominoes, all of whom were adults, albeit some of them young adults. They chafed under his leadership and despite the success of the group began fleeing when they couldn't take Ward anymore. The first to leave was Charlie White.

An item in the November 24, 1951, issue of *Billboard* noted, "Lou Kresetz [probably Lou Krefetz or, according to writer Charles Gillett, Lou Krefitz], manager of the Clovers (under contract at Atlantic Records), this week signed Charlie White, lead singer [sic] of the Dominoes (at Federal Records), to a personal contract. White will join the Clovers and will also be signed to a recording contract as a single by Atlantic."[21]

Ahmet Ertegun of Atlantic wanted the Clovers to move toward a bluesier sound and saw his chance when the Clovers' lead singer, Buddy Bailey, who had a mellow voice, was drafted. To take his place, Ertegun signed White, a singer with a raspier tone, to record with the Clovers. White was the lead on some great Clovers records, including "Good Lovin'," a #2 R&B hit in 1953, and "Lovey Dovey," also a #2 R&B hit the following year.[22]

White did a good job and the Clovers' records continued to sell well, but when Bailey came back from the service, Ertegun moved White to the Cat label, where he sang with the Playboys, a group that quietly faded into obscurity. Writer Birnbaum has an alternative take on White's departure from the Clovers, that he had personal problems and was fired in September 1953.[23]

At the turn of the new decade, with the Orioles in temporary descendance and the Dominoes in ascendence, there was still plenty of room for a number of other seminal doo-wop groups to blossom. The third great doo-wop group of the early 1950s was the Clovers, which between 1951 and 1954 boasted fifteen Top Ten R&B hits, including three #1 R&B records.

Baltimore record store owner Lou Krefetz brought them to the attention of Atlantic Records owner Ertegun. Atlantic was a little behind the curve in signing singing groups and Ertegun wasn't too sure about the Clovers since they, too, were trying to imitate the Ink Spots, a sound which Ertegun thought outdated. In the end he took a chance and signed them to his label. At first encounter, the Clovers wanted to sing the Billy Eckstine hit "Prisoner of Love." Ertegun didn't think that song would do much for the Clovers or for Atlantic Records so he wrote a song for the group called "Don't You Know I Love You," which went straight to #1 on the R&B charts. It was followed by "Fool, Fool, Fool," which also went to #1. Like the Dominoes, the Clovers also indulged in a bit of musical hokum with the novelty doo-wop song "One Mint Julep" ("The lights were burning low, there in the parlor / when through the kitchen door, up popped her father / he said, 'I saw you when you kissed my daughter' / better wed her right now, or face a slaughter").[24]

Although the Clovers sang some fabulous ballads, including the original "Devil or Angel," if the Clovers are remembered at all today, it's for their novelty hits "One Mint Julep" and their best-selling record from 1959, "Love Potion No. 9."

Billy's management style worked until it didn't work anymore. Take the case of James Van Loan, who took the spot in the Dominoes vacated by White. He was from a musically inclined family: his brother Joe took over the lead tenor spot in the Ravens after Maithe Marshall left the group; later, another brother Paul also sang with the Ravens. On a tour that reached El Paso, Texas, Van Loan walked away, still wearing his tuxedo. Ward was so angry he had Van Loan arrested for stealing—the tuxedo! Things would get worse for Van Loan.[25]

The November 11, 1954, issue of *Jet* ran the headline "Despondent Singer Found After N.Y. Disappearance." The small news item ran this way: "Singer Jimmy Van Loan, bassist with the Five Dominoes, was found wandering on a west Philadelphia street corner a week after he disappeared from a New York hotel, during a fit of despondency over the recent death of his mother. Dirty, disheveled and speaking irrationally, Van Loan was unable to explain what he had done since disappearance and was apparently suffering a nervous breakdown. He had disappeared after leaving a note for Dominoes leader Billy Ward, declaring he was 'sorry for the trouble I have caused,' but that he found himself 'singing at night and crying in the daytime,' since his mother's death last September."[26]

There was also an ongoing problem with Joe Lamont, who became ill and left the Dominoes for a period of time. His son Yusuf explained, "My father had health concerns, he had ulcers, which were probably stress induced. He returned to the group in 1953 and was helping Billy manage, but being on the road was hard on the body and my father was older than the other guys. In 1950, he was already thirty years old, while most of his compatriots were in their teens or early twenties. He wanted to get off the road; on the eastern seaboard it was almost a show a night and in the Midwest it was a lot of driving. After he left the group he joined the Nation of Islam, so there was not a lot of commiserating with the old guys."[27]

After leaving the Dominoes and before ending up with the Clovers, Charlie White started his own group called the Checkers (another group name taken from a game, like the Dominoes). What happened was, it took a while before White was able to join the Clovers, and when Syd Nathan figured out what was happening with White, he made contact and induced the former Dominoes singer to form a new group, which his King Records proceeded to record. Early in 1952, Bill Brown, lead singer on "Sixty Minute Man" and an important cog in the Dominoes' musical wheel, reached the limit of patience with Ward and left to join Charlie White. Although White ostensibly founded the Checkers, by early 1953 he moved on to the Clovers and Brown took over the leadership of the group. The Checkers recorded some interesting songs including "White Cliffs of Dover" a remake of Vera Lynn's hit song from 1942, and "Don't Stop Dan," which, of course, was a return engagement of Lovin' Dan from "Sixty Minute Man," but nothing much happened for the Checkers and the group disbanded in 1955.

Then there was Clyde. His circumstances were different from those of the other original Dominoes. When he joined the group, he was only a seventeen-year-old teenager, so all the good fame and recording success arrived when he was still learning how to be a known entity. The only part of the professional music business he knew was being under Billy Ward's tutelage, and to some extent Ward's strict management style gave Clyde's life a structure. So, at first, he didn't chafe as much as the other Dominoes, with Billy's rules. Teenagers, however, can be rebellious, and as they drift into adulthood pick up nuances and deeply feel the slights of perceived injustice.

Like Clyde, Bill Brown was a star with the Dominoes, yet he left the group. Billy, who kept track of all the competitive and potential talent, quickly enticed Raymond Johnson, an experienced bass singer, to take his place. He didn't last long and was replaced by another known talent, David McNeil, who had been the bassman for a moderately successful doo-wop group, the Larks. McNeil, who died in 2005, was one of the old doo-wop dudes who were interviewed by Marv Goldberg.

When McNeil was brought into the Dominoes, he was assigned by Ward to be Clyde's roommate, which didn't turn out to be such a good idea. McNeil, a music veteran, had profound discussions with Clyde about the advances and royalties coming to the singers, which in the Dominoes was zero. The Dominoes were on salary and stuff such as tuxedos came out of pay. Clyde got a good schooling from McNeil on what compensation should have looked like. As Goldberg wrote, "Dave [McNeil] was severely reprimanded for talking with Clyde about these verboten subjects."[28]

As writer Jon Hartley Fox explained, each of the Dominoes was paid a flat weekly salary, which meant they benefited little from the huge hits and lucrative coast-to-coast touring. The profits were to have been invested on behalf of the Dominoes; members knew nothing about that.[29]

Clyde was also getting heat from his father. Billy Ward didn't pay them (Dominoes) too well, so when Clyde came back home to Harlem, his father harangued him, "Man, you come off the road and you end up with no money. What's going on with those guys? Forget the Dominoes."[30]

Sometimes Clyde did ignore the rules. David McNeil told the story of a Dominoes tour in Los Angeles, when the group was playing the Club Oasis. Back at their hotel after the show, Clyde, McNeil, and Van Loan were standing around when they heard a tapping. They looked around and at a window they could see a small group of girls who had climbed up the fire escape. The trio of guys could sense a good evening ahead and they just walked out of the hotel—and stayed away for about two weeks until Ward had them picked up by the police.

Los Angeles was a den of disillusionment for Clyde. After El Paso, when Billy Ward had Van Loan arrested, the group kept going west to LA. Now, with Lamont out sick and Van Loan in jail, Ward was down to two singers. He picked up Grady Chapman to take Van Loan's place. According to McNeil, Chapman was given Billy Ward's white uniform and Clyde was unhappily moved to second tenor. Most West Coast fans of the Dominoes only knew their sound from the radio and records, not so much from publicity stills or live performances, so when Chapman sang lead tenor, and he could sound like Clyde, few knew that it wasn't Clyde. After the show, Chapman signed autographs as Clyde McPhatter, which further infuriated Clyde.[31]

Lamont's place was taken by popular local singer Jesse Belvin, who would become a national star as both a singer and songwriter. At that moment, he was on the verge of fame as his recording of "Dream Girl," a duet with Marvin Phillips, was about to become a major R&B hit. "Belvin for my dad is interesting, but I don't know if that is factual," Yusuf Lamont contemplated. "It's been said by a few people, I just can't verify. If it happened my dad would have told me about it, but that's not to say Jesse he didn't step in. My dad just said there was a rotating group of people."[32]

Johnny Otis was the big wheel for West Coast R&B, a kind of paterfamilias for all the R&B groups, and Lamont believed Billy Ward went to Otis's club, which was where he heard Jackie Wilson for the first time. If an event like Jesse Belvin sitting in for session work happened, then Johnny Otis would have been the facilitator. As it was, Jesse Belvin as a performer and songwriter was about to explode.

In February 1953, the Dominoes unusual song "The Bells" and Jesse and Marvin's "Dream Girl" chased each other up and down the important song listings. On February 14, *Billboard* reported "Dream Girl" was the eighth best-selling R&B record in the country, one position ahead of "The Bells." Not to be outdone, "The Bells" was third most played R&B song on America's jukeboxes, whereas "Dream Girl" was just #7.[33]

The upright, and maybe uptight as well, Billy Ward was hardened by the Dominoes' good fortune, which bent his thinking. The star of the Dominoes was not Billy Ward, it was Clyde McPhatter, and to some extent that grated and an undercurrent of jealousy permeated the group. Ahmet told Deborah McPhatter, Clyde's daughter, that Clyde was definitely fired because everyone loved him and Billy Ward "was very, very jealous of that."

Billy formed the Dominoes, managed the group, and wrote its songs, but Clyde was an electrifying performer, who would do things with his voice no one else was doing at the time. (The situation was akin to Harold Melvin and the Blue Notes in the 1970s, when Teddy Pendergrass was lead singer and resident heartthrob. Pendergrass pushed to have the group renamed Harold Melvin and the Blue Notes featuring Theodore Pendergrass. It wasn't enough and he quit a year later to go solo.) Ward had a big ego, was always fractious, and became greedy for fame as well, introducing Clyde as his little brother, "Clyde Ward." The biggest change came after "Have Mercy Baby" became a huge hit. The group's name was altered to Billy Ward and His Dominoes.

Clyde had been thinking of leaving the Dominoes for a long time. In a letter to his girlfriend Lorraine Lowe, dated November 19, 1952, Clyde wrote, "things are not working out well with the Dominoes and me. So, when I come home, I think I'm going to organize my own group. So, then maybe things will be better all way around."[34]

Clyde's aspirations happened slowly, because he didn't quit the Dominoes until April 1953. He always maintained he left on his own volition. Billy Ward, in an attempt to get ahead of the story, publicly claimed he fired Clyde after matters "came to a head" in Providence, Rhode Island.[35]

Joe Lamont, who would leave the Dominoes months after Clyde, not for personnel reasons but because of his health, was a witness to the denouement of the Billy and Clyde soap opera that had been consistent since the end of 1952. Lamont was not righteously anti-Billy like the rest of the Dominoes; he respected Billy and always said you knew what you were getting with him. He also witnessed what Billy and Clyde both realized, that Clyde was not long for the Dominoes. It always appeared that Jackie Wilson was an instantaneous replacement for Clyde but Lamont knew that Billy had made contact with Jackie for that just-in-case moment. Everyone close to the Dominoes suspected

Clyde would leave and Billy had Jackie waiting in the wings, so there was an overlap during the prelude to Clyde actually leaving. In fact, Billy brought Jackie Wilson in either for a tryout or rehearsal, depending how deep one was into Billy's motivation. Lamont was there at the time and was greatly impressed with the young man and quickly understood that Jackie Wilson was going to be a great addition to the Dominoes—at least for a limited run. He turned to Billy and said, "You better get some more rehearsals ready." Surprised by the comment, Billy answered, "Why?" And Lamont said, "Because you are going to have to replace this guy, too." Billy fined him for saying that.[36]

Deborah McPhatter had her own version of the story. "I had been told that before my dad left, that Jackie Wilson was in training for two weeks prior to my dad leaving. That two-week span that Jackie was supposed to be in training to take my dad's place with Billy Ward, leads me to believe that my father leaving the group was by a mutual understanding."

On the surface, you would think that Clyde and Jackie were friends, but not so. Clyde did not like Jackie Wilson at all. "I don't think it was necessarily competition with the music," said Deborah. "Jackie was kind of nasty, especially with the females."

She continued that the Clyde-leaving-Billy story "gets tricky because I've heard three different versions. In one version, Billy told my dad he was fired. Ahmet told me that Billy fired my dad. On the other hand, my dad told me, he wasn't fired, but he knew for a long time he wasn't happy with the Dominoes. He wanted to leave and in the end he just left. Knowing my dad and his personality, I can visualize him just throwing his hands up into the air and saying 'fuck it, I'm out of here.'"

Deborah said she met Billy Ward when she was a child, but doesn't remember him. What she does remember is that Billy Ward held a grudge against her mother, Lorraine Lowe from Bermuda. Lorraine was not the woman Clyde married in 1953, which was also the year Deborah McPhatter was born. "Billy Ward did not like my mother. She was educated, became a successful businesswoman, and Clyde trusted her. Billy saw the influence my mom had with Clyde."[37]

An alternative version of the Clyde/Jackie Wilson story, this one perpetrated by *Rolling Stone* writer Joe McEwen, has Jackie Wilson dropping by the Fox Theater in Detroit during a Billy Ward and His Dominoes rehearsal. Clyde had already left the group and the ambitious Wilson told Ward he was a better singer than Clyde McPhatter. That boast landed him an audition and to Ward's astonishment the gasconade proved credible. The problem with this version of the story is that Jackie Wilson was an unreserved Clyde McPhatter fan, saying, "I learned a lot from Clyde—that high-pitched choke he used and other things. I know they say Little Richard when they say Jackie Wilson, but he did not give me anything. Clyde McPhatter was my man." In addition, Doug Saint

Carter, Jackie Wilson's biographer wrote, "Clyde McPhatter would have by far the greatest impact on Jackie's emerging stage and recording abilities. Jackie, in fact, admitted publicly that he had fallen in love with McPhatter's voice."[38]

In the end, it didn't make a difference, except to Clyde's or Billy's ego, about who said it first, "I quit" or "you're fired," as the break was perfect for Clyde. He immediately signed with Atlantic Records. Billy Ward didn't do too badly, either.

Johnny Otis, born in 1921, over a long career did it all in the music industry—composer, producer, bandleader, and even a recording star. In the late 1940s and '50s, he was in the right place at the right time. A native of California, he migrated from the small town of Vallejo to Los Angeles, just at the time when R&B was exploding. Clubs and independent recording companies proliferated simply because there was so much homegrown talent in South-Central Los Angeles, not to mention the soon-to-be-famous who wanted to be a part of the LA music scene. In 1948, Otis opened an R&B nightspot called the Barrelhouse Club, which, like many Black-oriented venues, boasted an amateur night—and a lot of talent came through, everyone from Hank Ballard to Little Willie John to Etta James. Around 1951, a seventeen-year-old singer named Jackie Wilson played the club. When Otis saw him perform, he called Syd Nathan at King Records. This is the way Wilson remembered it: "Syd sent Ralph Bass. He heard me. He heard Little Willie John. He heard the Dominoes. He passed on me and Willie John, signed the Dominoes." Someone who was impressed by Wilson was Billy Ward, who took his name and telephone number. Wilson went to work at Lee's Sensation Club and forgot about Ward. Then two years later, in 1953, he got a call. It was Billy Ward, who wanted him to take over as the Dominoes' tenor and lead singer. In the swinging door of the group, Clyde left and Jackie Wilson walked in—a busy April 1953 for Billy Ward.[39]

New careers and new groups, lots of recordings, and the best and worst of personality traits frothed upward. That summer of 1953, the amorous Clyde McPhatter got married to a woman named Nora Thompson.[40] For Billy Ward, it was the usual mix of good and bad. To the positive, in August of that year, Billy Ward and His Dominoes were selected to entertain President Eisenhower at the Cherry Hill Country Club in Denver. Also on the bill were Bing Crosby and Bob Hope.[41] Meanwhile, old grievances continued: Ward told the press he was going to file charges with the musicians' union over disagreements he had with boxer Sugar Ray Robinson on their recent tour. The bitter Robinson-Ward feud, which started when Robinson was given top billing on a show, reached its peak during a Chicago engagement when Sugar Ray refused to pose for pictures with Ward.[42] That tiff spilled over into 1954, when Ward filed charges with the American Guild of Variety Artists and the American Federation of Musicians and asked for a release from his contract with the Joe Glaser Booking Agency. Ward accused the agency of mismanagement in booking, failure to represent the Dominoes properly, and charged that during the recent Sugar Ray Robinson–Dominoes tour, his group received improper billing. In response, Glaser called Ward a "troublemaker."[43]

In the summer of 1954, Billy Ward and His Dominoes were to share top billing with Nat King Cole at the "mammoth" Detroit State Fair. This was a perfect match, because once Clyde McPhatter left the Dominoes, Ward, who had an abiding affection for 1930s and '40s pop ballads, turned his group 180 degrees. For the most part, proto-rock 'n' roll was gone and smooth pop was in.[44]

"Billy walked away from the jump blues stuff to more huddle-around-the-radio, show-tunes fare," said Yusuf Lamont. That was because Billy was an unholy contradiction of being both old-fashioned and progressive. He realized the Dominoes needed to cross over to the pop charts if they were ever going to be bigger, better, and lucrative. To get to that wider appeal, Ward fixated on the 1940s, when young people huddled around the radio listening to those dreamy ballads on the Hit Parade. (Unfortunately, Jackie Wilson got caught in this loop as well and when he went solo, he would continue to sing ethnic chestnuts such as "Danny Boy" and "My Yiddishe Momme.")[45]

Ward began the shift while Clyde was still with the group. After "The Bells," the Dominoes released the highly romantic "These Foolish Things (Remind Me of You)," with Clyde at his unparalleled best: "A cigarette that bears a lipstick's traces / an airline ticket to romantic places / and still my heart has wings / these foolish things remind me of you."

Later in the year came a cover of "Rags to Riches," Tony Bennett's huge hit (eight weeks at #1 on the pop charts). "I know I'd go from rags to riches, if you would only say you care / And though my pocket may be empty, I'd be a millionaire."

This time out, Jackie Wilson took the lead. Both songs went to #2 on the R&B charts.

After some lean years, Billy took his group to different labels, first Jubilee and then Decca Records, where the Dominoes bagged the group's first big hit, "St. Therese of the Roses," to cross over to the pop charts since "Sixty Minute Man." The operatic song, with Jackie Wilson on the lead, went to #27 in the pop world and no listing on the R&B charts. The group's final two big hits, "Star Dust" and "Deep Purple," came in 1957. These over-the-top renditions were covers from the American songbook: "Star Dust" was a 1927 tune written by Hoagy Carmichael, and "Deep Purple" was composed by pianist Peter DeRose and published in 1933. There had been many, many resurrections of "Deep Purple" from the 1930s through the 1950s, while in the rock 'n' roll era, the most popular version was by brother-sister act Nino Tempo and April Stevens. It went to #1 in 1963.

Jackie Wilson was long gone when Billy Ward and His Dominoes sang "Star Dust" and "Deep Purple." The lead for both was Eugene Mumford.

When Ruth Brown crossed paths with Jackie Wilson for the first time, it was almost his last moments with the Dominoes. She wrote, "I had just met Jackie when he was with Billy Ward and the Dominoes as Clyde McPhatter's replacement. He darned near got himself fired that night after offering me a drink at the bar. Miss Rose Marks, manager of the group at the time, bawled him out in front of everyone, and that was the beginning of the end as far as Jackie was concerned."[46]

Wilson appreciated Billy Ward's strengths while acknowledging his deficiencies: "He was a choral coach at Carnegie Hall. He played piano and organ, could arrange, and was a fine director and coach. He knew what he wanted, and you had to give it to him. And he was a strict disciplinarian. . . . I studied under him about two years straight, and I stayed with the Dominoes until 1956."[47]

CHAPTER FIVE

MONEY HONEY

In 1951, the year that R&B/doo-wop crashed the airwaves big time, *Billboard*'s Rhythm and Blues record charts were dominated by three independent record companies: Atlantic, King/Federal, and Aladdin. The last company was six years old, having been formed in Los Angeles by Eddie and Leo Mesner. It started out as more of a jazz label before slowly migrating to R&B. Together the three companies produced more than half of the thirty top R&B hits that year. Aladdin could boast five of those songs: "Black Night" and "Seven Long Days" by Charles Brown, "The Glory of Love" by the Five Keys, "Bad, Bad Whiskey" by "Amos Milburn," and "I Got Loaded" by Peppermint Harris." Federal/King did almost as well, with four plus one Top Thirty songs: "Sixty Minute Man" and "Do Something for Me" by the Dominoes, "I'm Waiting Just for You" by Lucky Millinder, and "Flamingo" by Earl Bostic. "Bloodshot Eyes" by Wynonie Harris was a Top Thirty jukebox hit.

The winningest label was Atlantic with "Teardrops from My Eyes" by Ruth Brown, "Chains of Love" by Big Joe Turner, "Don't You Know I Love You" and "Fool, Fool, Fool" by the Clovers, and "Anytime, Any Place, Anywhere" and "Don't Take Your Love from Me" by Joe Morris. "Tennessee Waltz Blues" by Stick McGhee was a Top Thirty jukebox hit.

Two years later, a lot more labels swarmed into the R&B field, and a couple of the premier companies producing in that genre lost dominance. Thanks to Amos Milburn and his drinking songs, Aladdin mustered two Top Thirty songs, "Let Me Go Home, Whiskey" and "One Scotch, One Bourbon and One Beer," and one jukebox hit, "I'm Gone," by Shirley and Lee. Federal/King did one worse with just one song, "Soft" by Tiny Bradshaw, on the charts and "The Bells" by the Dominoes as a jukebox Top Thirty platter.

The only company to hold steady was Atlantic, which not only boasted the #1 R&B hit for the year, "(Mama) He Treats Your Daughter Mean," by Ruth Brown, but also a slew of other best-selling records: "Wild, Wild Young Men" by Ruth Brown, "Good Lovin'" and "Crawlin'" by the Clovers, "Honey Hush" by Big Joe Turner, and, perhaps the ultimate insult to Federal/King, former Dominoes lead singer Clyde McPhatter with his new group the Drifters and their chart-dominating song "Money Honey."

How did Atlantic Records, formed in 1947, become a powerful R&B label in so short a time and end up with Clyde McPhatter on its label? That's really a story about a couple of wild, wild young men—with a dream.

In the early 1940s, the Turkish brothers Ahmet and Nesuhi Ertegun boasted a comfortable life. Ahmet was a student while his older brother dabbled in different music ventures. They were in the United States because their father Mehmet Munir Ertegun was Turkey's ambassador to the United States. That carefree existence changed suddenly on November 11, 1944, when Mehmet was struck down by a coronary thrombosis. After his death, Mehmet's wife and daughter returned to Turkey, but his two boys stayed in this country. The two brothers were crazy for American jazz and blues music and dabbled in the industry, promoting shows and amassing a huge collection of 78 rpm records.[1] As it turned out, being an overzealous collector of obscure 78s bought for a nickel or a dime became a thousand-record accumulation. It came in handy because when Ahmet needed funds just for living expenses, he sold the records for $5 to $25 apiece. Nesuhi by this time moved to Los Angeles, got married and ran the Jazzman Record Shop.

Ahmet remained in Washington, DC, ostensibly to do graduate work at Georgetown University, but he was spending most of his time hanging out at Waxie Maxie's record store in the Black section of the city. This was Ahmet's real-life education, as there were waves of change rolling through the music world and a perceptive young man could pick up quite a bit of insider knowledge from the denizens of a big-city record shop, where collectors, performers, promoters, and sycophants gathered.

The first important change was in the supply of raw materials for record manufacturing. Due to World War II, there had been a shortage of shellac, a key ingredient in the making of a 78 record. With the war over, shellac was again available and a host of new record companies sprang up. The old "race" (rhythm and blues) genre had been all but abandoned by the major record labels as the music industry curtailed under the war effort. After the conflict ended, hundreds of small firms specializing in blues and R&B appeared, like plant seedlings after a long winter. Mainly, this odd phenomenon occurred because of two economic trends. First, there was a demand for new music among the younger generation of the late 1940s. Second, it was relatively inexpensive to create a music business and hundreds of record labels with some rhythm and blues recordings appeared in the post–World War II years. Most of these were tiny and ultimately evanescent.

One of those record entrepreneurs was Ahmet, who by 1947 had met enough of those would-be record titans to conclude he knew more about the record business than most of them. "I met these guys and I realized that none of them knew anything about the music," Ertegun recalled. "One of them had been . . . a jukebox operator who thought, 'Well, we're having trouble getting records so we might as well make some ourselves.' I met all these people and they had no idea of songs; they had no idea of musicians."[2]

Committed to starting a new record label, Ahmet first found an investor, Dr. Vahdi Sabit, a dentist whose patients included the Ertegun family. Ahmet still needed an experienced industry person so he got together with an old friend, Herb Abramson, who had worked at National Records, and induced him to join his nascent company. In October 1947, Atlantic Records was launched.[3] It did not go smoothly at the beginning as the rookie music entrepreneurs stumbled through a number of false starts. Then their luck changed—just in the nick of time. Well, some people say you make your own luck, and that was the case with Atlantic Records. The company was saved by Ahmet's propensity to befriend everyone in the music world, and some very quick thinking.

After two years in business, it was Ahmet's practice to dial up his distributors around the country to take the orders for Atlantic Records. In New Orleans, his distributor William B. Allen took his call. They chatted and Ahmet eventually asked for his order, which was only thirty singles. That was hardly a dent in the growing New Orleans market for R&B and Ahmet pressed Allen if he could push Atlantic Records a little harder. Allen liked Ahmet but he still had to deliver the bad news, that the New Orleans market, which, getting busier by the day with its own idiosyncratic take on R&B, was not very interested in anybody Atlantic was producing. Ahmet leaned in: so who was hot in New Orleans? Allen responded that there was a song selling on both the very obscure Harlem and Cincinnati labels that the market was mad for but for some reason no one could find copies. Allen was so desperate for copies he told Ahmet that if he could find a supply, he would take 5,000 copies. Amazed at the size of such an order for a song he never heard of, Ahmet told Allen he would see what he could do but he needed Allen to send a copy of the record, which was called "Drinkin' Wine Spo-Dee-O-Dee," by Stick McGhee.[4]

Since the labels were probably extinct, Ahmet came up with the brilliant plan to make an exact copy of the song on his own label. Country blues was not Ahmet's métier, so he was initially stumped as to who he would get to record the tune. Then he remembered he had met a musician in Harlem named

Brownie McGhee, who sang this kind of blues. He gave him a call and explained that he was looking for someone to cover "Drinkin' Wine Spo-Dee-O-Dee." Brownie exclaimed, "that's my brother's record." After Ahmet asked how he could contact him, Brownie answered, "he's right here." As luck would have it, Stick McGhee was staying with his sibling and Brownie put him on the line. Just to make sure Ahmet wouldn't be dancing on another record label's rights to the song, he asked Stick McGhee if he signed any contracts. As Ahmet would tell the story, Stick answered, "No man, I never signed anything. They gave me $75 and a couple of hot dogs."

Atlantic rerecorded the song with Stick McGhee and his brother singing backup. According to Ahmet, Atlantic vended 700,000 copies of the record and in those loosey-goosey times, and probably another 300,000 bootleg copies were sold. The record went to #2 on the R&B chart and even crossed over to the pop charts as well. It was the seventh best-selling R&B song of 1949. "Drinkin' Wine Spo-Dee-O-Dee" was a monster record and it made Atlantic, which then entered a prolonged winning streak. Soon the label signed up proto–rock 'n' rollers Ruth Brown, Joe Turner, and a talented blind musician named Ray Charles.[5]

From the very start of the new decade, young Ruth Brown and veteran Joe Turner with their jump-blues style were major Atlantic successes. Ray Charles would have his first big hit in 1953. The solitary singer was where Atlantic under Ahmet and Herb Abramson excelled, which was one reason Ahmet, in particular, did not favor the groups. Still, it wasn't difficult to read the tea leaves. The small-group sound backed with minimal instrumentation (later to be called doo-wop) was exploding. Teenagers, who bought into the new technology of the day, the inexpensive 45 rpm record, craved the sound. So, after taking a chance on the Clovers, which proved to be a major success story, Ahmet and Abramson expanded their search for another group.

By the 1950s, *Billboard*'s year-end compilations of the top songs were based on record sales and jukebox plays. In 1952, three song groups highlighted the Top Ten R&B tunes of the year. In seventh and eighth place were the Clovers' "One Mint Julep" and "Ting-A-Ling." Sitting at #2 was "Have Mercy Baby" by Billy Ward and His Dominoes.

The lyrics to "Ting-A-Ling" included the line "The way they rock 'n' roll and hold me, angel child." The usage of the term rock 'n' roll was still in the traditional sense a sexual reference. "Ting-A-Ling" was not a rock 'n' roll song. Neither was "One Mint Julep." Although rock 'n' roll in the sense as a genre of music didn't exist in 1952, "Have Mercy Baby" was about as close as one could get to it in the early 1950s. The Dominoes weren't an Atlantic group, but Ahmet leaned heavily into producing jump blues songs, which were a precursor to rock 'n' roll. He enjoyed the Dominoes sound and was in awe of its lead singer,

Clyde McPhatter. Ahmet confessed to Billy Vera that he loved "Have Mercy Baby."[6] To writer Gerri Hirshey he said, "I was mad for Clyde's voice."[7] And to Charlie Gillet he explained, "I liked his (Clyde McPhatter) high voice and the way he sang."[8] To others Ahmet gushed, "Clyde was a singer from heaven with the most lyrical voice."[9]

One of the great pop music legends, and a tale told often by Ahmet, begins this way. One day, early in 1953, while reading the newspaper, he learned that the Dominoes were scheduled to play Birdland in Manhattan. It caught his eye for two reasons. First, the venue was an odd booking for the Dominoes, since Birdland was a jazz club and the Dominoes were anything but jazzy. And second, Birdland might be worth a visit, if for nothing else than to see Clyde McPhatter in action. On the day of the Dominoes show, Ahmet made his way to 315 West 44th Street with great expectations, but after watching the Dominoes perform, he was extremely disappointed. Clyde McPhatter was not in the lineup and nowhere to be seen. After the Dominoes finished its set, Ahmet headed backstage looking for Billy Ward, finally cornering him.

"Where's Clyde?" he asked politely.

In response, Billy snarled, "I fired his ass."

"Uh, where is he?"[10]

Billy didn't know. Clyde didn't know either, but here was the hottest talent in the business now a free agent, and Ahmet knew he had to get to him with a contract offer before anyone else was aware he was no longer a member of the Dominoes.

In numerous recitations, the story stays mostly the same but the details blur. In an abbreviated version, Ahmet recalled. "Nobody knew [where he was], but he would probably be at home . . . got his phone number, called him up, had dinner the next day, and signed him up."[11]

For her book *Nowhere to Run: The Story of Soul Music*, Gerri Hirshey interviewed Ahmet Ertegun. She picturesquely wrote: "Ertegun embarked on one of his legendary talent hunts. Tracking down blind blues singers or a backwoods piano genius, Ertegun was often party to wild road rallies in taxi and limo, through Harlem or Louisiana bayous, into pricey clubs and cheap hotels. As a mogul in the making, Ertegun was tireless . . . about pursuing his musical infatuations. . . . The search for Clyde McPhatter led to a furnished room in Harlem. There the deal was cut."

Jerry Wexler, who went to work for Atlantic, noted that Ahmet was a night owl and he maintained musicians' hours, coming into the office in the afternoon and stalking clubs till the wee hours of the morning, combing the city for singers.[12]

Hirshey's retelling is close to the story Ahmet told Billy Vera, except with a little twist: "Ertegun runs out [of the Birdland] and goes up to Harlem where he asks everybody he knows where Clyde McPhatter could be found. Finally, someone knew where he was. Ertegun locates him and says, 'we would like to sign you to Atlantic Records.' Clyde answered, 'I'll make records for you if you promise me you will not play drums on the record like Mr. Nathan (Syd Nathan of King/Federal Records).'" Vera doubted this part of the story. "I don't think that's true at all. That was something Ahmet made up to make the story more colorful. I never heard of Syd Nathan playing on records. Don't forget he had great producers, Ralph Bass and Henry Glover, and they used top musicians."[13]

The press got wind of the Clyde McPhatter's on-the-run story late in May 1953 and played it as a music industry newsworthy item. *Billboard* buried its version of Clyde McPhatter going to a new label at the bottom of a busy news page, way in the interior of the magazine. Blink and the reader probably missed it. The small print headline read: "McPhatter Signs With Atlantic," and a straightforward, two-paragraph item read: "Atlantic Records added an important piece of talent to its R&B stable this week with the pacting [contract signing] of Clyde McPhatter, former lead singer of the Dominoes, and his new vocal group. McPhatter has been the lead singer of the Dominoes for the past few years and sparked the group on its waxings [recordings] of 'Do Something for Me' and 'Have Mercy Baby,' which he penned . . . the singer's contract is a long-term deal. McPhatter's first waxings with his new group will be released next month."[14]

In the same issue of *Billboard*, Bob Rolontz, who wrote "Rhythm and Blues Notes" and was one of the most knowledgeable and insightful writers on R&B scene, led off his May 30, 1953, column with the Clyde McPhatter story, except there were other things going on at Atlantic at the same time and he first began the column with those disparate changes, of course, not knowing these variants would eventually affect McPhatter's experience with his new label. Rolontz wrote that Jerry Wexler, an old associate of his at *Billboard*, had joined Atlantic Records as a partner and "will work with Ahmet Ertegun in all phases of the firm's business, including A&R (artist and repertoire), sales, etc."[15] The reason for Wexler joining the firm was that Herb Abramson had been drafted and was sent to Germany.

Wexler remembered the hectic times as happening in stages. "Before I arrived on the scene, Ahmet recruited a vocalist whose influence . . . would shape a whole generation of soul singers in the sixties, from Smokey Robinson to Marvin Gaye to Ronnie Isley to Curtis Mayfield to Aaron Neville. I'm talking about Clyde McPhatter."

(Wexler didn't do so badly either. His wife negotiated the deal with Atlantic, which included a corporate buy-in of 13 percent of Atlantic for $2,063.25. Ahmet took that money and bought a green Cadillac convertible, which he then gave to Wexler, who observed, "back then all record execs drove Caddies.")[16]

In the same column, Rolontz also addressed the Atlantic Records signing of Clyde McPhatter, adding that the label's new singer had already formed a new group.[17] Two weeks later, on June 12, 1953, Larry Douglas, whose syndicated column, "Theatrically Yours," appeared in Black newspapers across the country, succinctly repeated the important part of the McPhatter news to his readers: "Clyde McPhatter, former lead singer with the Dominoes, has formed a new group."[18] This was not necessarily major, but at least exciting, news in the music world of Black America.

As part of Clyde's agreement with Ahmet, who was now convinced of the viability of groups, Clyde was to form his own union of performers, which he did, apparently very quickly—actually too quickly!

"Clyde told me he had some friends who would form a group with him," Ahmet recalled. "He collected them together and brought them in for a session [recording]. We taped some stuff, but they weren't much good; not what I was looking for, which was a gospel sort of sound, which was how Clyde sang naturally."[19]

Probably as early as May 1953, Clyde was rehearsing this first group of backup singers, which were eventually brought in for a recording session. This was not a formal session in a true studio. In those days, Atlantic's offices were on West 56th Street, over an Italian restaurant, and instead of spending big dollars, Ahmet, Wexler, and engineer Tom Dowd just transformed Atlantic's work space into a temporary studio. To make room, they stacked desks. Camp chairs and microphones were brought in. A small RCA portable, four-position, mono-mix recording machine served as the console. The control booth was about four feet wide and fifteen feet long, room enough for Dowd and one other person.[20] It all sounded professional but not necessarily good. Nevertheless, the group was taken to a real studio in June 1953 for its next recording session. The better studio didn't make for a better sound, and Ahmet told Clyde this group didn't have it.

As a rule, vocal groups were not rehearsed, as most doo-wop producers lined up their groups in droves and pushed them in front of the mic to do their songs in one take, Wexler explained with some hyperbole. "There were no arrangements, and the band [actually the singers]—standard three rhythm plus tenor—hadn't even heard the tune and certainly not the key. As soon as one group finished two sides, another would be shoved forward on the assembly line. I'm glad to say we went our own way. We broke the mold and rehearsed. We even scrapped the first [recording] session. Neither the material nor the group members were worthy of Clyde McPhatter."[21]

"Clyde had pulled some gospel friends together and had done a session," recalled Bill Pinkney of the original Drifters. "It wasn't what the company was looking for, so 'Lucille' and 'Gone' were put in the can [shelved]. They [Ahmet and Wexler] said the sound was too light and not balanced. They said they wanted stronger, more gospel anointed voices."[22]

"So, he (Clyde) had another group of friends who were really good, gospel singers called the Thrasher Wonders, one of them [Andrew Thrasher] could sound just like the bass of the Dominoes," Ahmet said. "I told Clyde he should change his name. Clyde McPhatter sounded like a Western comedy actor—Andy Devine or somebody—but Clyde liked his name."[23]

Ahmet's memory is slightly off. Clyde went first to Gerhart Thrasher, who he knew from gospel group the Thrasher Wonders. Gerhart first recruited his brother Andrew. Clyde also wanted Bill Pinkney, so he sent Gerhart to find him. Gerhart told Pinkney that Clyde was putting an R&B group together and would like to talk with him, which he did. That's when Pinkney found out Clyde had signed a personal contract with Atlantic.

All the new recruits lived relatively close to each other in Harlem. "Clyde was on the west side of 127th Street near 7th Avenue, Gay [Gerhart] and Bubba [Andrew] were on 128th, and I was at 134th and Lenox Avenue," said Pinkney, looking back in time. "The guys were all young, in their late teens and early twenties. I was the oldest, at 26, so Clyde put me in charge, and I was the group spokesperson."

They would add a fifth member, William Ferbee, who was on the first recording session, but left right after that. He never toured with the Drifters nor recorded with the group again. When Ferbee left, Clyde shuffled Pinkney from top tenor to bass, Gerhart to tenor, and Andrew (Bubba) to baritone. That's how the Drifters ended up being a quartet.

The first rehearsal of the group was at Bill Pinkney's place, but they would end up practicing at each other's homes or at their friend Carrie's apartment, because she would make dinner for them. When they finally went down to the Atlantic offices, rehearsals were set up with Jesse Stone, who would be the arranger.[24]

At the time Atlantic had an office in a loft at 234 West 56th Street. As noted, there were just two desks in the space, one for Ahmet and the other for Herb Abramson, which became Jerry Wexler's when Herb went into the service. There was also a "miniature piano," so when people came into the office, they would play on it. When the Drifters came to record, they saw the desks being piled atop the other and chairs being brought in so the band had a place to sit. The engineer on these early recordings was Tom Dowd.[25] The new group used two microphones, with Clyde on one and the rest of the guys on the other. Ahmet always sought out the best in everything and for this first recording he brought in a couple of top-notch musicians including Sam "The Man" Taylor on tenor sax, and the top session guitarist on the East Coast, Mickey Baker, who in 1957 would team up with Sylvia Vanderpool to sing "Love Is Strange" as Mickey and Sylvia.

According to Pinkney, Ahmet and Jerry loved the results from that recording session so much, they offered the Drifters a contract on the spot.[26]

Moving from one record company to another was not as smooth a process as it should have been, especially amongst the smaller independents when there was a breakout star at the center of attention. The old record company scrapped to find a reason not to let the would-be star legally move on. That is what happened to Clyde McPhatter. When Atlantic Records announced the signing of Clyde, his old label sought to stall the change. As the June 13, 1953, *Cash Box* reported, "Federal Records created a situation in which both Atlantic and Federal claim exclusive rights to the chanter [singer]." What happened was, after Clyde obtained his formal departure from Billy Ward and His Dominoes, the singer showed Atlantic Records executives the signed release and was then inked to a long-term contract. Syd Nathan, president of Federal and King labels, was in New York at the time and upon being advised by his Cincinnati office of Clyde McPhatter signing with Atlantic, placed the matter in the hands of his attorney "for clarification." As Nathan told *Cash Box*, "While it is true that McPhatter has a perfectly valid release from Billy Ward and Rose Marks, it is also true that McPhatter has an individual contract with Federal Records. He belongs to us."[27]

Nathan had tried a similar legal move when Bill Brown walked away from the Dominoes. It didn't work with Brown, who moved on anyway, but Nathan's attorneys could gum up the process. A month later, *Cash Box* reported Clyde McPhatter was recording with his new (unnamed) group while King Records still maintained it had the rights to the singer.[28]

Tom Dowd was given the job of escorting Clyde over to King/Federal Records to get him out of his existing contract after some "wheeling and dealing," recollected Pinkney.[29]

Nathan's ploy failed with McPhatter as well. The August 29, 1953, issue of *Cash Box* finally let the cat out of the bag in regard to the naming of McPhatter's new group. A headline over a single paragraph news item read, "McPhatter Forms the Drifters."[30]

Allegedly the name was chosen because most of its members drifted from group to group.[31] When the lineup did the first recordings, it didn't have a name yet and the question overhanging everything was "What are we going to call ourselves?" At the time Pinkney summed it up for everyone: "Everybody seems to be taking on bird names. Is there a bird called a drifter?" He asked the question because he felt everyone in the group had been "drifting." Clyde responded by saying he didn't know if there was a bird called a drifter, but he liked that name and said, "Let's call ourselves drifters, The Drifters." The group all agreed.[32]

Ahmet and Jerry Wexler wanted a "cool name" for Clyde's new group and spent hours on the subject. "The Drifters had a disconcertingly bucolic ring for us, on the order of Bob Wills and the Texas Playboys," said Wexler, "But Clyde wouldn't budge: 'Drifters' it was."[33]

Although the *Cash Box* news story about McPhatter forming the Drifters was diminutive, it contained two important items of newsworthiness: first, that the Drifters would have their first record released within a week or two, and second, the group announced it had a new manager. The phrasing in the story was unusual in that it shifted the focus of the news to a supporting player instead of just on the group: "Clyde McPhatter ... formed his own vocal group called the Drifters, it was announced by George Treadwell, who signed him to a personal management contract recently."[34]

Whereas Billy Ward, along with Rose Marks, managed the Dominoes, Clyde was an entertainer and not business-focused by any means. Probably at the suggestion of Ahmet, Clyde brought in George Treadwell, a veteran of the music industry and labelmate Ruth Brown's manager, to take on similar duties. According to Tina Treadwell, Clyde and her father George Treadwell came to Atlantic at the same time.[35]

Born in 1918 in New Rochelle, New York (where Clyde would later own a house), George Treadwell was a handsome and talented trumpeter, who got his initial break playing in the house band at a Harlem nightclub and then with guys like Benny Carter and Cootie Williams. He shifted through a number bands before backing a young Sarah Vaughan soon after the close of World War II. The label on her single "I Cover the Waterfront" from 1947 credits Sarah Vaughan with George Treadwell's Orchestra. The record was great for Sarah and good for Treadwell. He was smart and ambitious and not a shrinking violet type. He married Sarah Vaughan and took on the role of her manager. They divorced in 1957. He also became the manager of Ruth Brown, which probably was how he met Clyde McPhatter. Later on, he would manage, at the end of their careers, Billie Holiday and Sammy Davis Jr.

As a manager, Treadwell was tough, shrewd, and could get past the inherent racism of the music industry. He was also avaricious. Tina Treadwell called him a good businessman.

This is the way Ruth Brown described him: "He certainly possessed the gift of gab and liked the finer things in life. Tall, a bit flashy, with a pencil-thin mustache and always impeccably groomed, George was a real Black Dorian Gray, who never lived long enough to complete the role he was playing."[36]

Treadwell smoked a couple of packs of Benson & Hedges cigarettes a day and died of lung cancer at age forty-eight. Tina's mother Fayrene Johnson, Treadwell's second wife, took over the group and moved her management office to London. Tina Treadwell now manages the Drifters touring group.

The usage of "Drifters" as a name for a singing group wasn't uncommon, especially in the country and western world. Perhaps it was for this defensive reason, and not anything nefarious, that when the name "The Drifters" was finally chosen by Clyde for his new group, Clyde and Treadwell formed a company called Drifters Inc. to manage and own the rights to the name of the new group (similar to Billy Ward and the Dominoes). Each of the Drifters' singers also had to contract with Atlantic Records as individual performers. Treadwell obtained a copyright on the group's appellation, giving some legal protection against fakers trying to sneak gigs as "The Drifters." Treadwell having his name on the copyright as well would have implications a lot sooner than expected.[37]

Time was money and as always, once talent was signed and secured, the rush to get a new record to the public was of paramount importance, especially for the independents. Even Atlantic's growing roster of R&B talent was thin compared to the major record companies. While the signing of new singers was important, that was half the battle. The talent needed to make money for the company. As *Cash Box* predicted, Atlantic was hell bent on bringing out a Drifters record as soon as possible.

Clyde might have been stuck on a name, but Atlantic wasn't hanging around waiting. It already had the unnamed group run through a list of songs. Early in August, Atlantic hustled a recording session, this one with the new iteration of the group, plus guitarist Walter Adams. The practice since the late 1940s was to have a group of four or five singers, plus one or two regular musicians to complement the vocalists. Five songs were recorded in this session: "The Way I Feel," "Money Honey," "Gone," "What'cha Gonna Do," and "Let the Boogie Woogie Roll." Every song boasted Clyde on the lead.[38]

The most unusual song was "Let the Boogie Woogie Roll." With Clyde in the lead, the Drifters start with an echo background, where they repeat Clyde on the refrain. Clyde sings "Let the Boogie Woogie Roll" and the Drifters respond, "let it roll, let it roll." Clyde sings, "I feel so sad," and the Drifters respond, "I feel so sad." Then the Drifters shift the background fill to the words "doo-wop, doo-wop, doo-wop," which some claim is the first appearance of that sound (or lyric) in pop music. What makes it really interesting is that the song wasn't released in the early 1950s, finally making an appearance around 1960.

Of all the songs recorded in that session, the clear stand-out was "Money Honey," a bouncy tune crossed with a bit of whimsy. It was an Atlantic in-house creation, arranged and written by Jesse Stone, who was one of the first hires by Ahmet when he formed the label back in 1947. Ironically, Stone, arranger and songwriter, was at the time the only Black person in the new company.[39] It was a brilliant hire by Ahmet as Stone, who was born in 1901, had been in the entertainment business since he was four years old and playing in his family's vaudeville show. By the 1920s, he had his own band, playing in Kansas City, the Midwest's hothouse of blues. He drifted through different bands, ending up in New York, where he met Louis Jordan and encouraged him to leave

Chick Webb's band and go out on his own. In turn, Jordan hired Stone to write his first arrangements and hired him and his band to back him up.[40] In the early 1940s, Stone scored his first big hits, "Idaho" for Benny Goodman, and "Sorghum Switch" for Jimmy Dorsey.

By 1945, Stone and his friend Herb Abramson decided National Records looked like greener pastures for both of them. It wasn't. As Stone told Nick Tosches, Al Greene, who headed National, wasn't "handling things right." Greene had a lot of great Black talent under contract (Billy Eckstine and the Ravens, for example) but he wasn't doing much with them. "Herb and I came up with the idea of starting a record company of our own," Stone remembered. "We figured we could do what a guy like Greene was doing. The only trouble was Herb Abramson didn't have any money and neither did I. Then, finally, Herb ran into Ahmet Ertegun. Ahmet had money. That was the beginning of Atlantic Records."[41]

Stone wrote many famous songs, including "Don't Let Go," for Roy Hamilton, "It Should Have Been Me" for Ray Charles, and "Your Cash Ain't Nothing but Trash" for the Clovers, but by far his most famous song was "Shake, Rattle and Roll" for Big Joe Turner (covered by Bill Haley and the Comets), a rock 'n' roll standard before the term "rock 'n' roll" became popular. Stone, in some regards, invented, but if not, at least refined, what became the basic rock 'n' roll beat.

When Ahmet unfurled Atlantic, his first inclination was that it should be a jazz label, and nothing really caught on. Eventually, he and Stone traveled to the South, visiting juke joints, honky-tonks, and music clubs to see what was going on, and they realized the young crowd wanted music that it could dance to. As Stone recalled, "I listened to the stuff that was being done down there and I concluded that the only thing that was missin' from the stuff we were recording was the rhythm. All we needed was a bass line. So, I designed a bass pattern, and it sort of became identified with rock 'n' roll—doo, da-doo, dum; doo, da-doo dum. I'm the guilty person who started that."[42]

Back in the spring, when Bob Rolontz caught wind of Atlantic hiring Jerry Wexler, he didn't realize that hire would be transformative for the record company and a big help to Clyde McPhatter's new career. It was Wexler who oversaw the first recording sessions for the Drifters.

Gerald "Jerry" Wexler was born in 1917 in New York City. He was an aimless street tough, college dropout, music aficionado, and draftee during World War II. After the war years, Wexler got a degree in journalism and in 1949 was hired as a reporter for *Billboard*, where he made one semi-lasting impression. When the magazine wanted to change the name of the Race Records chart, it was Wexler who tossed out the term "rhythm and blues," which the magazine adopted.

When Ahmet decided he needed someone to replace Herb Abramson, who would be gone for two years, he went to Paul Ackerman, a *Billboard* editor, and asked him for his advice. Ackerman said, "There are a number of people I could recommend, but there's nobody better than Jerry Wexler."[43]

Jesse Stone's lyrics for "Money Honey" were humorously charming, with the song constructed along a story line, or situational-blues set-up. Deconstructed, in part one, a landlord wants payment; part two, the hero goes to a girlfriend for money; part three, the girlfriend's response; and part four, lesson learned. As an example, the second verse unspools this way: "I was cleaned and skinned and so hard-pressed / I called the woman that I love the best / I finally reached my baby 'bout half past three / She said, "I'd like to know what you want with me." / I said, Money, honey."

Arnold Shaw, going full Jesse Stone, summed up the fiscal nature of the song: "'Money, Honey' made an acidulous comment on the connection between love and loot. McPhatter's approach was slyly humorous as he played the tomcat who had come to a most serious decision: no love for a pussycat without loot. It was a triumph of songwriting as well as triumphant performance."[44]

The song begins in baritone mode with a doo-wop groan, then Clyde's high tenor jumps in. The chorus stays profundo until about quarter of the way into the song, when the background singers elevate a little higher on the scale to get closer to Clyde's distinctive tenor. Wexler called the background doo-wop, sounding like aah-ooh, aah, ooh, "bagpipe harmonies." Writer Gillett suggested Hank Ballard and the Midnighters employed the same sort of sound on their popular, but suggestive, songs "Work with Me, Annie," and "Annie Had a Baby."[45] Musicologist Larry Birnbaum agreed, explaining, the Midnighters "had already adopted the Drifters' chant of "ah-ooh, ah ooh" for their 'Work with Me Annie.'"[46]

Birnbaum also writes that the melody of "Money Honey" is similar to Roy Orbison's "Ooby Dooby"; the chorus of "Money Honey" is akin to the one on Gene Vincent's "Be-Bop-A-Lula"; and the verse resembles Tommy James and the Shondells' "Hanky Panky."

On September 12, 1953, Atlantic Records bought a three-column ad for the bottom left side of Billboard's "Top Rhythm & Blues Records" page. The advertisement spotlighted the label's new releases with the exploding "Got to Sell Records" followed by ". . . with this new Atlantic Release!!" The ad copy then listed four songs Atlantic wanted to promote, including "The Tears Keep Tumbling Down" by Ruth Brown, "Sweet Talk" by Faye Adams, and "Heartbreaker" by Ray Charles. The fourth song was "The Way I Feel" by Clyde McPhatter and the Drifters with "Money Honey" on the B-side.[47]

In the listing, Ruth Brown, really the star performer of the Atlantic label, came first. After three Top Ten singles in row, "Tears Came Tumbling Down" tumbled down silently. "Sweet Talk" by Faye Adams met the same fate. This was her rookie outing. Her next song, "Shake A Hand," would be a monster hit. While Ray Charles already boasted his first R&B hit with "Mess Around," this next offering failed to chart.

That left Clyde McPhatter and the Drifters to salvage Atlantic's promotional efforts. In the same issue of *Billboard*, the magazine ran a page called "Reviews of This Week's New Records." On this page, the pop market section featured new cuts by Eartha Kitt, Connee Boswell, Bing Crosby, Hoagy Carmichael, and Betty Clooney (Rosemary Clooney's sister); the country and western section offered songs by Slim Whitman, Tex Ritter, and Hank Locklin; while the rhythm and blues column included new tunes by Ruth Brown, Fats Domino, and Joe Morris. This was a crowded page with forty different records in review, only one of which became a big hit. The standout listing simply read "Clyde McPhatter" without mentioning the Drifters, and the reviewer took Atlantic's B-side song, "Money Honey," and wrote it in as the A-side. The reviewer, who really had a feel for the R&B market, wrote: "The ork [orchestra] sets a real infectious beat behind the high piping of McPhatter for a powerful slicing for the market. This could pull well over the air and thru jukes [jukeboxes]. In addition to retailer loot." It's not as if the reviewer disliked the "The Way I Feel," but he knew which side of the single would be a hit. Placing "The Way I Feel" in B-side position, he expounded, "McPhatter's voice soars to stratospheric heights as he tackles this romantic ballad. An outstanding effort that's also due for plenty of action. This is McPhatter's first waxing for the label since leaving the Dominoes."[48]

Apparently, radio disc jockeys heard the same thing because a handful, too, flipped the record over and began playing "Money Honey."

A week later, *Billboard*'s writers, sensing a seedling with the potential to blossom, in the "New Records to Watch" feature, listed Clyde McPhatter's "Money Honey," with this supporting note: "McPhatter, former lead singer with the Dominoes, starts his disk contract with Atlantic with a disk that could grab a lot of loot. He's effectively backed by the Drifters."[49]

For the last week of September 1953, Faye Adams, now recording for Herald Records, boasted the #1 R&B song in the country, "Shake A Hand." Atlantic covered the loss as the Clovers' "Good Lovin'" and Joe Turner's "Honey Hush" were also in the Top Ten in sales. However, the gossip column eschewed all that good noise. The "Rhythm and Blues Notes" column began with this item: "Clyde McPhatter and the Drifters signed with the Gale Agency this week. McPhatter is the former lead singer of the Dominoes, and the Drifters is his new vocal group. He is now waxing for Atlantic Records; his first disk [single] for the firm was released last week."[50] Moe Gale, who owned the Savoy Ballroom, one of the top venues for African American artists, with his brother formed the Gale Agency, which through the 1940s managed top-flight African American artists including Chick Webb, Erskine Hawkins, Ella Fitzgerald, and the Ink Spots. The company was still very active in the early 1950s.

The trade magazine gossip columns kept the timpani thumping over Clyde McPhatter's new venture. *Cash Box*'s "Inside Harlem" column in mid-October 1953 reported: "Ticket agencies busier than ants on a lollipop selling ducats for the gigantic funfest sponsored by the Club International over at Hunts Point Palace, which stars Atlantic Records Ruth Brown; Clyde McPhatter and His Drifters of the same label."[51] Finally, on November 21, 1953, the ever-knowledgeable Bob Rolontz, in his column "Rhythm and Blues Notes," extolled: "After eight weeks in the top position on the *Billboard* bestselling and most-played R&B charts, the Herald waxing of 'Shake a Hand' with Faye Adams and the Joe Morris Ork was displaced by 'Money Honey,' Clyde McPhatter's debut slicing for Atlantic Records. McPhatter, former lead singer with Billy Ward's Dominoes, is backed by his new group, The Drifters."[52]

The 45 rpm record of "Money Honey" notes the artist as Clyde McPhatter and The Drifters. Underneath the record number to the right of the spindle hole are the words "Vocal Quartet."

"Money Honey" was not only the #1 R&B record in terms of sales, it was also the #1 played tune on America's jukeboxes, turning back "Shake a Hand" there as well. In addition to being a #1 record, the song stayed on the R&B charts for twenty-three weeks.

Dave Marsh, in his book *The Heart of Rock and Soul: The 1001 Greatest Singles Ever Made*, has an unusual take on "Money Honey," which he placed at #390 in his listing: "'Money Honey,' the Drifters' first chart record . . . immediately established the group as part of the new rock and roll movement. This had a lot less to do with Clyde McPhatter's style, which was the same daring, quavering chatterbox tenor it had been in the Dominoes, than with the song, supplied by the unforgivably, uncelebrated Jesse Stone . . . That takes nothing away from Clyde McPhatter, who's brilliant, or for that matter, from Sam The Man Taylor's incredible sax solo. But the finest achievement of all belonged this time to the guy who crafted the concept."[53]

Cash Box, a little late to the Clyde McPhatter party, in its "Rhythm N' Blues Ramblings" column, boasted of its poll of jukebox operators as to the top artists of 1953. The top two vote-getters were Atlantic's Ruth Brown and the Clovers. As to the top "money earner" for the year, the #2 record was Ruth Brown's "Mama, He Treats Your Daughter Mean" and #3 was "Good Lovin'" by the Clovers.

The columnist added, "Not to be lost in the maze of honors is the finishing of Atlantic's Clyde McPhatter & His Drifters in the number six slot in the (poll of) 'Most Promising Artists' of the year. When you consider that just a few months ago McPhatter's group was not only unknown but not even organized—then all we can say is 'Wow!' Congratulations to Herb Abramson, Miriam Abramson (Herb's soon-to-be ex-wife was important executive at Atlantic), Ahmet Ertegun and Jerry Wexler."[54]

Clyde never waxed nostalgic over the song, but he did adopt the phrase. An older Clyde had a bitter side and often said things in a very sarcastic manner. He used the phrase "Money Honey," but with the comma as "money, honey," on people who he felt owed him money. Said Deborah McPhatter, "in an agitated-slash-jokey type of way, he'd say with a bite, "I need my money, honey."

CHAPTER SIX

SUCH A NIGHT

Decades before hip-hop and the Tipper Gore advocacy of warning labels for songs in the 1980s, the first crisis faced by a post–World War II music undercard came in the early 1950s, and it was in response to the growing teen acceptance of rhythm and blues, which, indeed, boasted a wry, fun and occasionally "blue" take on such topics as sexuality and alcohol consumption in its songwriting, such as, for example, "Sixty Minute Man."

The first half-baked plan to take control of what the public should be listening to came in early 1954 when a group of R&B disk jockeys on the East Coast conceived the idea of forming a "club" to combat the playing of certain types of R&B songs on the air. The obvious target was records that might be considered "filthy" or in the popular lexicon of the time, "smutty," which one might say was due to parents of white teenagers hearing what their children were listening to on the radio. The other target was a bit more obtuse. Sounding righteous, the club would abolish songs that were derogatory in a racial sense. This was a reaction from Black middle-class parents listening to their children's music, who felt R&B's jokey, hipster jargon and double-entendre songs did not reflect well on the race.[1]

Taking the temperature of Black America, perhaps, was journalist Larry Douglas's rant in his October 1953 column, which was syndicated in the African American press, about rhythm and blues songs such as "Sixty Minute Man" being a "lower form of entertainment" as opposed to jazz, which was a "finer quality of music."[2]

The club was to function in this manner. When any member the group received a record that it considered a Double-D, derogatory or dirty, other deejays would be informed and asked not to play the song. The three targets of the group were sex in a suggestive manner, drinking, and songs that "hold the Negro up to ridicule." The prospective club members were not against blues records as such, but they were against a record in which "rock," "roll," and "ride" didn't deal with the rhythmic meter of the tune.

An article in a February 1954 *Billboard* magazine reported that the National Association for the Advancement of Colored People (NAACP) had been advocating for something similar to what the club was espousing.[3]

Just as in white America, African American parents of teenagers were caught in the cultural shift of the postwar years, where an increase in prosperity and more leisure time for teenagers happened at the same moment that there was a slowly evolving revolution in musical tastes. The problem was more acute, in some regards, for Black America, because radio—and in the late 1940s and early 1950s this was the primary way music was delivered into households—had begun to desegregate.

In 1954, *Sponsor*, a short-lived trade publication aimed at broadcasting advertisers, tried to educate its readership as to the growing "Negro" market. A September 2 issue of the magazine ran a story with the headline "Negro Radio Comes of Age." The article stated that over four hundred radio outlets aimed part or all of their programs at Negro listeners and already one hundred big advertisers placed substantial advertisements at all hours of the clock on Negro-appeal radio stations.[4]

Sponsor's September 20 issue checked in with deejays and program managers at Negro radio stations, asking what they played, what format was appealing, or what "copy approach" an advertiser should use. From KGFI in Hollywood, California, came this response: "As far as program choice is concerned, this audience, according to recent surveys, prefers personality disk jockey shows featuring rhythm and blues music. They liked the casual, friendly approach." At KWBR in Oakland, a responder answered, "Rhythm and blues is by far the most popular choice with the Negroes in this area and consequently it makes up the greater portion of our Negro schedule with shows running morning, afternoon and evening."[5]

Rhythm and blues was taking over the so-called "Negro" audience radio stations. This pushed out other formats such as jazz and gospel, and some of the rising Black middle class were unhappy with the changes. In 1954, the first counterpunch from the African American community came from the *Pittsburgh Courier*, a major Black newspaper that launched a tirade against "smutty" R&B records. Then Harry Mills of the venerable Mills Brothers went after popular disc jockey Alan Freed, who was now broadcasting in the Big Apple. He charged Freed, who was an early supporter of the Dominoes, with playing "off-color" records.[6]

Soon other Black newspapers jumped on the bandwagon. The influential *Detroit Tribune* entered the fray on November 13, 1954, with a front-page special: "The *Detroit Tribune* congratulates the *Pittsburgh Courier* in its exposure of smutty records fouling airwaves; But—your sex exploitation had God's condemnation." The story began this way: "Sin, sex and seduction are befouling the airwaves as never before through the medium of smutty records—and this has become shockingly more prevalent since rhythm and blues became big business."[7]

In November, the *Jackson (Mississippi) Advocate* reported that a prominent local citizen said he would help draft a committee of citizens to go before the City Council to request aid in halting the playing of "smutty and suggestive records over the air and on jukeboxes in public establishments where minors are permitted." The unnamed citizen screamed, "if nothing is done on the local level, I will be willing to take a group before Gov. Kennon for action." (The writer was mistaken; Robert Kennon was governor of Louisiana, not Mississippi, in 1954.)[8]

Picking up an article from a syndicated columnist, the *St. Paul Recorder* in December ran a front-page story with the comment: "Disc jockeys have a grave responsibility to remain within the bounds of good taste when it comes to smutty records. A national weekly newspaper has been carrying on a vigorous campaign against platter spinners who plug these disgusting records. The paper now has a jockey known as 'Moondog' on the carpet for letting distasteful lyrics on the air."[9]

"Moondog" referred to deejay Alan Freed, who was probably the best-known rock 'n' roll deejay in the country. He was even called the man who invented the phrase "rock and roll," which he didn't, but he certainly helped publicize the name of the new music sweeping America.

As Alan Freed's biographer John A. Jackson wrote, "Those whites were joined in their criticism of rhythm and blues by upper- and middle-class Blacks who were ashamed and embarrassed by the music's vulgarity and primitiveness."[10]

In 1953, the top songs on the pop charts included instrumentals such as "The Song from Moulin Rouge" and "April in Paris"; novelty numbers such as "(How Much Is) That Doggie in the Window"; and easy listening tunes like "Till I Waltz Again with You." All of these were a far cry from "Sixty Minute Man" or such 1953 R&B hits as "Baby Don't Do It" by the 5 Royales, "Let Me Go Home, Whiskey" and "One Scotch, One Bourbon, One Beer" by Amos Milburn, and "Wild, Wild Young Men" by Ruth Brown.

If 1955, with Bill Haley and the Comets singing "(We're Gonna) Rock Around the Clock" and 1956, with the coming of Elvis Presley, ushered in the spectacular rise of rock 'n' roll, then 1954 was the year when the forces of melodic good (post-swing) and evil (pre-rock) collided. Unwittingly at the forefront of this battle were two groups, Hank Ballard and the Midnighters and Clyde McPhatter and his Drifters.

Why these performers? Because in 1954, they issued some very hot, actually scorching tunes, that bumped up against the snowballing censorship movement, which was the last stand by traditionalists against the coming of a new music form.

Hank Ballard's group, the Midnighters, "cut three of the wildest records of 1954," observed writer Ed Ward, who added this explanation, "'Work with Me Annie' was a pretty unambiguous tune, with lyrics that did not seem to indicate that Ballard needed help around the office. If anybody was still confused, the follow-up record, "Annie Had a Baby," spelled things out, explaining she "can't work no more," as a result. Rounding out the Annie trilogy was "Sexy Ways," on which Ballard choked out a lust-filled vocal leaving little to the imagination when he said he loved her (gasp) sexy ways."[11]

Ward makes the point that the "Annie" records were mostly played on R&B stations and not pop music stations, presumably because no one at the time thought anybody but Black people paid attention to those songs, which was delusional. White teenagers were listening and liked this music so much that the trend line for radio listeners indicated a growing ascendency of R&B. By 1953, 25 percent of all the stations surveyed by *Billboard* were programming some R&B, or pre–rock 'n' roll.

As for Hank Ballard, he and his group had some kind of year in 1954: "Sexy Ways" was a #2 bestselling record on the R&B charts, while "Work with Me Annie" and "Annie Had a Baby" were #1 records.

It's hard to believe, but "Work with Me Annie" was originally even more ribald. Ballard, still known as Henry, not Hank, and the group known as the Royals, not Midnighters, came to record producer Ralph Bass at the Federal label with a song called "Sock It to Me, Mattie." As Bass told the story, he said, "Hank, that's too nasty, man. We can't do the song with that title because nobody will play it." Bass eventually suggested "Work with Me Annie."

Jon Hartley Fox, who wrote a history of King Records, never quite bought into that story because the title wasn't really the problem with the song so much as it was the lyrics, such as the well-remembered lines, "Annie please don't cheat / give me all my meat." In addition, the word "work" was common slang for sexual intercourse. Fox wrote, "If 'Sixty Minute Man' was the epitome of double-entendre humor, 'Work with Me Annie' came right to the point with no ambiguity."[12]

Hank Ballard was a fan of Clyde McPhatter, and some critics feel he used the same arrangement as the Drifters' "Money Honey," or what Atlantic's Jerry Wexler called the bagpipe harmonies of aah-ooh, aah-ooh, on "Work with Me Annie" and subsequent follow-up records.[13]

"Listening to the Midnighters, it's obvious that Hank Ballard was influenced by Clyde McPhatter," wrote Fox. "Ballard was not as smooth as McPhatter, but the young Detroiter, only seventeen when he wrote and sang "Work with Me Annie," had a distinctive and powerful voice and engaging style. Besides, where McPhatter was an R&B and pop vocalist, Ballard was a rock singer."[14]

Despite "Work with Me Annie" being banned by many radio stations, it rode the R&B charts for twenty-six weeks, buoyed by the lure of forbidden fruit, gossip, and jukebox plays. "Work With Me Annie" was the #1 most played song on jukeboxes for the first four weeks in July. Meanwhile, it was the #1 best-selling R&B tune from May 22 through the week of June 3.

As for "Annie Had a Baby," the song has its own mythology. Supposedly, a Los Angeles disk jockey, after playing "Work with Me Annie," joked that if listeners thought that song was great they should hear the Midnighters sing "Annie Had a Baby." Well, there was no such song, but so many requests came in for the tune that King Records got songsmith Henry Glover to write it. "Annie Had a Baby" was the #1 bestselling R&B song for two weeks in the autumn of 1954. Annie with her baby wasn't the most titillating song Glover transformed into a hit record. In 1951 he also scribed "It Ain't the Meat," which was initially recorded by the Swallows. ("It ain't the meat, it's the motion / that makes your daddy want to rock / it ain't the meat, it's the motion / it's the movement that gives it the sock.")

The two "Annie" songs and "Sexy Ways" were issued on the Federal label. Although these songs were very successful, the clean-up-the-airwaves movement managed to beat down even Federal. In November, *Cash Box* magazine reported that Syd Nathan, the president of the Federal and King labels, in an interoffice communication to his A&R staff, advised them that he was strongly against "blue" material and urged them to pass up such songs or revise the lyrics. Nathan pointed out the growth of R&B to its present stature and stressed the industry's moral obligation to the youth of America.[15]

The *Cash Box* columnists who covered the R&B field, specifically in New York, Chicago, and Los Angeles, proved as conservative as their counterparts in the Black newspapers. On October 30, 1954, "Rhythm N' Blues Ramblings" began its New York entry with unbridled support for Syd Nathan's new stance on blue lyrics. "The Midnighters on Federal Records came up with the fourth in the Annie series titled 'Annie's Aunt Fannie.' Operators [jukebox] and stores don't have to be afraid of this one as the lyrics are in good taste. A kudo to Syd Nathan for his grand move in the right direction."[16]

The same tone in the same column was taken up by the magazine's Los Angeles contributor, who wrote, "Many radio stations are now picking up the fight against dirty records. WDIA in Memphis is to be congratulated for starting the ball rolling. Also, WHEK in Akron."

The Los Angeles columnist had not been closely following the slow-moving crackdown on "smutty" records. The first radio station to publicly ban a "smutty" song was Detroit's WXYZ in March of the year. The station's deejay Ed McKenzie claimed the decision was made due to pressure brought through a flood of letters from mothers, teachers, and businessmen against offering such allegedly "suggestive trash" to teenagers.

Just what "suggestive trash" was banned in Detroit? A record entitled "Such A Night," recorded by the very popular Clyde McPhatter and the Drifters.

According to McKenzie, he introduced the song "with a bang" two weeks prior following requests from listeners, and played it along with cover versions by Johnnie Ray and Bunny Paul. The introduction of the song went off so well that he conducted a one-day telephone contest to determine the most popular version. The Johnnie Ray disk took top honors, closely followed by Bunny Paul with Clyde McPhatter and the Drifters trailing. Judging by the outcome, the station's demographics were clearly skewed toward a more mature audience. The phone contest gimmick strongly caught the attention of the station's older age group, resulting in a flood of letters protesting "Such A Night." McKenzie then made the decision to bar the song. Still, he rued his resolution of the problem as the younger listeners, fans of the Clyde McPhatter version, clamored daily for the station to play the record.[17]

The song came out of an early Drifters recording session on November 12, 1953. At the time the group recorded four new tunes, "Such a Night," "Warm Your Heart," "Don't Dog Me," and "Bip Bam." Clyde took the lead on all the tunes. Afterward the group went on a Midwest tour with Bullmoose Jackson.[18]

The group was still touring into the new year, this time in the South, where Black performers always had to tread carefully. Sure enough, it was the Drifters' turn. In 1954 the group was passing through Fredericksburg, Virginia, on their way to a gig in Atlanta. At the time, all the members would travel in Bill Pinkney's 1947 Cadillac, a four-door sedan. On a Fredericksburg street, a police car slipped in behind the Cadillac with the red lights flashing and siren buzzing. As Bill Pinkney recalled, there had been a robbery at a bank or finance company, and when the police saw a group of Black men in a Cadillac, it looked suspicious to them. No surprise: in the South, Black men in Cadillac always looked suspicious. The astute policemen took the Drifters to the scene of the robbery and no one could identify them as the robbers. The famous (not to the Fredericksburg police!) Drifters were standing around with their hands in the air when the less-than-brilliant cops said something like, "the robbers wore red clothing, let's just see what's in the trunk." So, Bill moved his hands down to get the keys. One of the cops thought Bill was reaching for a weapon and whipped his gun toward Bill ready to shoot. Bill saw the movement and immediately put his hands back up. The policeman spat out, "Boy, good thing your hanes [hands] went back up. You almost got it." Bill told him fast he was just reaching for the keys. After searching the car and finding nothing red, they let the Drifters ride on. As Pinkney recalled, "We didn't want to see Fredericksburg again."[19]

Despite misadventures while touring, there appeared to be very few bumps on the road to stardom for the Drifters at the start of 1954. "Money Honey" was still on deejay playlists when Atlantic pushed into the market "Such A Night," with "Lucille" on the B-side. The record would prove to be a two-sided hit, with "Such A Night" climbing to the #2 spot on the R&B charts and "Lucille" running all the way to #7. "Such A Night" was a very strong song and probably would have made it to #1 if some stations that decided not to play such a "smutty" record had taken a different approach.

The song was written by Lincoln Chase, who would go on to write some very scintillating cuts such as "Jim Dandy" for LaVern Baker and "The Nitty Gritty" for Shirley Ellis. In early 1954, he was still new to the music business. Starting in 1952, singers as diverse as Big Maybelle and Chuck Willis recorded his songs. Even Ruth Brown, who was hottest female singer on the charts at that time, took one of his songs, "Mend Your Ways." His first real success was "Such A Night."

For a song that would end up to be controversial, the lyrics were more romantic than risqué and very straightforward, with no double entendres. "Came the dawn and my heart and her love and the night were gone / But I'll never forget the kiss, the kiss in the moonlight / Oo-oo such a kiss, such a night / It was a night, oo-oo what a night."

It was the unsaid that bothered the critics: a man remembers the night he received a very passionate kiss from a woman. The lyric reads, "Oh how she could kiss; oh, what a kiss." Maybe it was too passionate. If Al Martino, the Ames Brothers, or Tony Bennett had sung that same song, it's doubtful there would have been a problem. Johnnie Ray's cover of the song got banned by the BBC in United Kingdom (it was still a #1 record there). In 1964, Elvis Presley's version of the song would go Top Twenty.

Writer Ed Ward explained the reaction to the song in 1954. "'Such A Night' may not have been as explicit as the Annie records but it still raised the hackles of censors just as much. After all, the reason Clyde remembered the night so well was that they did more than kiss, if the lyrics weren't lying."[20]

The Drifters' "Such A Night" was released in January 1954 with absolutely no clouds on the horizon. In fact, the trade publications were itching to get anything new on the Drifters. On January 9, 1954, *Cash Box*'s "Rhythm N' Blues Ramblings columnist struck first, writing, "Atlantic will issue a special release in about a week. Big news for the trade is that it will be two of Atlantic's big guns. Ruth Brown and Clyde McPhatter and his Drifters. This outfit's so loaded it's blistering."[21]

The columnist had good information because Atlantic did release a two-record bomb with Ruth Brown and Clyde McPhatter and the Drifters. As good as the latter group was, Ruth Brown at that point in her career was even better. She had her first big hit 1949 with "So Long," which climbed to #4 on the R&B charts. Then between 1950 and 1953, she could count eight Top Ten R&B hits including three songs that went to #1. At that point she was the Queen of R&B, earning the nickname "Miss Rhythm." Much to the dismay of Ahmet Ertegun, Atlantic Records would sometimes be known as The House that Ruth Built, which was a cute play on a moniker originally ascribed to Babe Ruth, with the "house" referred to being Yankee Stadium.

Even with all that, Clyde McPhatter would overshadow Ruth Brown in early 1954. In the January 24, 1954, issue of *Cash Box* magazine, its "Rhythm 'n Blues Reviews" column looked at a host of new R&B releases, which mostly broke down into familiar names such as Jimmy Reed, Howlin' Wolf, Little Milton, and Tampa Red; and groups, the Platters, Imperials, and Swans. In this column, *Cash Box* would highlight in its "Award O' The Week." one record it thought had the most chance to succeed. In the January 24 issue, the magazine chose three new records: "I Do/Good Things," by the 5 Royales, "If You Don't Want Me/ Love Contest" by Ruth Brown, and "Such A Night/Lucille" by Clyde McPhatter and The Drifters. Of all those records, the only one to become a hit was the two-song success story of "Such A Night" and "Lucille."

With the "Award O' The Week" selection came a longer review: For "Such A Night," the unnamed reviewer wrote: "Clyde McPhatter and the Drifters, who burst onto the record scene just a few months ago with the disk, 'Money Honey,' that went all the way to Number One come through with their second release and it has the earmarks of another smash. 'Such A Night' is a quick beat with an old Spanish flavor and Clyde does a lilty and gay job as he ecstatically describes the kisses and lips of his beloved. He's really squishy as he pitches this tale of woo. This one has it."[22]

Rival *Billboard* got around to reviewing the new Clyde McPhatter and the Drifters record the very next week. In its "New Records to Watch" slot, the reviewer wrote: "An exciting, punching reading of an unusual rocker could help put this effort over for the warbler as he tells of 'Such A Night.' The flip [B-side], penned by McPhatter himself, is also sung stylishly, while the Drifters lend the chanter solid support. A coin [jukebox reference] grabber."[23]

Out in the boonies, the *St. Paul [Minnesota] Recorder* boasted its own review: "Another group, hot in the chase for top honors, the Drifters with Clyde McPhatter, have a beguine-paced rhythm item, which is a sure-fire winner. Entitled SUCH A NIGHT, it's a lively bounce in the Latinish vein, which is very skillfully handled. Clyde, in his familiar head-voice style, romps ecstatically on the lead."[24]

To support the new release, Atlantic Records set adrift Clyde McPhatter and the Drifters. Into the chitlin' circuit the group strode, usually getting ecstatic reviews from the Black press as the tide had not turned on them yet.

In Jackson, Mississippi, the *Mississippi Enterprise*, on page 1 of its February 20, 1954, issue, heralded the coming of Clyde McPhatter with bold type and photos: "Attraction Monday, March 1, At Stevens, Gene Ammons & Clyde McPratter Drifters." Yes, someone at the newspaper didn't know R&B, misspelling Clyde's name and listing him after Gene Ammons. The underneath copy was worse: "GENE (Red Top) AMMONS ORCHESTRA, plus the hottest recording artist of today, CLYDE McPRATTER, the (Honey-Money Man) and his Drifters."

Feeling a bit guilty, the newspaper, the very next week, issued a new promotion, this time above the front-page headline. Sitting atop page 1 was: "Gene Ammons, Clyde McPhatter's Drifters at Stevens Mar. 1." The story debuted at the bottom of the front page, again referring to Clyde McPratter. On the jump, the copy was corrected as was the name of the Drifters' song from the week before: "But don't forget—GENE AMMONS, CLYDE McPHATTER (The Money Honey Man) and the DRIFTERS at Stevens Rose Room."[25]

Despite a few glitches in local newspapers, all the touring helped and "Such A Night" began its inexorable climb toward the top of the record charts. On March 6, 1954, "Rhythm N' Blues Ramblings" led off with the brief line, "Activity of the week is the pop diskeries [radio stations] discovery of 'Such A Night.' Tune has started to move like a rocket ship in R&B via Clyde McPhatter and His Drifters and now comes a Johnnie Ray version and Bunny Paul on Essex. The . . . tune is so exciting that we think you'll see quite a few more records out before long. Arrangements on both new releases follow the original McPhatter styling very closely. This column bets the Atlantic (Clyde's label) item catches a solid portion of the pop sales."[26]

Perhaps, having a hint of what the "Rhythm & Blues Ramblings" column was going to print, in the same issue, Atlantic Records took a quarter-page ad that made sure deejays and jukebox operators knew "Such A Night" by Clyde McPhatter was the original recording. The promotion began with the word "GET" and then repeated in bigger and bigger typeface "The Original." In descending order came the rest of the promotion: "From the rhythm & blues field comes the exciting NEW POP HIT 'Such A Night' by Lincoln Chase with Clyde McPhatter and the Drifters on Atlantic Records." A picture of the group accompanied the verbiage.[27]

The promotion and teenage clamor for pre–rock 'n' roll rhythm and blues, made the Clyde McPhatter and The Drifters' version a huge hit despite the covers. "Rhythm & Blues Ramblings" stayed on the story. In the very next issue of the magazine, the New York–based columnist of this feature wrote: "Atlantic gets a big pop, hype, on its Clyde McPhatter and The Drifters etching of "Such A Night." Disking by Johnnie Ray and Bunny Paul and the resulting airplay have helped the sales of McPhatter no end."[28]

"Such A Night" did shoot to #2 on the R&B charts. Could it have made it to #1?

One thing to consider, the R&B charts for much of February and March were dominated by Guitar Slim's bluesy "The Things That I Used to Do," which was the most played R&B song on the nation's jukeboxes for an astounding fourteen weeks. It was also the best-selling R&B tune for five weeks before being topped by Roy Hamilton's overly dramatic rendering of the pop tune, "You'll Never Walk Alone."

Meanwhile, the movement to slow the advancement of rock 'n' roll by focusing on smutty lyrics had picked up steam. Here are a few moments in the delirium:

- A Michigan congresswoman named Ruth Thompson introduced a bill in the House that would prohibit mailing any pornographic recording. The offense would be punishable by five years' imprisonment and a $5,000 fine. (The trouble with this bill was figuring out who would decide what was pornographic.)
- Great Britain's BBC bans "Such A Night" by Johnnie Ray after listeners complain about its suggestiveness. Song goes to #1.[29]
- The novelty tune "Riot in Cell Block #9" is banned by the CBS radio network. The song, penned by Jerry Leiber and Mike Stoller, was recorded by the Robins.
- Memphis loses its cool. First, WDIA, the nation's most powerful Black radio station, bans all records with suggestive lyrics and double entendres.[30] Then the Memphis police prohibit the Drifters' "Honey Love" from being loaded into jukeboxes due to suggestive lyrics.[31]

"Honey Love," another Drifters song that was more romantic than risqué, ended up getting the same treatment as "Such A Night." In October 1954, WDIA in Memphis banned the Annie records, "Honey Love," the Bees' "Toy Bell" (Chuck Berry's version would be known as "My Ding-a-Ling"), and ten other records. As Atlantic Records' Tom Dowd joked, "Southern outrage was such that you could have got arrested just for selling it ('Honey Love') or owning it."[32]

"Honey Love" was written by Clyde McPhatter with producer Jerry Wexler attaching his name to it under the pseudonym "Gerald." This was a shady practice by record producers as a way to grab a piece of songwriter royalties. Or as Deborah McPhatter declared, "the crook Jerry Wexler changed his name on the record and stole it [royalties]." Ironically, in the 1990s, Deborah was dating a trumpet player, who, during the summers when he wasn't on the road, worked in a group that played the Hamptons on Long Island. One year when he was playing at a marina in Greenpoint, Long Island, Deborah accompanied him. Sitting at the gig listening to the music was Mrs. Jerry Wexler and her boyfriend. Someone told her that Clyde McPhatter's daughter Deborah was also there, so Mrs. Wexler sought her out. "All she said was her name, who her husband was and that she was sorry." Deborah thanked her.[33]

"Honey Love," came out of a February 4, 1954, recording session that also produced "What'cha Gonna Do" and "Bells of Saint Mary's." In preparation, way in advance of the next holiday season, was a fourth song "White Christmas." The record would carry a new attribution: The Drifters featuring Clyde McPhatter instead of Clyde McPhatter and The Drifters.[34]

"Honey Love" was a little more explicit than "Such A Night." Key lyrics read: "I need it (I need it), When the moon is bright, I need it (I need it), When you hold me tight, I need it (I need it), in the middle of the night, I need your honey love." What Clyde needs is assumed, as is the definition of honey love.

The song was introduced in the spring of 1954 with "Warm Your Heart" on the B-side. A quick *Billboard* review on May 29 read: "'Honey Love' is a calypso-type opus that could start a new trend in the market. Infectious beat, clever lyrics and a spicy delivery add up to a powerhouse package."[35]

Calypso was a style of Caribbean music that was said to have originated in Trinidad and Tobago, although by the 1950s almost every island boasted its own form of a calypso beat. The year 1953 was a high point in the ascendency of that style of music in the United States as singer Harry Belafonte popularized calypso with best-selling records such as "Jamaica Farewell," a Top Twenty record in 1953. Belafonte's album *Calypso* in 1956 was the first long-playing (the LP) format record to sell a million copies. Although Bermuda is beyond the Caribbean in the Atlantic Ocean, calypso was popular there as well. Besides listening to Belafonte on the radio, Clyde would have heard calypso music from his girlfriend Lorraine Lowe and her family, who was from Bermuda. According to Deborah McPhatter, her mother was not only a big Harry Belafonte fan but knew his second wife, the former Julie Robinson.[36]

It was a short boat ride from "Jamaica Farewell" to "Honey Love."

The song lunged forward quickly. On June 12, "Rhythm N' Blues Ramblings" noted: "Atlantic's Drifters taking off in sensash [sensational] fashion with their newest 'Honey Love.' This is the third release for the group and there is no question about it becoming their third straight hit. Deck is taking off like a bolt in what has been a fairly sluggish market."[37]

The same unknown writer found a trend line in Atlantic label releases, observing the word "honey" had become a "magic word for the Atlantic menage" as the company hit big—really big—over the course of the prior year with "Money Honey" (Drifters), "Honey Hush" (Big Joe Turner), and the most recent, "Honey Love" (again, the Drifters).

By June, the R&B charts were crowded with some great, even classic, R&B tunes including "Shake Rattle and Roll" by Big Joe Turner, "You'll Never Walk

Alone" by Roy Hamilton, "Lovey Dovey" by the Clovers, "Sh-Boom" by the Chords, and "Goodnight, Sweetheart, Goodnight" by the Spaniels. Nevertheless, at the top of the R&B charts were the duo of semi-banned songs. At #2 sat "Honey Love" while resting snugly at #1 was "Work With Me Annie."

The very next week "Honey Love" took over the #1 spot and "Work With Me Annie" fell to #2. New to the Top Ten that same week was another semi-banned song, Hank Ballard and the Midnighters' "Sexy Ways."

At the start of December 1954, RCA Victor, one of the major record labels, reorganized its rhythm and blues division. The label was caught short by the growing popularity of R&B and decided to bring in a new executive as general manager of its Groove label while at the same time teeing off a talent search and stepped-up release schedule. RCA had been slow to make the move to R&B. Other majors had already jumped on R&B train. Decca took a new, aggressive stance on R&B bringing in songwriting wunderkinds Jerry Leiber and Mike Stoller to create some catchy music for the teen market. Capitol had already pushed strongly into the R&B field and was currently enjoying a big hit with "Ling Ting Tong" by the Five Keys. The other majors, Columbia and Mercury, were already on board with R&B. To illustrate how far behind the major labels were to the new music of America, not one major had a Top Ten R&B hit in 1953. RCA did find one act, the Du Droppers, that scored well in 1953 with two moderate hits "I Wanna Know" and "I Found Out."[38]

Three reasons for revitalized interest in R&B were an outlier revenue stream; geographic demand, especially from the South for R&B; and an ever-growing incursion of the genre into the pop music stream. At the beginning of December 1954, hot on the hit parades were such R&B hits as "Earth Angel" by the Penguins, "Hearts of Stone" by the Charms, "Tweedle Dee" by LaVern Baker, and "White Christmas" by the Drifters.

Back in February, if anyone was wondering why Atlantic would record a Christmas song, here was the sagacity of the company's thinking. Musicologist Marv Goldberg suggests that Atlantic recorded the song so far in advance because Ahmet Ertegun and Jerry Wexler were worried how songwriter Irving Berlin would react and, if the reaction was negative, he would deny Atlantic permission to record it.[39] "I mistakingly feared Irving Berlin's people would never approve," said Wexler. "They loved it."[40]

As Goldberg wrote, "And why not? He [Berlin] only stood to make more money from it."[41]

In the Drifters' version of "White Christmas," Clyde shares the lead with Bill Pinkney who employs his best, deep, doo-wop, bassman voice. Some writers suggest the Drifters copied their rendition of the holiday classic from the 1948 version of the song by the Ravens. Jerry Wexler, who produced the session, admitted the Drifters version was Ravens-inspired, although the Drifters dropped the swing style in favor of R&B.[42] Writer Charlie Gillett thought the Drifters' version of "White Christmas" was "extraordinary" and the best of the Drifters' February recordings.[43] The *Billboard* reviewer liked it, writing in mid-November, "This version of the Berlin favorite is one that should grab a lot of sales in the field for the next seven weeks. It features Clyde McPhatter and Bill Pinkney plus the boys. A real holiday item." On the B-side was another song from the February recording session, "The Bells of St. Mary's."[44]

The song rose to #5 on the R&B charts and crossed over to the pop charts, the first song by the Drifters to do so—even though it was at the bottom of that particular chart. The song was very strong in the cornerstones of the doo-wop world, the East and West Coasts. On Christmas day, "White Christmas" was #1 in New York, which was saying a lot considering the intense competition by some very great records. Trailing "White Christmas" in New York's R&B Top Ten were such tunes as "Teach Me Tonight" by Dinah Washington, "Earth Angel" by the Penguins, "Sincerely" by the Moonglows, "Tweedle Dee" by LaVern Baker, "Hearts of Stone" by the Charms, and "Mambo Baby" by Ruth Brown.

The Los Angeles contributor to *Cash Box*'s "Rhythm N' Blues Ramblings" column summed it up best, noting "This year saw a great number of Christmas tunes gain wide popularity throughout Southern California . . . Clyde McPhatter and the Drifters reap top honors for the biggest with their great arrangement of 'White Christmas.'"[45]

That was a Clyde McPhatter and the Drifters present that keeps on giving, even to this day.

CHAPTER SEVEN

BIP BAM

Back in 1969, the music writer Lilian Roxon published the *Rock Encyclopedia*, which became the cherished compendium for anyone interested in current and past musicians. When she got around to writing about Clyde McPhatter, she focused solely on "Money Honey," which she said at the time, "Is still held up as an example of how lively the rock and roll milieu was long before Elvis Presley's name brought it worldwide publicity . . . He [Clyde] was an integral part of early rock 'n' roll and did much to solidify the sound."[1]

Disc jockey Alan Freed was a big fan of Clyde McPhatter, first with the Dominoes and then with the Drifters, and when it was time to create rhythm and blues concerts for teenagers, he included both McPhatter-led groups in his lineup of stars. In the 1950s and into the early 1960s, the big shows for teenagers generally included a large number of singers and musicians who would perform one or two songs and then fade into the wings to be replaced by another hero of the hit parade.

The mythology behind Alan Freed is that one day in 1951 a local Cleveland record store owner named Leo Mintz came to Freed, who toiled at radio station WJW, with a proposition. Mintz's store, Record Rendezvous, boasted a steady sale of "race" records, or rhythm and blues songs marketed mainly to a Negro audience. By 1951, Mintz noticed an increasing number of white buyers coming into his store, and he approached Freed with the idea of creating a rhythm and blues radio show. While Freed wasn't all that familiar with R&B at that moment, Mintz said he would, in fact, buy the show, envisioning it as one giant commercial for his store. Eventually, Freed bought into Mintz's vision and on July 11, 1951, Freed debuted his rhythm and blues show and adopted a hipster show name, "Moondog." Less than a year later, Freed and Mintz decided to put on a concert in Cleveland, which would be called the

Moondog Coronation Ball. The stars of show were saxophonist Paul Williams (Hucklebuckers), Tiny Grimes (Rockin' Highlanders), Varetta Dillard, Danny Cobb, and the Dominoes (Billy Ward and Clyde McPhatter).

On the night of March 21, 1952, at the Cleveland Arena, concertgoers began to gather outside the venue, and gather and gather and gather. By various estimates 6,000 to 20,000 teenagers had amassed outside the arena. When they started pushing into the building, the Cleveland police pulled the plug on the concert.[2]

By one account the show was shut down after the first song of the night was launched by Paul "Hucklebuck" Williams. Another eyewitness said that Paul Williams finished his set and Tiny Grimes and His Highlanders made it onto the stage. Tiny Grimes had been a well-regarded jazz musician, but in the late 1940s he organized a ruckus combo called Tiny "Mac" Grimes and his Rocking Highlanders, which made a swinging, hipster version of the Scottish classic, "Loch Lomond." Grimes's merry band of African American musicians dressed in kilts and tams put on a wild show. After the Cleveland concert, the musician who would be known as Screamin' Jay Hawkins joined the band.

Generally, the practice in group concerts was that the top act at the moment would close the show. If Paul Williams and Tiny Grimes, who initially were billed as the stars of the Moondog Coronation Ball, were the first two acts, then the closing performers would have been the Dominoes. Paul Williams, Tiny Grimes, and Varetta Dillard were more in the rhythm and blues vein. The Dominoes recorded the proto–rock-and-roller "Have Mercy Baby" in January 1952 and although it wouldn't officially be released until April, as a preeminent deejay, Freed would have gotten an advance copy.

So, in effect, Freed could be given credit for putting on the first rock 'n' roll concert and inciting the first rock 'n' roll riot—and Clyde McPhatter was part of all that although it is still confusing as to whether the Dominoes made it to the stage that night.

Freed came to describe the music he played as rock 'n' roll, usurping the phrase as something he created, although it had been part of the Black vernacular for decades. At one point he even tried to copyright the phrasing. Others tried to out-name the new music. Atlantic's Jerry Wexler is credited with having *Billboard* magazine change the name of its Negro audience record chart to Rhythm and Blues. With that success, Wexler decided to take on Alan Freed. Borrowing a term being used to describe music popular in the South and Southwest, he decided to call this genre "cat music," thinking, perhaps, of the jazz term "hep-cat" and its abridged form "cat" or somebody who was "with it." He did explain in an essay that "cat music" would be "up-to-date blues with a beat, infectious catch phrases, and danceable rhythms . . . it has to kick and it has to have a message for the sharp youngsters who dig it."[3]

Atlantic decided to back up Wexler's creative impulse by carving out a new label called Cat Records. It only released eighteen singles over a limited lifespan, but one of those platters was the seminal doo-wop song "Sh-Boom" by the Chords.

Freed was so successful playing rhythm and blues or what he called rock 'n' roll that other white deejays around the country copied him in playing songs by Black recording artists. The real mark of his success was getting a new job at WINS, a radio station in New York, the biggest market in the country, with a major salary increase. *Broadcasting Magazine* reported Freed was under a percentage plus minimum guarantee and that he would receive $75,000 to $100,000 annually.[4] For the 1950s, that was a considerable compensation coup. In addition, the radio station agreed to let Freed use his show to promote what it called "dances" in return for 10 percent of the net income received by Freed from such entertainment.[5]

Since the Moondog Coronation Ball, Freed learned his lesson in promotion, and his shows, mostly spotlighting R&B artists, over the next two years were managed, sold-out affairs. There was a change in nomenclature as well. Freed began to call his show the "Rock 'n' Roll Party" while describing the music he played as R&B, but at some point he began calling the music he played rock 'n' roll, then associating the phrase to his name. When Freed came to WINS (his first radio show was in early September 1954), he also began planning his first New York concert for April 1955, which would be called The Rock 'n' Roll Jubilee Ball. Again, the term rock 'n' roll was not in general use. For example, when promoter Lou Krefetz organized a big touring show for early 1955, he called it the "Top 10 Rhythm and Blues Show."[6] No report exists as to how well the Lou Krefetz roadshow performed, but Freed's show was a monster success. As *Billboard* reported, "Disk Jockey Alan Freed's first 'Rock 'n' Roll' ball in the city was a complete sell-out for both nights at the St. Nicholas Arena." As for labeling the music, *Billboard* stuck with the common phrasing: the show "featured only rhythm and blues talent."[7]

For a $2 ticket fee, music lovers got to see extraordinary performers such as Fats Domino, Joe Turner, the Clovers, Harptones, Charles Brown, Ruth Brown, Varetta Dillard, and Clyde McPhatter and the Drifters. What's interesting about this lineup is that Freed chose doo-wop groups, traditional R&B singers, and a number of performers—Fats Domino, Joe Turner, Ruth Brown, and Clyde McPhatter and the Drifters—who had already crossed over the bridge to what Freed was calling rock 'n' roll.

There was something else unique in this blockbuster show, and it wasn't about Alan Freed. This time it was about Clyde McPhatter.

Like other group performers of the time, Clyde and the Drifters all dressed the same—to the nines in matching suits, white shirts, polished black shoes, and neckties. For the Rock 'n' Roll Jubilee Ball, the Drifters were still handsomely matched. Clyde, on the other hand, was in his army uniform. He had been drafted in 1954 and this would be one of his last shows with the group he founded. According to Marv Goldberg, he would make one more appearance with the Drifters, at the Cleveland Arena on Easter Sunday 1955.[8]

Clyde was drafted into the army on May 7, 1954, which was one year to the day after he signed with Atlantic. According to Bill Pinkney, the Drifters were on tour with another Atlantic Records performer, Big Joe Turner, when Clyde received the news. They were staying at the Hotel Belvedere in Atlanta, which was across the street from their venue, the Royal Peacock, a well-regarded stop on the chitlin' circuit.[9]

Clyde was no stranger to other African American musicians getting drafted. Out on the West Coast, Jesse Belvin got his notice just as he was beginning to ascend. Etta James, who grew up in the same Los Angeles neighborhood as Belvin and many other singers and songwriters, recalled, "Things were great for him [Jesse Belvin] until he got drafted into the Korean War. Seems like a dragnet came down and swept the best black boys off the street. They all disappeared at once, but Jesse was the one who left a mess of weeping girls behind."[10]

In 1957, ex-servicemen Jesse Belvin and Clyde would perform together at the Apollo, on a bill with Clarence "Frogman" Henry, Mickey and Sylvia, and three doo-wop groups.

A Black singer could get a little paranoid about the military draft. It did seem that as soon as you began to make it big in the music business, suddenly you were scheduled for military duty. Even the white singer who sang R&B, a guy named Elvis Presley, got his draft papers. Closer to home, Billy Ward had been in the service, and Bill Pinkney did his time as well.

Pinkney was with Clyde when he got his notice. "I sat Clyde down and talked to him about my military service," recalled Pinkney. "I told him he had to go, and that he had an obligation to answer the call to duty." They also discussed what to do about the Drifters after Clyde went into the service. Pinkney had already picked up some of the administrative duties for the group, including paying the guys, being a road manager and spokesman. He soon would be a recruiter as well. "You know I still hear Clyde's voice telling me to keep it together, keep it going," Pinkney would write before he died.[11]

Clyde's tour of duty was not the most onerous for a musician. He had been consistently stationed near enough to the Big Apple that he could come back to visit Atlantic Records and even do some recording.[12] The ever vigilant "Rhythm N' Blues Ramblings" column in the October 30, 1954, *Cash Box* magazine buttonholed Atlantic's Miriam Abramson, who spilled the beans that Clyde McPhatter had gotten a special pass, and a recording session in New York was immediately organized. At the time Clyde was still at the army base in Fort Dix, New Jersey, so coming home to New York was an hour bus ride.[13] Abramson was a little late on the tattle as the Drifters snuck into the recording studio a week before when they recorded four tunes, "Everyone's Laughing," "Sugar Coated Kisses," "Hot Ziggety," and "Three Thirty Three."

"Everyone's Laughing" was released as a single in 1955 with "Hot Ziggety" on the B-side. Both songs were written by Winfield Scott, who also penned "Tweedle Dee" for LaVern Baker and, with Otis Blackwell, "Return to Sender" for Elvis Presley. Unfortunately for the Drifters these songs either just weren't as good or were orphaned by the label. Neither side charted. "Everyone's Laughing" was a slow blues cut similar to what Johnny Ace had been doing very successfully until his death at the close of 1954. "Hot Ziggety" was another lift and corruption of a common colloquialism. "Hot diggety" was a popular expression going back at least until the early 1900s. Winfield Scott just dropped the D and added the Z. The arrangement was standard doo-wop with much Clyde call and Drifters echo. One year later, Perry Como would have a #1 song with the novelty tune "Hot Diggity (Dog Ziggity Boom)." This one was written by the songwriting team of Al Hoffman and Dick Manning, two men born in the old Russian empire before the Communist revolution. They also wrote "Papa Loves Mambo," another novelty hit for Perry Como.

"Three Thirty Three" was written by Clyde, and it was fairly explicit for the times. The three thirty-three refers to an address, which some listeners believe alluded to a house of prostitution. One interpretation of the lyrics goes like this: "You get a little bit of everything / wine, women and song / You can stay there for sixty minutes / I'll lay ya all night long." In lieu of all that was happening with the other Drifters songs in 1954, Atlantic wisely held back on releasing the tune. Bill Pinkney's observation about the song was "too risqué to be a single, and it was released only in an album later."[14]

This was Clyde's last recording session with the Drifters. As Jerry Wexler summed up, "Those first Drifters were together for a year, until Clyde went into the Army. By then we'd recorded two dozen sides."[15]

In early 1955, Clyde made Private First Class while being assigned to the US Army Coast Guard Artillery at Grand Island, near Buffalo, in western New York State. That makes sense because when Ruth Brown met Clyde for their assignation, she recalled that Pfc. McPhatter was "halfway through his stint for Uncle Sam in Buffalo," so that would have meant May 1955.[16]

Although drafted into the army, as he was stationed near Buffalo, Clyde could take his leaves and record with the Drifters or even perform with them if given enough days away from the base. By this time, however, he had already cut three songs that would be his last releases as a member of the Drifters, "White Christmas," "What'cha Gonna Do," and "Bip Bam."

Probably the most interesting is "What'cha Gonna Do," which wasn't released until 1955. As mentioned, Hank Ballard had an infatuation with Clyde McPhatter, and perhaps it's most noticeable in this song, because the arrangement is very close to Ballard's most famous song, "The Twist," which later became a hit tune for Chubby Checker and an international dance craze.

Jerry Wexler always claimed that Ahmet Ertegun wrote the tune and the record does attribute the songwriting to "Nugetre," which was Ertegun's pseudonym, but it could have been a tune acquired by Atlantic, which then gave Ertegun free rein to put his own name on the song. Wexler maintained that "What'cha Gonna Do," was the "greatest" tune Ertegun ever wrote, so for posterity's sake he still gets the songwriting credits.

Wexler also had this to say about "What'cha Gonna Do," that "'The Twist' was outright stolen from it, and we could have sued, but we never liked to draw attention to ourselves as writers"—possibly because they weren't the initial songwriters.[17]

This isn't to say that Wexler and Ertegun don't have supporters as to their songwriting capabilities.

"I was very close with Wexler; he signed me to Atlantic in 1967 and we remained friends until his passing," recalls singer, songwriter, and musicologist Billy Vera. "He was tough on employees but loved me. He was highly literate and my literary mentor. He was a tough businessman but fair. When Ben E. King offered to sell Wexler his song, Wexler refused, giving him an advance instead. His name is on very few songs, only when his contribution warranted it. As for Ahmet, Buddy Bailey of the Clovers told me Ahmet actually wrote their songs. Bear in mind, they were simple blues tunes with typical blues lyrics."[18]

Atlantic released "What'cha Gonna Do" in February 1955 with "Gone" on the B-side. The company, about the same time, issued Big Joe Turner's latest, "Flip, Flop and Fly," which came out in the wake of his #1 record, "Shake, Rattle and Roll." Turner, an old blues guy, had thoroughly made the transition to what Alan Freed was calling rock 'n' roll. And so had the Drifters, as "What'cha Gonna Do" was just as rock 'n' roll as anything by contemporaries Joe Turner, Bill Haley, LaVern Baker, and Ruth Brown.

Cash Box magazine highlighted both Atlantic releases in its "Award O' The week" inset of its "Rhythm 'N Blues Reviews" column. For the Drifters, the review read: "'What'cha Gonna Do,' is a rocking, driving jump with a gospel feel. Clyde's gimmicks, that mark him so distinctly from the rest of the field, to take a phrase from the song, 'knocks me out.'"[19]

Both Atlantic releases went to #2 on the R&B charts. "Flip, Flop and Fly" at first seemed the strongest of the two, but "What'cha Gonna Do," had staying power. For example, on April 16, 1955, *Cash Box*'s listing of the Top 15 R&B

songs in the country was jam-packed with classic tunes. "Flip, Flop and Fly" resided at #5 and "What'cha Gonna Do" at #7. Also on the charts were Johnny Ace's "Pledging My Love," Ray Charles's "I've Got a Woman," Etta James's "The Wallflower," Al Hibbler's "Unchained Melody," the Penguins' "Earth Angel," and LaVern Baker's "Tweedle Dee." In a top-to-bottom-of-the-page advertisement, it looked like the competition was only getting worse as Checker Record company was boasting of a new song called "Bo Diddley" by Bo Diddley.

Two months later, both Atlantic releases were still on the chart with "What'cha Gonna Do" at #5 and "Flip, Flop and Fly" at #7. Atlantic wasn't done. Also on the charts was a new tune by Ruth Brown, "As Long as I'm Moving."

Labelmates Ruth Brown and Clyde McPhatter would end up in all sorts of entanglements, but professionally they would often find themselves chasing each other up and down the record charts. The last of the three songs that would be a hit for Clyde McPhatter while still with the Drifters was released in 1954 and it was called "Bip Bam" with "Someday (You'll Want Me To Want You)" on the B-side. "Bip Bam" was released late 1954, still the early months of Clyde's military duty.

Musicologist Larry Birnbaum would call the song "a suggestive rocker."[20] That's an accurate description. The performers on the recording read The Drifters featuring Clyde McPhatter and it is his tune to carry. The songwriter is simply listed as "Calhoun," which could be a name or pseudonym. The underlying concept of the song is not original. It begins: "Bip bam, thank you ma'am / kisses taste like candy jam / you can see what a fool I am / When your lips meet mine, bip bam." The second stanza ends with the lines "Baby let me have some fun / won't you give me more than one / Lord, I love you, sugar plum / look out now 'cause here I come."

The made up "bip bam" phrase contained a one-word substitution from the idiom, "wham bam thank you ma'am," which gained in public popularity around the year 1950. The wording meant something done quickly. The phrase's meaning eventually got bent to convey a "quickie" in a sexual connotation. Country singer Hank Penny was an early enthusiast of the phrase, and in 1950 he released on King Records a song he wrote called "Wham! Bam! Thank You Ma'am." His lyrics read, "Wham! Bam! Thank You Ma'am, I hope your satisfied / you took my love and tore it apart and hurt me deep inside."

"Bip Bam" was recorded a year before in the November 1953 session that included "Such A Night," but Atlantic held on to it until it felt it was safe to release a song that could have been considered smutty and when they did the intention was for it to be the B-side song. A review in the *Minneapolis Spokesman* considered the Drifters' "Someday (You'll Want Me to Want You)" as the A-side when its critic wrote: "The Drifters in a manner that makes you think of the original Ink Spots have an excellent item in 'Someday' . . . Basso

Willie Pinkney comes through with a spoken recitation of the lyrics." As to the B-side, "Bip Bam," a quick note opined, "Clyde McPhatter leading the group in a rousing performance."[21]

On October 9, 1954, in *Cash Box*'s "Rhythm 'N Blues Reviews" it once again chose multiple selections for its coveted "Award O' The Week," this time honoring Atlantic with both choices, records by Ruth Brown and The Drifters featuring Clyde McPhatter. The busy Ruth Brown introduced "Mambo Baby," with "Somebody Touched Me" on the B-side. In regard to the Drifters, *Cash Box*'s selector of songs preferred "Bip Bam" to "Someday (You'll Want Me to Want You)" and listed it as the A-side, writing in hipster lingo: "The Drifters, featuring the most distinctive voice in the business, wax a pair that will surely help the business. The etch, a bouncer, 'Bip Bam,' that has infectious appeal sure to sell this platter. Item has a solid beat, tasty lyrics, potent ork [orchestra] backing, and the group." The reviewer was an obvious Clyde McPhatter fan. In his comments about "Someday," he (or she?) went Clyde-wild: "McPhatter very effective on this slow tempo saccharine wax. Deck employs a deep-deep bass recitation that acts as a counterfoil for the unique McPhatter pipes. This is one of the best McPhatter solo efforts so far. Could be a two-sider [both A- and B-sides become hits]."[22]

As good as "Bip Bam" was, it was no contest in comparison to Ruth Brown's "Mambo Baby." This song had two really good things going for it: first and foremost, it came out in the middle of America's mambo craze. The Cuban dance music began appearing in swing tunes during the 1930s and continued to pick up steam into the 1950s when it sashayed onto the pop charts. Rosemary Clooney had a Top Ten hit in 1954 with "Mambo Italiano," as did Perry Como with "Papa Loves Mambo" the same year. Second, the ditty was by the hottest female R&B singer on the planet, Ruth Brown.

Both songs were unleashed to the public at the same time and to some extent would go head to head. If this was a boat race, "Bip Bam" sprung a leak. While *Billboard* claimed the song was never strong enough to chart, *Cash Box* on its December 4, 1954, listing of the country's Top Fifteen songs, ranked the Drifters record as the predicted two-sided hit, coming it at #13 for "Someday" and #14 for "Bip Bam." Wow, two songs in the Top Fifteen! That could only be topped by Ruth Brown, who also had two songs in the Top 15. At #15, on the decline, was "Oh What a Dream," a former #1 tune. Her other song was "Mambo Baby," which was ensconced at #1.

The Drifters and Ruth Brown were dominant in 1954. In R&B jukebox plays, "Honey Love" was the most-listened-to song for eight weeks, from the end of July through mid-September when it was finally dislodged by Ruth Brown's "Oh What a Dream," which itself was the most-played song for another eight weeks. On the sales side, "Honey Love" was #1 for eight weeks until dethroned by "Oh

What a Dream." Then briefly "Annie Had a Baby" by the Midnighters and "It Hurts Me to My Heart" by Faye Adams hit top sales before being knocked out of the $1 slot first by "Oh What a Dream" and then by "Mambo Baby."

Clyde and Ruth first worked together in May 1954 when the Drifters backed her at a recording session for four songs: "Oh What a Dream," "Old Man River," "Please Don't Freeze" and "Somebody Touched Me." There's some speculation that Clyde, who was just drafted, wasn't at this session because his distinctive voice cannot be heard on most of these recordings, but Brown claimed he was one of the unbilled Drifters on her version of "Old Man River."[23]

With Clyde in the service, Bill Pinkney more or less took charge of the group and brought in teenager David Baughan to take the lead tenor spot. The good news about Baughan was that he sounded just like Clyde. The bad news was he was somewhat out of control. Johnny Moore was then lined up to replace Baughan, just in case.

As Pinkney tells the story, Baughan, known as "Little David," was able to do Clyde's part with amazing similarity but became hard to deal with. Just sixteen years old, he already had a drinking problem. In Cleveland, Bill discovered Johnny Moore. The next day, Little David woke up in the car to find Johnny Moore sitting next to him. Little David asked Bill who he was and Bill told him that Johnny was the new lead singer, thinking that David would straighten up. He never did.

Meanwhile, there was a push to make Clyde a solo act, and as part of that consideration he recorded two songs, "Love Has Joined Us Together" and "I Gotta Have You," with Ruth Brown, which were released in 1955 with "Love Has Joined" as the A-side.

The first suggestion that "Love Has Joined Us Together" might have legs was in November when a columnist in *Billboard* wrote that strong sales reports from key southern cities plus St. Louis, Detroit, Baltimore, Pittsburgh, and Cleveland indicated the record "is now threatening to jump into national listing if it gets a little more push." Oddly, the individual cities differed as to which side should have been the A-side, but, on the whole, most preferred "Love Has Joined Us Together."[24]

By mid-December, the song broke nationwide, making it into the Top Ten of tunes played by America's disk jockeys. "Love Has Joined Us Together," would end up climbing to the #8 position on the R&B charts.

Ironically, "Love Has Joined Us Together" mimicked real life as Clyde and Ruth Brown drifted into a relationship. Ruth Brown had a messy split with boyfriend Willis Jackson and was ready for love again. She wrote, "by the time we recorded 'Love Has Joined Us Together' . . . things had progressed to the stage where Clyde and I both knew something had to give. It was there in the way we greeted each other whenever we met, in the way we hugged when a session had gone, in the way I teased him about those little 'stingy brin' hats he used to wear. In the reluctant, lingering way we began to say goodbye."

When "Love Has Joined Us Together" began to get consistent airplay, Brown suggested to deejay Tommy "Dr. Jive" Smalls that he try to get Clyde down to New York, where she would join him to promote the record. Smalls had put together a concert he called a "Rock 'n Rhythm" show. Working in the New York metro area, he was an indirect competitor of Alan Freed and wasn't going to use Freed's signature terminology. The concert was at the Brooklyn Paramount Theater and would run a week from December 23 through December 29. On tap for the show were Bo Diddley, the Five Keys, the Cheers, the Turbans, the Flamingos, Pat Boone, and Ruth Brown together with Clyde McPhatter. Backing the troupe of singers was Ruth Brown's former boyfriend Willis Jackson and his sixteen-man band. That's when Clyde, rather than risk being seen in the city with Ruth Brown, asked her to join him in Buffalo.

The next day after their first night of lovemaking, Clyde bought Ruth a friendship ring. She recalled, "We dined and danced at the Moonglow Club until the early hours, made love all night once more, then prepared to say our farewells." The love affair lasted several more weeks, and when it was over they both moved on, staying friends until the very end of Clyde's life. (Bill Pinkney claimed he, too, had an affair with Ruth Brown, but Ruth never mentioned him in her autobiography.)

Clyde and Ruth did not sing together again until a show at the Apollo in 1968. Clyde arrived at the theater already in the tank and then continued drinking until he took the stage. His act dragged on and on, and pronouncements became more and more slurred. Whenever the orchestra cut, indicating it was time to leave the stage, Clyde would launch into another number. Finally, Ruth Brown was asked to get him off the stage. So, Ruth sashayed out, stood next to him and sweetly asked Clyde if he would like to sing "our" song, "Love Has Joined Us Together," as his encore. Before leaving the stage, Clyde spoke to the crowd, "Don't nobody but she and I know what there is between us."[25]

On February 18, 1955, a Larry Douglas syndicated column appeared in the *Arizona Sun*, an African American newspaper in Phoenix. It ended this way: "Ruth Brown, mother of a new little baby boy, is all set to return to the night club circuit." The little boy's name was Ronald. Ruth Brown called her son Ronnie, later shortened to Ronn. Over time, the person Ruth claimed to be the father of the child has not remained consistent.[26]

When Ruth first told the story of her baby, she was still with Willis Jackson and had watched him on a local television show. Afterward, she picked up the phone and called to congratulate him and before concluding the conversation added, "By the way, I got some surprise news. I'm expecting a child." His response was, "It's not mine." And it wasn't. The father, she said, was Drew

Brown. When Ruth and Clyde emotionally drew closer and closer, she wrote in her autobiography, he surprised her by volunteering to stand in as Ronnie's father. Ruth Brown was very fond of Clyde, and even though she was acutely aware of the gravity of her situation—to have a child and have no husband could be career killer—she thanked Clyde from the bottom of her heart, but turned down his suggestion.

In 1955, Brown married Earl Swanson, a saxophonist, and had a second son, Earl.[27]

It turns out there is an interesting twist to the tale of Ruth Brown's first child, Ronald. When she died in November 2006, the *New York Times* obituary made note that her first son, Ronald, was given the last name of Jackson (from Willis Jackson), but decades later, she told Ronald that he was actually Clyde McPhatter's son.[28]

Deborah McPhatter was most surprised to learn she had a half-brother. "My mom and stepdad knew Ruth Brown. I knew Ruth and she never said anything about having a child with my father. I read her autobiography, where she said she flirted and had sex with Clyde McPhatter. She also mentioned in the book that someone else was the father of Ronn."

In 2005, Deborah McPhatter broke her foot. She was home, leg elevated, in discomfort, and then her phone rang at seven in the morning. She picked up the receiver. Bill Pinkney was on the line and she greeted him, "Hey, Uncle Bill, what's up?" Bill took his time. "I was trying to reach you because I'm in Florida and there is a young man singing with us that is your brother."

Deborah laughed. She had been through this many times before. After Clyde's visage came out on a US postal stamp, about a hundred people contacted her claiming to be Clyde's son. There was even that incident after Clyde died when his last wife, Lena, adopted a cousin and claimed it was Clyde's child, which was patently absurd as one can't adopt a child after Clyde is dead and then say, "oh, this is Clyde's child." Nevertheless, if Bill was calling, she would be optimistic and told him she would talk with Ronn although she didn't believe the young man was Clyde's child. Weeks went by and Deborah didn't hear anything, sometimes wondering if this was Clyde's child, then who was the mother.

Eventually, Ronn called, saying, "I'm going to be doing a show in Boston. I would love if it if you came. We can talk." Deborah decided to make the trip and when she got to Boston, he came to the airport with a driver to meet her. "We got back to the hotel and we were sitting in the lobby and something funny was said. He threw his head back and started laughing," she remembered. "I thought I was going to faint. It was, oh my God, that is Clyde McPhatter because Ronn had a laugh just like my dad." At that point, feeling more secure that Ronn could be her half-brother, she asked who his mother was. At that point, one of the singers from the Flamingos ("I Only Have Eyes for You" from 1959) walks by. "My God," he exclaimed, "she looks just like your mother, Ronn." Deborah was on needles and pins. "Ronn, who is your mother?" she asked, and he answered, "Ruth Brown." I was speechless, because I had met her when she was in New York doing the Broadway production of *Black and Blue*."

Deborah added, "Ruth Brown never fessed up anything to me until a month before she died. She called me one night and said, 'I'm sorry. But, you and Ronn need each other.'" Brown didn't go into any detail about her relationship with Clyde. She made it seem as if it was a moment in time and then it was over. In her book, she said she never married Willis Jackson, but on the phone she said she did marry Willis.

"Ronn never knew Clyde," Deborah said. "I think Ronn is a year and half younger than me. Ruth Brown would have been in her prime then. Nora [first wife] was on the scene. Lorraine [Deborah's mother] was on the scene. Lord knows who else was on the scene. I don't think Ronn had a good relationship with Willis Jackson. He doesn't talk about him, although I have heard him say he knew something wasn't right about who his father was supposed to be."

"As for me," Deborah adds, "I was shocked to find out that Clyde McPhatter was my father. From the time I was three, it was always my stepdad in my life. I always referred to my stepfather as my father and I loved him to the moon and back. But there was my grandmother, who sometimes took care of me. She would take me to the Apollo and we would sit in the second-tier balcony in front of the theater. I was a child. I remember this guy would come out and it was like he was singing directly to me. That impression always stayed with me. I do remember when my other grandmother said, "Enough, I'm taking her to New Jersey to meet her father. I'm sick and tired of this man calling my house a 2 am or 4 am wanting to talk to Lorraine."

As a child, Deborah did meet Clyde. What she recalled was that everyone would wait for him to arrive but he didn't come until the next day or the next week. She sighed, "we didn't have a father-daughter relationship until about three weeks before he died. When he passed, I was a freshman in college."[29]

As for Ronn Jackson, he changed his name to Ronn McPhatter and became a singer with a new iteration of the Drifters.

CHAPTER EIGHT

TREASURE OF LOVE

As 1955 was coming to a close, *Billboard* magazine tried to sum up the music industry at that moment in time and, in a surprisingly frank admission, declared 1955 as the year rhythm and blues took over the pop field. To accentuate that pronouncement, in its headline the publication used the term "Virtual Surrender," as if the pop market virtually surrendered to R&B. Unfortunately, there was a qualifier in that declaration. While the trade magazine suggested the trend to R&B would continue strong with more original versions of tunes by R&B artists making it to all markets, there was still a flood of pop artists doing covers of R&B originals.[1]

If one looks at the top thirty songs of the year for 1955, only three actual R&B songs made the list: "(We're Gonna) Rock Around the Clock," by Bill Haley and His Comets, the number two best-selling song of the year; "Unchained Melody" by Al Hibbler, the twenty-first best-seller; and "Only You (And You Alone), the twenty-ninth best-selling song, by the Platters. Pop music, long starved of creativity, rushed into full rear-guard action with a host of male and female singers covering rhythm and blues songs—really the most interesting music on the radio. When *Billboard* declared R&B was taking over pop music, it was referring to two trend lines: that original R&B songs were making it to the pop charts but not yet dominating, and that pop singers were trying to stay relevant by singing what were originally R&B tunes.

Of the best-selling songs of 1955, one can find numerous covers of R&B songs by white pop performers, including: "Unchained Melody" (Al Hibbler) by band leader Les Baxter, "Sincerely" (Moonglows) by the McGuire Sisters, "Ain't That a Shame" (Fats Domino) by Pat Boone, "The Wallflower (Dance with Me, Henry)" (Etta James) and "Tweedle Dee" (LaVern Baker) by Georgia

Gibbs, "Hearts of Stone" (Jewels and Charms) by the Fontane Sisters, and "Ko Ko Mo" (Gene and Eunice) by Perry Como.

As the year 1956 unfolded, the term rock 'n' roll had not yet become universal, so some songs such as "(We're Gonna) Rock Around the Clock," which would later be termed rock 'n' roll, were still considered R&B by the trade publications. Meanwhile, the music industry was being wrenched through serious changes as teenagers, who listened to the radio and bought records, kept moving further and further away from the mellow post-swing sound and orchestra instrumentals that still inundated the pop side of the market.

Record Whirl, another short-lived music magazine of the 1950s, suffered from its own ideology, which was more conservative and pop music–oriented than the music teenagers were listening to. In its August 1956 issue, it published a commentary by a well-known deejay, Robert Q. Lewis, who had been in the business since the 1930s. It also had its own columnist interview Tommy (Dr. Jive) Smalls, a popular Black disc jockey in the New York metro area, who was being run aground by Alan Freed and other white deejays who followed in his footsteps.

The old pro Lewis noted, "there's plenty being written about the bad influence of rock 'n' roll but . . . go back a few years to another generation when rhythm and blues was the big thing . . . if anyone can point out to me any differences between that music and rock 'n' roll of today, why, I'll munch on that record."

Lewis assumed the role of an advisor to parents and suggested the teenage fascination with rock 'n' roll would be something they would outgrow, so be patient. He added, "today, with rock 'n' roll . . . almost all these fans are kids in their teens . . . while they're in the clutches of this feeling for rock 'n' roll you might as well not play any other brand of music."[2]

The record charts in 1956, including R&B and country and western, were completely invaded and conquered by a white singer named Elvis Presley. Dr. Jive, who had been playing R&B music for years, surprisingly also felt threatened by rock 'n' roll. "The sooner the term rock 'n' roll is dead, the better," he bellowed. "The term rock 'n' roll is a fad and will pass on in the next year or so. The trend will revert back to good rhythm & blues." Just to make sure he got his point across, he added with acidity, "Rock 'n' roll is basically rhythm & blues, however, in the past couple of years, pop artists started making these records and they were only poor imitations of rhythm & blues."[3]

In New York, the year 1955 ended with a battle of the box office as both Alan Freed and Dr. Jive hosted huge concerts during the holiday season and it appeared Dr. Jive got the best of the competition. Freed's backup orchestra was led by Sam "The Man" Taylor and Big Al Sears. And here it's a tossup as Dr. Jive's back-up group included Ruth Brown's ex-beau Willis "Gator Tail"

Jackson along with Mickey "Guitar" Baker. Alan Freed's performer lineup included Count Basie, LaVern Baker, Joe Williams, the Valentines, the Wrens, the Chuckles, the Cadillacs, the Heartbeats, Gloria Mann, and Don Cherry. A good group of talent, but not quite equal to Dr. Jive, who signed up Clyde McPhatter. Bo Diddley, Ruth Brown, Pat Boone, the Cheers, the Five Keys, the Flamingos, the Turbans, and the Four Fellows.[4]

As *Cash Box*'s "Rhythm N' Blues Ramblings" column averred, "There is no doubt that the simultaneous showings hurt the other at the box office, but the figures racked up in spite of the competition shows that the oft-predicted waning power of rock and roll is not yet a thing of the present."[5]

Indeed, the same column declared at mid-year that 1956 would be labeled the "year of rock and roll" and that the "buying of records according to the color of the artist was shattered beyond recognition as Fats Domino, Little Richard, Clyde McPhatter and many others crossed the [ethnicity] line."

Billboard magazine on interior pages often ran with five columns of print. It's "Virtual Surrender" article dominated the page in columns three and four because the first two columns all the way down to the middle of the page was taken by a promotion for the song "Adorable" trilled by a doo-wop quartet called the Colts. The ad read, "Thanks DJs, for spinning the original hit version!"[6]

"Adorable" was not only an adorable song, it was also a monster hit, closing out the last two weeks of the year 1955 as the #1 R&B song in the country. This very successful version of the song was not by the Colts. It was by the Drifters. As Bill Pinkney observed, "the Colts already recorded 'Adorable' but once the Drifters got hold of it, nobody mentioned that again." Indeed, despite the promotion in *Billboard*, the Drifters' version of the tune was so dominant that the Colts quickly drifted into obscurity.[7]

If one were to categorize all the #1 R&B songs of 1955, there were the single-performer rock 'n' roll tunes such as "Maybellene" by Chuck Berry, "Ain't It a Shame" by Fats Domino, "and "Bo Diddley" by Bo Diddley; the single-performer ballads such as "A Fool for You" by Ray Charles and "Pledging My Love" by Johnny Ace; and a whole lot of classic doo-wop. "Adorable" was solidly of the doo-wop genre.

The song was written by Buck Ram, a West Coast original, who did a lot of everything in the 1950s: songwriter, producer, manager, and record label owner. He was talented, shrewd, and was rarely outplayed in the music business game. He discovered the Colts and wrote "Adorable" for them, which he recorded on his own record label. The song did well regionally and was poised to become a national hit, but hit a roadblock when the Drifters' version proved more popular. One could say Buck Ram took a rare backseat with "Adorable," but he wrote the song so he actually scored with both groups. After the Penguins, a Los Angeles group, torched the record world with the classic doo-wop cut "Earth

Angel," Ram, who was already managing a newly organized group called the Platters, lured the Penguins away to his management company. Ram wasn't so much interested in the Penguins as he was with the Platters, but "Earth Angel" was such a big hit that he got a major label, Mercury Records, interested in signing the group. Ram told Mercury it needed to take both groups he represented, which it did. While the Penguins faded away, the Platters became the ultimate doo-wop group of the 1950s, mostly with songs such as "The Great Pretender" and "Only You (And You Alone)," which he wrote.[8]

This doesn't mean that Buck Ram was the most upright citizen in the transformative years of rock 'n' roll. As Billy Vera observed, "Buck Ram wrote a lot of songs, big ones. However, Danny 'Run Joe' Taylor, a songwriter with a dependency on the bottle, always claimed he wrote 'The Great Pretender' and sold it to Buck for $25. Buck was another manager like the Drifters' George Treadwell, who had his group on salary and paid them no royalties, which was highly unusual."[9]

Money issues would become a real problem for the Drifters, and a reckoning was coming. Meanwhile . . .

What made Pinkney especially proud of "Adorable" was that it was a Drifters song without Clyde McPhatter. The lead singer was Johnny Moore. Pinkney was now de facto head of the singing group, and as he promised Clyde, he would keep the group together. After Clyde departed for military service, the Drifters initially consisted of Pinkney, Gerhart Thrasher, Andrew Thrasher, and David Baughan with guitarist Jimmy Oliver.

As always, through the distorted feedback of historical testimonies from more than one participant, how Johnny Moore ended up with the group is a tale told differently by divergent players.

Marv Goldberg interviewed a number of the original Drifters before they passed away, and this is his retelling: In late 1954, while the group was in Cleveland for a show, Bill Pinkney was approached by Johnny Moore, who sang with a local group called the Hornets and was wondering if there would be any openings to sing with the Drifters. Bill didn't have anything to offer him, but on a return to Cleveland around Thanksgiving, when touring with Arthur Prysock, Annie Laurie, and Wilbert Harrison, Moore once again approached Pinkney. He auditioned and the next day got a call to get packing for a tour of the South.[10]

Bill Pinkney tells a different, weirder story. It's still Cleveland and the group was playing the Circle Theater with the same personalities Goldberg mentioned, Prysock, Laurie, Harrison, and the Paul Weston Orchestra. Pinkney feels the need for a bathroom break and heads to the men's room, where he overhears someone singing. Whoever it was sounded good. As it turned out, the voice belonged to Johnny Moore, and Pinkney asked if he was working.

The answer was yes, Moore was with the Hornets. Pinkney wasn't dismayed and inquired if he would be interested in singing with the Drifters. As Pinkney remembered, "He said to me, 'You got to be kidding me?' I told him no I wasn't, that Clyde had been drafted into the Army and we needed a good, reliable lead singer." Also, that if he was interested, he would quickly have to pack his bags because the Drifters were leaving on tour the next morning.[11]

At this point, the Drifters now had two lead singers, not because the group needed two but Pinkney wanted to show the misbehaving Dave Baughan that he could be replaced if he didn't straighten up. The ploy worked so well Johnny Moore left the group for a while. The absence didn't last very long. Pinkney contacted him again to return to the Drifters.

The B-side of the Drifters' "Adorable" was a bluesy song called "Steamboat." The song began, "You know I talked to the captain this morning / we're 500 miles from shore / and if you don't get a telegram or a letter / you know that woman don't want you no more." Pinkney took the lead on this one. The Drifters still had a lot of market momentum and this tune also climbed the R&B record charts, eventually becoming a Top Five song.

"Steamboat" was written by Buddy Lucas, a jazz musician and bandleader. He didn't write many songs and, in the rock 'n' roll era, became a valued session musician. He worked often with Dion after the singer left the Belmonts and launched a highly successful career as a solo artist. That's an unexplored connection in that one of the Drifters' three hit records in 1956 (with "Steamboat" and "I Gotta Get Myself a Woman") was "Ruby Baby." It was a Top Ten R&B tune for the Drifters, and in 1963 a #2 song on the pop charts for Dion. It might have made it to #1, but the Four Seasons' "Walk Like a Man" was too strong.

While the Clyde McPhatter–less Drifters started off with an adorable bang, the group was without a focus. Fans knew and adored the prominent and distinctively voiced Clyde McPhatter and without him the Drifters were opaque. It didn't help that the group had no key leading singer, a fan favorite like Frankie Lymon of Frankie Lymon and the Teenagers, who boasted a monster hit in 1956 with "Why Do Fools Fall in Love." Johnny Moore sang lead on "Adorable," Bill Pinkney on "Steamboat," Gerhart Thrasher on "Your Promise to be Mine" and then it was Johnny Moore and Bill Pinkney again on subsequent records. Also, the trend line for the group was weak. Although the first releases by the new Drifters were all hits—"Adorable" went to #1, "Steamboat" to #5, "Ruby Baby" to #10, and "I Gotta Get Myself a Woman" to #11—the progression was in the wrong direction.

George Treadwell, who managed the Drifters, was not a patient man, and he was very good at reading the tea leaves that floated his way from the burgeoning teenage market. When push came to shove, Treadwell always shoved.

Although the new Drifters could boast a successful turn after Clyde McPhatter moved on, without royalties their salaries were not commensurate with their status nor their needs. The individual Drifters began grumbling about their wages and turned to Pinkney, still the unofficial leader of the group, to do something for them. Pinkney took their issue to Treadwell's New York office manager. He wouldn't give. There was more. After that meeting, the manager called the other Drifters together and told them that Pinkney was being fired. Pinkney didn't know this as he was driving south to Washington, DC, for the Drifters' gig at the Howard Theater. At the theater, Pinkney walked backstage carrying his uniform when he was met by his driver, who told him, "They got rid of you and fired Bubba (Andrew Thrasher) as well." The driver, Lacy Hollingsworth, told Pinkney what happened. Since Pinkney asked for more money, Treadwell decided to fire him and when Bubba heard about it, he pitched a fit, screaming, "How can you fire Bill? He is the Drifters." He got dismissed as well.[12]

The denouement of the original Drifters evolved over the next few years. In 1957, the Drifters consisted of Charlie Hughes, Johnny Moore, Tommy Evans, and Gerhart Thrasher. This group bragged one Top Ten hit, "Fools Fall in Love." Then Moore and Hughes got drafted and were replaced by Bobby Hendricks and Jimmy Milner. This lineup had one moderate hit, "Drip Drop." Dion, who seemed to have a private line into the George Treadwell–Drifters mix, in 1963 had a Top Ten hit with a rockin' remake of "Drip Drop."

In 1959, Treadwell tired of the whole Drifters mess and canned everyone. Then he discovered a group called the Five Crowns, hired them all and renamed the combo the Drifters.

Now, let's turn back to "Virtual Surrender," that *Billboard* article from November 1955, the one that declared 1955 as the year R&B took over the pop field. In the news story itself, the writer mentioned the R&B songs and artists who did well in '55. Johnny Ace's "Pledging My Love" was the most played R&B song of the year. The disc jockey favorite for the year was "Ain't It a Shame" by Fats Domino, who was also voted the favorite male R&B artist of the year. Ruth Brown was the favorite female artist and the voters' choice for best group was the Drifters. There was a caveat in the last selection. The columnist wrote, "the first vocal group in the listings, despite what seemed like an overwhelming predominance of the group diskings [recordings], is Atlantic's Drifters, who still, in the minds of most spinners [deejays], are identified with their former lead, Clyde McPhatter, who now is waxing as a single."[13]

It was nice of the *Billboard* columnist to ascribe the confusion surrounding the Drifters and Clyde McPhatter to deejay naivete, but the magazine staff seemed to have had the same problem. In mid-January, the trade publication had to run a correction note: "In the *Billboard* last week the national rhythm and blues retail and disk jockey charts erroneously credited 'Seven Days' to the Drifters. Sole artist credit should have gone to Clyde McPhatter."[14]

Clyde had been drafted in March 1954, and his military service would last two years. During the period of time when he was out of the scene, it was obvious Clyde would sever ties to the group he founded.

The impetus for Clyde to go solo may have first become apparent as early as the autumn of 1954, when, with Clyde on leave and in the studio, the Drifters recorded "Everyone's Laughing," "Sugar Coated Kisses," "Hot Ziggety," and "Three Thirty Three." This would be the last recording session of Clyde with his group, although he would appear with them at the start of 1955. The Clyde-go-solo pot was boiling, although nothing apparently happened for the remainder of the year.

When Atlantic Records issued "What'cha Gonna Do" with "Gone" on the B-side in February 1955, the Clyde situation started to get tricky. The record is attributed to Clyde McPhatter and The Drifters. However, in March, just the following month, Atlantic issued an advertisement that read "Clyde Rides Again!; WHAT'CHA GONNA DO, Clyde McPhatter, Atlantic #1053." Clearly, the promo spotlighted Clyde as a solo act. This superseded an ad for the same song from the prior month that touted the song as being a Clyde McPhatter and Drifters song. In March, Clyde was back in New York on leave, and Marv Goldberg suggests this was the time the Drifters were told Clyde was going out on his own. "Actually, it's impossible to know when they were informed," Goldberg writes, "but at least we know that it was worked out with Clyde at this time," citing the change in the advertising copy as proof.[15]

There may have been something else happening behind the scenes that also led to Clyde's divorce from the Drifters, and that was a change in managers. As noted, George Treadwell managed the Drifters, but, at some point, Clyde met Irvin Feld. The record store owner had branched out into producing concerts and managing talent. Perhaps in expectation of going solo, he signed with Feld, who convinced him to go it alone. The clinching point from Feld was that he could get promoters to pay more for Clyde as a solo act, reportedly $3,500 a week, which was more than Treadwell was getting for the Drifters as a group.[16]

When all that happened is still difficult to ascertain. One theory is Atlantic Records engineered the move, which was possible since Ahmet Ertegun and Feld knew each other from before there was such a thing as Atlantic Records. More than likely, taking on a new manager came about because Feld, who, among many other things, was also an agent with the General Artist Corporation (GAC), a big New York–based talent agency. Kenneth Feld, Irvin Feld's son, who eventually took over his father's business, suggests in regard to Clyde that the Rubicon was crossed when his father affirmed with no equivocation,

"I will book you as a separate performer"—thus the ongoing rumors of Clyde McPhatter as a solo performer was suddenly a reality.[17]

Irvin Feld was born in 1918, and by the time he was in his twenties was selling cosmetics door to door in Baltimore. What he wanted to do was establish himself in Washington, DC, and an opportunity arose when the NAACP (National Association for the Advancement of Colored People) was seeking someone to open a pharmacy in one of the District of Columbia's African American neighborhoods. With financing from the NAACP, Irvin opened the much-needed pharmacy. To attract patrons, he put speakers in the windows and played "race" music, gospel, jazz, and blues. Due to the music, people in the neighborhood started coming to the new pharmacy, but they mostly wanted to buy records so Irvin changed the store into a music shop. When the young Ertegun brothers began hanging out in DC record stores, that's when Feld and Ahmet Ertegun first met.

The music store, Super Music City, did so well that Irvin opened two more. At the same time, he would record local talent such as gospel singers in a small studio he built in one of his stores and release the tunes on his own record label, Super-Disc Records. He also recorded country and western artists, including musician Arthur Smith. In 1945, Smith's "Guitar Boogie" became the first million-selling record produced by a small, independent record company. The tune went on to sell three million copies and the performer transitioned into Arthur "Guitar Boogie" Smith.

Irvin also became a consultant to RCA Victor Records, freelanced as an agent for GAC, and around 1955 began putting together tours for Black performers, at first in the DC-Baltimore-Richmond-Pittsburgh loop. That grew into the Biggest Show of Stars tours with many of the top R&B acts in the country. This was an aggressive road show with eighty one-nighters, which he would do twice a year. Feld's business eventually expanded into other types of shows, and in 1967 he bought the Ringling Bros. and Barnum & Bailey Circus, then left the music business.

The official announcement of the McPhatter-Drifters split was in midsummer 1955. *Cash Box*'s lazily written story on the subject read as if was directly quoting the Atlantic Records press release: "Atlantic Records this week [July 23, 1955], announced that Clyde McPhatter, who rose to prominence as the lead singer of the Drifters vocal quartet, will henceforth be featured as a recording star in his own right. At the same time, the Drifters will continue their own recording career with Atlantic, with tenor David Baughan replacing McPhatter as the lead voice."[18]

This led to some fancy footwork by Atlantic. From the last recording session of Clyde with the Drifters, two songs, "Everyone's Laughing" and "Hot Ziggety," were pulled to be released as a single. Although Clyde recorded these tunes with the full Drifters group, Atlantic rushed to get the record into market as solo recordings by Clyde McPhatter. The extra promo on this news was that both songs "were written especially for Clyde's talents by Winfield Scott, creator of LaVern Bakers big hit 'Tweedle Dee.'"

Whatever the Drifters might have felt about being left off the credits to the songs, they just had to let it go and move on in the new direction. "There wasn't anything we could do about it, regardless of how we felt," said Pinkney. "It wouldn't have made any difference. There was no discussion of 'Everyone's Laughing.' We never knew what was being released. We were always on the road and didn't know until several months later. We didn't know Clyde was going on his own. When he went into the service, we thought he'd be back. The idea was strictly George Treadwell's."[19]

In the news stories about Clyde McPhatter going solo, Atlantic Records had to also address the fate of the Drifters. As *Cash Box* reported, the group had been engaged in a series of highly successful one-nighters and theater appearances on their own since Clyde entered the service in 1954. The article concluded that the Drifters would "continue to perform under the aegis of George Treadwell and the Gale Agency. Their first disk without Clyde will be issued by Atlantic as a special release early in August."[20]

Atlantic Records didn't help in the continuing confusion, running ads, for example, associating subsequent Clyde releases with new Drifters releases, such as one promotion touting "Love Has Joined Us Together," his duet with Ruth Brown, and the Drifters' "Adorable." One could say that Atlantic didn't really know what it had with the McPhatterless Drifters as a recording act until "Adorable" and "Steamboat" were released in October 1955 to great success. Whatever George Treadwell might have thought about losing Clyde as a client, he knew how to get the best out of the existing Drifters.

As Bill Pinkney lamented, "We didn't know anything about the potential for more income or that we had rights that could and should have been protected. None of us knew about the legal side—trademarks, copyright and publishing."

Treadwell also got the worth out of Clyde McPhatter. When the Drifters was founded, George Treadwell made sure the name of the group was copyrighted to Clyde and himself as they were business partners. Shadow groups of singers would haunt legitimate groups through the 1950s and into the '60s. If, for example, a group called the Nimrods had a hit and was touring the East Coast, a shady tour promoter on the West Coast would quickly put together a group called the Nimrods and have them tour venues in California. This was easy to do because most R&B fans had never seen photographs of their favorite singers and didn't know what they looked like. By copyrighting, it afforded legal claim to the name and a lawsuit or cease and desist order could be issued against the shady enterprise.

With Clyde going his own way and Treadwell remaining as manager of the Drifters, it was obvious to Treadwell that Clyde would be, in a certain sense, competition to the Drifters, so he needed to get full ownership of the rights to the group, and he convinced Clyde that was what needed to happen. "It is my understanding that George Treadwell did pay my father for his share of the rights to the Drifters," reported Deborah McPhatter. "However, I don't know what the dollar amount was."[21] Tina Treadwell concurs that Clyde ended up selling his shares of Drifters Inc. to her father.[22]

This didn't mean that Clyde thought whatever settlement they had was fair. Bill Curtis, Clyde's longtime drummer, claimed that Clyde would never talk about what Curtis called "the Treadwell situation" as Clyde and Treadwell "weren't on good business terms."[23]

The acrimony was mutual.

When Tina Treadwell was a young girl, her family lived in Englewood, New Jersey, near Clyde's parents and in walking distance to Clyde's house. "One of my best friends lived two doors down from Clyde McPhatter. I was playing with my friend at his house when there was a party at Clyde's house. I ended up with my friend at the party," Tina recalled. "When my father found out, I got the worst whupping I ever got. My dad was not happy that his daughter was inside Clyde McPhatter's house without her parents."

Looking back, Tina suggested, "Once Clyde left the group not only did the Drifters have a history of success but my father took the group overseas. There was resentment from Clyde."

She added, "I was born in 1958 and my father died in 1967. My father and Clyde's relationship had been acrimonious. From what I understand, at some point Clyde's career was no longer going the way he wanted and he was drinking. That changes your personality."[24]

Considering the success of the Drifters through the next decade, Clyde would regret his decision to end his "ownership" of the group's name, but at the time it seemed like the prudent thing to do. Treadwell was a hands-on manager and the Drifters did exceedingly well over the years while he shuffled players in and out as if he was playing gin rummy with talent. According to one person who knew him, he didn't have a good reputation because of the way he treated his singers, putting them on salary and taking all the royalties. He famously fired one group of Drifters, hired another group of singers and called them the Drifters and that group, under lead singers Ben E. King and Rudy Lewis, was probably the most successful iteration of the Drifters.

In 1958, a reporter cornered Treadwell and was able to secure a rare interview. The story began in complimentary fashion: "In the last five years more than 50 quartets have sprung from fame via one record hit, and died just as quickly as public favorites. Among those to successfully survive as a consistent money maker in the record field have been the Drifters quartet."

One of the reasons for their staying on top while others come and go, the reporter attributed to their "shrewd" manager, George Treadwell, who said, "Each member of the group is capable of soloing and unlike most foursome vocal groups, one man doesn't bear the burden. I never have any trouble in booking the Drifters because promoters know that they're a surefire click at the box office. They've always held their own on big shows in competition against other acts."[25]

As for Clyde, things were happening quickly for him as well. In March 1956, Atlantic Records made a big splash in signing Guitar Slim, who had a big hit in 1954 with "The Things I Used to Do." Underneath all that excitement, Ertegun made sure he solidified his existing roster of performers. So, at the same Atlantic announced the signing of Guitar Slim, the company also reported it had renewed contracts with the Clovers and Clyde McPhatter. As *Billboard* reported, "The artists renewing with the diskery [recording company] are Clyde McPhatter and the Clovers, both consistent performers in the best-selling ranks. McPhatter, who is leaving the U.S. Army shortly, formerly recorded with the Drifters group, but in his last few Atlantic releases has been building solidly as a single."[26]

His manager, Irvin Feld, also swung into action, getting Clyde on a big tour that Feld organized. Bill Simon, who authored *Billboard*'s gossipy R&B column "Rhythm-Blues Notes" on March 14, 1956, wrote, "Clyde McPhatter, a wonderful guy and a great artist, was released from the Army last week. He'll be joining the big new Irving [sic] Feld Rock and Roll package."[27] Also on that tour were labelmate LaVern Baker, Bill Haley and the Comets, and the Platters, which made it an integrated tour.

Billboard's Bill Simon was back again with a follow-up Clyde McPhatter story in the May 26, 1956, issue of the magazine, when he wrote: "Some of the cats will never forget hearing him sing 'Because' at Herb Abramson's wedding. Maybe he'll record it one of these days."[28]

Atlantic's cofounder Herb Abramson also had been drafted, but, except for some excellent recordings he did with Clyde, his return to civilian life was rougher than his tour of duty.

Abramson, a cofounder of Atlantic Records, was drafted a year before Clyde, in 1953, so his return to civilian life was in 1955. In those two years a lot had changed at Atlantic Records and with Abramson's personal life. The two mixed.

During his tour of duty, Abramson was sent to Germany, and when he came back to the states, he brought a girlfriend with him. He and Miriam divorced, and that was also a professional problem because Miriam, who also had been with Atlantic from the start, handling the company's financing among other duties, had become one of the top three executives at the company, which went from being Ahmet Ertegun, Herb Abramson, and Miriam Abramson to Ahmet, Jerry Wexler, and Miriam. As Wexler wrote, "When Herb returned, his marriage to Miriam was over, straining the atmosphere in the office. Moreover, since Atlantic's inception, Herb had been president. Even during his Army stint, he retained his title and drew full salary . . . there would be personality problems, and finally the partners decided that Ahmet would be company president."[29]

This was Abramson's memory of his return. When he left the company in 1953, his office was next to Ahmet's, and when he returned it was Jerry Wexler who sat next to Ertegun and there was no room for a third desk. "We had an interesting setup," Abramson recalled, "Ahmet and Jerry had an office at one side, and I had an office at the extreme other side, and in the middle there was a conference room."[30]

Also, into this volatile situation came Ahmet's brother Nesuhi. After flirting with going with one of Atlantic's chief competitors, Ahmet talked him into coming over to Atlantic. Nesuhi and Abramson did not get along.

The solution was to give Herb a label of his own, which was called Atco. As writer Ed Ward noted, "Atco was an ideal niche for the returning soldier who had missed out on Atlantic's rise to glory."[31]

During that rise to glory, an impediment to Atlantic's success story arose because the success of Elvis Presley attracted a tidal wave of young, white male performers into the new world of rock 'n' roll. Atlantic didn't have any great white hopes in its lineup until it signed an up-and-coming young singer/songwriter named Walden Robert Cassotto, better known as Bobby Darin.

In 1956, Darin, who had been a Bronx high school student writing songs with classmate Don Kirshner, a future music publisher and producer, signed with Decca Records. His first shot at stardom, a cover of "Rock Island Line," crashed, and in the aftermath, Abramson picked him up, dusted him off, and signed him to Atlantic Records. While everyone liked Darin at the company and thought he had tremendous talent, Abramson couldn't get anything going with him. Over a two-year period, Abramson produced six singles by Darin, all of which struck out. Abramson decided he was going to drop him from the Atco label.[32] Ertegun, however, liked the kid and decided he would have a go at producing Darin, and in less than two hours, recorded three sides including "Splish Splash," a novelty song that Darin wrote with popular New York disc jockey Murray the K (Murray Kaufman). Teenagers went for the splashy tune in a big way. The record sold 100,000 copies in the first month of its release, over a million total, and climbed to #3 on the pop charts in 1958.

That was the start of a stellar career for Bobby Darin and the beginning of the end for Abramson at Atlantic Records. As Atlantic's engineer Tom Dowd recalled, the success of Bobby Darin was "the beginning of a whole new era," as it gave Atlantic its first breakthrough into the white side of rock 'n' roll." Adversely, for Abramson, said Dowd, "it was the end of the road. Herb just looked around and said, 'I'm not where these guys are' and left." It was a little more complicated than that. After long deliberations, Atlantic bought out Herb for about $300,000. Miriam and the original investor Dr. Sabit, were also bought out, leaving the company in ownership of Ahmet, his brother Nesuhi, and Jerry Wexler.[33]

While Abramson wasn't able to establish the career of the talented Bobby Darin, he was able to successfully launch Clyde McPhatter on his journey as a solo performer.

This was a meld of two young music industry veterans who had returned from active duty. As Ahmet Ertegun biographer's Robert Greenfield wrote, after Clyde returned from the army, Herb Abramson produced a hit record entitled "Seven Days" and then had Clyde cut "Treasure of Love."[34]

Where Abramson was a step behind the record market with Bobby Darin, he was at the right place with Clyde psychologically and in terms of where Clyde needed to be, as he was now a seasoned performer. Jerry Wexler once said of Clyde that it was his dream to transcend the R&B category and take a place in show business alongside the Perry Comos and Nat King Coles of the world.[35] Although Clyde was only twenty-four years of age for most of 1956, he had been in the music swirl since he was a teenager, and Abramson adopted a less rock 'n' roll and more mainstream approach with Clyde. "Seven Days" was a song that could have been recorded by Al Martino, Perry Como, or Eddie Fisher or any other white pop singer of the times, although it would have been slightly different as Clyde still could give it that R&B patina to make it a better record. Clyde despondently crooned: "Seven days, seven days, and there's not a word from you / . . . The phone won't ring at all, the clock is standing still / my tears are like raindrops, upon my windowsill." An unnamed vocal chorus supplied the background, which was the same for the B-side, a song called "I'm Not Worthy of You," written by Clyde.

An early *Billboard* review, with scattered jive talk, in December 1955, read: "Another strong McPhatter platter enters the race for the gravy and this could break fast. There's a great chorus and full ork [orchestra] sound, and most of all, McPhatter is his same great chanting self. A strong production that shapes up as an all-level entry. Flip [B-side] is 'I'm Not Worthy of You,' a well-delivered weepy styled ballad."[36]

The slow, heartbreak tune, "Seven Days," did not break Clyde's heart, as the tune shot all the way to #2 on the R&B charts in 1956 and crossed over to the pop charts, slotting in at a respectable #44. It would have been tough for "Seven Days" to make it all the way to #1 on the R&B charts as three monster hits dominated the bestseller list from January to May: "The Great Pretender" by the Platters, "Why Do Fools Fall in Love" by the Teenagers featuring Frankie Lymon, and "Long Tall Sally" by Little Richard. Still, "Seven Days" was the twenty-third best-selling R&B tune of 1956. The song probably has as many critics as fans, yet "Seven Days" did two important things. First, it established Clyde McPhatter as a soloist, and second, it cleared the way for "Treasure of Love," a much better song.

In April 1956, two white singers crashed the R&B charts, Elvis Presley with "Heartbreak Hotel" and Carl Perkins with "Blue Suede Shoes." This was a moment of great rock 'n' roll and pre-soul music classics. Hot on the radio were such songs as "Long Tall Sally"' from Little Richard, "Please, Please, Please" by James Brown, "Why Do Fools Fall In Love" by the Teenagers featuring Frankie Lymon, and "Drown in My Own Tears" by Ray Charles. There were also some fine doo-wop records including "Magic Touch" by the Platters, "Little Girl of Mine" by the Cleftones, "Eddie My Love" by the Teen Queens, and "Church Bells May Ring" by the Willows.[37]

Into this mix came "Treasure of Love" with "When You're Sincere" on the B-side. The track was written by the songwriting team of Joe Shapiro and Lou Stallman, who were enjoying their best year ever in 1956. The two also penned an even bigger hit for Perry Como, a little tune called "Round and Round," which went to #1 on the pop charts in 1957. Starting in the 1940s, Como could boast ten #1 records. This would be his last and the only one in the rock 'n' roll era. Whereas "Round and Round" was a bouncy tune sung with an effervescent delivery by the usually insouciant Como, "Treasure of Love" was Clyde in all his soulful earnestness. The song boasted an unusual start, bare-naked guitar strumming. Then it's Clyde's crystal-clear voice: "The treasure of love is easy to find / it's waiting for you if your hear-r-r-r-t isn't blind." A chorus, more 1950s pop than doo-wop, accentuates Clyde's singing. The key to the song's success is an unlikely mix of Clyde's voice, chorus, and the strumming guitar.

An early review in *Billboard* focuses on that McPhatter sound: "Here's another great two-sided disk by the velvet-voiced McPhatter. The warbler [singer] sings with poignancy and feeling on 'Treasure of Love,' an attractive ballad." The review also noted that Clyde was backed by a pop vocal group and a big band.[38]

By May, the two new R&B songs that were attracting a lot of record sales were Little Willie John's "Fever," later to be an even bigger hit for Peggy Lee, and Clyde's "Treasure of Love." The trade magazines suggested the "Treasure of Love" market action was due to the legion of Clyde fans. *Billboard* concluded, "McPhatter, out of the Army only about as long as his latest record has been available to the public, is getting a resounding welcome back to civilian life. His fans are snowballing 'Treasure' into a big hit for him."[39]

Cash Box, through its "Rhythm 'n Blues Ramblings" column, initially leaned more to his record company's hot streak when explaining the success of "Treasure of Love," saying, "Atlantic continues to swing at a torrid pace. The diskery now pops up with what should be Clyde McPhatter's greatest side yet—and his first real heavy impression on the pop market. Clyde sings 'Treasure of Love' against a terrific arrangement and the result is overpowering."[40]

In the May 5, 1956, issue of *Cash Box*, the magazine placed two songs in its coveted "Award O' The Week" insert of record reviews, "Fever" and "Treasure of Love." The reviewer absolutely gushed over the McPhatter song: "Clyde McPhatter turns in a powerhouse marching tempo, 'Treasure of Love.' A beautiful melody, gospel flavored, simple and easy to remember, stirring in the feeling it imparts, tender in the treatment, and marital in spirit. It is an exciting thing to listen to."

After "Seven Days" and now "Treasure of Love," all things began to roll in Clyde's direction as a singer in his own right. With success, fans quickly forgot about his association with the Drifters. A deejay survey in *Billboard* that asked the question "Who are the favorite artists or bands in your locations?" listed Clyde as the third favorite behind the Platters and Little Richard in the R&B category.[41]

Cash Box never included the names of the columnists who wrote "Rhythm 'N Blues Ramblings," but they were some of the most insightful followers of R&B in the country. Early on, the New York voice of the column predicted "Treasure of Love" would affect the pop market as well as the R&B charts, and he was correct. In June, the same columnist noted, "Clyde McPhatter, sizzling like butter in a frying pan as his 'Treasure of Love' makes like it is going to be Number One on the pop and R&B charts, opened at the Apollo Theater this past weekend."[42]

Meanwhile, over at the competition, a *Billboard* charting of the fastest climbing songs in the pop market included mainstream singer Patti Page with "Allegheny Moon," former teen sensation Teresa Brewer with "A Sweet Old Fashioned Girl," rock 'n' roller Gene Vincent with "Be-Bop-A-Lula," and at #1, Clyde McPhatter with "Treasure of Love."[43]

The pundits were a little too optimistic. "Treasure of Love," went to #1 on the R&B charts, but just to #16 on the pop charts, which was still Clyde's best posting in the mainstream music world. In some local markets, "Treasure of Love" was a monster recording. A listing of the top songs of 1956 from a New York City radio station that concentrated on the new rock 'n' roll (either WINS or WABC) listed "Treasure of Love" as the sixteenth top song of the year, one spot behind Elvis Presley's "Hound Dog" and one ahead of Shirley and Lee's "Let the Good Times Roll." *Billboard*'s list of the top R&B songs of 1956 placed "Treasure of Love" at #15, one behind "Don't Be Cruel" by Elvis Presley and one ahead of "Eddie My Love" by the Teen Queens.

One fascinating story from 1956 involved both Clyde and Elvis. In June, *The Carolinian*, a Black newspaper in Raleigh, North Carolina, ran a story with the headline "McPhatter, Presley in Song 'Fight.'" This was a wire service article out of Cleveland that the newspaper picked up, and it began picturesquely with this lead: "The rafters rocked and rolled at the Arena last week when two of the nation's top rhythm and blues artists appeared on the same stage in a three-day battle for the mythical title of King of the Rock and Rollers."

When all was said and done, the promoters decided to jointly give the crown to Clyde and Elvis, although the reporter who scribed the story observed McPhatter fans were in the majority. An applause meter on stage gauged the reception accorded each artist after his turn at the "mike." Apparently, according to the meter, Clyde had a slight edge in the applause. However, the promoters, wishing to avert a probable riot among the ardent Presley fans, decided to have two crowns made. The story concluded, it was the first time that Clyde, "a recent GI who headed the Drifters quartet at one time, and Presley, the hottest rock and roll shouter in the country, had met." Probably the last time as well. Elvis would famously go into the military in 1958, two years after Clyde returned to civilian life.[44]

At the end of 1956, *Billboard* attempted to summarize the musical trends of the prior twelve months, and it was obvious to the magazine that the Black singers, who were traditionally segregated to the rhythm and blues radio stations and record listings, had completely invaded the pop charts in what truly had become the year rock 'n' roll came of age.

The magazine recapitulated: "Looking closely at the 25 rhythm and blues platters that made the pop charts, it is interesting to note the great variety of rhythm and blues artists and styles that found pop acceptance. It was not only the slicker, pop-oriented singers like Clyde McPhatter and Otis Williams ('Ivory Tower'), who hit the pop market, but also those working in the traditional style like Shirley and Lee, Little Richard and Fats Domino. Their impact, in fact, has virtually changed the conception of what a pop record is."[45]

CHAPTER NINE

WITHOUT LOVE (THERE IS NOTHING)

According to rock 'n' roll mythology, in 1955, when aspiring doo-wop group the Teenagers showed up for an audition with record producer George Goldner, the lead singer Herman Santiago was late. The quintet, all teenagers, intended on singing a tune Santiago and another member of the group, Jimmy Merchant, wrote called "Why Do Fools Fall in Love." When Goldner showed signs of exasperation with the tardy singer, Frankie Lymon, the youngest member of the group, stepped up, saying he could do the lead because he helped write the song.[1]

There are additional origination stories. Another tale has it that the song, originally called "Why Do Birds Sing So Gay," was written by a neighborhood girl, whose boyfriend showed it to a local singing group thinking it would make a good song lyric. In this version of the story, three members of the singing group, Frankie Lymon, Herman Santiago, and Jimmy Merchant (the other members were Joe Negroni and Sherman Garnes), were walking home from school when they audibly freestyled the poem into a song and improvised better lyrics centered on their various girlfriends. The result was "Why Do Fools Fall in Love."[2]

The record itself listed the singers as The Teenagers Featuring Frankie Lymon and the songwriters as (Frankie) Lymon and (George) Goldner, the owner of the label, Gee, which produced the record. What happened was that the slippery Goldner told the group that only two names could be listed on the copyright, so he arbitrarily credited Frankie Lymon and himself as the songwriters. This was a scam, but, nevertheless, a common practice in the 1950s and early 1960s, when young Black artists, who knew little to nothing about music legal matters or royalties, were taken advantage of by avaricious record producers, who would insert their names as co-songwriters so as to co-opt royalties.[3]

The song was so popular with teenagers that it was the sixth bestselling R&B song of the year, nine slots ahead of Clyde McPhatter's "Treasure of Love." The difference between the two was that "Why Do Fools Fall in Love," which mixed elements of doo-wop and rock 'n' roll, was so popular it was the twenty-eighth best-selling song for 1956 on the pop charts as well. The two acts would also boast a second best-seller on the concluding R&B charts for 1956: Clyde's "Seven Days" and the Teenagers' "I Want You to Be My Girl."

Over the course of a year, Clyde and Frankie Lymon and the Teenagers would spend a lot of time together, as the performers were immediately tossed into the revolving drum of Irvin Feld's new package tour. The Teenagers' Jimmy Merchant befriended Clyde. "I knew him well," he said. "Initially, we did many shows together during a two-month tour in 1956."[4]

One month after Clyde left the service, Feld booked him on what was then a ground-breaking package tour, which was called The Biggest Rock n Roll Show of 1956. Rock 'n' roll tours would end up to be a prosperous business for Feld. "My dad created the Biggest Show of Stars (renamed in 1957) tours," recalled Kenneth Feld. "He would do eighty one-nighters in both the spring and fall tours. He was the first to tour rock 'n' roll, and his tours were the first time white and black acts were mixed. Frankie Lymon would tour with white groups, for example. The talent was there working together."[5]

Feld's initial foray into the national touring circuit boasted a fantastic lineup of talent: Bill Haley and the Comets, Clyde McPhatter, Frankie Lymon and the Teenagers, the Drifters, the Platters, Bo Diddley, LaVern Baker, Big Joe Turner, the Turbans, Shirley and Lee, Roy Hamilton, and the Five Keys.

The whole cast consisted of African American performers except for the headliners, Bill Haley and the Comets, which meant it was to be an integrated show. In the early 1950s, there had been individual integrated R&B shows and even the earliest of the Alan Freed rock 'n' roll movies always had white and Black performers. However, this was a package tour that would not only travel mid-America but head into the South as well. For Feld, this was uncharted rock 'n' roll territory. How extensive was this tour? It would move from the Northeast to Canada to the American South, back up through the Midwest, ending in New England.

The most worried performer in the group was probably Bill Haley, who wrote in his diary, "This tour is all colored but our act. With the racial situation in the South broiling . . . I hope my nerves hold up."[6]

He was right to be nervous. The opening night of the tour was on April 20, 1956, ten days after Nat King Cole, while doing a show in Birmingham, Alabama, was attacked by four white men who rushed the stage and began throwing punches, knocking Cole to the ground. On the fifth performance of the tour, in Scranton, Pennsylvania, Haley was punched in the face as he left the stage. This would have been a show for a largely white audience, so the assault would not have come from a Black person.

The Feld tour wasn't without controversy, as individual shows were canceled because of protests, pickets, and violence. In Greenville, South Carolina, a second show was canceled due to a bomb threat. In Rochester, New York, fans attempted to pull Bill Haley from the stage.[7]

Even with all that *sturm und drang*, the tour was considered a great success. The opening show in Hershey, Pennsylvania, attracted six thousand teenagers. That night, *Look* magazine photographer Ed Feingersh took what was perhaps the ultimate early rock 'n' roll picture. He stood on stage with his camera looking out to a sold-out auditorium while in the forefront Bill Haley and the Comets are in throes of music euphoria; Haley on his guitar, the saxophonist wailing away while leaning backward like bad yoga, the bass player seemingly climbing his instrument and the drummer fully engaged. Anyone seeing this picture would immediately know why the new rock 'n' roll was suddenly so popular.

Before the show arrived in Miami, the local Black newspaper, the *Miami Times*, played up the angle of rock 'n' roll insurgence: "What's this? A strange virus! No indeed, it's the most exciting music beat of the century . . . the music that has quickly been adopted by the American public as the greatest. And the news of the Biggest Rock 'N Roll Show of '56 coming . . . has really caused a sensation."[8]

The unnamed reporter skipped right past Bill Haley, the Platters, and the rest of the performers to focus on two of the acts, Clyde McPhatter and the Teenagers. "The . . . show scooped the business by getting Clyde McPhatter for his first appearance since he entered the Army. Clyde's record 'Seven Days,' which he made while still in the service, is already tops on the hit parade."

About the Teenagers, the reporter wrote: "The Teenagers, hit maker of the tune, 'Why Do Fools Fall in Love,' which incidentally was written by 13-year-old Frankie Lymon, lead tenor of the group . . ."

The logistics for the tour weren't great. Bill Haley and the Comets rode in their own Cadillac with a Decca van carrying their instruments. All the other performers rode the bus, and because many establishments wouldn't serve Black people, meals and night sleeping were often on the bus. This wasn't just in the South. After a performance in Columbus, the troupe was traveling on the Ohio Turnpike. Bill and his band stopped at a restaurant for a meal. The bus, traveling minutes behind, pulled up as well, but the eatery wouldn't serve the Black performers. A fight ensued and everyone had to leave very quickly. Often during the tour, Haley and the Comets had to buy food for all the singers, who weren't allowed in restaurants.[9]

The tour was catnip to nascent rock 'n' rollers. In Philadelphia, 11,000 fans jammed the Arena for two shows. At the Forum in Montreal, 16,000 fans came out, 13,000 fans in Toronto, 9,000 in Pittsburgh, 10,000 in Atlanta, 14,000 in Charlotte, and 22,500 in Detroit. As the headliner, Bill Haley and his Comets earned almost $1,500 (over $17,000 in 2024 dollars) a show, which was a considerable payout in the 1950s, a period of low wages in America.[10] (In 1955, the median income for men was $3,400.)[11] There are no numbers as to how well the African American acts were paid, but touring was really the primary source of income for these performers, especially as many were not getting much in return from having a successful record.

With such a huge turnout in its city, the *Detroit Tribune* reviewed the show, noting, "The Olympia was filled almost to capacity with teen-agers and adults who were eager to hear the music that's sweeping the country with its crazy rhythm." Then the column focused on Clyde McPhatter: "The song 'Money Honey' sent the bobby-soxers screaming as Clyde McPhatter sang it in his unusual tenor voice, which brought him fame."[12]

The columnist added, "Clyde, formerly of Billy Ward's Dominoes and also of the Drifters, is now singing as a single. Before ending his performance, Clyde and his once Drifters did one of their old hits, 'What'cha Gonna Do.'"

The Biggest Rock n Roll Show of 1956 was true to its billing, a "big" show in the sense that a number of the acts could boast #1 R&B hits, including Clyde McPhatter. Few, if any, would be able to repeat as hitmakers. Clyde would, and his career would continue to go on to greater success. Clyde would also become a regular on subsequent Feld tours. One year later, on the spring 1957 Biggest Show of Stars tour, Feld, trying to avoid the hassles of the first tour, created an all African American performer program, dropping Bill Haley and headlining with Fats Domino. McPhatter shared the bus with Chuck Berry, LaVern Baker, the Five Satins, the Moonglows, and Bill Doggett, among others.[13]

Frankie Lymon would be back on the tour in the fall 1957 edition after going the Clyde McPhatter route. Lymon's producer, the market savvy but unreliable George Goldner, decided Lymon should be a separate act from the Teenagers, and early in 1957 he made that happen. At this point, Frankie Lymon's and Clyde's careers would diverge, although, sadly, they both would end up in the same place physiologically, with addiction problems, which would, in different ways, eventually prove fatal.

The start of 1957 held very good news for Clyde. One of his songs, "Without Love (There is Nothing)," which was released in December of the year before, was quickly climbing the charts. Clyde would start the new year with a hit record.

Time has diminished many of Clyde's best songs. Some of those old enough to remember the tunes have good memories of Clyde's oeuvre. Singer Billy Vera, who had great regard for Clyde's solo career songs, holds "Without Love

(There is Nothing)" in particular high regard, saying "it is just a magnificent song." It is, to put it in the vernacular of the time, a "chirping" of sorrow. Although the tune begins with a piano solo, it has a near-country vibe at the beginning. The listener almost expects to hear one of those expository tales such as told by country singer Marty Robbins. Instead, the listener hears: "I have conquered the world / all but one thing did I have / without love I've had nothing at all." This is all accented by a mournful choir. Yet the tune glides on McPhatter's unusual voice, which slides from tenor to something deeper and more mature.

The tone of the song is a reflection of the songwriter's Weltanschauung. It was written by Danny Smalls, another talented soul with addiction issues. He tended to write songs that were often from a dope addict's persona, if not perspective. If one listens closely to the words of the song, it's filled with self-pity. The singer is basically saying not just that he has nothing, but that he is nothing.[14]

The first review of the song in *Billboard*, on December 1, 1956, caught the songwriter's lament: "Here's a beautiful styled weeper-ballad that offers the singer one of his most powerful vehicles to date. Its churchy sound and emotional build-up are memorable features."[15]

Rival *Cash Box* placed the song in its "Award O' The Week" category of its "R&B Reviews" column. Also, in the "Award O' The Week" were songs by the Moonglows and Clovers, but Clyde's tune was the only one to become a hit. The reviewer effused, "Clyde McPhatter seems to have hit the formula again with 'Without Love.' It is a very strong and moving tune given the benefit of McPhatter's tender treatment. McPhatter . . . now itches again for the big pop and r&b disk with this simple but effective waxing [recording]. It is our opinion the deck [A-side] will move McPhatter into the hit category once again."[16]

As rock 'n' roll was on the rise across America, Clyde and his Atlantic Records team continued to go against the grain, with a more mature, slow-and-easy pop sound. The days of "Have Mercy Baby" and even "Money Honey" were in his rearview mirror. He was now more like a Black Frank Sinatra, if Ol' Blue Eyes had the idiosyncratic range of Clyde McPhatter.

If "Without Love (There is Nothing)" wasn't convincing enough of the change in McPhatter's approach to music, then the B-side of that record nails down the transmutation. It's a song called "I Make Believe" and is pure pop with all the R&B bleached away. The tune was given short shrift by the trades. All *Billboard* had to say about it was that the song "has a tenderness and heartfelt sincerity that will appeal to a wide audience. The poppish backing is an asset."[17]

Not according to the *Cash Box* reviewer, who did not appreciate the song but still tried to be positive. The critic wrote "I Make Believe" is a "strictly pop side that comes off beautifully, but without the something extra that makes 'Without Love' outstanding."[18]

The weakness of the B-side tune was a surprise, since the song wasn't a throwaway. It was written by Ivory Joe Hunter, a fine singer/songwriter also on the Atlantic label. The jovial performer was born in 1914 and by the 1930s briefly started his recording career. It is said he wrote more than seven thousand songs, a handful of which were peerless hit records, including "I Almost Lost My Mind" from 1950 and "Since I Met You Baby" from 1956. "Empty Arms" could be on that list as well, but some of Hunter's thunder was stolen by Teresa Brewer, who covered the tune and had a Top Twenty hit with it. Hunter's big hits were slow, bluesy crawls, but Clyde's version of "I Make Believe" had no blues. It was pure pop.

The weak B-side didn't make a difference as "Without Love (There is Nothing)" took off quickly. By the end of December 1956, *Billboard* spotlighted two new records that were tearing up the charts in local markets, Little Richard's "The Girl Can't Help It" and Clyde's "Without Love (There is Nothing)." The trade publication commented, "This disk has been building up strength quite rapidly in the past two weeks. It now looks well established in New York, Philadelphia, Los Angeles, St. Louis, Baltimore, Pittsburgh and other cities. Has good chart potential in both the pop and r&b fields."[19]

Next to this commentary, Atlantic Records placed a one-column, top-of-the-page to bottom promotion trying to give Big Joe Turner's new record some zest by piggybacking it with other new releases, and in screaming type read: "Look Out Charts! Here's Joe Turner with 'Midnight Special Train' and 'Feeling Happy,' Watch It Join These Red Hot Hits: Ivory Joe Hunter's 'Since I Met You, Baby,' LaVern Baker's 'Jim Dandy,' Clyde McPhatter's 'Without Love,' The Clovers' 'I'm a Lonely Fool,' Chris Conner's 'I Miss You So,' Chuck Willis' 'Juanita.'"

Clyde's "Without Love (There is Nothing)" rose to #2 on the R&B charts. As good as it was, it stood no chance of #1 as Fats Domino absolutely dominated the best-seller list in early 1957 with "Blueberry Hill," "Blue Monday," and "I'm Walkin.'" As to radio and jukebox play, the two songs that dented the Fats Domino monopoly were from Clyde's Atlantic stablemates: Ivory Joe Hunter with "Since I Met You Baby" and LaVern Baker with "Jim Dandy." Then by early March, a little song called "Love Is Strange" by Mickey and Sylvia conquered as well.

The better news was that "Without Love (There is Nothing)" crossed over to the pop charts, where it became a Top Twenty hit, the second Clyde record in a row to do so (with "Treasure of Love"). If the game plan was to take Clyde McPhatter mainstream, it appeared to be working.

Atlantic tried to mix things up for Clyde in 1957 by switching between songs with gusto and the heartfelt, basically lively romantic tunes that were scoring so well with record buyers. Early in the year, Atlantic released a more beat-driven Clyde song, "Thirty Days," with "I'm Lonely Tonight" on the B-side, but it got lost in the success of "Without Love (There is Nothing)," and doesn't appear that Atlantic gave it much support. After "Treasure of Love" and "Without Love (There Is Nothing)," Atlantic Records went back to the lighter, danceable side of Clyde with a tune called "Just to Hold My Hand." The songwriting credits say Perryman and Robey. More than likely the first writer was Willie Lee Perryman (Piano Red) although his brother Rufus Perryman (Speckled Red) was a musician as well. Robey is Don Robey, who was the head of Duke/Peacock Records, and his credits are a steal.

The April 13, 1957, issue of *Cash Box* magazine, which generally was very supportive of Clyde McPhatter, once again put his new release in the "Award O' The Week" category alongside songs by Bill Doggett, who had a huge instrumental hit with "Honky Tonk" in 1956, and Bo Diddley. Predictably, the reviewer was high on Clyde's new ditty, writing: "Clyde McPhatter comes up with one of his most impressive releases in many months. 'Just to Hold My Hand' is a middle beat jump with an engaging melody—and McPhatter reads it in great style . . . From all indications, this side should be a 'big' seller, perhaps his best since 'Treasure of Love.' The flip (B-side), 'No Matter What,' is a slow beat . . . easy lilter. However, for the sales charts, it's 'Just to Hold My Hand.'"[20]

Two weeks later, *Cash Box*'s "R&B Ramblings" column observed, "Atlantic is really on the move with 'C. C. Rider' by Chuck Willis and Clyde McPhatter's 'Just Hold My Hand.'"[21] Clyde's song did well, rising as high as #6 on the R&B charts, and crossing over to the pop charts, coming in at a respectable #26. It was competitive at Atlantic, and Willis would get more pats on the back because "C. C. Rider," a superlative rendition of an old blues tune, was a surprising hit, topping the R&B charts in 1957 and vaulting to the pop charts where it nestled down at #12. The song didn't make *Billboard*'s top fifty best-selling songs of the year (there was a lot of teenage dross that made the list in '57: Pat Boone's update of "Love Letters in the Sand," "Young Love" by Tab Hunter, "Rainbow" by Russ Hamilton), but the New York City rock and roll station (WINS or WABC) placed "C. C. Rider" as the #13 top song for the year. One tune by an Atlantic Records artist did better, "Since I Met You, Baby," by Ivory Joe Hunter. Time and tide have not treated "Just to Hold My Hand" well. It's near-forgotten, while "C. C. Rider" is considered one the great R&B tunes of the 1950s.

In July 1957, Clyde opened a record store in New Rochelle, New York, where he had a home, although he wasn't there often. New Rochelle was a pleasant suburban community just north of New York City in Westchester County. This was big news for the trade publications and *Cash Box* magazine ran a photo of Clyde in his store surrounded by teens looking awfully glad to be near their hero. Actually, the opening of the store caused a near-riot, and also in the photo was a policeman, who looked more confused than bemused.

A headline above the photo read "McPhatter's Tune Shop," and the caption read: "Atlantic recording star, Clyde McPhatter, who recently opened his own record outlet at 437 North Avenue ... was swamped by hundreds of teenagers who stampeded the store to see the disk star and get his autograph. Police were on hand to handle the huge throng."

Also in the caption was a brief recap of Clyde's career. "McPhatter, who made his first big climb up the success ladder with Billy Ward and his Dominoes, later joined Atlantic as lead of the Drifters. Today, as a soloist, he is one of the label's top record sellers and is currently on the boards with his click [record] 'Just to Hold My Hand.'"[22]

Clyde's record shop generated plenty of news, good and bad, over the next several years. Nora McPhatter made the news as the manager of the store. One news story that appeared in numerous Black newspapers reported: "While Clyde McPhatter takes to the road to coin a fortune with his much sought after voice stylings, he wife, Nora, isn't doing bad herself in the money department operating the town's (New Rochelle, New York) biggest record store."

According to Nora, Clyde opened the store because she was looking for something to keep herself busy while Clyde toured. Since the opening in 1957, the shop had become a central spot for the "teenage rock and roll addicts." They meet and discuss what's new in the big beat world, buy the latest records and get a chance to converse personally with McPhatter when he is town, which was rare. As for Nora, the reporter observed, she had always shunned the spotlight and that even at her Tune Shop, she is quiet and reserved and many mistake her for one of her clerks because she doesn't display a bossy attitude.[23]

Then the bad news. A *Jet* magazine story from May 15, 1958, reported: "More than $750 in cash and five boxes of record albums worth $260 were stolen from singer Clyde McPhatter's record shop in New Rochelle, N.Y., his wife Nora, reported to police. Because no doors were forced or windows broken, police believe the robbery was committed by a former employee who may have had a key to the premises."[24]

Alan Freed, the maverick radio deejay who had been promoting rock 'n' roll since his Cleveland days in the early 1950s, also pioneered the music's entry into mainstream entertainment, which at the time consisted of television and motion pictures. In 1956, he hosted a CBS television show called *The Camel Rock and Roll Party*. The "Camel" in the title didn't refer specifically to the dromedary but to the popular cigarette brand with a camel logo. Yes, a show for teenagers sponsored by a cigarette company, which hoped all those bad boys who carried their cigarettes in the shoulder roll-up of their t-shirts would be smoking Camels. The format was a typical variety show with one guest singing one song to be replaced by another. Among the guests, were Clyde McPhatter, Frankie Lymon, and labelmate LaVern Baker. Lymon would cause Freed trouble down the line. Freed would host another show called *The Big Beat*, which premiered in 1957 and, although doing well in the ratings, was quickly canceled when segregationists went after the ABC network because Frankie Lymon was shown on television dancing with a white female from the audience.[25]

In regard to non-radio public entertainment, Freed's most conspicuous efforts were in motion pictures, where he starred as himself in five movies that featured rock 'n' rollers. These films were popular with American teens, many getting a first chance to see their musical idols in performance. The first of his movies in 1956 was *Rock Around the Clock*, featuring, of course, Bill Haley and His Comets. The Platters also made an appearance. Also, that year, *Rock, Rock, Rock*, featuring Frankie Lymon, LaVern Baker, and numerous others, arrived in theaters. Clyde would make his big-screen debut in the 1957 release *Mister Rock and Roll*.

On October 11, 1957, the African American newspaper *St. Paul Recorder* ran a review of current happenings in the world of R&B. Among the short items was this: "Rock 'N Roll Beat, Alan Freed's *Mr. Rock and Roll* movie offers some brand-new tunes by such artists as Chuck Berry, Clyde McPhatter, LaVern Baker and Little Richard, and the great Lionel Hampton."[26]

Alan Freed performed a benevolent service for Clyde, allowing him to sing, in *Mister Rock and Roll*, both sides of a new single (the 45 rpm) that Clyde introduced in September of that year. In the movie, a shot of an appreciative audience applauds as a voice-over announces, "Next, here's a real favorite guy; Clyde McPhatter sings 'Rock and Cry.'" Clyde then steps out of the stage curtains. The spotlight is on him. He looks very sharp with a dark, tailored suit, white shirt and patterned tie. The camera then moves to a close-up of a very handsome, and apparently happy, Clyde singing an upbeat song. His smile lights up the stage.

For Clyde's second number, we see Alan Freed in the recording studio. He is sitting at his desk, reading from a sheet of paper, "Here we go with Clyde McPhatter and 'You'll Be There.'" A quick shot of a record on a turntable. Then it's Clyde in the same setting, earnestly singing the ballad "You'll Be There." This time, the camera frame begins in a close-up and then pulls back to see Clyde performing on the same stage setting as "Rock and Cry."

The underlying purpose of Freed's movies was to say to the world, look, rock 'n' roll singers are not rowdy teens but good people who have talent. Clyde McPhatter, in that regard, was an excellent choice in that he was not a teenager, but still young, amiably handsome, distinguished, and presented himself as a sincerely upright person.

Clyde McPhatter must have been a fan favorite of the *St. Paul Recorder* readership, because on November 1, 1957, the newspaper published a new blurb employing a melodic phrase that had become a cliché, the rhyming of McPhatter and the word "platter." It read: "McPhatter New Platter on Tap: For Rock and Roll fans, effervescent Clyde McPhatter is out with a thing called 'Rock and Cry' with a flip [B-side] titled 'You'll Be there.' It will be there on the R&R [rock 'n' roll] scoreboard for some time to come. Atlantic Records produced the waxing [recording]."[27]

A sub-genre of pop music, songs with an Afro-Caribbean (also called Latin) beat, became very popular in the mid-1950s mostly due to the wild success of singer Harry Belafonte. The year 1957 was the peak for this type of music with best-selling tunes such as "Day-O (The Banana Boat Song)," a big hit by two different performers, Harry Belafonte and the Tarriers, and "Marianne" by the Easy Riders. Clyde took a shot at this genre with his "Rock and Cry."

Although it had a terrible title, "Rock and Cry" was a good song. The trouble is, it just might have been too late for the Caribbean party, because it generated almost zero excitement. When *Cash Box* featured the song on its "Award O' the Week," up against "Keep a Knockin'" by Little Richard and "Jailhouse Rock" by Elvis Presley, it flipped the record, putting "You'll Be There" as the A-side and "Rock and Cry" as the B-side. The reviewer wrote: "Clyde McPhatter releases two sides from the flicker [movie] *Mr. Rock and Roll*, one of which looks like a power laden wax [song] destined for great pop and r&b heights. The deck [A-side], "You'll Be There," is a dramatic slow-beat shuffle that finds Clyde at his singing best. The chanter [singer] is given a big choral backdrop, together with a socko [terrific] arrangement, and the combination of all three makes a powerful offering."[28]

The same reviewer was not too enthusiastic about the B-side song. "The flip, 'Rock and Cry,' is a quick beat rocker, Latin tempo wax [recording] that strengthens the release. Infectious dance side the kids can get close to. Two good McPhatter etchings [recordings]—but for sustained action we look to 'You'll Be There.'"

Whether the radio deejays played "Rock and Cry" or "You'll Be There," it didn't make a difference because the single attracted little attention. It did not even chart on the R&B listings. The single did make the pop charts, but at the lowest rungs.

This a far cry from what Clyde was used to and certainly a great distance from his—arguably—most successful recording of 1957, "Long Lonely Nights."

At the start of the 1950s, there seemed to be such a dearth of interesting, catchy, or tuneful new songs that when a platter appeared that music publishers and talent managers thought had hit potential, singers would be rushed into recording studios around the country to be the earliest to come to market with a version of that song. As a result, there was always a scrum. In March 1950, the top records played on America's jukeboxes could have meant one of ten versions of "Music! Music! Music!" (top hit for Teresa Brewer), one of ten versions of "Rag Mop" (top hit for the Ames Brothers), or one of fourteen versions of "Chattanoogie Shoe Shine Boy" (top hit for Red Foley).

Except for the race by white singers to cover successful R&B, the mosh-pit of song seemed to have settled down. Rare tunes such as "Ko Ko Mo," originally recorded by the African American duo Gene and Eunice in 1954, also attracted a lot of covers. Seventeen different artists took a whack at that song, from white crooners to country and western warblers to other R&B acts to novelty-song enthusiasts. The most successful version of the song was by the laid-back crooner Perry Como in 1955.

Singer/songwriter Lee Andrews Thompson would have his own latter-day version of a record rumpus in 1957. Like Clyde McPhatter and Ben E. King, Lee Andrews (he would drop the Thompson) was born in North Carolina, in the town of Goldsboro, which in the 1950s tallied a population between 21,000 and 28,000 souls and was located about forty miles southeast of Raleigh. The Thompsons were a musical family. Lee Andrews's father, Beachy Thompson, sang with the famed gospel music group the Dixie Hummingbirds, and Lee's two boys stayed in the field as well. Donn T. became a singer/songwriter while Ahmir Thompson, who goes by the name Questlove, was a founding member of the band the Roots, and is an Academy Award winner.

In 1953, when he was still a teenager, Lee Andrews formed a doo-wop group in Philadelphia, calling it Lee Andrews and the Hearts. A year later, they first recorded on a small label, Rainbow Records, with three records: "Maybe You'll Be There" and on the B-side "Baby Come Back," written by Andrews; "The Bells of St. Mary" with the Andrews original "The Fairest" on the B-side; and chestnut "The White Cliffs of Dover" with another Andrews tune, "Much Too Much," on the B-side. Clearly, Rainbow Records did not trust Andrews's skill as a songwriter enough to give him A-side credit. But, he had the chops.

Lee Andrews and the Hearts boasted three songs of note. In 1958, "Try the Impossible" was a Top Forty tune on the pop charts. One year earlier, "Tear Drops," was a Top Twenty hit. The group's most famous record and the one that should have been the group's most successful recording was "Long Lonely Nights."

The song, penned by Andrews with three other names attached, was originally released on a small label called Mainliner. It showed potential and Chess picked it up for distribution, also acquiring the master. It was a doo-wop dream from the start. The romantic ballad begins: "Long, long and lonely nights / I cried my eyes out over you / wondering if I did wrong / and why you left me with a broken heart." Smart operatives quickly grabbed at the song, resulting in two other acts recording it as well, the Kings on the Baton label and Clyde McPhatter on Atlantic Records.

The three versions of the song hit the market about the same time. As *Cash Box* observed, "all three are worthy efforts and the scramble is now on for the valuable airplay." Lee Andrews and the Hearts placed "The Clock" on the

B-side, "an infectious, quick beat novelty." The Kings went in a similar direction with "Let Me Know" on the flip, which was "a quick beat bouncer delivered with a cute vocal reading."[29] Clyde went outside the box, recording the standard "Heartaches" with a bumpy Latin beat.

Cash Box blew the whistle for the start of mayhem. "Watch the rumble develop," it wrote. "Somebody or everybody is going to get a big seller with 'Long Lonely Nights.'"

Atlantic ginned up the competition from the start. In the same issue of *Cash Box* as those record comments, the label placed a full-page advertisement twenty pages ahead of the "Long Lonely Nights" discussion. Ostensibly, it was promotion for the company, reading "The Hottest Artists Are On Atlantic." The illustration was primitive, a record in the middle of the page surrounded by a listing of ten Atlantic Records artists and their new songs, such as "Mr. Lee" by the Bobbettes, "Empty Arms" by Ivory Joe Hunter, and "C. C. Rider" by Chuck Willis. Other artists riding the circle included Ruth Brown, Ray Charles, LaVern Baker, Joe Turner, Chris Connor, and the Drifters. At the very top of the circle was "Long Lonely Nights" by Clyde McPhatter.[30]

The small Baton label couldn't keep up with Atlantic and Chess, and the Kings' take on the song disappeared quickly. The version by Lee Andrews and the Hearts didn't do badly, riding to #11 on the R&B charts and crossing over to the pop charts, climbing to an honorable #45 listing. It would have done better except Clyde McPhatter's rendering split the market for the song. On the pop charts, Clyde's version didn't do as well as the platter by Lee Andrews and the Hearts, coming in at #49. On the R&B charts, there was no contest; Clyde's version went to #1. Although there is not much difference between the Clyde and Lee Andrews's treatments of the song, over the long, long and lonely nights between 1957 and today, it is the Lee Andrews version that is mostly remembered.

Clyde's McPhatter's parents, George and Beulah McPhatter. All photos courtesy of Deborah McPhatter.

Clyde McPhatter photo card.

Clyde with his father, George McPhatter.

A Dominoes album when Clyde McPhatter was lead singer (1952).

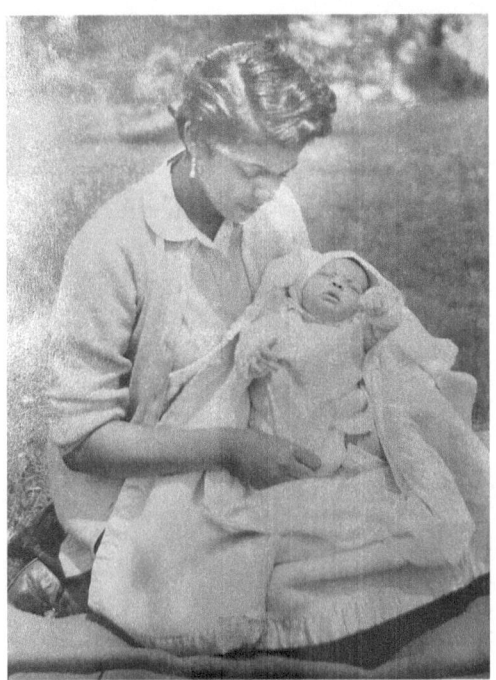
Clyde's daughter Deborah baby picture.

Deborah McPhatter with her mother Lorraine Lowe.

Promotion for Topeka stop of the Show of Stars Tour (1957).

Clyde McPhatter was one of the rock 'n' roll stars to appear in the movie *Mister Rock and Roll* (1957).

Newspaper advertisement for a Clyde McPhatter show at Detroit's Flame Show Bar (1958).

Clyde McPhatter headlining at a Rockland Palace, New York, concert (1958).

Newspaper advertisement for trunk tour stop at Detroit's Graystone Ballroom (1960).

The Guildford stop on McPhatter's first tour of the United Kingdom (1960).

Album Poster of Clyde's 1962 hit song "Lover Please" on Mercury records.

Advertisement for an upcoming performance at The Forty Thieves Club in Bermuda. (1962).

Clyde McPhatter headlining a late 1960s concert.

Clyde McPhatter in his midthirties.

Clyde McPhatter at work.

Deborah McPhatter's mother Lorraine, Clyde's nephew Winfred "Brother" Tolor, and Clyde's daughter Deborah.

The Clyde McPhatter US Postage stamp issued in 1993.

North Carolina Music Hall of Fame 2009 Induction Award Plaque.

Clyde McPhatter's daughter Deborah holding her father's gold record at the North Carolina Music Hall of Fame.

Deborah McPhatter, board chair at the NC Music Hall of Fame.

E: info@rbhof.com
PH: (313) 669-8388

July 1, 2023

RE: 2023 National Rhythm & Blues Hall of Fame Enshrinement Ceremony:

Dear Deborah McPhatter,

Congratulations! On behalf of the National Rhythm & Blues Hall of Fame Foundation board of directors, we are pleased to inform you that your father Clyde McPhatter has been posthumously selected to be honored and enshrined into the 2023 inaugural class of the National Rhythm & Blues Hall of Fame.

We congratulate you on this well-deserved recognition, and we are very proud of the outstanding achievements you have had in the music industry. We are all fortunate to have benefited from your many contributions.

We cordially invite you and a guest to attend the 2023 National Rhythm & Blues Hall of Fame Enshrinement Ceremony to be held on Sunday, September 24, 2023, at the Hawk Center located at 29995 W. 12 Mile Road, Farmington Hills, Michigan 48334 (Metro Detroit) VIP Media Red Carpet begins at 3:00 p.m. and the Enshrinement Ceremony starts @ 4:00p.m.

Your room for (2) nights and ground transportation to/from airport to hotel and to/from hotel to the venue will be covered by the National Rhythm & Blues Hall of Fame. Each inductee will receive two (2) tickets that will be left at the door under your name, additional tickets can be purchaesd by going to www.RBHOF.com

The 10th Annual Hall of Fame V.I.P. White Party will be on Saturday, September 23, 2023, @ Bert's Warehouse 2727 Russell Street Detroit, Michigan. Each inductee will receive two (2) tickets to both events, your tickets will be left at the door under your name for both events. Additional tickets can be purchased by going to www.RBHOF.com

Sincerely,

LaMont "ShowBoat" Robinson
Founder/CEO
National Rhythm & Blues Hall of Fame

WWW.RBHOF.COM

Clyde's induction letter for Rhythm and Blues Hall of Fame.

Clyde McPhatter's R&B Hall of Fame Gold Record.

ROCK & ROLL HALL OF FAME

November 14, 2024

The McPhatter Family
c/o Deborah McPhatter
7428 Cairnesford Way
Wake Forest, NC 27587

A pivotal figure in the evolution of rock & roll music and the social landscape of youth culture, Clyde McPhatter was the first artist to be inducted twice into the Rock & Roll Hall of Fame. In 1987 he was inducted in recognition of his incredible career as a solo artist, and again in 1988 as a member of the legendary vocal group the Drifters.

Clyde McPhatter is regarded as one of the most significant vocalists of his era, both for his solo work and as a member of the Drifters. As lead singer of the Drifters, McPhatter's smooth, emotive voice and gospel-infused delivery helped define the group's sound—bridging the gap between gospel, blues, and pop to lay the foundation for what would become "soul" music. He was instrumental in shaping the group's early hits, including the classic "Money Honey," which went to Number One and was later recorded by Elvis Presley. As a soloist, he was an emotional powerhouse, saturating each performance with drama of the highest order. His high tenor and passionate execution had a notable influence on later vocalists like Jackie Wilson, Sam Cooke, Smokey Robinson, and Aaron Neville. McPhatter's boycotting of shows where the audience would be segregated by race and his appeal to both black and white audiences also helped to blur the lines of racial segregation in popular music.

We are honored to celebrate Clyde McPhatter and his impact and influence on rock and roll every day at the Rock & Roll Hall of Fame.

My Best,

Greg Harris
President & CEO
Rock & Roll Hall of Fame and Museum, Inc.

Union Home Mortgage Plaza, 1100 Rock & Roll Boulevard, Cleveland, Ohio 44114 | 216.781.7625 | rockhall.com

Clyde's induction letter for the Rock and Roll Hall of Fame.

Deborah McPhatter's daughter Dama Conti with her husband David and children Sydney and Joshua.

CHAPTER TEN

A LOVER'S QUESTION

When the *Carolinian*, a newspaper targeting the African American population of Raleigh, North Carolina, published its cute story about Nora McPhatter running Clyde's record shop venture, it focused on just how successful the singer had been. It was in some regards an aspirational story of a Black man from North Carolina succeeding in the music world and accruing riches along the way. As mentioned, the lead paragraph began with Clyde taking to the road to "coin a fortune" with his performances. The same story recounted a bit of Clyde's career, noting: "Rated as a hot attraction by promoters because of his winning style and pleasing personality, McPhatter's box-office value was noticed seven years ago when he was a member of the Dominoes quartet."[1]

In those seven years, Clyde had been skillful enough and, perhaps, lucky enough as well, to retain that box-office value. In late summer 1957 Clyde headlined at the Howard Theater in Washington, DC, one of the premiere venues for Black performers, where he proceeded to set all sorts of records. He attracted 23,450 people to his shows, and they forked up $37,950 ($414,000 in 2024 dollars), which was a record. The previous house record holder had been set five years before when bandleader Buddy Johnson's show brought in $32,600. According to a story in the *Jackson (Mississippi) Advocate*, "In two years the debonair McPhatter has become the hottest box office attraction in show business." The newspaper also reported, in reference to Clyde's Howard Theater shows, "six cops were on constant duty to handle the standing room only crowds. Three of them were at stage-box to guard McPhatter against the mobs of teenagers who sought to snatch his handkerchiefs from his pockets as souvenirs or crowded around him for autographs."[2]

A show like Clyde's at the Howard usually meant a week's residency. The way remuneration at the Apollo, the crème-de-la-crème of the Black theater circuit, worked was that a headliner in the 1950s would be paid a flat fee (later that would change to royalty-based payment) for as many as five shows a day, seven days a week. That would earn the performer about $7,500 (about $85,000 in 2024 dollars). Clyde was at the peak of his career in 1957, and from his tenure at the Howard he would have earned between $5,000 to $7,500 for the week. [3] Again, this was a period of steadily climbing but still low wages in the United States, especially for African Americans, so to that ethnic group $7,500 for a week's work would seem like a fortune, which is why it was a focus of so much of the Black press.

Clyde was twenty-five years old in 1957 and looked his age if not younger. The teenagers who listened to his music when he was with the Dominoes were now young adults. The newest generation of Black teens, now accustomed to rock 'n' roll and songs from Black and white singers on the same radio station, behaved toward Clyde as did those who discovered him at the start of his career.

The African American–oriented newspapers of the 1950s kept their readers informed about the comings and goings of Black performers because that's what younger readers wanted to read. The same newspapers also tried to target the young readers with special features. The *Miami Times*, for example, ran a column called "Teen Talk," and in January 1957 the columnists interviewed a senior at a local high school. When asked who was the interviewee's favorite vocalist, the answer was Clyde McPhatter.[4]

The *Carolina Times* in Durham, North Carolina, established a "Letter Box" where teenage "pen pals" could write to the newspaper. On November 17, 1957, one entry read: "I would like to become a Pen Pal. I enjoy reading the AFRO Youth Page. I am 16 and a senior. My hobbies are dancing and playing cards. My favorite singers are Clyde McPhatter, Moonglows, Charts and Del Vikings."

Another teen on the same day wrote, "I have just cut Clyde McPhatter's picture out of this week's AFRO. He is boss!"[5]

In December of every year, *Cash Box* magazine polled its readers in what it called "The Final Count." One of the categories to vote for was "Best R&B Male Vocalist of 1957." The answers at the close of 1957 were unusual in that top vote-getters were guys who had been around for a while: Little Richard, Chuck Berry, even Ivory Joe Hunter. Depending on interpretation, Clyde's positioning could be considered good or mediocre, as his vote total placed him as the sixth most popular R&B singer. Two white singers made the R&B list, Elvis Presley and a young newcomer, Paul Anka, at eight and sixteen respectively.[6] Elvis was understandable. Ever since he began recording his R&B crossover music, he was popular with Black teens. Paul Anka was a white pop singer. Sure, Anka had a #1 hit in 1957 with "Diana," but that was nowhere near R&B. So how did Anka attain ethnic crossover status? He had to thank Irvin Feld.

On September 26, 1957, the *Arizona Sun*, a Phoenix newspaper for the local Black community, ran a headline on an interior page that read "Show of Stars at Phoenix Coliseum." Yep, the Irvin Feld package tour was coming to town. According to the column, which appeared to be based on a Feld press release, the two-and-one-half-hour show would star Fats Domino and Paul Anka, who was referred to as the sixteen-year-old boy whose "Diana" is in the #1 spot of hits. The column added with extreme fantasy, "Anka, who is replacing Elvis Presley in the teenage popularity poll, will feature many of the tunes he has written."

A subsequent paragraph noted, "Also appearing will be LaVern Baker, the "queen of the blues." Lumped in as "other headliners" were Clyde McPhatter and fourteen-year-old Frankie Lymon on his first personal appearance tour since leaving the Teenagers.[7]

With the rise of so many talented white boys singing rock 'n' roll, Irvin Feld had no choice but to reintegrate his shows. The fall edition of his Biggest Show of Stars of 1957 tour was jammed packed with a lot of old pros and hot new singers: Clyde McPhatter, Frankie Lymon, Fats Domino, Chuck Berry, Buddy Holly and the Crickets, the Spaniels, the Drifters, the Everly Brothers, LaVern Baker, Jimmy Bown, Buddy Knox, the Diamonds, Johnnie and Joe, the Bobbettes, and Paul Anka.

When Feld put together his first tour for 1958, the only holdovers were Clyde McPhatter, LaVern Baker, and Paul Anka. A slew of newcomers were added, including soon-to-be superstars Sam Cooke, the Everly Brothers, and Jackie Wilson, the man who replaced Clyde in the Dominoes but had since launched a solo career.[8] Clyde touring with Jackie Wilson was not a problem. The clash of personalities would come from an unlikely source, Paul Anka.

At some point, Clyde McPhatter began suffering a change of countenance. Since the start of his career, he had been known as a friendly, welcoming, and charming young man. His carefree smile contained more wattage than an ice cream parlor. Except for the numerous ladies he left in his wake, including wives, everyone seemed to love Clyde. Ruth Brown, who had an affair with him, called him "sweet."

Unfortunately, as the years went on, Clyde descended into alcoholism, and along with that disease came the associated personality changes such as irresponsibility, anger, and unreliability. His randy behavior started shifting more to men than women.

Where did that all begin? Touring for Black performers was ridiculously difficult, made even worse by Jim Crow segregation. The days and nights were long, and the only breaks seemed to be drinking, card games, and sex. If you were part of a package tour, it was the same one to three songs every night. As bad as it was for men, it was worse for women.

The Shirelles—Shirley Owens, Doris Coley, Beverly Lee, and Addie "Micki" Harris—first scored with a regional hit "I Met Him on a Sunday" in 1958. Beverly Lee was seventeen years old and immediately went on tour.

When The Shirelles were on the Dick Clark bus tours in the South, Dick Clark himself would go into the restaurants, place orders for the Black singers, and deliver the meals, Lee recounted. The Shirelles learned early on to travel with food. Experienced musicians brought along a hot plate. Bo Diddley would cook on the road; his specialty was fried chicken wings. You had to be very crafty in finding ways to eat. At some places where the tour stopped they couldn't use the restrooms and the bus would have to pull up alongside the road. The guys would be on one side of the bus and girls on the other behind a tree, or someone would hold up a coat. Some of the promoters would be rude. The Shirelles learned quickly that you would have to get your money right away because promoters would run out with your earnings. At a package show, the headliners would know to get their money immediately—be paid before the show went on. When the Shirelles toured the South, they would leave their New Jersey home at 3:00 a.m. or 4:00 a.m. in the morning and had to make sure they had food with them, because they knew they couldn't stop at white restaurants. They usually had fried chicken and canned goods such as sardines or Vienna sausages, crackers, juice, and water because they knew they were in for long rides.[9]

For the men, travel meant a lot of drinking in the off hours, so it would have been easy to pick up a taste for almost anything with alcohol. Clyde's issues ran deeper. His father was a cold personality, and as a response Clyde would attach himself to older, intelligent men with very strong, determined personalities, who would not only attend to him, but point the way to music success—men like Billy Ward, and in the mid-1950s, Irvin Feld.

Paul Anka would describe Feld as "very smart . . . with his own inimitable vibe. He always dressed in silk suits, a cigarette dangling from his mouth . . . he was up day and night, worked very hard, and sold what he believed in. He was a salesman in the sense that he could persuade you to see things through his eyes. A true believer. Smart, shrewd, and aggressive, but also trusting."[10]

According to Ken Feld, when his father first booked Clyde for his tours, he was not officially his manager at that time. "Clyde came out of the service and was on the tour immediately. He was alone, needy, and he approached my father to manage him. Part of the problem was that there were a lot groups on the tour but Clyde was 'a lone ranger.'"[11]

Bill Curtis, who was Clyde's drummer for a decade, puts Irvin Feld's management of Clyde close to the beginning of Clyde's solo career. "To some extent he got Clyde McPhatter famous as a solo act. Irvin Feld treated Clyde just like a son."

The close father-son relationship didn't last very long, and the ending was complicated. "Clyde started drinking a little bit after that," Curtis claimed.

What happened to the Irvin Feld and Clyde McPhatter relationship to cause it to sever so severely? The answer is Paul Anka.

Clyde was like family to Irvin Feld, and then Feld found this teenage boy with talent in Canada and "started to devote a lot of time to this new kid [Paul Anka]," Curtis recalled. When he found this other singer, Feld started taking some of the emphasis off Clyde, putting all his attention on the new kid. Clyde didn't like that. In fact, he resented it and took solace in the bottle.[12]

As a teenager in Ottawa, Canada, Paul Anka found a way to get backstage at a rock 'n' roll concert. After cornering Chuck Berry and Fats Domino, he was about to be thrown out when Anka spotted Irvin Feld and called out to him. "You're Mr. Feld." The man turned and answered, "Yes?" The aggressive fifteen-year-old took out a piece of paper, wrote down his name, address and telephone number and handed it to Feld, telling him that he's Paul Anka, a songwriter, and he has this tune called "Diana." Feld said, "Okay kid," and spun away as quickly as possible.

About a year later, Paul Anka, with high hopes, traveled to New York, walked into the Brill Building with a sheath of songs, and caught the attention of Don Costa, who liked his song "Diana" and signed the young Canadian to a contact. Since Irvin Feld, whom Anka called Irv, owned record stores, he got to hear a lot of demos, one of which in 1957 was "Diana." He liked it and played it for his brother Izzy and partner Allen Bloom.

"Irv had a hunch about 'Diana,'" Anka recalled. "He had a great ear for talent ... he must have heard something he liked because he signed me to go on one of his tours, much to the objection of Al [Allen Bloom] and his brother Izzy. They were looking for a new act for their 'Show of Shows.' Al and Izzy wanted this guy named Teddy Randazzo [later a very successful songwriter], who had some kind of a record out at the time that was doing well. But Irv was the boss and he stuck with his decision to take me on tour."

Irv used to pick the show's stars, Anka explained. "I honestly think Dick Clark learned a lot from him. All Irv ever did was see what the Blacks were buying in his stores, and those were the acts he'd pick for his rock 'n' roll tours. He told me he kept my number from that show in Ottawa, but he probably didn't know who the hell I was until I walked into his office."

Between tours, Anka lived with Feld and his family, which wasn't always pleasant because Feld's wife had troubling psychological issues and would rage at him almost daily. Since Anka was away from his own family and was a minor, Feld became his legal guardian on the tours. When in the States between tours, Anka continued to stay at Feld's, sharing a room with his son

Kenny, even though he was seven years older. "I became the big brother he never had," says Anka.[13]

"When 'Diana' came out my father actually became Paul's legal guardian so he could tour and work in the United States," Ken Feld said. "My father was his manager as well. Paul is like an older brother to me. We still stay in touch."[14]

Irvin Feld officially became personal manager for Paul Anka in February 1958, taking over the job from Paul's father, Andrew Anka. The booking, or talent, agency for Paul remained General Artists Corporation (GAC).[15] On Feld's tour things were not always copacetic. "Clyde McPhatter, who had been the lead singer of the Drifters, was also managed by Irv," Anka wrote in his memoirs. "And he was insanely jealous of me and my success. He was a bitter, angry guy for someone who sang such sweet songs."[16]

Beyond Clyde's personal issues including feelings of abandonment by his pseudo-father, jealousy was certainly a valid disposition. Remember Clyde's record earnings at the Howard Theater. That paled in comparison for what Feld did for Paul Anka. The Bronx, New York, at one time boasted a theme park called Freedomland. It wanted to hire Paul Anka, and Feld secured for him a $100,000 deal just for a weekend's work. The contract was so outlandish that when Feld called GAC, Anka's talent agency, to write up a contract, the agent wrote it for $10,000. Feld straightened that out quickly. He also booked Anka for tours outside the United States.[17]

The end of Clyde working with Feld wasn't easy. Ken Feld, who was a youngster when this happened, still recalls that period of time and the stress on his father. "Clyde was difficult, highly temperamental. My father was his personal manager, and once he started managing Paul Anka at the same time, Clyde became jealous of that, of Paul's success at a young age. But, they [Clyde and Paul] were different personalities. It really became impossible for my dad, and that's why he gave up Clyde, because of his demands."

Ken said he can still remember waking up in the middle of the night and hearing his father talking on the telephone with Clyde McPhatter in what he called "high tension conversations." Ken reiterated, "Clyde was a temperamental guy."[18]

The Feld-McPhatter relationship wasn't just a one-way street of bumps. Feld was also under pressure from numerous other facets in his life. The rock 'n' roll tour business began to get very competitive with new players entering the market. On the home front, Feld's wife, Adele, committed suicide in midsummer 1958; she was just thirty-one years old. Meanwhile, on the back-office side of the pop music business, economics forced major talent, booking, and management companies to consolidate.[19]

One of the first big mergers was GAC taking over the Gale Agency, which had been a major talent manager for R&B artists. Among the names on the

Gale roster who would move to GAC were Clyde McPhatter, LaVern Baker, Chuck Berry, Al Hibbler, Roy Hamilton, Buddy Johnson, and Della Reese.

Billboard magazine, in its story on the GAC deal, noted that Tim Gale helped many R&B acts break into the pop field "via his auditorium tours of which he was an early pioneer." His "Biggest Shows" tours back in 1951 and 1952 helped set the pattern for the pop and rock 'n' roll units touring in the later 1950s "and are often considered to have created more employment for rock and roll acts than any other type of showcase."[20]

Then in June 1958, it was announced that GAC had "absorbed" the Feld Brothers' Super Attractions business. The new operation would be known as GAC-Super Productions. Irvin Feld would join GAC and Tim Gale, who formerly owned the Gale Agency, would be in the new subsidiary. The Felds kept several of their operations separate from the deal. From the news story that appeared in *Billboard* on June 9, 1958, the pop music package tours were already on the wane with Feld's increasing fascination with touring and promoting the Ringling Brothers & Barnum & Bailey Circus, which he, his brother, and one other investor bought in 1967 for $8 million.[21]

Rock 'n' roll stalled a bit in 1958 as well. Sure, there were Elvis, Chuck Berry, Danny and the Juniors singing "At the Hop," and plenty of hopped-up doo-wop ditties such as "Get a Job" by the Silhouettes and "Book of Love" by the Monotones, but if one looked at the Top Ten best sellers of the year, the roster looked very, as they used to say, "square." The #1 song for the year was "Volare (Nel Blu Dipinto Di Blu)" by Italian singer Domenico Modugno. Also in the Top Ten were David Seville with the kiddie novelty tune "Witch Doctor," and bandleaders and pop singers Perez Prado, Billy Vaughn, Perry Como, and Dean Martin. If it weren't for Elvis, the Everly Brothers, the Champs, and Tommy Edwards in the Top Ten, one would have thought rock 'n' roll was dead. Perhaps it was. With the deaths of several rock 'n' rollers, payola scandal, Elvis in the army, and adult backlash to rock 'n' roll, 1958 has come to be known as "the year the music died." Even Atlantic Records looked shaky. As Jerry Wexler lamented, for all his company's cleverness, after Chuck Willis ("C. C. Rider") and Ivory Joe Hunter ("Since I Met You Baby"), records sales plummeted and panic set in.

The company finally got straightened out because Atlantic did what it always did: it found the next best-sellers. Two records got it back in the game. Again, Wexler told the tale. "These two tunes were so winning, so widely popular, so immediately irresistible, no one could keep them off the air." The first of the company-saving songs was "Yakety Yak" by the Coasters, and the second was "Splish Splash" by Bobby Darin. Each sold more than a million records and contributed to company coffers $400,000 to $500,000 in revenue, respectively.[22]

Whether it was because of belt-tightening at the record company or touring schedules or emotional issues with Clyde, the record company only released three records by him in 1958, although it recorded at least twice that number of new singles and at least two of what it called EPs (extended play, 45 rpm). One of the EPs was a duet with LaVern Baker. The company also released Clyde's first true album, *Love Ballads*, which included a number of older recordings such as "Bip Bam," "Long Lonely Nights," and "Rock and Cry."

At the start of 1958, *Billboard* celebrated Atlantic Records' tenth anniversary with a number of stories. On one page was a feature on Miriam Bienstock, cofounder Herb Abramson's former wife. Not to be diminished, Miriam was listed as company vice president and also a cofounder of Atlantic Records. The headline read: "Atlantic's Money Man Is a Woman."[23] Atlantic Records repaid the favor by taking advertising space in the same issue. The promotion on page 41 headlined with "Happy New Year: New Decade." Part of the underlying copy read: "This is our 10th anniversary in the music business and we are celebrating by issuing four powerhouse records that we know will start off another decade of progress for us."

One could see why the executive team at Atlantic was in a panic at the start of 1958. The four "powerhouse" records all died an inglorious death. Only one of the four in the promotion was by newcomers, a trio by the name of the Jaye Sisters, who sang "Going to the River" with "Pitter Patter Boom Boom" on the B-side. The other three singers were all established stars—yet nothing! Ivory Joe Hunter introduced "Baby Baby Count on Me" with "You're on My Mind"; Ray Charles hit the market with "Talkin' 'Bout You" and "What Kind of Man Are You"; while Clyde McPhatter went with "No Love Like Her Love" and "That's Enough for Me."

The songwriters for "That's Enough for Me," which might have been introduced at some point as the A-side tune, were Johnny Otis and Brook Benton. Otis was a veteran of the industry, at one time or another being involved in every facet of the business, from club owner to orchestra leader, to manager, radio host, and singer. He helped a lot of people get their start in the music world and was never shy about taking credit for a song he helped bring to market. Otis introduced aspiring songwriters Jerry Leiber and Mike Stoller to singer Big Mama Thornton, who had a monster hit with their song "Hound Dog" three years before Elvis Presley. Otis, who produced the record, added his name as the third songwriter. Leiber and Stoller went to court to get his name omitted—and won!

Otis seemed to hit it off with a music aspirant, Benajmin Francis Peay, who would change his name to Brook Benton, and the two would sign off on a number of successful songwriting efforts starting in the mid-1950s.

Born in 1931, Benton, a New York boy, first began as a gospel singer before switching to group doo-wop and then going out on his own a solo singer. Around the mid-1950s he started writing with Johnny Otis. By 1957 Benton was on the RCA label and like Clyde McPhatter appeared in Alan Freed's movie *Mister Rock and Roll*. In 1958 Benton celebrated his first major hit, "It's Just a Matter of Time," which summed up his career up until that moment. After 1958, he became a star singer and sought-after songwriter. His last big hit was "Rainy Night in Georgia" in 1970.[24] He could have kept going, but Benton too had drinking problems. Bill Curtis summed it up this way: "Brook Benton created his whole career around Clyde, even to the drinking. Brook was an alcoholic."[25]

Around the time of "It's Just a Matter of Time," which rose to #3 on the pop charts in February 1958, Benton along with his writing partner Johnny Otis tossed "That's Enough for Me" to Clyde. It was a pleasant, mid-tempo, pop song that was left dangling by Atlantic Records. Clyde sang, "I don't want a bank account / 'cause I get by on a small amount / I got you, pretty baby, that's enough." Clyde got his wish; he didn't add to his bank account with this song.

He did much better with his second entry for 1958, a song called "Come What May" with a Clyde-penned tune "Let Me Know" on the B-side. The first review of the song came in the *Billboard* column "Review Spotlight on . . ." in the April 7, 1958, issue. This was a crowded house, with many important songs hitting the market at the same time including Elvis Presley's "Wear My Ring Around Your Neck," Chuck Berry's "Johnny B. Goode," and the Everly Brothers' "All I Have to Do Is Dream." As for "Come What May," the review was positive: "A solid entry by the artist. It's a swinging up-tempo side strongly presented by McPhatter with excellent ork [orchestra] backing. It can also go in R&B markets. 'Let Me Know,' the flip [B-side], is a weeper ballad."[26]

Two weeks later *Cash Box*, as was its practice with Clyde McPhatter, put the song in its "Award o' The Week" column of "R&B Reviews." Altogether, the page rang up sixteen reviews including songs by Fats Domino, Ivory Joe Hunter, Jimmy Reed, Joe Turner, the Bobbettes, and the Moonglows. The only hit record out of the bunch was "Come What May." Ironically, as it would turn out, a major word used on the page was "gay." This was not in reference to homosexuals but in the original context of being happy. One of the reviews was for a group called the Gay Knights. The exuberant review of "Come What May" began this way: "Clyde McPhatter just inherited a million dollars, or his stock rose twenty points, or he hit a homerun with bases loaded—but whatever it was he's in high spirits as he sings the gay, quick-beat bouncer, 'Come What May.'" The reviewer continued in this spirited vein: "McPhatter literally is walking on air as he sings his joyous song of love. He sells his mood so completely that the listener will clap hands, sing along or in some way get into the act."[27]

Despite the vibrance, it was the *Billboard* reviewer who really better understood the potential of the song, much more than the *Cash Box* critic, when he noted that "Come What May" was a good tune for the R&B market. As it turned out, the song did very well in the R&B world, climbing to #3 on the charts. "Come What May" did cross over to the pop markets, where it ran into a buzz saw of competition, hence its middling positioning at #43. As to those songs that came out the same week as "Come What May," "All I Have to Do Is Dream" was the #2 best-selling song of the year, "Wear My Ring Around Your Neck" the twenty-second best-selling song, while "Johnny B. Goode" wasn't even a Top Fifty bestseller, although now it is considered one of the classic rock 'n' roll songs of the 1950s.

Clyde needed to raise his game if he wanted his own tunes to compete with those popular and wonderful songs. Surprisingly he did—with a little help from Brook Benton.

The tale of the hit song "A Lover's Question" begins this way. Brook Benton was listening to a friend, musician Jimmy Williams, as he carried on and on about his latest unsettled romance. Wílliams asked Benton so many questions that, after a while, Benton said, "You've got a lover's troubles, but I think I've got a song." The phrase "lover's troubles" morphed into "lover's question," and Benton and Williams filled out the rest the song right then and there. They thought it a good tune and took it to a song publisher, Dave Dreyer, who said he would see if he could get it recorded.

At that time, Clyde was rehearsing at Atlantic's studio on 57th Street in Manhattan. He would be recording four songs, one of which was "I Can't Stand Up Alone" by country singer/songwriter Martha Carson.

Next door to the studio was an adjoining office, and sitting there were Ahmet Ertegun and Jerry Wexler. Dave Dreyer stopped by unannounced, saying he had a demo of a song called "A Lover's Question," which he thought might interest Atlantic. They said sure, let's hook it up, and the record was placed on the hi-fi. Ertegun and Wexler were in accord. Not only did they like the song but thought it perfect for Clyde McPhatter, so they called him in to hear it. Clyde gave it a thumbs up, and one of the planned songs to be recorded was scrapped with "A Lover's Question" being the substituted tune.

"Wouldn't it be funny if this last-minute entry was the hit?" Clyde said jokingly. The music gods were listening.[28]

For Clyde's next single Atlantic paired "A Lover's Question" with "I Can't Stand Up Alone." While the latter was a good song, part gospel and part R&B, it wasn't quite what the teenagers were buying. On the other hand, "A Lover's Question" was pop music magic, from its bouncy "bum-ba-bum- bum" lead to Clyde's imploring query, "Does she love me with all her heart / should I worry when we're apart / it's a lover's question, I'd like to know-ow-ow-ow."

Cash Box on September 20, 1958, had so many songs it needed to review, it cut itself short just writing full or half reviews for thirteen songs and mentioning five more. There were some stellar songs in the grab-bag including Eugene Church's "Pretty Girls Everywhere" and Bobby Darin's "Queen of the Hop," but the main focus was on Clyde's McPhatter's "A Lover's Question"/"I Can't Stand Up Alone." The ecstatic and prescient review went like this: "Watch out for Clyde McPhatter's new pairing. It has that hit look written all over both ends of the disk. On one half he wants to know if the chick's affection is 100% pure as he asks 'A Lover's Question.' It's a bouncy effort that Clyde and the vocal crew glide over in top drawer, pop-oriented style. The other half, tagged 'I Can't Stand Up Alone,' from the pen of Martha Carson starts out slow and then breaks into a fast-paced opus. It's an inspiring gospel-flavored item that McPhatter and the chorus put across with telling effect. Both sides are gonna cover a wide market. Get with 'em!"[29]

"A Lover's Question" entered *Billboard*'s "Honor Roll of Hits: The Nation's Top Tunes" (America's Top Thirty bestsellers) on November 10, 1958. Also new to the charts that week were the novelty song "Beep Beep" by the Playmates, "I Got Stung" by Elvis Presley, and "Topsy I" by Cozy Cole. Entering the chart one week ahead of "A Lover's Question" was Bobby Darin's "Queen of the Hop." Two weeks ahead was Ricky Nelson's "Lonesome Town," and three weeks ahead was the Teddy Bears' "To Know Him Is to Love Him."[30]

"A Lover's Question" would climb to #6 on the pop charts and #1 on the R&B listing.

In its annual summation of the year's trendlines, *Billboard*'s Howie Cook looked back on the year 1958 and decided there was no definitive trend, and the charts showed the hit songs were of a "vastly different nature and origin, indicating that the road to Hitsville is still a wide-open path" including what Cook called "rockaballads, rockabillies and instrumentals." Among the songs he singled out for diversity were Conway Twitty's "It's Only Make Believe," which Cook termed a rockaballad and "one of the most recorded types of pop tunes this year"; the Playmates' "Beep Beep," which originally was part of the group's nightclub routine that's "hardly danceable . . . but the kids took to it immediately"; and "A Lover's Question" by Clyde McPhatter, "his biggest [hit] in recent years."[31]

CHAPTER ELEVEN

LOVEY DOVEY

When American cities were de facto segregated through most of twentieth century, a large African American neighborhood functioned like a small town with its own main streets, unique businesses, and eateries. Sometimes, there were also popular music venues where African American performers, singers, and musicians would perform for a Black audience. As a group, these clubs, especially in the East and southwest of the Mississippi River were called the chitlin' circuit, and many a rhythm and blues act made its way on the circuit, down the East Coast, across the South into Texas, and then swung north into the Midwest or west to the Pacific Coast. It was a long, hard ride, but for Black musicians it was where the money was to be made.

As the battle for civil rights picked up steam and more and more institutions and cities desegregated, African Americans could now eat, shop and watch live shows anywhere in a metropolitan area, but the old main streets in the ethnically defined neighborhoods declined. Something similar happened in the world of popular music. As the rolling trunk shows of a dozen or more rock 'n' roll performers, which by the mid-1950s had desegregated, began to dominate the tours, some of the old chitlin' circuit venues declined along with the Black entrepreneurial businesses that supported those clubs.

Music writer Preston Lauterbach makes the case that rock 'n' roll might not have come into existence without the whole support system of the chitlin' circuit. He wrote: "Though the moguls' names are not recognized among the important producers of American culture, their numbers rackets, dice parlors, dance halls, and bootleg liquor and prostitution rings financed the artistic development of breakthrough performers" including Joe Turner, Wynonie Harris, B.B. King, Ike Turner, Johnny Ace, Little Richard, and James Brown. Lauterbach added, "as money and power flowed through the ghetto during the 1930s and 1940s, creativity and musical innovation followed. But, as Black downtowns atrophied and disappeared thereafter, not only was their influence diminished, their mark faded from America's cultural history."[1]

Irvin Feld might have pioneered the rock 'n' roll trunk tour, but big-name promoters followed, including Alan Freed and Dick Clark. It was a very competitive business. As Bill Curtis, Clyde McPhatter's longtime drummer, observed, "those big shows would put ten (or more) acts on the stage. It was killing the small promoters, many of whom were Black. When those big shows came to town, they would clean out the chitlin' circuit. A town couldn't support two of those shows."

A 1950s singer as renowned as Clyde McPhatter, as a singular performer, might come into a town for a series of concerts. It would be well advertised and promoted in advance, and since the concert business was so competitive, a big tour would catch wind of the scheduled performance and book the same city a week or two before McPhatter's show, essentially, as Curtis said, "to drain the town."

In 1959 Clyde, who was now a veteran performer, could see that the live-show business had changed since he began with the Dominoes back at the beginning of the 1950s and devised a new plan for himself going forward. He got together with another promoter named Henry Wynn and said to him, "if we pool together such headliners as Sam Cooke, Jerry Butler, Lloyd Price and myself, we can compete against those other shows," and that's exactly what happened. As Curtis reminisced, "they did that for quite a while."[2]

For Clyde McPhatter, the year 1959 began like most other years since he was released from the service. He was booked on an Irvin Feld package tour, this one with the familiar title, Biggest Show of Stars of 1959, Spring Edition. Reflecting on the competition for rock 'n' roll voices, this tour was somewhat smaller in scope with the usual names such as Clyde McPhatter, Frankie Lymon, Bo Diddley, Lloyd Price, and LaVern Baker, and some newer folks including the Coasters, the Crests, Little Anthony and the Imperials, the Chantels, Wade Flemons, and Bobby Hendricks[3] (former singer with the Drifters; hit record, "Itchy Twitchy Feeling," in 1958).

The only difference between this tour and others preceding it was that Irvin Feld and his brother Israel (Izzie) became part of the promotion. In July, the *Evening Star*, a Black-customer-based, Washington, DC, newspaper, secured the two for a major feature. The article noted that Feld-packaged shows toured the nation and the world, largely under the aegis of General Artists Corp-Super Productions Inc., as the Felds "only recently merged with GAC to form the third largest theatrical agency."[4]

The Anka-McPhatter turmoil also seemed settled as Irvin explained, in the process of packaging shows, that he also became agent-manager for Paul Anka, "a 17-year-old actor-composer-singer," and Clyde McPhatter, a twenty-seven-year-old singer. "Keeping up with these boys is enough," Irvin said with a sigh. "I've been asked to manage other talent but I simply can't."

The story did mention that Irvin Feld was a widower, had two children named Kenneth and Karen, traveled extensively to oversee investments, lived with his brother and his wife, and was piloting a move to reestablish the Ringling Brothers-Barnum & Bailey Circus as a touring attraction.[5]

There would be another Biggest Show of Stars, the winter edition, which would include Clyde McPhatter, but Irvin Feld's interest in rock 'n' roll tours diminished as he got more and more involved in the circus world.

As for Clyde's big idea about joining forces with the likes of Sam Cooke, who since 1957, when he boasted the #1 hit record, "You Send Me," had become a major star, that seemed to be working out.

Part of Clyde's independent tour program hinged on the relatively unknown Henry Wynn, who was a regional promoter, although Wynn's record was somewhat spotty.

A news item from 1960 had Wynn involved in a failed show that was to open in Greenville, South Carolina. According to the story, the Greenville Memorial Auditorium was rented to a Jim Crocket, who planned to promote his show in Greenville, Charlotte, and Greensboro.[6] He had contracted for a package show from Universal Attractions in New York and it was to include recording artist Jimmy Jones, a hot singer with two big hits in 1960, "Handy Man" and "Good Timin'," and who sung in what one writer said was a "smooth, yet soulful falsetto modeled on the likes of Clyde McPhatter and Sam Cooke."[7] Advance publicity did not include any mention of Jimmy Jones, so Crocket questioned the New York firm and learned that the package was put together by Henry Wynn of Supersonic Attractions out of Atlanta. According to Crocket, the tour played Greensboro and Charlotte but lost money so Wynn closed down the Greenville show, but only after people had already taken their seats.[8]

Wynn endured. According to an *Atlanta Daily World* story, "During that era in the early 1970s through the early 1990s, Atlanta's nightlife was run by men like Charlie Cato, Henry Wynn, Eddie Ellis, Frank Matthews and Bumpy Johnson. They could have been classified as hustlers, but mainly they were all interested in promoting live bands throughout the city. And that was a good thing, especially for the Black musicians and patrons."[9]

Back in 1959, Wynn's Supersonic Attractions was trying to compete with the likes of Irvin Feld and Dick Clark. In 1959, Wynn's package tour called Supersonic Attractions of '59 headlined Sam Cooke and Jackie Wilson and included other Black singers such as Hank Ballard and the Midnighters, Marv Johnson, the Falcons, Jesse Belvin, Baby Washington, and Johnny "Guitar" Watson.

Supersonic Attractions was formed in 1959 and by 1962 helped fulfill Clyde's vision. It's Biggest Show of 1962 featured Clyde, Sam Cooke, Jerry Butler, the Drifters, Chuck Jackson, Little Eva, Chris Montez, Tommy Roe, the Miracles, the Orlons, Dee Dee Ford, Barbara Lynn, and Don Gardner.[10]

Clyde's entrepreneurial efforts not only managed to get off the ground but were lucrative. The gossipy *Jet* magazine reported, "The complex situation that singer Clyde McPhatter finds himself in, as an owner of the touring rock 'n' roll [show] that he's headlining, he had to pay himself $4,500 weekly [$47,000+ in 2024 dollars] as the star or else be guilty of violating his contract."[11]

Financially, Clyde McPhatter was doing better than fine. In 1959, Clyde moved into a brand new $45,000 eight-room ranch home complete with swimming pool in Englewood, New Jersey. At Christmas 1958, he gifted his mother and father a $25,000 home in Teaneck, New Jersey, not far from his new house. Clyde told the press he planned on building a complete recording studio in his extra-large basement at a cost of about $15,000.[12]

Clyde was attached to many real estate rumors in the late 1950s. *Jet* magazine had him listed as one of the buyers interested in purchasing the "swank" White Horse Lodge in upstate New York, for sale at $60,000 ($640,000 in 2024 dollars).[13]

When Detroit's Paradise Theater came up for sale in 1961, Clyde's name appeared again as one of the buyers. This would have been an interesting deal, as the Paradise was probably the most important venue for Black performers outside of Manhattan's Apollo Theater during the 1940s. According to the Detroit press, several Black recording stars would be given an opportunity to invest in the corporation that would own the theater. Names in the offing included Clyde, Sam Cooke, Ruth Brown, LaVern Baker, Jackie Wilson, Louis Jordan, Roy Hamilton, Della Reese, and Brook Benton.[14]

In fact, anything Clyde expended *mucho dinero* on was news. The *Arizona Tribune* reported Clyde spent $1,000 for a new wardrobe before opening in New York.[15] And the *Minneapolis Spokesman* reported that Clyde celebrated the "overnight success" of his "Ta Ta" recording by gifting his wife, Nora, with a new bracelet to the replace the $1,500 (bracelet) she had recently lost.[16]

After "A Lover's Question," Clyde rolled into 1959 with strength and momentum, yet an underlying discordancy haunted the veteran singer. He had been a favorite singer with *Billboard* and *Cash Box*, the trade publications that followed the music industry, so it was unusual when a negative story turned up.

Billboard ran a regular column called "Night Club Reviews," and in the February 23, 1959, issue, the veteran columnist Bob Rolontz took an unusual, more critical view, of Clyde's performance, a debut at Max Gordon's Village Vanguard in Manhattan. Almost apologetically, Rolontz wrote, "When he was good—and he is a mighty good singer—he was outstanding; when he was bad it was due to a poor selection of material. On his first show he picked almost all of the wrong tunes and only showed off his fine vocal style when he sang 'I Can't Go on Alone' and 'A Lover's Question'—tunes with feeling. The slick, Sinatra-type items were not for him . . . McPhatter is best on folk songs, serious standards, blues and spiritual items, and when he lines up a program with these songs and gets enough club experience, he could build into a solid nightclub attraction."[17]

Clyde may have wanted to be the Black Frank Sinatra, but the problem was, he was still being managed as a rhythm and blues act. In his heart he knew it, which was why the rise of white teen singer Paul Anka and the deflection of his manager Irvin Feld's attention hurt him so profoundly.

When Feld put together his first Biggest Show of Stars for the year 1959, Clyde was still a mainstay, and Paul Anka was not on the show. Feld was taking the young singer in another direction and that could best be seen in the issue of *Billboard* magazine from November 16, 1959. In one column called "Music as Written," a very brief item reported, "Clyde McPhatter opens at the Howard Theater in Washington on November 20." The Howard was an anchor on the old chitlin' circuit, a venue for a mostly African American audience.

On the same page, in another column, came this more laudatory verbiage about Clyde's management-company-mate and competitor: "Paul Anka has conquered still another European country. His recent opening at the Olympia Theater in Paris created a storm of excitement, which resulted in the gendarmes coming to the rescue. He returns to the U.S. November 24. Paul has two strong ballads in his latest ABC-Paramount release, It's 'Time to Cry' b-w 'Something has Changed.' Incidentally, both tunes were written by the very versatile performer."[18]

At the end of 1959, when *Cash Box* published its column "The Final Results" in which it tallied the results of its annual survey, Paul Anka and Lloyd Price were tied for first, one position ahead of Elvis Presley for "Best Pop Male Vocalist of 1959." Clyde McPhatter made the list at #24, one position behind Sam Cooke. As to the Best R&B Male vocalist of 1959, Clyde McPhatter did better, coming in at #5, one spot behind Jackie Wilson.[19]

The survey included two listings for individual songs. For "Best Pop Record of 1959," the #1 song was "Mack the Knife," Bobby Darin's turn away from teen ditties and a pop remake of a 1928 song from the German musical *The Threepenny Opera*. Paul Anka was on the list at #8 with "Put Your Head on My Shoulder." The real bite, however, was the #5 song, "There Goes My Baby," by Clyde's old group, the Drifters, which was now led by Ben E. King. This iteration of the Drifters came after George Treadwell fired the old Drifters and brought the Five Crowns in as their replacements. King (under his real name

Benjamin Earl Nelson) wrote the song with Lover Patterson, but manager Treadwell attached his name to the song (the old royalty exploitation trick). No Clyde McPhatter song was on the list, although he did drop "Since You've Been Gone" on the charting for "Best R&B Record of 1959." It was a middling placement far, far behind the #1 song, the Drifters' "There Goes My Baby."

Although Clyde was still a young man in 1959, just twenty-seven years old, he had been in the business since the rise of doo-wop and proto-rock 'n' roll at the start of the 1950s. White, pretty-boy teenagers (such as Frankie Avalon, Jimmy Clanton, and Fabian) were flooding into the pop market while R&B was in a state of flux, with less rock 'n' roll and more versatile balladeers such as Sam Cooke and Jackie Wilson, who could rock out when necessary.

Over the prior couple of years, Atlantic Records and Clyde McPhatter's trend line in the pop music world had been spotty. Back in 1956, Clyde's career took a huge leap forward when "Treasure of Love" crashed the Top Twenty pop market. Then for the next two years, he struggled to attain that kind of crossover performance although still scoring beautifully on R&B charts. "A Lover's Question," in 1958, was Clyde's biggest hit record on the pop charts, a kind of career-saving song. Now one year later, the big question was how to go forward.

Atlantic was not the same company as when Clyde signed with the label in 1953. R&B groups such as the Coasters and the new Drifters were now dominant at the company, but Ertegun and Wexler were making plenty of room for white singers such as Bobby Darin. Meanwhile, longtime labelmate Ray Charles at the end of 1959 would leave Atlantic for a bigger label, ABC-Paramount.

For a while, Atlantic had the successful songwriting duo Jerry Leiber and Mike Stoller on the payroll until a question about being underpaid led to a parting of the ways. Ertegun and Wexler played as fast and as loose with finances as any independent record producer at the time. Ruth Brown, who had been one of Atlantic's mainstays since it opened its doors, in the 1980s took the company to court for moneys not paid. As she noted, "there's something wrong when a singer has been popular for twenty-five years and hasn't seen a penny since 1963."[20]

Leiber and Stoller originally produced "There Goes My Baby" (a song Jerry Wexler hated), so they could have lent their talents to Clyde. That didn't happen. They were busy elsewhere. Here's where things get interconnected. The Clovers, Atlantic recording artists, were one of the great doo-wop groups of the early 1950s with songs such as "Don't You Know I Love You," "One Mint Julep," "Good Lovin'," and "Devil or Angel." When the group's contract with Atlantic expired in 1957, they left, eventually signing with their manager's label, Poplar, in 1958. The following year, Poplar was acquired by United Artists Records, who brought the Clovers into the studio, where the group recorded a Leiber and Stoller song, "Love Potion No. 9." It would be the biggest hit of the Clovers' career.

Meanwhile, over at Atlantic, it was decided that Clyde should record an old Clovers record, "Lovey Dovey," from 1953. That's the doo-wop tune with the lyrics "you're the cutest thing that I ever did see / I really love your peaches, wanna shake your tree," which magically appeared in "The Joker," the Steve Miller hit from 1974. "Lovey Dovey" was also a record on which Ahmet Ertegun gave himself a cowrite.

The Clovers took "Lovey Dovey" to #2 on the R&B charts with an imaginative cutting: a bouncy doo-wop lead, slick saxophone work, and a blues piano riff. Clyde twisted the song into a mid-tempo rocker. It turned out to be a decent, if not pedestrian, recording by Clyde.

For the B-side, Atlantic chose a Doc Pomus and Mort Shuman song called "My Island of Dreams."

In the 1950s and early '60s, the hottest young songwriters could be found in either one of two office structures in midtown Manhattan, the Brill Building or 1650 Broadway. Record publishers, producers, and songwriters inhabited these two midrise buildings, where the interiors were cut up into virtual warrens of musical activity.

The term "young songwriters" was spot-on because many were teenagers, some not even out of high school. The musical progenies generally set up as a two-person team of lyricist and composer. Some of the more famous included male-female partners such as Carole King and Gerry Goffin, Barry Mann and Cynthia Weil, and Jeff Barry and Ellie Greenwich. Their model was Leiber and Stoller, who were still active songwriters and producers. In the latter role, they needed songwriters for the resurgent Drifters and enlisted the team of Doc Pomus and Mort Shuman. While "My Island of Dreams" didn't' work well for Clyde, the two were absolutely in synchronization with the Drifters, writing for the group such hit songs as "This Magic Moment" and "Save the Last Dance for Me."

The Drifters with Ben E. King, who would soon go solo, were now the top of the pops, while Clyde was working through some late-career struggles. This isn't to say "Lovey Dovey" teamed with "My Island of Dreams" was a failure, because it wasn't. The week it was released the record found itself up against some decent competition: Chuck Berry's "Almost Grown" with "Little Queenie" on the B-side, Jackie Wilson's "That's Why (I Love You So)," and the Crests' "Six Nights a Week." Paul Anka, the same week, even had a new song, "I Miss You So," which was a middling performer.

The *Billboard* review on "Lovey Dovey" / "My Island of Dreams" was quick: "McPhatter has a solid, new version of his [no, it was a Clovers' song!] old hit that looms as a strong contender. The rocker is solid with appeal over a driving backing. 'My Island' is a celestial-type rockaballad with a hula flavor that is also a prospect."[21]

"Lovey Dovey" went to #12 on the R&B charts and to just #49 on the pop charts. In a rare miss for Paul Anka, his "I Miss You So" climbed higher, to #33 on the pop charts.

For Clyde's next song, Atlantic went back to the Brill Building, this time to the songwriting team of Neil Sedaka and Howard Greenfield. Sedaka was balancing songwriting for others with a nascent pop career. As a singer, he had his first hit record in 1958 with "The Diary" and his second, "Oh! Carol," in 1959. At the same time, he and Greenfield were writing teen tunes such as "Stupid Cupid" for Connie Francis.

Sedaka and Greenfield wrote a mild rock 'n' roller called "Since You've Been Gone," and Clyde took it to the recording studio. The B-side recording was "Try Try Baby," with the songwriters listed as Ahmet Ertegun and Jerry Wexler. "Since You've been Gone" was a better cut for Clyde, who gave it the ol' McPhatter verve: "You told me you loved me, but honey you lied / you left me here crying, how can I go on / since you've been gone." The *Billboard* review was strong: "McPhatter effectively decks out a potent, dual-mart lover's lament that rides along at a quick 'Gotta Travel On' clip. Strong piece of material on the deck that has that big hit look."[22]

"Since You've Been Gone" was, indeed, a hit but not a "big hit." While it only managed to ride to #4 on the R&B charts, it performed better on the pop charts than "Lovey Dovey" at #39.

Clyde McPhatter would chart one more Atlantic Records–produced single in 1959 and even after attracting Brook Benton as cowriter, it was another mid-tier performer. Although the song, "You Went Back on Your Word," was anchored by a basic rock 'n' roll beat, it sounded like everything else Clyde was singing at the time. The B-side was another Ertegun/Wexler-credited throwaway song, "There You Go." Brook Benton's tune managed to get as high as #13 on the R&B charts, slightly better than "Since You've Been Gone," but it had little carryover to the pop charts, slotting in at #72. In comparison, Brook Benton, writing for himself, charted six records in 1959, including two Top Ten hits, "It's Just a Matter of Time" and "So Many Ways."

Clyde's contract with Atlantic Records was due to terminate early in 1959, and it wasn't a secret that bigger labels were interested in signing the singer. After five years with Atlantic, maybe the string had run out with Ertegun and Wexler. Clyde's last recordings were tired in concept. He had been in the game a decade, which was already longer than most hitmakers. The question was, in a changing world of pop music, did he have anything left to offer? It doesn't appear that Ertegun and Wexler thought so. There is no record of Atlantic fighting to keep Clyde on Atlantic. Since he was still relatively young, a lot of A&R men across the industry were already heading to their comptroller's office to see what could be offered. Atlantic was not going to compete.

A small continuation, on the jump page of a February 1959 *Billboard* magazine, concluded a feature on a man named Ray Ellis, who had come over to M-G-M Records to head A&R. The closing comments noted, "Ellis was active as a free-lancer, particularly with Atlantic, where he worked closely with Clyde McPhatter . . ."

Ellis wasn't well known yet, although he should have been. Born in 1923, Ellis entered the music industry as a musician, playing in jazz bands with Gene Krupa and Paul Whiteman. As it turned out, his real talent was as a composer and arranger. Columbia Records producer Mitch Miller, who was intuitive about nascent talent, plucked him out of the band life to help arrange for the pop music world. Ellis would end up doing the arrangements on bestsellers as diverse as the Four Lads' "Standing on the Corner" in 1956, Johnny Mathis's "Chances Are" in 1957, and Bobby Darin's "Splish Splash" in 1958.[23]

At the start of 1959, Ellis was working the market, but M-G-M Records needed help and Ellis knew how to make hit records. Just a month after Ellis sat down in his new office, *Billboard* slipped in a filler toward the bottom of page 4. The small one-column headline read "Snares McPhatter." This was Ellis's first big move in his new job. The label signed Clyde to a long-term contract with a guarantee the press reported to be in excess of $50,000 a year (along with unidentified fringe benefits). Behind the scenes, there had been a bidding war as Warner Bros. and United Artists had made strong offers for Clyde's services and had dangled very attractive contracts.[24]

Although a little late to the Clyde McPhatter breaking news, *Cash Box* was able to add more meat to the bone. A week after its rival broke the news about Clyde, *Cash Box* got to M-G-M Records' "prexy" [president], who said, "instrumental in bringing the former Atlantic Records star to M-G-M was Ray Ellis, newly appointed A&R head."[25] As it turned out, Ellis had arranged and conducted several of McPhatter's hits with Atlantic including "Seven Days," "Treasure of Love," "Without Love," and his last big hit "A Lover's Question."

Cash Box quickly followed up its account of the Clyde McPhatter changing labels story with a photo. Three gentlemen, all with suits, white shirts, and ties, stand alongside a sitting Clyde McPhatter in a handsome plaid jacket and dark tie. Clyde has a pen in hand. The smiling, standing gentlemen, now important figures in Clyde's professional life, were from left to right Irvin Feld, Clyde's manager; Arnold Maxim, president; and Ray Ellis, recording chief. The cutline on the picture read: "Clyde McPhatter of 'Lover's Question' fame seems very happy as he signs with the label."[26]

Why wouldn't he be smiling as it was the most lucrative contract of his career?

According to *The Carolinian*, the Black newspaper in Raleigh, North Carolina, "McPhatter decided to cast his lot with M-G-M. Though not a rock-and-roller in the strictest sense of the word, McPhatter became popular in this era of the 'big beat' and has been closely identified with it.... Knowing Ellis to be 'just what the doctor ordered' when it came to supervising his music, McPhatter happily went over to the 'Leo the Lion' label."[27]

As always when a label signed a new act, it was hell-bent for leather to get the singer into the studio to start earning back some of the advance. Clyde would be in the studio recording before the month was out.

What looked to be a perfect marriage of a record company and musician or "just what the doctor ordered" turned out to be nothing more than a mirage.

M-G-M was a middle-of-the road label with more big band–type performers under contract than rock 'n' rollers. Before the signing of Clyde, its biggest youthful singer was Connie Francis, who for every teen-ditty would resurrect an old chestnut. In 1959, Francis would have huge hits with the novelty song "Lipstick on Your Collar" and the resurrection of the 1928 Paul Whiteman classic, "Among My Souvenirs." In August 1959, M-G-M ran a full-page promotion in *Billboard* advertising all its sixteen great new 33 ⅓ (rpm) records. Except for albums by Clyde McPhatter (*Let's Start Over Again*), Connie Francis and the Impalas (the hit song "Sorry [I Ran All the Way Home]" in 1959), the other singers promoted were not musicians any self-respecting teenager at that time would listen to. They included Maurice Chevalier, Harry James, David Rose, Jimmy Newman, Joni James, Jaye P. Morgan, and even Ray Ellis, who boasted an album titled *I'm in the Mood for Strings*.[28]

As promised, M-G-M Records was able to push out a Clyde record as fast as possible. He signed a contract in early March, and a news brief at the end of the month in *Billboard* revealed a record distributor discussing up-and-coming records: "'I Still Get a Thrill' by Joni James is hot. 'I Told Myself a Lie' by Clyde McPhatter on M-G-M is strong."[29] Joni James had a minor hit in 1959; it wasn't this record. As for Clyde, this record went nowhere as well. "I Told Myself a Lie" was so mainstream, it didn't even make the R&B charts. The hint this was not anywhere near R&B was on the credits, which read orchestra and chorus under the direction of Ray Ellis. If that wasn't enough of a clue where Clyde was headed, then the B-side would have been the answer: "(I'm Afraid) The Masquerade is Over," a reimagining of the 1939 recording by Larry Clinton.

Things didn't get any better for M-G-M's next Clyde release, "Twice as Nice," with "Where Did I Make My Mistake" on the B-side. On August 10, 1959, *Billboard* magazine ran a full page of what it called "& Tomorrow's Tops," basically songs it viewed as potential hits. There were three categories: "This Week's Singles," "Best Buys" (records poised for a breakout), and "Bubbling Under the Hot 100" (records that had been building momentum and would soon chart). Two songs of note in "This Week's Singles" were "Mack the Knife" by Bobby Darin and "Poison Ivy" by the Coasters; two songs of note for "Best Buys" were "I'm Gonna Get Married" by Lloyd Price and "Sleep Walk" by Santo and Johnny; and three songs of note on "Bubbling Under" were "(Till) I Kissed You" by the Everly Brothers, "The Angels Listened In" by the Crests, and "Twice As Nice" by Clyde McPhatter. All became big hits except for "Twice as Nice," which barely managed to make the Top 100 records, posting only as high as #91 and, again, no listing on the R&B charts—but Ray Ellis with orchestra and chorus did get another credit.[30]

Ray Ellis and M-G-M Records tried again, this time with a song appropriately called "Let's Try Again" with "Bless You" on the B-side. This was a perkier recording, and the effect was much better than the previous efforts. "Let's Try Again" made the R&B charts, falling in at #13 and did much better on the pop charts, at #48.

The label would release two more Clyde McPhatter singles in 1960, without much success. Its last McPhatter platter [record] was not a half-hearted effort. "This Is Not Goodbye" was penned by Neil Sedaka and Howard Greenfield. The B-side tune, "One Right After Another," was written by Otis Blackwell, who wrote some great rockers including "All Shook Up," "Fever," and "Great Balls of Fire." The record disappeared without a trace. M-G-M Records just couldn't find the right rhythmic formula to keep Clyde's career in motion.

To be fair, there was the usual confusion instigated by the prior record company. The tactics could be considered vengeful, but more than likely just opportunistic. Atlantic would continue to issue whatever Clyde McPhatter recordings it never considered worthwhile in the past but, hey, why leave them on the shelf when M-G-M is promoting the singer?

A gossipy note from *Cash Box*'s "Record Ramblings" column began this way: "MGM's Clyde McPhatter to headline at Blinstrubs in Boston . . . Atlantic, his former employer, has a chart item in Clyde's recently released 'Since You've Been Gone' . . ."[31]

To muddy the waters even more, Atlantic later in the year issued a Clyde McPhatter album, simply called *Clyde*. *Cash Box*'s album review read: "A compilation of the artist's previous singles for the label presents McPhatter in a light that will delight his many fans. Included are such hits as "Since You've Been Gone" and "A Lover's Question" plus "Lovey Dovey." Now there were two Clyde McPhatter albums in the market, in addition to Atlantic's first Clyde McPhatter album, *Love Ballads*, from the year before.[32]

In 1960, Atlantic Records released three more Clyde McPhatter singles, only one of which, "Just Give Me a Ring," charted—at #96 in the Top 100 list of best-selling songs. One of the more desperate singles was "Deep Sea Ball," which a British writer called "goonish," backed by "Let the Boogie Woogie Roll," credited to Ahmet Ertegun and Jerry Wexler.[33]

British music journalist Peter Doggett summed up Clyde's career at the start of the 1960s: "He [Clyde] had apparently enjoyed working with the producers Ahmet Ertegun and Jerry Wexler, but he knew that he could get a bigger advance elsewhere. His decision to abandon his solid Atlantic roots and move to M-G-M looks, with hindsight, like a disaster. But at the time, it made industry headlines for the size of Clyde's advance, and no-one—except the Atlantic producers, perhaps—can have imagined how quickly McPhatter's stock would fall."[34]

It was obvious to Clyde things were not going well, and he took his woes to a friend, Clyde Otis, one of the first Black executives at a major record company. Born in 1924, Otis served in the Marines during World War II and then afterward came to New York where he found success as a songwriter. In 1958, Mercury Records hired Otis to head A&R, where he cowrote and produced many of Brook Benton's best efforts including "It's Just a Matter of Time," "Kiddio," and "The Boll Weevil Song."[35]

Clyde McPhatter was not happy with his album, nor his progress at the label, so sometime in the summer of 1960 he met with Clyde Otis, whom he had known for years. The two decided Clyde needed to switch labels again, although it would be his third in less than a year. Clyde got his contract dissolved and quickly signed with Mercury. Otis immediately got Clyde into the studio and over the course of two days recorded enough songs for an album. Music writer Harry Bacas got an early listen to the songs and wrote a column saying, "The songs are unlike anything Clyde McPhatter has done before. They are standards, mostly ballads, arranged and conducted by Glenn Osser."[36]

The album, released in 1960, was called *Ta Ta!* Back of the album liner notes were partly boastful and partly a declaration of Clyde's maturing approach to song: "To his legion of fans, a more versatile McPhatter emerges. A McPhatter that glibly skips from a light rock 'n' roll-ish ditty to a stirring love song. A McPhatter that switches from an original love ballad to 'Ta Ta,' his first Mercury release and more important, a big one on the popularity charts."

The liner notes also offer a bit of reality, that the songs were selected by the two Clydes, McPhatter and Otis, who were longtime friends, and that McPhatter had to be pushed into doing six of his own songs: "Why Was I the One You Chose," "Who's Worried Now," "What's Love to Me," "For All You've Done," "Everything Gonna Be All Right," and "I Need a Love Like Yours."

Then the liner notes go a bit off-track: "And even in the most modern idiom, McPhatter shows two faces—one, the love balladeer on "Let Me Shake the Hand" and "Why Was I the One You Chose"; the other, a modern minstrel in rollicking mixture of soul and song."[37]

Otis kept Clyde in the studio for two more days, recording songs in his usual "big-beat" style, but with one difference: a complement of strings.

Bacas interviewed Clyde, who told him he wasn't starting anything new by being a rock 'n' roll artist recording with strings. "A general movement has been growing in the record business toward changing rock 'n' roll and giving it a broader appeal," Clyde averred. "It's a very good sign, too. Anything that doesn't progress has to die and it was time for rock 'n' roll to change. Whatever it does will be an improvement."[38]

It was certainly an improvement for Clyde. His first Mercury effort looked like a winner. The song, "Ta Ta," was cowritten by Clyde. In July 1960, *Cash Box* took a look at a bunch of new songs from popular singers with the potential to become hit records. In the mix were releases by Freddie Cannon, Skip and Flip, Don Gibson, Little Anthony and the Imperials, Charlie Rich, and Clyde McPhatter. Only Clyde's "Ta Ta" lived up to its potential.[39]

The *Cash Box* reviewer intuitively understood all the recording nuances Mercury was bringing to the Clyde McPhatter show: "The exciting Mr. McPhatter makes his debut under the Mercury banner and comes off with a torrid first showing that could develop into his biggest single to date. 'Ta Ta' is . . . a rockin' romantic blueser with the popular Mercury string-sound in the backdrop. Exciting and clever instrumental work showcases Clyde's vocal maneuvers beautifully."[40]

Inking Clyde was a gamble, but the word on the street was that Mercury was happy with its new singer. Maybe "happy" was an understatement. According to one press report, Midwest-Mercury prexy Henry Friedman was "elated" with action on Clyde's "Ta Ta" as well as Brook Benton's "Kiddio." Considering the tough, crowded-with-good-songs market when "Ta Ta" and "Kiddio" were released in late summer 1960, elation was the unexpected prize. Competition at the time included Chubby Checker's "The Twist," Elvis Presley's "It's Now or Never," the Ventures' "Walk Don't Run," Sam Cooke's "Chain Gang," Johnny Burnette's "Dreamin'," Brenda Lee's "I'm Sorry," and Roy Orbison's "Only the Lonely," among many other fine tunes.

The jaunty, full-orchestrated "Ta Ta" put Clyde back on all the charts. It zoomed to #7 on the R&B listings and crossed over to the pop charts, climbing to #23. Clyde sang, "When I hold my baby tight, with all my might / I tell I will never let her out of my sight / she says 'Ta Ta' just like a ba-aa-aa-bee." The song wasn't exactly an advocacy for feminism, but it did sell a lot of records. As did Brian Hyland's "Itsy Bitsy Teenie Weenie Yellow Polka Dot Bikini," another song on the charts at that time that cast a dubious shadow on femininity. Hyland did a little better than Clyde; "Itsy Bitsy" had climbed to #1 on the charts.

CHAPTER TWELVE

THERE YOU GO

In January 1956, it was announced that "(We're Gonna) Rock Around the Clock" became the first record to sell one million copies in the United Kingdom. Just about a year later, Bill Haley and the Comets boarded the *Queen Elizabeth* ocean liner for a transatlantic voyage to the British Isles. Things would get a little crazy, man, crazy. The first sign of disequilibrium was when the boat arrived at Cherbourg, a small port city in Normandy, France. Over a hundred British journalists, photographers and assorted media men and women were waiting for them, trying to get the early scoop on the famous rock and rollers from the United States. The masses all boarded the boat for the last leg of the journey to Southampton, England, where a frenzied crowd of teenagers awaited Bill Haley.

After the passenger ship arrived in Southampton, the logistics were a little tricky. Bill Haley and his group, including musicians and wives, had to shift to Rolls Royce limousines for a one-mile drive to Southampton's rail station, where they would board a train to London. The mile to the station was hellish with teenagers accompanying the line of cars, jumping on the vehicles, trying to open doors, and banging on windows. At the train station a phalanx of policemen had to form a protective corridor to get Bill Haley and his band to his train car through a raving mob of five thousand teens shouting "We want Bill."

The media wasn't of much help. The *Daily Mirror* had run a competition for tickets to board the Southampton-to-London train, and it was jam-packed. Finally, the train arrived at Waterloo Station in London, where another two thousand teens were waiting. When the train stopped, the frenzied crowd slammed their way through a police cordon to engulf the Bill Haley entourage. Once again, the police formed a moving shield line to get the group into waiting limousines.[1]

The first concert by the group was on February 6, 1957, at London's Dominion Theater. It was a sold-out performance.[2]

Before visiting England, the Bill Haley and the Comets tour had traveled first to Australia, then home for a few weeks before arriving in England. It would move on to Dublin, where about 4,000 fans rioted with bottles being thrown at police and store windows smashed. According to Haley biographer Peter Benjaminson, after two straight months of touring through Australia and then Great Britain, sales of "(We're Gonna) Rock Around the Clock" totaled six million copies, and the band was pulling in royalties totaling $30,000 a week. About 350,000 fans had seen the rock and rollers through the course of their tour, one of whom was a young man from Liverpool named Paul McCartney.[3]

Rock 'n' roll had officially arrived in the United Kingdom. A British trade publication called *Record Mirror* tried to sum up the tumultuous year in music witnessed by the United Kingdom in 1957. A headline stretching across two pages read: "A Cavalcade of Rock & Skiffle." The latter music was a combination of folk, blues, bluegrass, even jazz, and very popular in Britain. Indeed, the subhead to the story explained, "Throughout 1957 rock 'n roll may have had the edge so far as Britain's listening was concerned but skiffle was a clear leader as regards to play-it-yourself." The first part of the article was all about Bill Haley and "(We're Gonna) Rock Around the Clock," which estimated sales of that record as of that writing in December 1957 were closer to eight million copies.[4]

Bill Haley was the first real rock 'n' roller to tour Great Britain, but there were precursors. Back in 1954, the Crew-Cuts, a white group from Canada, covered a song, "Sh-Boom," by Black doo-woppers the Chords and turned it into a monster record. The song, as vocalized by the Crew-Cuts, wasn't exactly rhythm and blues, but it was close enough. The Crew-Cuts went on the road (and boat!), including to England. When the Canadians pulled into Liverpool, Paul McCartney went down to the Empire Theater and stood at the back door waiting for the Crew-Cuts to come out. He said, "I met the Crew-Cuts . . . and they were very kind and very nice and I thought, 'Well, that's possible then, stars can talk to people,' and I remembered that later."[5]

Whether Bill Haley and His Comets were actually the first of American rock 'n' rollers to come to Great Britain is debatable, because in December 1956 Pat Boone arrived for a tour that would last through January 1957. The question music historians still debate is whether Pat Boone was really singing rock 'n' roll or just a pop version of rock 'n' roll tunes. He included in his show his own versions of "(We're Gonna) Rock Around the Clock" and even the Clyde McPhatter–led Drifters' big hit "Money Honey," which he would sing in what he would call a tasteful way. Boone would explain himself this way: "Rock 'n' Roll is a good outlet . . . and it will stay popular as long as people are not ashamed to like it, but I condemn those who perform it on a stage in a distasteful way... I move around the stage, I snap my fingers and I stamp my feet, but I refuse to do anything to offend anybody."

After the Pat Boone and Bill Haley expeditions, the United Kingdom in 1957 opened up to American acts of all types: country-pop singer Mitchell Torok, who sang "Caribbean" in 1953, arrived, and he was followed by the Platters, who boasted an extensive program that began in March and lasted into May. Their first show was in York, where the group played to a capacity crowd, taking six curtain calls at the first show.

The Platters' tour overlapped with another aggressive musical journey by an American group, the arrival of Frankie Lymon and the Teenagers, or as they were promoted in the United Kingdom, The Teenagers with Frankie Lymon. This tour wasn't as crowded with dates as the Platters, but it lasted longer, from March through June. R&B groups were the thing in 1957, as the relatively unknown Freddie Bell and the Bellboys from Philadelphia also came to England. They toured with the UK's homegrown rock 'n' roller, the popular Tommy Steele. The Bellboys must have had a good show because, while they never had a hit record in the United States, their "Giddy Up a Ding Dong" was a Top Five tune on the UK singles chart.

Next up in Britain for a summer tour was Charlie Gracie, who had a couple of big hits in 1957 with "Butterfly" and "Fabulous." To close the year, who else but Paul Anka arrived for a December tour. Among the songs Anka sang on that visit was "White Christmas," although it is not known if he sang it straight or like the Drifters' doo-wop version. He did sing "Diana," appeared on British television, and picked up a gold disc to commemorate a million copies of his record "Diana" sold in the United Kingdom.[6]

Paul Anka, the Platters, Pat Boone, and Charlie Gracie all returned to England over the next two years. Connie Francis would be a frequent visitor and even the songwriting team of Doc Pomus and Mort Shuman, who wrote a couple of Clyde McPhatter songs, did a tour as well, although by this time Pomus and Shuman were more known for writing "A Teenager In Love" for Dion and "I'm A Man" for Fabian.

In 1959 Clyde McPhatter was still working his usual tour stops, where he continued to be popular. By August he was back in his home state of North Carolina, where he was now heading a show that also included Bo Diddley, the Crests, and Chubby Checker. Clyde in his home state was always news to the local Black press, and the *Carolina Times* (Durham, North Carolina) played it this way: "Clyde McPhatter, the hottest Negro record star alive today, headlines the show. When Clyde swings forth with his bouncy tunes, which are favorites the world over, the audience sings along, clapping hands and patting feet."[7]

"The world over?" As popular as Clyde McPhatter was in the United States, he was barely known outside of North America. Even in rock 'n' roll-rabid

United Kingdom, he was inconsequential except for the few rhythm and blues diehards who had been tracking blues singers since the early 1950s and could probably list every Dominoes song he had ever sung.

Clyde caught a break (sort of!) in December 1959, when the British music magazine *Disc* ran what might have been one of the first reviews of a Clyde McPhatter song in the United Kingdom. This one was about "You Went Back on Your Word." However, the reviewer considered "There You Go" as the A-side. The good part of the review read that Clyde "comes out again, this time rocking comfortably on 'There You Go.' Vocal group and a honking saxophone accompany Clyde this time but there seems to be little about this half that would make it stand out from the rest of the crowd. 'You Went Back on Your Word' has more punch to it. A steady beat number with a directness of approach that should find it a niche in the jukes."

The bad part of the review was borderline homophobic. Perhaps a neutral observation, perhaps an allusion—the reviewer noted, "That high-pitched, almost feminine voice of Mr. McPhatter . . ."[8]

All that aside, why the sudden Clyde McPhatter song review? Two weeks later *Disc* ran a tiny news item with a headline that read "Bobby Darin for TV." The one-paragraph story read: "Silver Disc winner, Bobby Darin, touring Britain next spring with Duane Eddy and Clyde McPhatter in a package show, will probably take in a *Sunday Night at the London Palladium* TV spot during his visit."[9]

That was good news in a time of strife for Clyde. Whether radio deejays chose "You Went Back on Your Word" or "There You Go" as the A-side song, it was not a major hit, nor was anything else he was recording for M-G-M. In February, a *Billboard* column called "Distributor News" led with an item that seemed suspiciously like a record company plant. It quoted a record distributor who speculated on what songs showed signs of becoming a hit. The distributor claimed, "heading the list for M-G-M are 'Mama' with B-side 'Teddy' by Connie Francis, 'Pretty Eyed Baby' by Dick Caruso, 'Think Me a Kiss' by Clyde McPhatter and 'Angela Jones' by Johnny Ferguson and 'What Do You Want' by Adam Faith." [10]

Here's what's strange about the paragraph. Connie Francis's "Mama" / "Teddy" did become a two-sided hit. "Think Me A Kiss" charted but not very strongly. No one ever heard from Dick Caruso and Johnny Ferguson again, and Adam Faith was a British singer with no following in the United States. (In 1965 his song "I'm Alright" would be his only record to chart in the US Top 40.)

That paragraph was a quiet lead-in for a story *Billboard* would track the very next month. First, on March 7, came this item: "Bobby Darin, Clyde McPhatter and Duane Eddy will tour England, Germany, France and Italy starting March 17."[11] A week later, a story about American singers going to Britain carried this note: "One of the most talked-of attractions on the current London scene is the triple-threat package of Bobby Darin, Clyde McPhatter and Duane Eddy, which opens there next Friday."[12] Finally, a small news blurb carried this headline: "Darin, Eddy Leave for British Tour." Somehow, Clyde was suddenly forgotten. Even the one-paragraph story discarded his name. "Bobby Darin and Duane Eddy departed last week for a month's co-starring tour of England and Scotland. This will mark their first personal appearance in the British Isles. Pair will perform in Lewisham, Edmonton, Leicester, Glasgow, Liverpool, Birmingham, London, Leeds, Sheffield, Manchester, Castel and Guildford."[13]

Fear not, Clyde was definitely part of this tour, and his participation made this 1960 journey important in regard to American acts coming to Britain.

Whether one considers Pat Boone or Bill Haley the first of American rock 'n' roller to come to Britain, the pattern going into 1958 was for promoters to bring over a single act, a Little Richard, a Jerry Lee Lewis, a Platters, a Buddy Holly and the Crickets, and so on. The first attempt to export to the United Kingdom what was the standard trunk show in America came from a non-tour management company. Johnny Otis, musician extraordinaire and just about everything else in the music business, put together one of his Johnny Otis Shows for a tour of Britain beginning in April 1958. The idea was to take to Europe some of the regulars from his Johnny Otis runs in the United States, people like Marie Adams with her group Three Tons of Joy, Mel Williams, Don and Dewey, and Jimmy Nolan. Contracts had been signed with one of the bigger tour operators in the UK, but when the show got postponed for a week due to work permit problems, it all fell apart. Apparently, the influential Musicians' Union had refused to grant permits, and without those important papers the Ministry of Labour would not sign off on the tour.

The next attempt to bring over a trunk tour to the UK came from Alan Freed. This tour was supposed to begin on October 11, 1958, and continue for twenty-one days. Among the acts expected to appear in London were Chuck Berry, the Champs, Danny and the Juniors, Screamin' Jay Hawkins, and Jo-An Campell. Freed was dealing with a London agent named David Rabin, who had an option clause for final acceptance. In the end, Rabin bailed and the tour didn't happen.

Everyone in the transatlantic music business suddenly got cold feet and the only tours by Americans to the British Isles were again by single acts. The first break in this pattern occurred at the start of 1960 when double headliners Eddie Cochran and Gene Vincent arrived in Ipswich, England, at the start of a lengthy program that would finally end in the city of Bristol in April.[14]

"Britain in the 1950s was a very different place to the USA and there was a great reluctance by the promoters to book rock 'n' roll acts at all," explained Ian Wallis, who literally wrote the book about early rock 'n' roll tours to Great Britain.

Initially, the US acts that did visit Britain (Bill Haley, Charlie Gracie, the Teenagers, Buddy Holly, and others) were placed on variety shows—similar to the old Ed Sullivan television program in the United States—appearing with comedians, ballad singers, magicians, or novelty acts like performing dogs. British promoters did not understand that a show solely comprising teenage music would be financially viable.

"The Bobby Darin, Duane Eddy, and Clyde McPhatter package and a similar one with Gene Vincent and Eddie Cochran at the beginning of 1960 were the first to feature more than one U.S. act, but equally as important the British support acts were aimed at the teenage market," Wallis added. "They were rock 'n' roll shows rather than variety shows that included a rock 'n' roll act. This proved that the demand was there, and we [the British] then enjoyed a few years of rock 'n' roll package shows, featuring U.S. acts, several of whom were welcomed to Britain for the first time, often a few years after they had peaked as chart acts in the States."

There were limitations. The biggest reason Great Britain never experienced the big Alan Freed or "Caravan of Stars" type package tours was purely down to cost. In those days, air travel was too expensive and American acts would arrive by ship, like Bill Haley. This was a slow and complex procedure and to make financial sense the act needed to work in the United Kingdom for a lengthy period, hence some of the four-month-long tours. There was no way a show with many U.S. acts could possibly work financially. Even three performers on a UK tour were a gamble.[15]

Back in the United States, GAC (General Artists Corporation), which was now managing Clyde McPhatter, devised a compromise program for England, a small group of prominent American performers with diverse backgrounds.

This was GAC's first European rock 'n' roll package tour. It was also the first package show containing three rock 'n' roll acts aimed at the United Kingdom. GAC was a little smarter than prior American promoters who wanted to bring multiple acts. It did a number of things right. First, although the three Americans were rock 'n' rollers, guitarist Duane Eddy was borderline country, Clyde McPhatter was old R&B, and Bobby Darin was straight-up pop. Second, while Duane Eddy was backed by his own group of musicians, Clyde and Bobby Darin used British musicians—Bob Miller and the Millermen—as their orchestra throughout the tour, thus pleasing the very chauvinistic Musician's Union. Third, the tour added a British act, Emile Ford and the Checkmates. And fourth, the tour was modest in scope. It would begin in Lewisham (South London) on March 18, swing through Scotland and hit most of Britain's biggest cities before ending up in Guildford, suburban London, on April 10.

"Emile Ford and the Checkmates were a big act in the UK, and Bob Miller and the Millermen were there to back McPhatter and Darin, but were given spots of their own," recalled concert attendee Spencer Leigh, who would go on to work for the BBC from Liverpool (home of the Beatles) and write numerous books about rock 'n' roll. He was fifteen years old in 1960 and went to the show with his friend Andrew Dobie.

"Five acts were normal, but three Americans were very unusual," Leigh continued. "I don't know how the promoter had swung that with the union, possibly by saying they were providing work for the Millermen. No one was booed, but Emile Ford was definitely the best received. Darin, I learned later, was irritated by the fact that Ford had his own superior sound system and he wouldn't let Darin use it."[16]

The ecstatic March 14, 1960, *Billboard* article mentioning the tour noted, "the jubilant bookers and promoters are reporting the biggest rush for tickets since Bill Haley's tour just three years ago."[17] This wasn't an exaggeration as British, Scottish, and Irish teenagers rushed to see this show, many attending a rock 'n' roll tour for the first time, having missed Bill Haley because they had been too young.

The main attractions were Duane Eddy and Bobby Darin. Most British teenagers had never heard of Clyde McPhatter. A passing reference to the new incarnation of the Drifters might have brought him a bit of ancillary fame, but the Clyde McPhatter–less Drifters hadn't yet translated to the British music scene.

"To be honest, I doubt that many British teenagers would have been familiar with Clyde McPhatter prior to his arrival in 1960," Wallis said. "The Drifters' records had been released in the UK, but they had not had any chart hits before 1960. When they did finally break through this side of the Atlantic, it was with the later material by Ben E. King or Johnny Moore."[18]

"The whole bill was the attraction," said Leigh. "Duane Eddy's 'Peter Gunn' was an amazing record and I knew Bobby Darin would be a great showman. It was fantastic, especially when Duane Eddy started playing before the curtain opened. I later found out that this was Lee Hazlewood's (Eddy's manager/producer) idea. I knew of Clyde McPhatter but at that time I only knew of his records like 'Think Me a Kiss,' as the Drifters' catalog before 'There Goes My Baby' was not played on the radio here."[19]

Also attending the shows was Brian Smith, who would soon be aiding and photographing American and British rockers. By the time of the Eddy-McPhatter-Darin tour, Smith was a young but experienced concertgoer.

"I saw my first live-music shows in the mid-1950s, courtesy of a friend's older brother and his pals, who were jazz fans," Smith explained. "They took my friend and me to many shows, introducing us to skiffle and blues, all this before rock 'n' roll. I saw Chris Barber, who brought to the UK—and backed-up—many American blues singers on tours in the UK as well as playing double bass with Lonnie Donegan on "Rock Island Line." It was always a big mantra of mine that Donegan, directly through skiffle, then indirectly through all the Brits who were first in skiffle groups (like the Beatles and the Stones), possibly put more guitars into more hands than anyone who ever lived."

As to the concert, which was in an old cinema: "With rock 'n' roll came the new 'package tours,'" Smith expounded. "These were two shows a night, six nights a week on the old vaudeville/music hall circuits. Most common stops were the one-nighters in cinemas. That's how we Brits first saw Bill Haley, the Platters, Charley Gracie, Buddy Holly, and the Everly Brothers."

For the Eddy-McPhatter-Darin tour, at Brian Smith's stop, there were two shows. He went to the first show alone just to experience Duane Eddy, and then returned for the second show, hanging with friends. "These were our big nights out, so most us wore suits and ties," he said. "Most everyone was smartly dressed."

"I was sixteen and, as I said, I was there mainly for Duane Eddy," Smith continued. "He was my first big guitar hero. His first LP (*Have "Twangy" Guitar Will Travel*) was my first acquired album, too! Instrumental rock 'n' roll was in its heyday, and he was the biggest. Clyde McPhatter had an unusual name and at that time was only known to many of us for the recent hit, "A Lover's Question." I only learned of his Drifters' connections and history much later. Duane was magic, but the biggest, general applause of the night was for Clyde McPhatter doing "Without Love."[20]

The promotional flyers for the Eddy-McPhatter-Darin tour were very old school with no illustrations, only screaming, eye-catching typeface. For the Empire Theater presentation in Liverpool, which were back-to-back evening performances, "The Biggest Show Ever!" flyer promoted the stars in descending order of star status. First was Bobby Darin in red type against a black background with a boxed insert of his well-known songs. Then came Duane Eddy, with yellow type against a black background also with a boxed insert. Then Clyde McPhatter in red type with no black background and no boxed insert. It was as if he had been forgotten and then his name squeezed into the flyer at the last minute because below him on the promotion was Emile Ford and The Checkmates in yellow type with a black background and a boxed insert. Bobby Darin's and Duane Eddy's wording included the phrase "From America—First Ever Visit to Britain," while it appeared Clyde McPhatter had to be explained to the prospective audience: "The American Recording Star whose success includes 'Bless You' and 'Let's Try Again'" (a moderately successful single in the United States, which must have gotten a release in the United Kingdom as well).

The in-depth show booklet that could be bought at the concert sported an unimaginative cover, headshots of the five stars of the show against a red background. The headshots had white swirls behind. At the top of the booklet were Emile Ford and Duane Eddy, in the middle of the page Bobby Darin, and at the bottom Bob Miller and Clyde McPhatter. The inside head-and-shoulder photo of Clyde showed an extremely debonair gentleman dressed in a dark suit with highlights on the lapels and four buttons at the bottom of the sleeve. He has a dark crossed tie at the top of a starched white shirt. The smiling Clyde leans against his right hand, which is holding a cigarette. Clyde was beginning to bald and had taken to wearing a wig, but in this photo his hair looks natural or at least touched up to appear natural.

The one-page bio, which was headlined, "The Boy Who Followed a Star," was over-the-top laudatory:

- "The reason for Clyde's ever-increasing popularity is due in the main to three things—his fine voice, his natural as well as acquired knowledge of music, and his personality. His voice is something that lingers in the memory. Moreover, he knows how to put it over. His countless fans confess it does something to them.
- "He is friendly, earnest, and sincere artiste. Like all such people he is sensitive to the reactions of audiences, but behind the flashing smile there is plenty of grit and determination.
- "There is a lot more to be written in the future, for while his rise to stardom has been rapid [yikes, actually a ten-year journey] it is no flash in the pan."[21]

On the opening night of the Eddy-McPhatter-Darin tour at the initial venue in Lewisham, the very first American star British teenagers would see was Clyde McPhatter. This is how Wallis wrote up the moment: "He [Clyde McPhatter] impressed with a short act that got off to a strong start via a powerful 'Money Honey.' The ex-Drifter than continued with 'Just to Hold My Hand,' 'Without Love (There is Nothing)' and a knockout 'Think Me A Kiss.' The Millermen played too loud, but Clyde's wonderful high-pitched voice still rose above them and he closed with a moving 'Have Mercy Baby.'"[22]

Another Brit who eventually played an ancillary role in helping American pop singers on their British tours, including befriending Jerry Lee Lewis, was Graham Knight. He was on the scene as a teenager as well. "I saw Clyde McPhatter when he toured with Bobby Darin and Duane Eddy," said Knight. "I liked his 'Without Love.'"

Knight added, "That tour was a sell-out. It was promoted by Arthur Howes and the Grade Organization, the biggest booker in the UK."[23]

What made this tour successful, besides the stars, was that it was backed by a couple of the savviest managers and promoters in the British entertainment industry, Leslie Grade and Arthur Howes. The old pro was Grade, who with his brother Lew created the largest talent agency in Europe after World War

II. In the 1950s, the Grades began producing television shows before moving into cinema as well.

The aggressive upstart was Arthur Howes. Here's a quick Howes story. Two years after this tour, in October 1962, he got a call from Brian Epstein, who was managing a new band called the Beatles. They had just unleashed in the U.K. their first single, "Love Me Do." Epstein was hoping Howes would book the Beatles on one of his touring packages. Howes said sure, he would do that. In return for this favor, Epstein offered Howes the option on all Beatles tours in the future.[24]

Things would definitely get crazy on those future Beatles tours, but this current tour of Eddy-McPhatter-Darin was also not without problems.

The guitar-savvy instrumentalist Duane Eddy was definitely an attraction for the dedicated who enjoyed fine musicianship, but the headliner for this tour was Bobby Darin, who was climbing music charts on both sides of the Atlantic with "Mack the Knife." He was no stranger to the Brits as his swimfest of teenage romance tunes, "Splish Splash" and "Queen of the Hop," were as popular in Newcastle as New York.

Even by 1960, the preeminent model for a music career was that of Frank Sinatra, who first struck it big in the 1940s and was still going strong on the airwaves, headlining at nightclubs and starring in motion pictures. Not only did Clyde McPhatter yearn to step up to the mature Frank Sinatra level but so did Bobby Darin. With the roaring success of "Mack the Knife," Darin decided it was time to make his move. He caught the British teenagers by surprise—and they weren't happy about it.

As Spencer Leigh looked back, he said, "Darin was not what some of the rockers wanted, but I thought he was fine."[25]

The first hint that something had been amiss was in a small item in *Billboard* on March 28, 1960, which carried the headline "London Bow Big for Darin, Eddy, McPhatter," but a line in the story read "Darin had a rough passage for the first house but adapted his act, bringing his hits in earlier . . ."[26]

By the next week, the rabid British press came at Darin with fangs bared. The popular music rag *Melody Maker* blanketed the top of its front page of April 2, 1960, with a squealing, antagonistic headline: "Darin Slams Back at British Rock Fans." The story began, "Bobby Darin this week hit back at the rock rowdies who have dogged his British concert tour with Duane Eddy, Clyde McPhatter . . . 'I'll never tour Britain again in a rock 'n' roll package show,' Darin told *Melody Maker* . . . 'The guys in the show are great but the tour was just one big mistake for me. I am trying to sell myself as a personality, not a 'big talent.' I am a ballad singer more than a beat singer. I have found the British audience the noisiest I have played to anywhere in the world . . . that barracking in Lewisham on my first show was the most shattering thing that has ever happened to me as a performer."[27]

Darin had begun his performance with a couple of finger-snapping non-rockers. Then he crooned instead of rocked on "Dream Lover" and "Clementine." By then, the audience began to twitch. When he next transitioned to the hoary chestnut "My Funny Valentine," the heckling began. Darin was not a novice performer and he knew he had to change the script. He next launched into the big beat of "Splish Splash," then "I Got a Woman," "Beyond the Sea," and "All Night Long."

As Wallis surmised, "Darin was neither the first nor by any means the last to learn that rock 'n' roll audiences want rock 'n' roll and not a poor man's Sinatra."[28]

Yet, the British audiences were forgiving. On April 23, 1960, in a prerecorded performance, Bobby Darin appeared on British television with a gig called *This is Bobby Darin*. He was the host of the show and, it turned out, a good person to tour with as he introduced other artists including Duane Eddy and Clyde McPhatter. The latter performer singing "Think Me a Kiss."[29]

By that time, the Eddy-McPhatter-Darin tour had broken up and everyone had gone their separate ways. On April 11, 1960, Darin flew back to the United States. He already had a weeklong gig scheduled at the Deauville Hotel in Miami Beach, then a couple of more stops before landing at the swanky Copacabana in Manhattan. Duane Eddy did even better. After his swing around the British Isles, he was able to extend his tour to debut on the European continent with bookings in France, Spain, and West Germany.[30]

As for Clyde McPhatter, it was back to the usual grind. By the end of April, he was headlining a show and dance at College Park Auditorium in Jackson, Mississippi. A blurb in the local newspaper read: "Students of Madison County Training School and All Schools in the community are invited to see the Lloyd Price, Clyde McPhatter, LaVern Baker show [also Bo Diddley, Joe Turner, Little Anthony and the Imperials, Sonny Turner and the Coasters] coming to College Park Auditorium . . . Buy your advance tickets early for only $2.00."[31]

CHAPTER THIRTEEN

LOVER PLEASE

A Friday night in May 1961 and another Sam Cooke/Clyde McPhatter tour arrived in Memphis, Tennessee.

At this point in time, Cooke was at the top of his game, one of the biggest names in popular music. He had hit big in 1957 with the #1 record "You Send Me," a string of moderate hits over the next three years, and then came back strong with "Chain Gang," a #2 record in 1960. Another Cooke tune, "Cupid," was beginning to take off. Cooke had begun the year with engagements in the Bahamas, and when he came back to the states, he and Clyde organized the current tour, adding the always popular Hank Ballard, and then other performers along the way.

Also on the tour was a new female singer named Aretha Franklin. The young songstress with a powerful voice signed with Columbia Records the year before. The big record company was not a good fit, as it tried to mainstream Franklin, not only in the tunes chosen for her to sing but where she was to perform as well, not hitting the chitlin' circuit until she was booked for one-week engagements at the Royal in Baltimore and Howard Theater in Washington, DC. For the tour Sam Cooke took her under his wing and she was enamored with him, saying, "It was Sam's tour as far as I was concerned. He followed me [on stage] and he just wore people out. He wrecked every place that we went . . . When he would come on, the building would just erupt."[1]

When the tour arrived in Memphis, it was a couple of hours before the show was scheduled to begin. The whole entourage was staying at the Lorraine Motel, the best accommodation in Memphis for visiting African Americans. For performers, it was also an advantageous location, as it was just a few blocks from Ellis Auditorium, a big venue in the city. As Clyde and Cooke stepped into the motel's lobby to check in, they were informed a telegram had arrived earlier and was waiting for them.

The NAACP (National Association for the Advancement of Colored People) had been directing efforts to desegregate music venues, taking particular umbrage at places that segregated audiences into Black sections and white seating. The NAACP had targeted the Ellis Auditorium ahead of the Cooke/McPhatter tour and the telegram informed the two singers that not only was the auditorium to be segregated for the show, but seating would be even more rigid. Sam Cooke's biographer Peter Guralnick laid out the scenario, "Negroes restricted to the left of the first, second and third balconies, thus limiting not only sight line and participation [there would be no coloureds dancing on the floor] but keeping their numbers to fewer than 1,000 in a crowd of 4,000."[2]

Clyde had already been through skirmishes of this type. As his drummer Bill Curtis commented, "Clyde integrated a couple of cities. In Raleigh, a club there had a section for Black people. His family wanted to come and see him perform. Clyde didn't want them put into the segregated section, he wanted down front, and if the club wasn't going to open up, he wasn't going to perform. He stood his ground and they eventually opened up the club to a mixed audience."[3]

According to *Jet* magazine, the Jim Crow structure at this particular club was more dire than Curtis remembered, and Clyde canceled a four-day nightclub engagement in Raleigh because "Negro patrons" were barred. The magazine reported, "The Mercury Record star said that when he arrived in town for the date, promoted by a white disk jockey, he learned of the 'no-Negroes' edict and promptly announced his decision to the owners of Thornton's Danceland Café." A life member of the NAACP and a follower of the southern student sit-in movement, McPhatter told *Jet*: "I think it's time for performers in the higher income brackets to take a definite stand in the battle for racial equality even if it hits them in the pocketbook."[4]

A similar battle happened with a nightclub in Atlanta called the Copa, said Curtis.[5]

At the time, in March 1963, the Atlanta situation was a major coup for Clyde. A headline in the pages of *The Carolinian* trumpeted, "Militant Artist Ends Atlanta Bias." The news story began: "Confronted with a jimcrow [Jim Crow] situation that could've resulted in his losing $3,000, Clyde McPhatter talked with the owner of the swank Copa niteclub here and persuaded him to drop his bias attitude toward Negro patrons."

Clyde had been booked into the café for a week's engagement, then afterward learned not only weren't "Negroes" welcome but that he was the first "colored attraction" to play the club. When local Black leaders learned of the situation at the Copa, they informed Clyde that if he performed there, they would picket the club. Clyde was not only a lifetime member of the NAACP but had made several appearances before the youth groups of the civil rights organization and donated to their cause. He decided to solve this problem for everyone concerned.

"When I pointed out the breaking down of Jim Crow barriers throughout the South in schools, public places and on transportation lines, he [Copa owner] relented," Clyde told *The Carolinian*. "A picket line wouldn't solve any of his or my problems, so he agreed to just quietly let any orderly guest come in."

Clyde then phoned several civil rights leaders in town and told them that they and their guests were welcome, and the picket line demonstration plans were canceled.[6] *Jet* observed, "Singer Clyde McPhatter instituted his own brand of militancy down in Atlanta and successfully talked management of the Copa night club to drop racial barriers."[7]

The Carolinian concluded its story: "That night about 15 Negro parties were admitted without incident. One waiter was heard to remark that 'they were much better behaved than many white parties he had served and their tips ran higher than he was accustomed to.'"[8]

In the September 1963 issue of *Ebony* magazine, a story headlined "Negro Entertainment" summarized: "The Negro entertainer of old usually has been forced to sell his wares to prejudiced audiences . . . The goals of the Negro entertainer of 1963 are essentially the same as those sought by his predecessor during the past century: to be judged strictly on talent, to discard undignified identities and stereotypes and to demand and assert his own humanity. The story of the Negro in the entertainment arts has been a growing affirmation of . . . citizenship. His final goal will not be reached until his story cannot be isolated from the larger panorama of American entertainment as a whole . . ."[9]

In 1960 Memphis's population stood at just under 500,000, with at least a quarter of that population being Black. In addition, the Beale Street area of the city had been a tremendous cauldron of blues music for decades. Nevertheless, Tennessee was a state committed to Jim Crow, and Memphis was always problematic to Black performers in transit.

"One night we were driving through Memphis, really just outside the city, and we got caught up between two cars," Curtis recalled. "They got us boxed in, and the car behind was bumping us. We couldn't get past the car in front. That's when we decided not to come through cities like Memphis at night again."[10]

Then there was the night of April 3, 1968. Clyde and Curtis were staying at the Lorraine Hotel for a Memphis gig. They stepped out on the balcony and saw Martin Luther King Jr. and his entourage. Everyone waved hello. After the show, Clyde and his band left town for another gig. On the road they were listening to the car radio and heard Martin Luther King Jr. was shot.

Sam Cooke had his own Memphis war stories. The last time he was in Memphis before the March 1961 tour, his car ran out of fuel. He sent his brother to get some gas and waited with the car. As he was standing by the side of the road, a white policeman pulled up and told him to move the car. Cooke explained the situation, but the policeman didn't care. "Well, push it, then." As Cooke told the story, he informed the policeman that he was a singer, his name was Sam Cooke and he didn't push cars, adding for emphasis, "If Frank Sinatra was here, you wouldn't ask him to push no car." Meanwhile, Charles arrived and tried to distract his angry brother before the situation got out of hand. Sam Cooke, shook him off and barked at the cop. "If it was all that important, you push the fucking car. You may not know who I am, but your wife does. Go home and ask your wife about me."[11]

While that incident ended positively, Cooke understood that African American performers did have to tread carefully in the South. The year before, a Cooke/McPhatter tour was going through Birmingham, Alabama, when their New York–licensed bus started drawing attention from a white streetcorner mob. Since some white acts were on the tour, the passengers on the bus were mistaken for a group of Freedom Riders.

What to do about the Memphis show posed a quandary for Clyde and Cooke. Clyde's view was that Black performers were no better than indentured servants in a business that was dominated by white people and governed by greed. On the other hand, by refusing to play a show from which you were contractually committed could have adverse consequences, "from legal and financial pitfalls to the one result no entertainer ever wants to contemplate, the alienation of a substantial portion of his audience."

Clyde and Cooke went around and around on this, eventually deciding they weren't going to play before a segregated audience. Over time, this confrontation has been recognized to be a bravura Sam Cooke moment as Cooke biographers often accentuate the Memphis story as part of the singer's change from pop music idol to one committed to the cause of desegregation. The biographers then forget about Clyde, who had been on the desegregation road longer.

Guralnick wrote about the incident, first quoting Cooke's brothers who said, "Ordinarily Sam knew just how far to push the buttons and he knew what buttons not to push because it might hinder his career. This time he didn't give a fuck about his career as we were right in the middle of it." According to Charles Cooke, Sam had told him to check out the audience, which was segregated with all the Black people in the balcony. Then Sam Cooke said, "Shit, forget it. Cancel it." Guralnick writes that he (Sam Cooke) released a statement to the Negro press declaring that it was against his policy and the policy of his promoter to play to a forced segregated audience.

The Cooke pronouncement read: "This is the first time that I have refused to perform at show time simply because I have not been faced with a situation similar to this one . . . [to the NAACP] I hope by refusing to play to a segregated audience it will help to break down racial segregation here and if I am ever booked here again it won't be necessary to do a similar thing."[12]

Another heroic Cooke bio reads: "He [Cooke] returned to Memphis, and another segregated audience at Ellis Auditorium. He refused to play unless the audience members were seated together. His requests were denied and he was met with threats, but he didn't back down. Two hours before the show was scheduled to start, Cooke cancelled it."[13]

Over time, the Memphis confrontation has been completely co-opted by the legend of Sam Cooke. Where were Clyde and the other performers when all this was happening?

No slight to the wonderful Sam Cooke, but when the press got wind of the Memphis situation, after a calming lead paragraph, it reported a much different scenario: "Top singers Sam Cooke and Clyde McPhatter this week refused to perform before a segregated audience in the municipality-owned Ellis Auditorium here [Memphis]. NAACP President Jesse H. Turner wired Mr. McPhatter, an active NAACP life member, informing him of the Jim Crow seating arrangements. The NAACP message was delivered to Mr. McPhatter upon his arrival here, a few minutes before show time. The NAACP expressed opposition to the seating plan. Mr. McPhatter agreed, as did the other stars who were asked what could be done at such a late hour. After a brief conference with NAACP Field Secretary L.C. Bates, the stars [McPhatter and Cooke] elected not to perform. They were joined by vocalist Aretha Franklin and the Olympics, a singing group."[14]

In Memphis, the NAACP came to Clyde McPhatter, not Sam Cooke, because he had been active in civil rights issues going back to the end of the 1950s. According to Curtis, Clyde was an advocate and supporter of the Atlanta Student Movement, which mobilized the city's university students to end segregation in public facilities, and on March 15, 1960, over two hundred students sat-in at eleven restaurants in downtown Atlanta.[15]

Early in July 1960, Clyde addressed the NAACP at its convention in St. Paul, Minnesota, and as one press report noted, he shared the spotlight with "young NAACP freedom fighters from across the land during youth night."

Referring to student protest leaders, Clyde said, "The NAACP is proud of the young people who, rather than continue to endure the humiliation of Jim Crow, are willing to risk verbal abuse, physical assault, expulsion from school and imprisonment in Dixie dungeons."

Clyde even commended white civil rights activists, saying, "The NAACP hails the young white students, who, rejecting prejudice, have stood shoulder to shoulder with Afro-American youth in this irresistible crusade."[16]

In December 1960, *Jet* magazine reported, "Adding their efforts to Atlanta sit-in demonstrations, singer Clyde McPhatter, John Wesly Dobbs, 77, father of opera star Mattiwilda Dobbs [who got out of his sick bed to join the march], and the Rev. Martin Luther King Sr., carry protest signs in picket lines." A photo showed all three with their particular signs. Clyde's read: "The presence of segregation is the absence of democracy: Jim Crow Must Go!"[17]

Atlanta wasn't the only city where Clyde protested.

During the 1963 civil rights campaign in Birmingham, Alabama, white supremacists bombed the A. G. Gaston Motel, which catered to Black patrons and at the time was the headquarters of the Southern Christian Leadership Conference's directors Martin Luther King Jr., Ralph Abernathy, and Fred Shuttlesworth. Fortunately, they weren't injured. Again, Curtis recounted, he and Clyde were at the Gaston Hotel, and "we got caught up in that and then we marched."[18]

Back in Tennessee, African Americans in Fayette and Haywood counties started registering to vote en masse. In response, white merchants, principally the gas dealers in the area, stopped delivering to Black gas station owners and farm fuel users. According to the press, Gulf Oil distributor Rube Rhea removed the oil tanks from one Negro gas station owner and told suppliers from other oil firms to do the same to their Negro clients as long as they persisted in their right to exercise the ballot.

Clyde and organist Bill Doggett, who had a huge hit in 1956 with "Honky Tonk Parts 1 and 2," started a counterprotest, urging fellow artists, who like them drove thousands of miles between gigs on one-night tours, to join them in a "selective patronage" campaign against certain gas companies including Gulf, Texaco, Amoco, and Esso. McPhatter and Doggett publicly returned their Gulf Oil credit cards. In a joint announcement, Doggett and McPhatter stated, "As members of the NAACP we feel that all show people should give them their unqualified support in their campaign, which we support, to get Negroes to stop buying gas from those who don't care about our civil rights."

It was not an empty gesture. By one estimate at least $5 million was spent yearly by theatrical people on the road for gas and oil. Said McPhatter and Doggett, "The least we can do to help is to refrain from the purchase of these companies' products."[19]

In 1967, *Ebony* magazine sought to dispel the notion that it was the financial support from white donors that kept civil rights organizations afloat. In a story headlined "Lifers Dispel Myth of Laxity," the magazine editorialized: "A long-standing rumor that Negroes are unwilling to pay the cost of their own freedom cannot be substantiated by facts, according to the NAACP, for the organization's records show that its first two life members were Negroes: John B. Nail, a Harlem real estate man, led the way back in 1927, along with Dr. Ernest Alexander, and among them many prominent in American life—Marian

Anderson, A. Philip Randolph, Count Basie, Harry Belafonte, Chuck Berry, Althea Gibson, Dr. Martin Luther King, Clyde McPhatter . . ."[20]

The environment for Black entertainers was still perilous in 1967. When Deborah McPhatter and her mother accompanied Clyde on tour that year, one of the stops on the chitlin' circuit was Tifton, Georgia. Deborah took the opportunity to visit a local Black-owned shoe store to get a pair of sandals repaired. She dropped off the shoes, which were never to be seen again. Afterward she wrote this note on the ticket: "Summer of 1967, KKK ran us out of town. Had to leave shoes. My father with band and 'mommie.' Thought I was going to die! Will never forget."

Deborah McPhatter, who grew up in the Northeast where her life circulated between New York and New Jersey, sardonically noted that tour journey was "educational." She had friends and family who were white, so to see signs for the first time that read "for colored only" or "for whites only" was shocking to her. Laughing about it decades later, she said, "Never did get the sandals out of repair. The car and van for Clyde's family and band members came and got us as the KKK marched down the street. Loved those darn sandals; my dad had them made for me in the Village [Greenwich Village, New York City]."[21]

Like other Black entertainers of the era, Clyde had to balance his activism against his career. He still had to spend time in recording studios and go on the road to perform. His songs had to be good enough to attract the attention of teenage record buyers, and his shows had to be entertaining despite long, long road trips. He was no longer a young man, but he was in a young man's game, pop music. He didn't have options. Aging white singers like Perry Como and Andy Williams could host television shows or, like Frankie Avalon and Rick Nelson, appear in movies. Some aging Black performers could move on to nightclubs, Las Vegas, or prestigious art centers such as Carnegie Hall in New York. Clyde was not old enough to be esteemed like a Count Basie or jazzy enough like a Sarah Vaughan.

While signing with Mercury gave Clyde's career a boost, he was still on the downside as a hitmaker. His last major record was "A Lover's Question" from 1958, and his last crossover song to dent the charts in a substantial way was "Ta Ta" in 1960. For whatever reason—too much time on the road, civil rights activism, or personal demons—1961 was a washout year. Too little time in the recording studio meant just a handful of songs to be released, only one of which, "I Never Knew," attained what could only be called mediocre success.

Help was on its way and came from a place so far from Clyde's frame of reference that it could have been sent, for all he knew, from another planet. And initially Clyde didn't know much of anything about the celestial gift, which was a song called "Lover Please," other than that he didn't like it.

In 1974 singer/songwriter Billy Swan had a #1 hit record, a little tune called "I Can Help." In his long slog to fame, Swan had a number of brushes with good fortune, including writing the song "Lover Please." He was born in 1943, in the small burg of Cape Girardeau, Missouri, which is located near the borders of Illinois, Kentucky, Tennessee, and Arkansas. He grew up on country music before switching allegiance to rock 'n' roll. It seemed his destiny was to be a Nashville musician or songwriter because by the time he was teenager he could play multiple instruments from piano to guitar. At the age of sixteen he wrote a poem for English class that would become the basis for "Lover Please."

Swan's first big break came in the early 1960s. He was in a local band called Mirt Mirty and the Rhythm Steppers, which, as just the Rhythm Steppers, recorded "Lover Please," on the Louis label, created by Bill Black, who not only was Elvis Presley's bass player but led his own group, Bill Black's Combo, which charted five Top Twenty instrumental hits in a row from 1959 to 1961.[22]

The Louis label was created in 1962 and was based in Memphis. Black was an esteemed musician (later in the Rock and Roll Hall of Fame). His involvement attracted the Mercury Records representative in the area, and when he heard the song by the Rhythm Steppers, he thought it might work for one of his company's performers. The record went first to corporate headquarters in Chicago. They, too, liked the tune and passed the record to New York, home base at the time for Shelby Singleton, Mercury's recording director, with a note that the song was perfect for Clyde McPhatter and he should record it.[23]

Singleton was the right person to handle this request. Considering the southernish origins of the Rhythm Steppers, its version was straight rockabilly. Singleton, who was from the South, in 1960 was named the head of Mercury's Nashville office. He was so good that he was also made the head of A&R in New York as well. In June 1962, *Billboard* spotlighted him in a column called "Man Of The Week," noting "A typical day in Singleton's peripatetic life is to do a recording session in New York in the a.m., fly to Nashville for a session in the afternoon, and fly back to New York that same day to edit tapes in Mercury's New York offices. At 29, Singleton has become a fireball among A&R men."[24]

That year Mercury promoted Singleton to company vice president. Why not? One of his major successes in 1962 was Clyde McPhatter's "Lover Please," which fell into his lap. Since he was steeped in country, rockabilly, and R&B, he could transition the tune from rockabilly to ebullient, soulful pop.

Singleton listened to the Rhythm Steppers song several times before phoning the singer. "Clyde," he said, "I'm sending you over a record I want you to listen to. Learn it today, and we'll record it tomorrow night. We have to move fast." Singleton was thinking the Rhythm Steppers version or another rockabilly remake could hit the market before Mercury made its move.

An unexpected roadblock was Clyde, who didn't like the song, telling Singleton "It's no good. This song is not my kind of thing." Part of the problem was that so many of Clyde's recent records had been done with big string orchestras, and he had gotten used to recording lush ballads. He wasn't sure he wanted to go back to a basic rock 'n' roll recording session. Singleton finally convinced him to at least try out the song. Clyde acquiesced, and Singleton quickly organized a recording for the next night.

Clyde and a group of musicians, engineers, and producers gathered at Capitol Studios in New York, and as can be expected with such a rushed schedule, things didn't go well at the start. Clyde was still griping that he didn't like the song. The original arrangement called for two guitars, drums, bass, piano, two saxes, two trumpets and a small chorus. After a few tries, Singleton ditched the trumpets and one of saxes and had those guys hand-clap instead. The bonus here was the remaining sax player. Singleton had hired King Curtis, one best sax players in the business, who played, as Singleton told the press, a "yakkety" saxophone that had a "flutter-tongued effect."

Singleton was a man on a mission, and that was to beat to market anyone else who might have been thinking of recording the song. The Clyde McPhatter interpretation had to be established as "the version" in the public's mind, so he kept the engineers working through the night, processing tape. The next morning, the first one hundred pressings were ready for shipment to radio disc jockeys. In a blink of an eye, young Billy Swan was going to have a hit record, and so was Clyde McPhatter.[25]

What Singleton saw in "Lover Please" was the possibility of merging a song with Southern origins with a New York recording style. He felt the Nashville sound and the New York sound began in different places but could be made to work together. According to Singleton, the Nashville sound derived from musicians recording extemporaneously, where the singer goes over his or her song with the pianist and the musicians take it from there. New York musicians mostly used written arrangements. In September 1962, Singleton brought Clyde McPhatter to Nashville for recording sessions at the RCA Victor Studios.[26]

"Lover Please" hit the turntables of deejays early in 1962, with the first trade publication reviews coming on February 10. *Cash Box* chose eight new songs for its "Pick of the Week," only two of which became hits, "Dream Baby (How Long Must I Dream)" by Roy Orbison and "Lover Please" by Clyde. The review read: "We'll bet our bottom dollar that Clyde McPhatter has one of his biggest sides in quite a while with this one. Tabbed 'Lover Please,' it's a tremendous twister that has the vocal and instrumental sound of success. Great arrangement."[27]

The key word in this review is "twister," which referred to the dance called the twist. Chubby Checker's song, "The Twist," went to #1 in 1960 and then returned to the charts at the end of 1961, becoming a #1 song all over again, ushering in the first wave of rock 'n' roll dance crazes. "Lover Please" had a twistable dance beat, which was something the *Billboard* reviewer highlighted: "A snappy rhythm number with a handclapping beat. McPhatter shouts out the message in fine style. Good dance number, with upward modulation that helps it build."[28]

In April, *Cash Box*'s listing of the top R&B songs in the country showed "Lover Please" still holding firm at #4. The top three songs were all dance tunes: "Slow Twistin'" by Chubby Checker, "Mashed Potato Time" by Dee Dee Sharp, and "Twistin' the Night Away" by Sam Cooke.[29]

There was one other oddity about the record. The B-side song was written by Clyde and his longtime guitarist and music coordinator Jimmy Oliver, who according to Bill Curtis had worked with Clyde since his days on 124th Street in Harlem when he was doing doo-wop on street corners.[30] Doo-wop groups often worked with a regular guitarist, who appeared on stage with them. The original Drifters boasted guitar man Walter Adams, who in 1953 died of a heart attack, and Oliver officially took over that slot. Oliver stayed with Clyde until April 1962, when he left for what one writer said was "unspecified reasons." The gossipy "New York Beat" in *Jet* magazine simply wrote, "Singer Clyde McPhatter and his long-time accompanist Jimmy Oliver came to a parting of the way."[31] Curtis suggested that, by this time, Clyde was becoming a difficult person to be around, especially when on the sauce.[32]

Mercury Records, sensing a big hit from Clyde, booked full-page ads in the trade publications. The *Billboard* promotion touted the star and the song to deejays and jukebox owners. This was publicity aimed at the industry, not consumers. In varying typefaces and sizes, the sparse verbiage read: Clyde Pleases . . . ; "Lover Please" (large letters); Clyde McPhatter; Mercury 71941 (small letters); A Big Money-Maker; Here's another Big-Profit Hit by Clyde McPhatter; Mercury Records logo.[33] For *Cash Box*, Mercury featured a head and shoulders shot of Clyde with similar sparse wording. The message line was changed to "A Sure 'Money Maker.'"[34]

Clyde hit the road again. On February 23, he was in Washington, DC, where the local newspaper caught up with him: "Singing star Clyde McPhatter hit town Wednesday for a fast swing through the disc jockey studios and three, night-time, teen-age hops. He was promoting his latest record, 'Lover Please.'"[35]

After years of trying to be more urbane, with ballads heavy with strings and backed by full orchestras, this late-career song put him back in front of teenagers. The good thing, of course, was that teenagers listened to the radio and bought his records. As a solo artist, "Lover Please" was the biggest hit of his career since "A Lover's Question" four years before. The song climbed to #7 on the pop charts and to #4 on the R&B listing.

Shelby Singleton wasn't going to let the Clyde McPhatter moment go to waste and by spring had pushed a follow-up Clyde record into the market. Nothing new this time. Instead, he plucked the Thurston Harris hit, "Little Bitty Pretty One" from 1957, and had Clyde record it. The song always had a powerful groove, and Clyde's approach didn't change it much—the new version was just less bluesy and more pop than the original. Still, Clyde was hot and the song climbed to #25 on the pop charts but was a no-show on the R&B lists.

Then things got incestuous at Mercury.

In September, Mercury released another Clyde McPhatter single with "Maybe" on the A-side and "I Do Believe" on the B-side. Both songs list Margie Singleton as a cowriter. *Cash Box* review noted, "The exciting, fast-moving 'I Do Believe' moves along at a sizzling twist [an over-used word in 1962] clip. Great assist from the Merry Melody Singers . . ."[36]

Margie Singleton was Shelby Singleton's wife and was not only a songwriter, but also one of the Merry Melody Singers. She wrote the B-side tune, "Next to Me," for Clyde's hit song "Little Bitty Pretty One."

"My husband at that time, Shelby Singleton, started bringing Black artists to Nashville to get a different sound," said Margie Singleton, conjuring up her past. "There was no place for Black people to stay in Nashville except one crummy motel, so we would let the singers—Brook Benton, Damita Jo, Clyde McPhatter—stay in our house while they were here to record. I played 'Next to Me' to Clyde. He liked it and recorded it without much change. I'm basically a country-blues artist. That's where my heart is."

With Clyde, things could suddenly go off-track, and in Nashville things did.

"We were in our offices looking for songs for Clyde, Shelby was in the next room," Margie retraced the moment. "I was singing a song for Clyde when he grabbed me and kissed me."

Margie was both surprised and offended. Black or white, in the South, it was not, err, "gentlemanly" to grab a married woman for a buss on the lips. "Clyde was a great artist, and I had already given him the song 'Next to Me,'" she said. Then remembering the kiss incident, she added, "I didn't think too much of Clyde as a person."[37]

It's hard to say what Clyde was thinking, or not thinking, at that moment. The year was 1962, the location was the South, and he decided to kiss a white woman. Just seven years before, fourteen-year-old Emmett Till was lynched in Mississippi for allegedly offending a white woman. Margie Singleton may have been "the white girl that wrote the blues" and taken a liberal attitude toward race relations, but she was born in a small Louisiana town and married Shelby at thirteen years of age. When Margie told her husband about the incident, he wisely advised, "don't make a fuss."

She didn't and the two ended up working together on many projects. The singles and albums they did together just didn't congeal.

"Maybe" with "I Do Believe" did not chart at all. Nor did Clyde's last release in 1962, "The Best Man Cried" with "Stop" on the B-side. Both of those cuts were credited to Clyde McPhatter with the Merry Melody Singers.

"I formed the group, the Merry Melody Singers, with three of the Jordanaires, the group that often served as the background singers for Elvis Presley on recordings and live performances," said Margie. "It was Gordon Stoker, Bill Matthews and Ray Walker, me and Nellie Kirkland, who had a high, beautiful voice. Sometimes Priscilla Mitchell, who was married to singer Jerry Reed, sang with us. We called her Prissy."[38]

A bit of trade publication puffery about Shelby Singleton included this note: "Margie Singleton, who has recorded on the Mercury label for a long time. She is known as a singer, but also writes songs, among them many important tunes."[39] Margie Singleton had been recording country songs since 1957. She signed with the Mercury label in 1960. Her biggest hit, "Keeping Up with the Joneses," was a duet with Faron Young. As a songwriter, she wrote a couple of hits for Brook Benton. In 1949, she married Shelby Singleton. They divorced in 1965, and Margie moved to United Artists Records.

In 1962, Mercury Records released two Clyde McPhatter albums. The first was called "Lover Please," which featured the best-selling song. With "soul" music in ascendence, the second album was called "Rhythm and Soul," and the credits read Clyde McPhatter with the Merry Melody Singers.

The *Cash Box* review read: "Clyde McPhatter has won many laurels in the past for his distinctive, highly-personal style of singing the blues and this new Mercury LP outing seems destined to earn the chanter a flock of new fans. With some first-rate backings from the Merry Melody Singers . . ."[40]

For as much as Shelby Singleton pushed his wife, the very talented Margie Singleton, into Clyde's professional orbit, nothing worked for them in concert with each other. Margie worked well with Brook Benton, writing his hit "Lie To Me," and Damita Jo—"I just loved her," said Margie—there was no incoming tide for Clyde. Perhaps the disconnect began with the unwanted kiss from Clyde or Shelby Singleton trying, unprofessionally, to reward his wife by getting her to write for a big star. Shelby, who gets kudos for reviving Clyde's career, also should be credited with helping to kill it as well, because after "Little Bitty Pretty One" a penumbra drifted over Clyde's association with Mercury—the law of unintended consequences.

In the year-end *Cash Box* survey of R&B records and artists, Clyde McPhatter was still in the mix, although beginning to slide. For "Best Male Vocalist," Clyde was listed at #14. Ahead of him in 1962 were singers associated with him or his prior groups, Sam Cooke (#3), Brook Benton (#4), and Ben E. King (#13). Behind him was Jackie Wilson (#19).

As to the "Top R&B Records of 1962," Clyde's "Lover Please" only came in at #40. Among the songs ahead of it were King Curtis's "Soul Twist" (#7), Sam Cooke's "Twistin' The Night Away" (#9) and "Having a Party" (#36), and Ben E. King's "Don't Play That Song" (#21).[41] However, it did chart better than Brook Benton's "Lie to Me" (#50), which was produced by Mercury Records, cowritten by Margie Singleton, and backed by the Merry Melody Singers.

CHAPTER FOURTEEN

CRYING WON'T HELP YOU NOW

The Apollo Theater in Harlem, once the premier venue in America for African American performers, first opened in 1913 as a burlesque showcase, and the patronage was white. After it was purchased by Sidney Cohen in 1934, it became "the" place to perform for Black singers and entertainers. The very talented, merely talented, and, with its amateur night, sometimes the not-so-talented took to the stage there. The audience was appreciative of good singing, dancing, and comedy, and if you had it, you were enthusiastically welcomed there, and that welcome was nondiscriminatory in terms of sexual orientation. If you were good, it didn't matter if you were straight, gay, transgender, or from another planet, you were welcomed on the stage.[1]

Unlike in white America, the Black entertainment structure, from the Jim Crow era onward, was surprisingly liberal in its attitude toward homosexuality. Black burlesque shows such as the Brown Skin Models, which often featured males dressed as women, trouped across America playing the chitlin' circuit even in the most conservative states of the South and Midwest. Popular R&B singers of the late 1940s and early 1950s such as Larry Darnell and Bobby Marchan got their start in these burlesque shows.

Down in New Orleans, the famed Dew Drop Inn, which opened in 1945 as a venue for African American performers, boasted drag queen Patsy Valdalia (Irving Ale) as one of its longtime masters of ceremonies. In the 1960s, one of the most popular attractions at the Apollo was the Jewel Box Revue, a troupe of female impersonators.

A list of LGBT luminaries who performed at the Apollo is deep and brilliant. Alberta Hunter, who was a lesbian, is said to have appeared at the Apollo around 1930, which was before the audience shifted from white to Black. In the following decades, an unofficial list of LGBT performers who appeared at the Apollo would include Billie Holiday, Johnny Mathis, Nina Simone, Sister Rosetta Tharpe, Little Richard, Big Mama Thornton, Billy Preston, Bessie Smith, Arthur Conley, Luther Vandross, and Clyde McPhatter.[2]

Not everyone on the list would be thrilled at the inclusion of their name. Clyde McPhatter was one of those who would be unhappy to see his nomenclature on that docket. Since no gay man has come forward to say he was Clyde's lover, there is no personal testimonial support that Clyde was homosexual, and many people who knew him would swear up and down that he was a straight dude. Conversely, other people who also knew him well attest to the opposite and that he struggled mightily to control a more natural sexual orientation. Ruth Brown called Clyde bisexual. Maybe she got it right. He allegedly had two children with two different women whom he did not wed and did not have kids with three women he did marry.

As mentioned, Clyde was befriended and had his career aided by two men, Billy Ward and Irvin Feld, who became father figures to him—and the crazy murkiness of Clyde's personal life begins here.

In November 2005, the *Washington Post* ran a column about contentiousness between Kenneth Feld and the Washington, DC, business magazine *Regardie's*, which folded in 1992. The *Post*'s article recounted *Regardie's* "unearthed family secrets that had been whispered about in Washington for decades," that Kenneth's father Irvin Feld was "a closeted homosexual" and that was the reason his wife killed herself. Kenneth was quoted as saying: "to say Irvin was a homosexual—what did that prove? That charge is an absolute lie . . . I can't buy the statements about his alleged sexual preference contributing to my mother's death."[3]

Irvin Feld had two children from his marriage.

Billy Ward was a good friend to Johnnie Ray. He was also the one who recruited Clyde McPhatter to the Dominoes. According to someone who knew Ward in the mid-1950s, he, too, was a closeted gay person. Ronald Isley of the Isley Brothers said of Ward, "He was a genius, but was 'funny.'" When asked what he meant by 'funny,' Isley said, "He was a nice-looking guy who never married. We knew he liked men." When asked the confirmation question whether Ward was gay, Isley answered to the affirmative, "Yes."[4]

This doesn't mean that Ward was not intimate with his business partner, Rose Marks—the rumor that they were having an affair certainly provided him cover.

Singer/songwriter Billy Vera, who has been in the music business since the 1960s and seemingly knew everyone, tells this humorous tale about soft-blues singer Charles Brown, who was gay.

First a little background. In 1944, Cecil Gant, a Black serviceman, had a huge record with "I Wonder." His tenor voice arranged against a slow-piano beat would set the standard for the soft sound of the blues that would develop in the late 1940s and early 1950s. The singers, of which Charles Brown was an early practitioner, were later called the "sepia Sinatras" or blues crooners. Perhaps, the pinnacle of this type of music was Johnny Ace's recordings in the early 1950s, but other singers included Percy Mayfield, Ivory Joe Hunter, and Charles Brown. Outside of a solo career, Charles Brown is most known as the lead singer for Johnny Moore's Three Blazers, as Clyde McPhatter was the lead singer for Billy Ward's Dominoes. The best known of the Three Blazers tunes is the eternal "Merry Christmas Baby."

In 1949, Brown married popular Black singer Mabel Scott. Vera, who knew Scott in her later years, once asked her, how did she not know her husband was gay. Her answer: "He was on the road a lot, and I was on the road a lot. We didn't really see much of each other." They divorced in 1951. Brown would marry again.[5]

Between Frank Sinatra and Elvis Presley, the biggest teen idol with the wildest and most adoring fans was Johnnie Ray, whose song "Cry" jumped to the top of the record charts in 1951. Screaming teenage girls turned out in the thousands to watch Ray's very personal, primal performances, all the while singing the most lachrymose of songs.

Although for a moment in time Ray was America's reigning heartthrob, he was also homosexual. He knew it, the folks around him knew it, and the police knew it. In 1951 Ray was arrested in Detroit for "soliciting and accosting," which was defined this way: "Any person who shall accost, solicit or invite another in any public place, or in or from any building or vehicle, by word, gesture or any other means, to commit prostitution or to do any other lewd or immoral act, shall be guilty of a misdemeanor."

On May 14, 1952, a gossip column by Louella Parsons screamed, "Cry Girls Cry: Johnnie Ray to Wed." Eleven days later Ray married Marilyn Morrison in New York. In attendance was the city's mayor Vincent Impellitteri. Marilyn was pregnant at the time, but months later she lost the baby. They separated, not filing for divorce until 1954.[6]

Little Richard was never one to hide his homosexuality, yet he too had girlfriends and even married. Before she died in 2022, famed burlesque dancer Angel Lee (Audrey Sherborne) told this story. "I met Little Richard when I was sixteen. I was just graduating high school. I didn't start my affair right away; it took a moment for him to get there. It was when I had just left my parents. Little Richard was fun." Lee didn't leave Little Richard until she met Screamin' Jay Hawkins, but they remained friends for years afterward.[7]

Little Richard met Audrey Sherborne around 1956. Three years later he married Ernestine Harvin Campbell. That marriage lasted four years. Little Richard admitted, "I was a neglectful husband . . . we were not compatible the way we should have been . . . I never loved her in the way a man should love his wife. I loved her more like a sister. Ernestine was jealous and she had reason enough to be, because I wasn't a husband. I didn't give her any attention. I was gay and I wasn't concerned."

For her part, Ernestine offered, "We had normal husband-and-wife relations, definitely. That's why it was so easy for me to discount anything that anyone said to me at that time about him. If he was gay, he was very good about hiding it from me!"[8]

Apparently, Ernestine was the only person in America who didn't know Little Richard was gay.

In midcentury America, the music industry operated similarly to the motion picture industry in regard to homosexuality: don't ask, don't tell. There was good reason for this. The opprobrium of homosexuality, especially for men, was so strong that any hint of such behavior was considered a career killer, which was something Clyde had to consider because he too was a heartthrob, especially to African American teenagers, who would shriek just as loudly when he performed as did white teenagers for Johnnie Ray.

Strangely affected and flamboyantly attired, Liberace signaled who he was to those with intuitive receptors; to everyone else he was a handsome, entertaining musician. In "Mr. Sandman," their hit song from 1954, the Chordettes addressed Liberace's hetero-attractiveness in these lyrics: "Mr. Sandman, bring us a dream / Give him a pair of eyes with come-hither gleam / Give him a lonely heart like Pagliacci / And lots of wavy hair like Liberace."

In the mid-1950s Liberace was an extremely popular entertainer, not only in America but in the United Kingdom as well. When he arrived in London for a tour in 1956, a columnist in the *Daily Mirror* wrote: "I've spoken to sad but kindly men on this newspaper who have met every celebrity arriving from the United States for the past thirty years. They all say that this deadly, winking, sniggering, snuggling, chromium-plated, scent-impregnated, luminous, quivering, giggling, fruit-flavored, mincing, ice-covered heap of mother love has had the biggest reception and impact on London since Charlie Chaplin arrived at the same station, Waterloo, on September 12, 1921."[9]

The most offending phrase in the diatribe was "fruit-flavored," as "fruit" was a derogatory phrase for a homosexual in the United States. So, in effect the columnist was saying publicly that Liberace was a homosexual—at the time a career killer.

Liberace sued for libel. You could assume someone was a homosexual, even know for sure that was the case, but apparently you could not say such a thing in public. The case was finally brought to a conclusion in 1959. Liberace won and was awarded 8,000 pounds (just about $200,000 in 2024 dollars), at the time the largest libel settlement in British legal history.[10]

Liberace achieved his victory by lying. He declared he was not a homosexual and that even the thought of it offended him. His other strategy was to appear in public with women, most famously with Sonja Heine, the three-time Olympic gold medal winner and herself an entertainer. Together, they were fodder for the tabloids and chewed up a lot of press presence. Liberace told his biographer, Scott Thorson, that they actually had an affair, but Thorson didn't fully believe that assertion.[11]

Years later, Liberace explained the reason for his deceitfulness: "In 1956, people were destroyed by that accusation. It hurt me. People stayed away from my show in droves. I went from the top to the bottom in a very short time, and I had to fight for my life."[12]

The British press had learned to be careful. In 1959, when *Disc* magazine lined up sixteen songs for commentary, the columnist Don Nicholl placed his review of two Rock Hudson songs from the film *Pillow Talk* just before his commentary about Clyde McPhatter's new single "There You Go" / "You Went Back on Your Word." Addressing the closeted actor, Nicholl wrote, "Rock's voice is light and a little stagey, but not unattractive." At the time, it was not publicly known that Rock was gay—and the same might be said of Clyde. Nicholl's review, as noted, got more to the unmentionable point, when he began with, "That high-pitched, almost feminine voice of Mr. McPhatter."[13]

If he saw the review, Clyde ignored it. He certainly didn't sue. But the United Kingdom would prove difficult on his return trip in the late 1960s.

In the repressive 1950s, performers who were homosexual split off in two directions. The first group tried to hide this part of themselves and often attempted to live the life of a straight person. The psychological harm of trying to be someone he or she wasn't was immense, which is why, when journalists and music enthusiasts try to define the reason why the smiling, gregarious Clyde McPhatter descended into drink and irascibility, it was often attributed to his attempts to hide his true self.

As a pop music reviewer with psychologist tendencies wrote: "Clyde's life was also complicated by depression. In the 1950s, in America, no one spoke openly about any sexual orientation other than heterosexuality. It was often written that Clyde believed his fans had deserted him, leading to his depression and increased drinking. That 'conventional wisdom' was established at a time when sexual orientation was not openly discussed and few fans knew what his peers in the entertainment industry understood—that Clyde was bisexual . . . Because Clyde was the son of a Baptist minister and was close to his family, and because the Baptist Church at that time had no tolerance for what would have then been considered 'sexual deviation,' Clyde may also have felt he had disappointed or embarrassed his family."[14]

Billy Vera, who was heterosexual, spent a lot of time around homosexual performers and music industry folk. He said about Clyde McPhatter, "I never heard that he was gay."[15] The famed lead singer of the Drifters was Rudy Lewis, who Vera did say was a closeted homosexual and whose life, like Clyde's, ended in shambles with death coming far too soon.

When Clyde left the Drifters, he was replaced as lead singer by a number of talented individuals such as Johnny Moore and Bobby Hendricks. By 1958, the Drifters were failing, complaining to, and about, management and, even worse, getting into a fight on stage at the Apollo. Bill Millar wrote in his history of the Drifters, "Frequent bickering with George Treadwell had created a deep and irreconcilable rift. The Drifters were sacked *en masse*." There was a downside to all that. Treadwell had a contract drawn up in 1954 to present the Drifters twice yearly, for ten years, at the Apollo. Not wishing to break the contract, Treadwell looked around, noticed a group called the Five Crowns, that was on the lower bill of an Apollo show, hired them and changed their name to the Drifters. Two of the new Drifters would stand in as lead singer: Charlie Thomas, and most importantly, Benjamin Earl Nelson, better known as Ben E. King. The latter lasted two years as a member of the Drifters before he too went off on a solo career. He was replaced by Rudy Lewis, who would be the lead on such great Drifters' hits as "Some Kind of Wonderful," "Up on the Roof," and "On Broadway." The last song was released in 1963. While Lewis was successful in keeping his homosexuality a secret, his health deteriorated quickly through a heroin addiction and other disorders. He died in 1964 at the age of twenty-seven.[16]

"Rudy Lewis, the drug use, dealing with the trauma of not being able to be who you are, a lot of that happened before I was born (in 1958)," said Tina Treadwell. "But, I do know he was incredibly talented, had a beautiful voice. He was never like the other guys, going out with women. He stuck to himself and ended up in Harlem dead of a drug overdose."[17]

There was a second choice, another way to go if you were homosexual singer. For that post–World War II generation of R&B singers who would lead the country into the new world of rock 'n' roll, many were forthright about who they were. The surprising broad-mindedness of the R&B crowd and its fans allowed a number of homosexual performers to go their own way and do it successfully.

The first of the new breed, teen-minded, gay R&B singers to score nationally was Larry Darnell (Leo Edward Donald), who in 1949 boasted two monster hits, the first being "I'll Get Along Somehow," which shot to #2 on the R&B charts. When he followed that up with a song called "For You My Love," the initial review in *Billboard* was tepid at best: "Strong-voiced shouter hollers an okay up-tempo blues with fair combo backing."[18] Somehow the reviewer got everything wrong about the song. "Strong-voiced" was a little much for Darnell, whose voice rolled toward a higher range, although not quite the pitch that Clyde McPhatter would hit a year later with the Dominoes. And "hollers" was more derogatory than accurate. The song was recorded on Regal Records, and the 78 rpm record reads "Jump Blues with Band." This was the sound of quick-paced R&B that would become rock 'n' roll by the mid-1950s. "For You My Love" shot to #1 on the R&B listings.

A music historian wrote of Darnell, he became a "sex symbol with his good looks, sly smile and songs of romance and heartbreak, yet he was fairly openly homosexual."[19]

In 1949 Fred Mendelsohn and the brothers David and Jules Braun founded Regal Records in New Jersey. The focus was on rhythm and blues and, looking for new talent, the trio traveled to the South, ending up in New Orleans. They learned quickly that the best place to spot great R&B was at the Dew Drop Inn. As Mendelsohn told an interviewer, "This was the club for Black artists." So, they were standing around when Larry Darnell took the mic and sang "I'll Get Along Somehow," an older tune popularized by Black bandleader Andy Kirk. "He [Darnell] added a recitation that sent the dames screaming and hollering," Mendelsohn continued. "We brought him to New York and recorded the song as a Part 1/Part 2 record . . . we also cut 'For You My Love.' And we put both records out at the same time, also something that was unheard of. *Billboard* had an R&B chart of 10 records. Darnell had two at the same time—in the number one and number three slots."[20]

New Orleans, especially the Dew Drop Inn, was more accepting of unfettered homosexual entertainers than the rest of the country, yet Darnell was a popular performer everywhere. In October 1949 he was at the Village Vanguard in New York, which was open to anyone with talent.[21] Then about a month later he was booked at the Showboat, a Philadelphia Club that catered to African Americans. Darnell teamed with Bill Johnson and His Musical Notes. His November show followed Showboat appearances by Bull Moose Jackson, Mercer Ellington, Sticks McGhee, and Amos Milburn.[22]

Regal Records folded in 1951, and although Darnell quickly signed with OKeh, he was never a hitmaker again.

Bobby Marchan followed a similar route to stardom as Larry Darnell. He was born in 1930, which made him just two years younger than Darnell. They were both from Ohio and left the state as teenagers to perform with traveling burlesque troupes. For Marchan the escape vehicle was the Powder Box Review, where he was a female impersonator. Then, like Darnell, Marchan found a home in New Orleans, where he performed at the Dew Drop Inn and the competition, the Club Tiajuana. His first record, "Have Mercy," was released in 1954. It was a deep blues cut, not at all similar to the Dominoes' rockin' and rollin' "Have Mercy Baby."[23]

Johnny Vincent, who owned Ace Records, caught Marchan's act at a drag show and offered him a contract under the mistaken belief that he was a woman. Nothing much happened with Marchan's career until 1957, when he had a regional hit with "Chickee Wah-Wah." Later that year he joined with Huey "Piano" Smith ("Rocking Pneumonia and the Boogie Woogie Flu") to form the uproarious group Huey "Piano" Smith and His Clowns.[24]

As a soloist, Marchan's biggest hit was "There's Something on Your Mind," which climbed to #1 on the R&B charts in 1960.

New Orleans record producer Carlo Ditta remembers meeting him backstage at the Dew Drop Inn. "Just a very nice person; a real sweet guy. We talked a long time. I was a big fan of 'Something on Your Mind.'"[25]

Another New Orleans singer, Frankie Ford, who was a gay white man, took a different tack, starting out initially as a teen heartthrob before coming out. Ford in 1959 had a million-selling hit with "Sea Cruise," which was written and recorded by Huey "Piano" Smith. Joe Caronna, who was a partner in business with Ace Recording honcho Johnny Vincent, wanted a singer named Frank Guzzo (soon to be Frankie Ford) to cut a new vocal track on "Sea Cruise" after it was recorded by Smith.

As Frankie Ford told the story, he was in Philadelphia working on a song called "Cheatin' Woman" when Joe Caronna told him to fly back to New Orleans. "Bobby Marchan was about to leave Huey 'Piano' Smith and the Clowns and Smith needed someone to sing lead vocals on Huey's records. Huey didn't like to travel, and he would send someone else in his place. After we cut 'Cheatin' Woman' with 'Last One to Cry' on the B-side, which was a regional hit, and Huey still in New Orleans, he decided to make me the lead on 'Sea Cruise,' saying 'Frankie needs a record right now.' 'Sea Cruise' had a hard driving sound, but what really got everyone's attention was the up-front sound effects, harbor sounds, a buoy bell."[26]

An alternative explanation claims Caronna thought the "big-voiced" teenager could be America's next teen idol and recorded Ford singing "Sea Cruise" then dubbed in his voice over the Smith track.[27]

Record credits read Frankie Ford with Huey "Piano" Smith and Orchestra. "Sea Cruise" was a Top Twenty song. Ford played the teen idol, going on the road, seemingly forever. Ford's career got sidetracked in 1963 when he was drafted. When he returned two years later, the Beatles and the British Invasion had conquered America. As the years went on, Ford began to display the more flamboyant side of his personality. Ditta, who seemed to know everyone in the New Orleans record business, when asked if Ford was gay, answered "very."[28]

Or as Drifters singer Terry King observed, "Frankie Ford, everyone knew he was gay. He was like Liberace."²⁹

Singers who were homosexual could tell who else on the tours were as well. When the Shirelles toured, their bodyguard and roadie was a guy named Ronnie Evans, who was gay. "When we appeared on the Jocko Henderson show for the first time, one of the back-up dancers on the show was a rubber-legged young man named Ronnie Evans," the Shirelles' Beverly Lee explained. "A few years later, when the Shirelles were becoming big stars, Luther Dixon (our record producer) recruited Ronnie to be our chaperone, bodyguard, sometimes emcee or master of ceremonies when we were on the road. His job was to look after us."³⁰

Billy Vera toured with the Shirelles as their arranger and bandleader. He knew Ronnie well. "One time at the Sahara in Las Vegas, this little guy with a lump [gun] under his left armpit finds me and said, 'My wife is upstairs in the room crying her eyes out, because you pinched her ass in the casino.' I said, 'that's not my style.' He harrumphed, 'You calling my wife a liar?' Just then Ronnie comes down the stairs dressed like Little Richard in a black jumpsuit. I said, 'Ronnie, this dude thinks I pinched his wife in the casino.' Ronnie answered, 'Oh please, child, that's my friend Billy, he's with me.' The guy gets up in Ronnie's face and calls him a queer. Ronnie could fight and when things started to get bad, Ronnie said, "Listen motherfucker, there are two things I like to do in this world, fight and suck dicks. And we are going to do one or the other if you come at me. Don't bother to pull that piece out from under your shoulder or I'll stick it so far up your ass it'll take an army of doctors to pull it out.' The guy didn't know what to do, so he turned and walked out of the room."

Once when Evans was asked how did he know who would do it (have sex) with him, he answered without explanation, "we can tell," adding "if they're drunk, they will play with you." Evans knew all the gay performers, even the ones who to their audience and fans appeared as straight, married, and/or closeted. Asked who was secretly gay, Evans said Marvin Gaye and one of the Impressions.³¹

Even to the next generation of soul singers, there were still a lot of performers who tried to mask their homosexuality. Terry King, who sang with the Charlie Thomas–led Drifters for almost fifty years, when asked about Clyde McPhatter, said he only met McPhatter once when King was a teenager. Charlie Thomas, however, knew Clyde well and sometimes talked about his bisexuality. "It came up, but very subtle," said King. "Charlie would mention it in a certain way. He knew Clyde was gay. Whatever he said to me, I kept to myself. I never exposed anyone, because it was a private thing. This industry is so strange. People had to keep their homosexuality hidden."³²

Even if they weren't having affairs, gay performers had a natural camaraderie and friendship for others who they knew were gay. Johnnie Ray, after appearing with the Dominoes with Clyde McPhatter in Chicago, was desperate to tour with them. When it was still career-risky for white and Black singers to be photographed in joyful proximity, *Ebony* magazine in March 1953 ran a four-page spread titled "Negroes Taught Me to Sing." A photo accompanying the story showed Johnnie with Billy Ward and his Dominoes "crying" together backstage at Chicago's Oriental Theater. Johnnie Ray and the Dominoes were on a five-shows-a-day bill, and between performances the movie theater played *Flesh and Fury*, which about summed things up as Johnnie's already ignored wife, Marilyn, flew in for the first shows. Whether Johnnie Ray and Clyde or, as it turned out, Billy Ward, were more than sociable is unknown.[33]

Clyde was, however, tight with Bobby Marchan.

John Wirt, Huey "Piano" Smith's biographer, tells this story. Bobby Marchan delighted in calling men "miss" or feminizing their male names, and he did this so often that Huey "Piano" Smith caught himself doing the same. Said Smith, "Bobby [Marchan] had told me what time to come call [on] him from a card game, because he wins all the time. I called [on] Bobby and Clyde McPhatter opened the door. Then I said, 'Clydie Mae, is Bobby in there?' Maybe Clyde didn't hear me. He didn't say anything. But Bobby got me calling the man Clydie Mae!"

Wirt, when asked if anything other than a card game was going on in the apartment, answered that, when Smith told him the story, "Huey didn't mention anything about Clyde being gay, although it was well-established that Bobby was gay. I assumed they were on the road [touring] together." Wirt added that neither Huey Smith nor any of the other Clowns were gay, although someone had written that Gerri Hall, a female member of the Clowns, was a "butch." Hall had been married. Her ex-husband was the brother of Fats Domino's wife. The popular pianist was also from New Orleans.[34]

As to his home town, Carlo Ditta observed, "The French Quarter was always filled with gays since the 1940s and 1950s. They had lesbian joints as well. New Orleans is not a prude town. In the Black area, the Dew Drop Inn always had a female impersonator night. Back then, the African American population wasn't as fucked up over gays as the white people. Bobby Marchan was very well-known to be gay as was Little Richard and Esquerita."[35]

Esquerita?

In the later 1940s, gay performers were switching successfully and unsuccessfully between appearing in drag, performing in revues as dancers, and sometimes trading sex for money. In some ways they never left behind their careers as outrageous entertainers and when the new decade arrived with renewed interest in rhythm and blues, they made their moves to that music scene. The most successful of these players was Little Richard (Richard Wayne Penniman), and he was schooled on his journey by two other excellent gay musicians, Esquerita [Eskew Reeder Jr.] and Billy Wright.

By the time Clyde made it big with the Dominoes in 1951, Billy Wright, who had an enormous influence on Little Richard and helped get him his first recording session, was on the verge of stardom. Instead, the changing R&B market was shifting away from straight blues to group tunes (early doo-wop), jump blues (pre–rock 'n' roll) and soul crooners, and although Savoy Records continued to record him, Wright got lost in the shuffle, which is an appropriate metaphor since one of Wright's more memorable tunes is "Stacked Deck" about a deck of cards.

Wright first scored in 1949 when his "Blues for My Baby" shot to #3 on the *Billboard* R&B chart. He would have another Top Ten R&B hit that year, "You Satisfy," which was the B-side of "Blues for My Baby." Despite three new recordings in 1950, nothing happened for him. Then in 1951, two of his songs, "Stacked Deck" and "Hey, Little Girl," were Top Ten R&B hits.[36] He was still getting some very good gigs, appearing at the San Diego County Fair in July 1951 along with headliners Les Paul and Mary Ford.[37]

When compared to what was happening with flashy newcomers the Dominoes, one could understand how Wright's days as a hitmaker were tenuous. *Cash Box* would do regional record reports in the early 1950s, and in May 1951, when the Dominoes' "Do Something for Me" was, for example, #1 in New Orleans, Wright's "Keep Your Hands on Your Heart" was #5. Savoy, Wright's record company, saw that "Keep Your Hands" was already plateauing, so on the same page as the chart it ran a promotion for "Stacked Deck" with "Mercy Mercy" on the B-side. In June, *Cash Box* surveyed seven cities, and "Rocket 88" was clearly dominating the charts. Coming up quickly was the Dominoes' "Sixty Minute Man." Billy Wright's "Stacked Deck" was only charting in Houston. By August 4, "Sixty Minute Man" was the #1 R&B song in the country, and Savoy decided to release Wright's "Hey Little Girl"/"Find My Baby."[38] Two weeks later "Sixty Minute Man" was still #1 and in the trade publications Savoy promoted Billy Wright and "Hey Little Girl," which was a fine jump blues number in the spirit of the times.[39] It would be his last record to chart.

Originally, Billy Wright's birth year was listed as 1932, but more recent research now has him being born in 1918 in Atlanta. Once again, although it seems counterintuitive, Wright, too, as a teenager found a comfortable environment for his homosexuality in the drag shows that were popular in Black clubs and tent shows throughout the South. The pattern was the same for Wright as for Darnell and Marchan. He worked as a dancer and a female impersonator before making the leap to chitlin' circuit singer.

A music historian doing a deep dive into Wright's song "You Satisfy" wrote, "Wright was one of the many young gay males who found their first opportunities in music performing in drag as female impersonators in the many tent shows that toured the South during the first half of the twentieth century

... it also, of course, afforded homosexuals one place where they might be accepted, even celebrated, in a world that otherwise discriminated against them at every turn."[40]

Where and when Little Richard met Wright is as fuzzy as Wright's birthdate. It's often written that Little Richard met Wright when he was performing in the "Hot Harlem Review," a traveling drag show. That doesn't seem correct, as Wright was a seasoned and successful singer when they met and would have put those shows in his past. One Little Richard biographer has them meeting in 1952, which can't be right either, because in 1951 Wright was able to use his influence to get Little Richard his first recording session, and the backing band was Wright's session musicians.

That was the first thing Wright did for Little Richard. The other influence was less tangential, more style and showmanship. As the 1950s unfurled, the heavily slicked, combed-straight-back hair, sculpted atop the head would become the style of the decade, as it was adopted by the white "greaser" crowd and then teenagers everywhere. As early as the late 1940s, Black performers on the creative edge, such as Wright and Esquerita, sported outrageous versions of this "do" with the hair stacked one or two inches high and held fast with pomade. Little Richard copied this look, as well as adopting Wright's use of stage makeup and eyeliner.[41]

Said Little Richard, "He [Wright] influenced me a lot. He really enthused my whole life. I thought he was the most fantastic entertainer I had ever seen. ... His make-up was really something. I found out what it was and started using it myself. It was called Pancake 31."[42]

In the 1980s when he was the music editor for the *East Village Eye*, James Marshall found a down-and-out Screamin' Jay Hawkins working a seedy bar in Manhattan and interviewed him. A notorious fabulist, Hawkins's testimonies cannot be fully trusted, but he did tell Marshall he had seen Bobby Marchan, Larry Darnell, and Esquerita in the same drag review in Youngstown, Ohio.[43] Darnell, Hawkins added, had hit big with "There's Something on Your Mind," so this would have been around 1949. Hawkins and Esquerita would have a rocky association. Not so with Little Richard, who met him a few years after the alleged Youngstown show.

This is the way it happened. Little Richard was hanging out at the bus station in his home town of Macon, Georgia, trying to pick up someone for sex. One night Esquerita came in. He was traveling with a lady preacher called Sister Rosa, who was selling "blessed" bread. Esquerita played piano for Sister Rosa. The two men made a connection and they went to Little Richard's house, where Esquerita immediately sat at the piano playing way up on the treble and with a fantastic bass the song "One Mint Julep," a big hit for the Clovers in 1952.

"He had the biggest hands of anybody I'd ever seen. His hands were about the same size of two of my hands put together," Little Richard recalled. "It ["One Mint Julep"] sounded so great. I said, 'Hey, how do you do that?' And he says, 'I'll teach you.' And that's when I really started playing . . . I learned a lot about phrasing from him. He really taught me a lot."[44]

Esquerita's career never took off. Marshall met him in the 1980s and befriended the musician. "He was really a nut," said Marshall. "He had twenty different gigs a week, everything from playing piano in hotel lobbies to dancing in a drag place. At that point he was about 50 years old."

Marshall's best story is about one night when he and Esquerita went off to see Screamin' Jay Hawkins, who Esquerita claimed was a friend. Screamin' Jay was playing a club on Third Avenue in Manhattan. "As soon we walk in the door, I realized it was a mistake," Marshall said. "Hawkins looks at me as if to say, 'why did you bring this asshole.' Sure enough, by the end of the night they were having an argument about money. Apparently, Esquerita still owed Hawkins money from the 1950s. They ended up in the middle of Third Avenue. One of them had a knife, the other had a bottle, they were slashing at each other. Hawkins had a funny, expressive face and he gets this weird look. Then he just clocks Esquerita with a left hook to the side of the head and knocked him out cold. That was the end of the fight."[45]

Rudi Protrudi, lead singer of the punk band the Fuzztones, also befriended Esquerita about the same time. "I was a very big Esquerita fan. At the time, he had a gig at Tramps two or three nights, and I had gone to see him. I told Screamin' Jay Hawkins, who said they used to hang out together and that they shared a jail cell at one time. Hawkins used to jam at clubs together with Esquerita on piano and Hawkins on sax. They would dress to see who could be the most outrageous and from what I understand these clubs were real underground sleazy dives."[46]

Esquerita died from complications from AIDs soon afterward in 1986.

Little Richard took Esquerita's style of playing piano and made it his story. While he had earlier recorded on other labels, his big break came in 1955 when Specialty Records signed him to a contract and sent Robert "Bumps" Blackwell to record him in New Orleans. At first things didn't go well. Blackwell thought Little Richard was too tame. "If you look like Tarzan and sing like Mickey Mouse it just doesn't work out," Blackwell said. Anyway, Blackwell called for a break and he, Little Richard, and the band went over to the Dew Drop Inn. The place with was crowded with girls—and boys. Little Richard saw a vacant piano, sat down, and launched into a risqué tune, "A wop-bop-a-loo-mop, a good goddam—Tutti Frutti, good booty . . ." This was the sound Blackwell was looking for. Specialty cleaned up the lyrics and "Tutti Frutti" became Little Richard's first hit record.[47]

This period of time overlapped with Clyde's military requirement, 1954 through 1956. It was also during this time that Clyde pursued relations with women. He married Nora Thompson and had an affair with singer Ruth Brown. Clyde and Brown were stablemates at Atlantic Records at a time when the company dominated R&B with Ruth Brown, Clyde McPhatter and the Drifters, Big Joe Turner, the Clovers, LaVern Baker and Ray Charles.

Brown was equal to them all. She first charted in 1949 with a song called "So Long" and continued scoring major hits throughout the 1950s. At the time she met Clyde, she was a veteran of the chitlin' circuit when it was dominated by male singers. She knew every type of Black male entertainer personality and made peace with them all. She was a lousy judge of men for her own affairs and marriages, Otherwise, she was as perceptive as a professional psychologist, except that she was not one to sit quietly on her opinions.

In regard to her manager George Treadwell, she wrote, "George was an ex-trumpeter with Mr. B's [Billy Eckstine] short-lived forties orchestra, married at the time to Billy's ex-vocalist, Sarah Vaughan. When they broke up, he married again, and after his death it was Faye Treadwell who inherited the Drifters name. He [George Treadwell] was what you would call a pretty boy and in many ways he reminded me of Clyde McPhatter; there was a manly side but a softer, feminine side as well."

In reference to Clyde, she opined, "Clyde was shy and sweet, and despite his high, girlish voice and mannerisms there was innate manliness about him I found tremendously appealing." She first worked with Clyde when he was one of the unbilled Drifters singing background on her recording of "Old Man River." Afterward, they became friends. In 1955, the two recorded a couple of duets and the formerly platonic relationship turned up the heat. During a break in his military duties they met in Buffalo for a weekend spent under the covers. They were an item for a while longer and then it was over, but they remained friends.

Brown knew Clyde well. She wrote, "Like everyone else I had heard rumors of his bisexuality, and I believe towards the end he was ashamed and terrified of the outside world having his gay tendencies confirmed. He began drinking to drown the guilt and shame he felt, sinking his career into the doldrums."[48]

She wasn't the only one with that opinion.

Yusuf Lamont, whose father Joe Lamont was an original member of the Dominoes, said he and his father used to talk about Clyde a lot—and about related stories. For example, Yusuf claimed that in the Black churches homosexuality was not uncommon at all, especially for "the so-called pretty boys, high-voice guys, the tenors."[49] James Cleveland, the King of Gospel, and probably the most well-known gospel singer, composer, musician and African American minister of the 1960s through the 1980s, was gay. In 1992 Cleveland's foster son filed a lawsuit against the Cleveland estate, claiming that Cleveland abused him over a five-year period and infected him with the AIDs virus. According to *Jet* magazine, "As a result of Cleveland's acts of sodomy, [Christopher] Harris was infected with the virus . . ." The article also said that Cleveland had been a practicing homosexual for several years.[50]

About Clyde in particular, Yusuf Lamont observed, "He was living a double life. Not being able to live his life out loud combined with career setbacks, that will drive you to drink."[51]

However, there were people close to Clyde who said he was not gay. His nephew, Wilton "Brother" Tolor, said Clyde was straight, and talk of him being homosexual could have come from those close to him. Said Tolor, "You got backstabbers in every family."[52]

The person who traveled on the road with Clyde for the longest time, Bill Curtis, reported he never saw Clyde with men. "He was not bisexual. Clyde had a girlfriend every city," said Curtis. "He was definitely a ladies' man. I never saw him act like he wanted to be with a man."

Concerning rumors of Clyde being gay, Curtis added, "That was his persona on stage. He acted that way on stage"[53]—which was probably not the best way to squelch rumors of gayness or bisexuality.

If there is any confirmation as to whether Clyde was gay or bisexual, it is probably what happened to him in England. In 1967, Clyde decided he could revive his career by relocating to the United Kingdom. It wasn't a smooth transition, and Clyde was lonely and drinking more. Things weren't going well. Bill Millar, who wrote a history of the Drifters, in a magazine article on Clyde McPhatter, scribed, "Clyde was gigging around Britain and Europe to progressively smaller audiences, and gradually sinking lower. He really hit the depths when he was arrested and charged with loitering."[54]

Actually, it was more serious than that. Clyde was arrested for "loitering with intent." In the United Kingdom, the concept goes back to the Vagrancy Act of 1824, which was written to prevent suspects and infamous thieves from lingering about certain places, and, as later claimed by gay organizations, was used to criminalize men who were found in areas where men picked up each other for sex.

Ian Wallis writes, "The case against him went to court but then collapsed, though not before embarrassing revelations had been made as to the pitiful state of his finances."

Graham Knight, who had seen Clyde perform on his first trip to England in 1960, added, "a big fuss when he got arrested at a public toilet. Back then homosexuality was still a crime in the United Kingdom."[55]

And magazine editor Tony Burke noted, for foreigners, "back then the cops would find a way to kick you out of the UK if you were caught importuning."

More or less, that's what happened. The UK Home Office decided not to renew Clyde's work permit, forcing him to return to the United States.[56]

Little Richard first toured the United Kingdom in 1962 on a bill with Sam Cooke and Gene Vincent. His band included keyboard whiz Billy Preston, who was also gay. As for Gene Vincent, he wasn't supposed to be there because his UK work permit had expired, but he played anyway. Little Richard came back every few years to play in the United Kingdom, and it was probably on his 1969 tour that Graham Knight met up with him. They talked about Clyde's arrest, and Knight revealed, "Little Richard told me that Clyde McPhatter had a terrible reputation in America and that he was an alcoholic like Gene Vincent."[57]

While in the UK, Clyde would write often to probably the only woman, besides his mother, who he really had deep and abiding affection for, Lorraine Lowe, the mother of his only daughter, who had long been happily married to another man and thus unattainable. He poured his heart out to Lorraine in many missives from London, and it appears she knew of Clyde's sexual orientation. In a letter to Lorraine dated August 25, 1968, Clyde wrote, "I have started so many letters to you, but somehow always recall you saying to me in all your letters, 'Clyde be a man'—not to be facetious dear (I mean that) but there too, I wonder how many times I've said that and to whom. I can still recall you saying to me so often, 'Clyde, make up your mind.'"[58]

And in another letter, Clyde wrote, "But Lorri, let me say this to you, heretofore I've been reluctant to write because I didn't know how you would weigh what I wrote to you.... May I remind you again, you've always said to me, you could except [accept] me when you felt you were receiving the Man [underlined twice] Clyde."[59]

After Clyde died, Ruth Brown spent some time analyzing Clyde with his pianist Cliff Smalls. "We discussed the anguish Clyde had felt on returning from his less-than-triumphant British tour at the end of the 1960s, the shame he experienced after being arrested for 'loitering with intent,' even though the charges had been subsequently dropped."[60]

As to what happened in England, that arrest for loitering with intent may not have happened as reported or, perhaps, there was a subsequent police incident later that same year. It's difficult to tell without seeing an original arrest record.

According to Wallis, after July 1969, Clyde's "only publicity arose from a rather unseemly incident when he was arrested for loitering with intent."[61] However, a January 1, 1970, document from the London Metropolitan Police that was forwarded to the Home Office (Immigration and Nationality Department) affirmed Clyde was charged with a crime on December 12, 1969. The report stated: "McPhatter was seen by police loitering near parking meters. When he was stopped and searched, he was found to be in possession of a screwdriver for the use in connection with theft." The report also noted that, according to his passport, Clyde should have left the United Kingdom on or before November 21, 1969.

That incident appears to be more like police harassment, as eventually Clyde was not imprisoned nor fined. Two charges were dismissed while other charges (it doesn't specify, but these could refer to the passport problems) were "conditionally discharged." In addition, that same report states, "He is a present employed . . . earning £500 per week." That was considerable money in those days, so why would he be breaking into parking meters for coins?[62]

If there was an original, official report of Clyde's arrest for loitering, it has long since disappeared. Since this memo is the only documented report from 1969, two Clyde police incidents sometimes get conflated.

Deborah McPhatter did briefly discuss Clyde's sexuality with Ruth Brown. "She [Ruth] did not go into that kind of detail with me. She made it seem like he was . . . [Deborah wouldn't say the word] and that was the end of it."

As to talking with her father about the rumors, she said, "You don't walk up to your parent and ask, 'Are you gay?'"

Then she added, "I've read and heard so much disrespect about my father. I've heard so much emphasis on his sexuality. He's gay, he wasn't gay. That's of no interest to me. His voice and what he contributed to the world of music is what is important to me."[63]

Louise Murray has been around the music industry since her days as a member of Hearts and their hit song "Lonely Nights" in 1955. She is married to Donald Gatling, who came very late to doo-wop, subbing as a member of the Jesters in the group's later years and producing doo-wop shows. As a teenager, Donald grew up with the original members of the Jesters, and at some point, they assigned him the rights to the group's name. He knew a lot of doo-wop performers and when asked about homosexual members in those 1950s groups, he threw up his hands as if to say what a stupid question, and exclaimed, "they were all gay."[64]

Well, not all. But, some. And maybe, or maybe not, Clyde.

CHAPTER FIFTEEN

DEEP IN THE HEART OF HARLEM

The 33⅓ and 45 rpm record formats were introduced in 1948 and 1949, respectively, replacing the hard, shellac, easily breakable 78 record, which had been the dominant format since the Gramophone Company made it the company's standard in 1912. Both formats succeeded, but it was the 45 record, or single, that ended up as the defining listener technology of the 1950s, as it was inexpensive, represented just one hit record with a bonus song on the second side (B-side), and was a natural fit for the hundreds of thousands of phonographs and jukeboxes in America. The 33⅓ format, or LP, made its own way in a kind of alternative universe. For the most part, the top-selling albums of the 1950s were Christmas compilations by popular singers, soundtracks to Broadway plays, the movie versions of those theatrical productions, and anything by Elvis Presley. Occasionally a superior jazz product would crash the charts, such as *Kind of Blue* by Miles Davis or *Brubeck Plays Brubeck* by Dave Brubeck.

The peak year for the single was 1974, when 200 million records were sold. Coincidentally, that year slightly more albums were sold than singles. More impressive was the fact that revenues from album sales were about double that of singles.[1] This was always the attraction for record companies. The potential revenue from album sales was so much greater than that of the single, which is why in the 1950s the record companies would promote a popular singer such as Johnny Mathis or Marty Robbins through albums that supported their best-selling singles. It was like doubling the revenue from one recording or of a full recording session.

By the early 1960s, alternative music formats such as jazz, instrumental, and folk music could regularly be supported by albums, with the occasional breakthrough featuring popular performers. Increasingly, music companies began to issue albums in support of singles releases. After the Beatles, singles and albums supported each other in the marketplace.

The album format in the 1950s and into the very early 1960s did one other thing: it gave a presence to older singers, who were no longer hitmakers but still had a deep fan base.

In 1957 King Records rushed out a kind of greatest hits album from the time when Clyde sang with the Dominoes. It was called *Clyde McPhatter with Billy Ward and His Dominoes*. The liner notes on the back of the album sleeve had some nice things to say about Clyde: "The dynamic vocal style of McPhatter was recognized by the general public when he first appeared as lead singer in the original Dominoes vocal group." That was only a feint. All the verbosity in the liner notes was really about Billy Ward, including this line: "Billy Ward's arrangements and coaching helped McPhatter along the road to success."[2]

With Clyde McPhatter still popular with teenagers, Atlantic Records began to issue McPhatter albums, the first, *Love Ballads*, coming in 1958.

When Clyde moved to M-G-M, it, too, issued a McPhatter album, *Let's Start Over Again*. However, Mercury Records really made albums part of the Clyde McPhatter plan. The company, having a very broad base of record acts and performers, understood the potential of the album. As an example, in 1964, Mercury took out a full-page ad in the trade publications touting its recent album releases including comedy (Moms Mabley), folk (the Freedom Singers), country (Faron Young), soundtrack (*Porgy and Bess*), classical (*Rossini Overtures*), popular (*House Party-Discotheque*), and the past—and maybe future—hitmaker, Clyde McPhatter with his album *Live at the Apollo*.[3]

For Clyde, who recorded with the Dominoes and Drifters on different labels, there were always the odd leftover songs or hit compilation albums from prior record companies that would be released, but starting in the late 1950s, his present record companies at a particular time would invest constantly in McPhatter albums, none more so than Mercury. In 1960, with his first hit record, "Ta Ta," on his new label, Mercury Records that same year issued its first McPhatter album, also called *Ta Ta!* Then came *Golden Blues Hits* in 1961, and with the great "Lover Please" hit single, the company issued in 1962 an album of the same name, *Lover Please!*

With the mature McPhatter no longer creating hit records, Mercury tried to take advantage of the consistent trend to record albums by the once famous, who it perceived still had a welcoming fan base. Clyde, who had been recording since 1950, certainly fit into that category. The trouble was, how to best position Clyde as a mature and cosmopolitan singer. Mercury experimented but really never figured it out. Starting in 1962, it issued *Rhythm and Soul* with the Merry Melody Singers, trying to catch the rise of soul music. Then in 1964 came the urbane-sounding *Songs of the Big City*, and finally that same year an album recorded from a live performance, *Live at the Apollo*.

The latter was clearly an attempt to re-create one of the best-selling and trend-setting albums of the early 1960s, James Brown and his Famous Flames' *Live at the Apollo*, which was released—reluctantly—by King Records in 1963. According to legend, King Records dismissed Brown's concept of recording his Apollo show, so he funded it himself. King eventually conceded and released the album, which then spent over a year on *Billboard*'s album chart, rising as high as #2. To this day, it is considered one of the greatest albums of the 1960s.

This isn't to say Clyde's albums were derivative. Clyde could never be confused with James Brown. He had his own voice and style, and the Mercury albums are not without fans. Dutch musicologist Dik de Heer noted, "The Mercury stint was his [Clyde's] last fruitful period, but Clyde could have been much bigger if he had focused on the newly emerging soul music [for which his voice was perfect] instead of clinging to his vision of MOR [middle-of-the-road] success. *Songs of the Big City* and *Live at the Apollo* were excellent albums."[4]

The *Billboard* review of *Songs of the Big City* was noncommittal: "McPhatter sings songs of longing and meaning that are very much of social conscience themes. Besides his current singles, 'Deep in the Heart of Harlem,' and 'Second Window, Second Floor' he also sings such formidable tunes as 'Spanish Harlem' and 'Up on the Roof.'"[5] The latter two songs still tied him to his past, as "Spanish Harlem" was initially and successfully recorded by Ben E. King and "Up on the Roof" by the Drifters.

From the late 1950s through the 1960s, Clyde pushed different formats, although his big dream was to have a successful and ongoing nightclub career, which is why he kept falling back to middle-of-the-road despite the fact that his last big hit, "Lover Please," was rock 'n' roll. In comparison, Ben E. King and the Drifters stuck to what they did best, play in the pop music world. Ben E. King, who had hits in 1962 and 1963 with "Don't Play that Song (You Lied)" and "I (Who Have Nothing)" ran into an elongated period of being off the charts and then had one of the biggest hits of career in 1975 with "Supernatural Thing—Part 1." As for the Drifters (with lead singers Rudy Lewis and Johnny Moore), they bragged three of their biggest hits ever, with "Up on the Roof" in 1962, "On Broadway" in 1963, and "Under the Boardwalk" in 1964.

Billboard was enamored with the Drifters' longevity. Groups tended to arrive with fanfare, belting out a hit record and then disappearing just as quickly, but the Drifters with an ever-changing lineup of singers had been at it for over a decade.

In December 1964 the entertainment industry trade publication ran a complimentary feature on the group, noting: "The Atlantic Records' group's 10-year record is especially impressive considering the important personnel loss it had over that period. First, its lead singer Clyde McPhatter went out on his own;

a few years later, another lead singer, Ben E. King decided to hit the solo trail. Historically, when a lead singer exits a group, it usually marks *finis* to their activities... not so with the Drifters. They have been averaging about a million copy sales on their big hit singles, and their albums, which Atlantic brings out on top of their singles, using the same title, have been steady sellers."[6]

Well, if you write about someone, it's the kiss of death for the subject's career. The Drifters boasted three Top 40 hits in 1964, "Under the Boardwalk," "I've Got Sand in My Shoes," and "Saturday Night at the Movies," and then it was over for the group as hitmakers. It was a good run.

When the year 1964 unfurled, it looked to be just like any of the prior three or four years in pop music, with a little bit of everything, no discernible trend line, and a great distance from the last innovative year, 1956, when rock 'n' roll first conquered America. When Clyde's "Deep in the Heart of Harlem" hit the record charts at the start of the year, he, like the music industry in general, was looking for a sense of revival. "Deep in the Heart of Harlem" dropped into shallow waters, coming in at a lowly #95 on the *Billboard* Hot 100 list. Many other veteran singers were also struggling. Duane Eddy tried "The Son of Rebel-Rouser." It barely made the chart at #100. Connie Francis's "In the Summer of His Years," after two weeks was still at #85. Bobby Darin's "Be My Little Girl," after three weeks, only managed to get to #73.

What was succeeding at the start of the year, at least in terms of the Top Ten songs, were some old trend lines: first, a big presence from the young, hirsute white boys such as Bobby Vinton ("There! I've Said It Again" at #1), Bobby Rydell ("Forget Him" at #9) and Johnny Tillotson ("Talk Back Trembling Lips" at #7); the girl groups still going strong with the Mermaids ("Popsicles and Icicles" at #6) and Martha and the Vandellas ("Quicksand" at #8); smooth R&B and dance R&B grooving with Lenny Welch ("Since I Fell for You" at #4) and Shirley Ellis ("The Nitty Gritty" at #9), and even basic rock 'n' roll with the Kingsmen ("Louie Louie" at #2).

By the next month much of that would be on the highway to hell: the white soloists, the girl groups, and even old-style rock 'n' roll would wind down. Only R&B would survive under a new genre title, "soul music," which would be dominated by two labels, Motown from Detroit and Stax out of Memphis. Clyde would catch no break with that new R&B sound.

The cause and culprits were the Beatles and the British invasion. Remember Bobby Vinton's tepid #1 hit, "There! I've Said it Again." It was bounced by a little song called "I Want to Hold Your Hand." The Beatles had arrived in America and immediately conquered the record charts. Next up at #1 was the Beatles' second hit, "She Loves You," which was followed by another Beatles song, "Can't Buy Me Love." For the week of April 4, 1964, the top five songs in America were all from the Beatles.

For a while, the radio stations and record charts were aflutter with new accents, old sounds, and everything in between. The Beatles were knocked out of the #1 slot by Louis Armstrong singing "Hello Dolly," a show tune. *Billboard*'s album reviews from mid-1964 included new releases by Elvis Presley, England's Dave Clark Five, pop singer Bobby Vee, folk group the Village Stompers, a joking nod to surf/car music with *Rods and Ratfinks*; soundtrack music from the James Bond movie *From Russia with Love*, and Clyde McPhatter's *Songs of the Big City*.[7]

For a singer such as Clyde McPhatter, who had been around since the pre-dawn of rock 'n' roll, it was hard to find a place in the music world. Despite the Beatles and the British invasion, R&B in the form of soul music thrived. In 1965, Black performers such as the Four Tops, Mel Carter, Ramsey Lewis, the Supremes, Barbra Mason, and James Brown all had major hits. Mercury just could not get Clyde there, and in August 1965 he and the recording company ended contractual obligations. Clyde moved on to the Amy-Mala-Bell aggregation.[8]

Ironically, "Lover Please" had a comeback in 1965. Adam Wade redid the song. The *Billboard* review observed, "Happy, hand-clapping revival of the Brook Benton song, made famous by Clyde McPhatter."[9] This is just about the same week that Mercury released its last Clyde McPhatter song, "Crying Won't Help You Now." The most successful song releases that week included the Rolling Stones' "The Last Time" and the Dixie Cups' "Iko Iko." Almost two months later, *Billboard* listed "Crying Won't Help You Now" as one of its "breakout" singles. Other breakout singles that week included Barbara Mason's "Yes I'm Ready" and the Supremes' "Back in My Arms Again."[10] Clyde's "Crying Won't Help You Now" didn't break out. It rose no further than #27 on the R&B charts and not at all on the Hot 100.

In some ways, changing labels was a step down for Clyde, as he was moving from a major record company to a smaller independent. While it was a risk, Bell Records with its associated labels Amy and Mala was in revival mode during the 1960s and doing a good job of it.

Bell Records was named after its founder Benny Bell, who in 1952 sold his enterprise to Arthur Shimkin, a well-known record producer in the 1960s and 1970s. Shimkin was driven to do something great with his new company and hired renowned jazz trumpeter and bandleader Sy Oliver as music director. In 1959 Al Massler became president of Bell and he created two new subsidiaries, Mala and Amy records, both of which specialized in rock 'n' roll and R&B. In 1961 Larry Uttal, who owned Madison Records, folded his company into Bell Records and then purchased Bell outright about a year or so later.

Uttal, like many music executives in the 1950s and 1960s, did not have an exceptional reputation, some calling him either shrewd or ruthless. Nevertheless, he was successful because he did a have a good ear for music. On his

Madison label he released a single by a raw but talented young man named Paul Simon and later would record another talented up-and-comer named Daryl Hall, who would eventually join with John Oates to form Hall and Oates. Before he folded the Amy label in 1969, such artists as the Guess Who, Lee Dorsey, Del Shannon, and Clyde McPhatter recorded on the label.[11]

In 1965 Clyde recorded his first songs for the Amy label and for some reason it was decided he should revive Connie Francis's #1 hit from 1960, "Everybody's Somebody's Fool." This was an interesting cut, with a lot of talk-singing, a full chorus of background singers, and even a twangy guitar. Clyde was his usually empathetic self, but with a slightly deeper voice. The record went nowhere, as did all of his other four singles from his Amy years, 1965 to 1967.

Cash Box on November 5, 1966, did make Clyde's "A Shot of Rhythm and Blues," with "I'm Not Going to Work Today" on the B-side, as one of its "Picks of the Week." Sixteen songs were chosen, but only two were hits, "Mellow Yellow" by Donovan and "Sugar Town" by Nancy Sinatra. The bored reviewer for the Donovan and Nancy Sinatra songs called both "easy-going" before predicting good things ahead. For Clyde McPhatter, the reviewer made no prediction of good fortunes, but he was definitely caffeinated, exclaiming: "From out of rock's past comes Clyde McPhatter holding a bright candle dubbed 'A Shot of Rhythm and Blues.' The funky, slow-paced highly danceable blueser should set lot of toes tapping and lots of throats humming."[12]

"A Shot of Rhythm and Blues" was recorded at Rick Hall's Fame Studios in Muscle Shoals, Alabama.

Clyde's last single, from 1967, summed up his emotional state. The A-side was "I Dreamt I Died" with "Lonely People Can't Afford to Cry" on the B-side. These songs were very much of their times, recorded in a jaunty rock style. They were cowritten by Paul Vance, who was a prolific songwriter over four decades, writing a variety of hit songs including "Catch a Falling Star" for Perry Como, "Itsy Bitsy Teenie Weenie Yellow Polka Dot Bikini" for Brian Hyland, and "Playground of Your Mind" for Clint Holmes. Vance couldn't pull a rabbit out of the hat for Clyde though. The single with the melodramatic titles appeared as a two-side downer.

Clyde released no new albums during his Amy years. It was time to try something new. In 1967, Clyde decided to try to restart his career in Europe, which was not an unusual choice. One of his contemporaries, Mickey "Guitar" Baker of Mickey and Sylvia ("Love is Strange" in 1956) fame, moved to France in the 1960s and almost never returned to the United States. Baker was a quiet gentleman like Clyde and never really spoke about his move to Europe, although speculation, of course, centered on more creative music making, and getting away from the increasingly vitriolic fight for racial equality in the United States.

What also might have influenced Clyde's decision to go to across the pond, to Great Britain in particular, was the international success of the Drifters. The official Drifters group made it to England for the first time in 1965. In that year, the group was led by Johnny Moore with Charlie Thomas, Eugene Peterson, Johnny Terry, and guitarist Billy Davis. The Drifters boasted a successful two-month tour, and the group even got their picture taken with Brian Jones of the Rolling Stones.

In January 1966 the Original Drifters arrived in Britain for a one-month tour. This group was led by Bill Pinkney with Gerhart Thrasher, Bobby Hendricks, and Bobby Lee Hollis. The promoters were so pleased with this tour that the Original Drifters came back to England in the spring for a two-month tour.

While that group was touring through the midlands of England, so was Ben E. King, and like the Original Drifters, King returned again, this time in late autumn for a second tour and then for a third tour in the spring of 1967.[13]

In the UK the recognition continuum between Clyde McPhatter and Ben E. King and also the Drifters (Original and official) was immense. The oeuvre of the later Drifters of "There Goes My Baby" to "On Broadway" and "Under the Boardwalk" and Ben E. King of "Spanish Harlem," "Stand by Me," and "I (Who Have Nothing)" was well-known in the UK. Not so much Clyde McPhatter. His work with the Dominoes and first incarnation of the Drifters was far in the past and his singles, even "Lover Please," were tangential to British Isles teen record-buyers.

When Clyde McPhatter arrived in England for a two-week tour in May 1967, it was somewhat unexpected. As American-performers-touring-Britain musicologist Ian Wallis wrote, "The arrival of Clyde McPhatter for a couple of dates in the UK was one of the big surprises of 1967. Clyde had toured with Duane Eddy and Bobby Darin in the spring of 1960, but had since made little impact with record-buyers in Britain. In fact, his name was rarely mentioned."[14]

The May 20, 1967, issue of Britain's *Melody Maker* magazine, on its upcoming shows page, offered an advertisement from the Cue Club, located in London's Paddington area, which was promoting "The Clyde McPhatter Show." Tiny wording added "From America." This didn't appear to be an A-lister venue, as preceding Clyde was a group with the unlikely name Count Suckle and Sound System. Coming in after Clyde was a band called Rick 'N' Beckers.[15]

The UK promoter, Roy Tempest, at first didn't quite know what to do with Clyde in terms of backup bands and companion acts, but it all got straightened out and Clyde's musical journey appeared to be a successful run, so much so that Clyde decided to relocate to London, which he did in early autumn of that year. In a letter dated October 14, 1967, Clyde wrote to Deborah McPhatter's mother Lorraine, reporting on the hassles and hustles of his new locale: "I had trouble with the fellows playing my music, but we worked at it and it sounds good, but not as good as I would like to hear it played. It'll work its way out though . . . Last night we played a town about 140 miles from London named Nottingham. Tomorrow, believe it or not, we play Birmingham, but we always come back to London after each engagement. We open at the Palace Theater in London, Monday, for one week, then we will play at the air force base here after which I will fly on to Germany where I won't be doing anything but armed forces bases. After that I hope I'll get a chance to see some of Sweden before I come home . . . however, the Sweden visit is not definite."[16]

According to Wallis, Clyde's two-week tour skipped Birmingham, and in London, the venue was the "Whiskey a Go Go" (not to be confused with the original Whiskey a Go Go in Los Angeles). The tour did just okay, suffering from two major impediments. First, the always-popular, at least in Britain, Ben E. King was touring at the same time. Second, as an indication of where rock 'n' roll (or simply "rock" music) was headed, Clyde played a club in the town of Dunstable, England. The next evening, a relatively unknown guitarist named Jimi Hendrix was the headliner.[17]

Clyde didn't make it to Sweden. He sent a letter to Lorraine on October 16, 1967, from London, which, in itself, was unnerving. He wrote, "When I arrived in London, I went to a doctor for an injection of penicillin. I also had him write me a prescription for 'deximil' (dextroamphetamine) tablets, they're for tension. The reason for the 'dexies' was that I wasn't sure of my music being played to my satisfactions, and I didn't want you to get upset about it." [18]While the drug can be useful in regard to attention focus and behavior control, it was often misused in the 1960s, and it was addictive. According to Bill Curtis, Clyde "also got on the pills with the booze."

Nevertheless, things were looking up for Clyde. In an undated letter, probably from late 1967, Clyde wrote to Lorraine, "I've been so busy, moving from pillow [sic, pillar] to post. I've finally found a very lovely apartment. Well, it's not all that lovely, but it's nice for one who is alone (and lonely) . . . it hasn't been as easy as I thought it would be to get a place without signing a long lease."[19]

As far as his music was concerned, in the same letter, Clyde continued, "I just signed a recording contract for Decca (they have a branch here). I shall have a record released the third week of May. It will also be released in America."

It's good to be optimistic, but it is not great to fool yourself. Clyde did sign with Decca, but he would end up recording on the company's stereo-technology, experimental label, Deram. Others on the label in the 1967–68 period included the Moody Blues, Cat Stevens, and Ten Years After—completely different cats.

In January 1968, Clyde, still lonely but feeling good about the new year, wrote to Lorraine: "I hadn't realized the change that has come until I read your letter. I'm now aware that as the result of my being away like this, it has given me the opportunity to reflex [sic, reflect] and really see myself objectively and also seeing and realizing that there are people that really care. I'm almost certain now that things are going to turn out okay."[20]

Clyde was on the Continent when he wrote this letter because he added, "I can hardly wait to get to England and try out some new material. I think you're going to like it . . . I'm not supposed to start work until next Friday, 2/2. But as I told you on the phone, I'm going to record while in Europe, so it will give me a week to get things organized before the session."

Clyde needed to get a lot more organized, because when he came back to England, he was refused entry because he failed to secure a work permit and scheduled club appearances had to be cancelled. Finally in February all the paperwork was straightened out, and he did a short two-week tour. After that, gigs were harder to arrange, as there still wasn't a great interest in the singer.[21]

Melody Maker's "Clubs" page showed London's Whiskey a Go Go promoting two Clyde McPhatter shows on February 8 and February 13, 1968, sandwiching a band called Glenroy Oakley and The Oracles.[22]

Clyde had beautiful handwriting, but a missive that appears to be from March 1968, shows a penmanship that was in decline. He was in Spain when he wrote the letter and appeared to be stressed: "You must have surmised during our telephone conversation that things just weren't going right in England for me. The agent that had me to come over seemed to have made a complete change as far as our relationship was concerned. The band that he put with me was awful, the places that I was playing was just as bad as the band. In other words, I was going thru hell. So, I signed a contract with another agent in England . . . tomorrow I leave Spain to go back to England to record. I don't know how long I'll be in Europe; I met some people while I was in Germany."[23]

He didn't stay in Continental Europe and came back to Britain. He did a couple of clubs in May and then nothing until later that summer of 1968. Wallis reported: "He [Clyde] was struggling on all levels. Bureaucracy was still giving him work permit problems and, although he could still work occasionally at military bases, he was not exactly inundated with offers. To make matters worse, he was drinking heavily and probably not in the best shape to take advantage of any opportunities that did arise."[24]

In the August 24, 1968, issue of *Melody Maker*, a London company called Class Managements Ltd. boasted in a promotion, "Artistes represented by this office: The Foundations (3 hit Records), The Flirtations ('Someone Out There'), The World of Oz ('King Croesus') and Clyde McPhatter ('Only a Fool')." One had to wonder just how classy Class Management was if "Only a Fool" was the only song the company considered to use as a promotion for Clyde McPhatter.[25]

Clyde had two recording sessions with the Deram team in the spring and fall of 1968. As Drifters biographer Bill Millar concluded, the recording session yielded seven tracks, most of which were indifferent ballads penned by staff writers and A&R men, like Wayne Bickerton and Less Reed, who thought they could write songs. These recordings were, Millar opined, "duly swamped with syrup-y arrangements." Two singles were culled from this material, the ballad "Only a Fool" released in 1968, and "Baby You Got It" released in 1969, both of which Millar dismayingly reported "bombed out of sight."[26]

As a result of the lack of chart success, Clyde's contract with Decca (Deram) was annulled by mutual consent, and in 1969 he signed with B&C Records. The letters in the corporate name stood for Beat and Commercial, and it was an offshoot of Trojan Records created by British Jamaican Lee Gopthal and Chris Blackwell of Island Records. In 1967, Gopthal's Pyramid label released a song by reggae artist Desmond Dekker called "Israelites," which topped the British charts and was a Top Ten tune across the pond, making it the first reggae hit in the United States.[27]

In 1969 Clyde cut his only single for B&C Records, a tune called "Denver," with "Tell Me" as the B-side. Reviewer Peter Jones of Britain's *Record Mirror* liked this recording, noting, "Yet another Record of the Week. A sensitive and interesting reading, a good song by one of the more loved voices. He digs deep here, specially at this tempo. A nice, nice record."

Jones was right. This was a fine effort. It begins a bit lushly with a "Ferry Cross the Mersey" vibe and then settles down into a mixed pop/soul beat. Just how much resonance the city of Denver had in England in the year 1969 is hard to figure, as it is hard to explain why B&C would make this Clyde's first, and, as it turned out, only release by the company. Clyde did sound good, though.

Up until the mid-1960s, Clyde's consistent earnings from his company contracts, recordings, and live shows had created for him a pleasant lifestyle. A week in residence at the Apollo Theater (minimum thirteen shows) in 1966 netted him $24,000 (over $231,000 in 2024 dollars).[28] By all accounts, he was generous to his family and donated to civil rights organizations. The money didn't last, and as Ian Wallis noted, one of the ancillary negatives from Clyde's arrest for loitering with intent was the public exposure of Clyde suffering from a tenuous financial situation. Looking at a couple of remaining financial forms one can see why. For the year 1963 Mercury Records paid Clyde almost $16,000 in royalties.[29] In 1968, a royalty statement from BMI (Broadcast Music Inc) showed Clyde earned $2.18.[30]

The cobwebs in Clyde's wallet didn't diminish while he resided in London. It wasn't helpful that his drinking problems were more obvious and his reputation for being unreliable increased.

"I knew a lot of the smaller promoters that booked him in the UK in the sixties," said Graham Knight. "But he had a terrible reputation for missing shows due to drinking too much. I knew he was here for quite a while, but he ended up being abandoned by almost all the bookers."[31]

Although by 1969 his club appearances were becoming fewer and fewer, in January and February bad tidings were in abeyance as he was booked into multi-night appearances in bigger cities such as Manchester and Liverpool, and also in Staffordshire. Wallis, quoting a local Manchester newspaper, said the shows were sold out and the crowd appreciative. After a handful of club bookings in March 1969, the string petered out until July, when he played his final gigs in the UK.[32]

Although the loitering charges either had been dropped or, as some reported, "acquitted," the incident happened and it was probably part of the reason why the UK Home Office (the government department that oversees security and immigration) did not renew his work permit. Clyde returned to the United States in 1970.

If anything, Clyde came back to his East Coast haunts even in worse financial condition than when he left for London. Fortunately, he still knew a lot of people in the industry, and he contacted an old friend, Clyde Otis, who had helped him in the past.

Otis was a giant in the industry, first as a very successful songwriter and then with Mercury Records, where he was the first African American to be head of A&R at a major record company. Physically he was a giant as well, standing 6'4". He produced or wrote thirty-three chart-toppers for Mercury, working with everyone from Timi Yuro with "Hurt," Brook Benton with "Just a Matter of Time," "The Boll Weevil Song," and fifteen other hits, and Dinah Washington, with her late career masterpieces "What a Difference a Day Makes" and "This Bitter Earth." In 1961 Otis left Mercury and formed the Clyde Otis Music Group, working with major artists such as Aretha Franklin.

Clyde Otis left Mercury for a couple of probable reasons. One theory is that he was poached by Liberty Records, which offered a higher salary. A second possibility is that he and Mercury had a difference in philosophy as to who should own the rights and retain the income from the records Clyde Otis wrote or produced. Mercury thought it should and when Clyde Otis wouldn't budge, a split occurred. Mercury didn't blink because it had an ace up its sleeve. It had a hot, young producer coming up by the name of Quincy Jones.

Clyde Otis was born in Mississippi, dropped out of school to work the cotton fields, and then joined the marines, which got him out of the South. When he returned to the States after his service, he washed up in New York driving a taxi. He had a talent for music, and an encounter with a fare, who was in the music industry, proved all the luck he needed. He gave the customer a demo, which eventually became a song recorded by Nat King Cole. He attained the elevated management position at Mercury because he brought to the recording company such talent as Brook Benton, Dinah Washington, and Timi Yuro.

Isidro Otis, Clyde Otis's son, remembers Clyde McPhatter used to stay at his family's house when working with his dad. "A lot of artists did that when recording with my father," Isidro remembers. "I was young and don't have many recollections of Clyde McPhatter except that he seemed to be real 'cool.' He had that swagger about him. A lot of the artists like Brook Benton and the Isley Brothers became like family. Not Clyde. I asked my mother about Clyde, and all she could remember was that he recorded with my father. She had no stories to tell."[33]

Clyde Otis had his own production company, Argon Productions, and that's how Clyde McPhatter came to Decca; Otis brought Clyde to the recording company as an Argon artist. According to Isidro Otis, Argon first recorded the album *Welcome Home*, which was shopped to a few major labels. Then Otis had Clyde meet Tom Morgan at the US offices of Decca Records, who signed him with an advance of $25,000, a lifeline for Clyde.[34] Clyde Otis was one of the first African Americans to retain publishing rights to his songs, and in regard to the tunes he produced for Clyde McPhatter, these were actually leased to Decca.[35]

Early in August 1970, *Billboard* briefly noted, "Clyde McPhatter is back in the country on Decca with a new album, *Welcome Home*, produced by Clyde Otis. Featured is McPhatter's new single 'Book of Memories.'"[36]

This wasn't a throwaway album; a true effort was made to make the album a quality offering. One of arrangers was Belford Hendricks, a compatriot of Clyde Otis since the late 1950s, who collaborated with Nat "King" Cole, Sarah Vaughan, Dinah Washington, and Aretha Franklin, among many others. For some, Clyde Otis was one of greatest arrangers/producers of R&B in the twentieth century. Isidro Otis concedes, "That's impressive to hear, but I'm sure my father would say his partner, Belford Hendricks, should probably earn more of the credit as the arranger. With all those many songs recorded under my father's auspices, a lot of credit should go to Belford."[37]

Clyde's album offered twelve songs, of which only "Our Day Will Come" (a #1 tune by Ruby and the Romantics in 1963) was most familiar. Otherwise, many of the tune titles reflected Clyde's state of mind: "A Mother's Love," "The Ties That Bind," "Mr. Heartache," "Someone to Believe In," and "Book of Memories." A couple of singles were released from the album.

"In my opinion," wrote Bill Millar, "some of the best performances of his career."[38]

Ed Ochs, who authored the "Soul Sauce" gossipy R&B column in *Billboard*, agreed: "Decca is out with Earl Grant's last LP and a fine comeback album by Clyde McPhatter. He's better than ever."[39]

Not everyone was on board with that assessment. *Ebony* took Clyde to task, noting, "The man who founded the Drifters in 1953 and then made it as a single is back in the U.S. after spending three years in Europe. His is an intimate, rather high, ballad voice but he seems uncertain as to what he wants to do with it on this spotty set. Yet he comes through on 'I'll Belong to You' and 'Our Day Will Come.'"[40]

In mid-summer 1970, *Billboard*'s "Soul Singles" chart boasted three classic songs at the top of the list: "Signed, Sealed, Delivered (I'm Yours)" by Stevie Wonder, "Get Up, I Feel Like Being a Sex Machine (Parts 1 & 2)" by James Brown, and "War" by Edwin Starr. Down list, there were a host of other great tunes by Clarence Carter, Aretha Franklin, the Jackson 5, the Spinners, the Chi-Lites and Diana Ross. Somehow there was room on the charts and radio playlists for a great comeback. Unfortunately, it was not Clyde McPhatter. It was Gene Chandler, who had sung the #1 hit "Duke of Earl" back in 1962. Chandler would return in 1970 with his last major recording, "Groovy Situation." On the lower end of the Soul Singles charts, other R&B veterans slipped in as well, including B.B. King, Rufus Thomas, Esther Phillips, and Dyke and the Blazers.[41]

Into this swirl, Decca released two singles consisting of songs from the *Welcome Home* album: "Book of Memories"/"I'll Belong to You" and "Why Can't We Get Together" / "The Mixed Up Cup."

The album didn't create an iota of an impact and neither did the singles, which couldn't even make it to the pop charts. Clyde Otis was not happy with the results of the Decca deal and terminated the Clyde McPhatter agreement after just one album release. He continued to keep Clyde McPhatter afloat, getting him gigs with rock revival concerts and small club dates.[42] The problem was that Clyde McPhatter was emotionally and psychologically falling apart and had been for years.

His daughter Deborah observed, "I'd seen him extremely hurt and upset with people in the business. More drinking when there was a letdown or when Lena [his wife] would act up, having all kinds of people in the house, which would piss him off, and that she was screwing other musicians. As a youngster I knew he drank because I was told he drank, but I also knew the difference in his personality when he drank." Deborah added that she never saw her father handle a bottle of liquor in front of her.[43]

When Deborah was a teenager, she had witnessed her father cuss out management over being "shorted" at the famous Forty Thieves Club in Hamilton, Bermuda. Unfortunately, financial discrepancies with club managers were a common occurrence everywhere. Except the Forty Thieves Club was a big deal in its day, almost like a visit to Las Vegas. Dionne Warwick, Damita Jo, B.B. King, Mel Torme, Aretha Franklin, Ike and Tina Turner, Tom Jones, Ramsey Lewis, Marvin Gaye, the Temptations, and many more famous names all played the club. In the audience it wasn't unusual to find rock royalty, such as John Lennon of the Beatles or Keith Richards of the Rolling Stones. A promotion in the island's *Bermudian* from 1963 shows Kitty Kallen coming to the club's stage at the beginning of July, the Mello-Larks in the middle of the month, and Clyde McPhatter opening on July 30.[44] (There's no date on the clipping but Kitty Kallen boasted a career comeback in 1963 with the success of her recording "My Coloring Book.")

Clyde wasn't the only performer to have complaints about the Forty Thieves Club. Mel Carter, who had a big hit in 1965 with "Hold Me, Thrill Me," said, "I performed there once and it was not a good experience for me and my manager."[45]

What happened on the night Clyde and management went toe-to-toe? He had played the club many times, but on this particular night he was inebriated, which was never good. To be fair to Clyde, the Forty Thieves Club earned its name. Other than money issues, what could have gotten Clyde to the point of anger, said Deborah McPhatter, trying to bring back to mind the events of that night, "No disrespect, but the forty or so white men who owned that club and everything on Front Street in Bermuda were given the name (Forty Thieves) for a reason. They have been known to do shady deeds. Sure, my father drank and over-drank, but he wasn't a 'shit-starter.'" Someone told Deborah that Clyde's problems at the club might also have had something to do with the white female he was seeing. Said Deborah, "I do remember seeing such a lady with him, but I have no idea who she was."[46]

"Clyde was an easygoing person, very generous and nice to be around—when he wasn't drinking," said Bill Curtis. "When drinking he was very nasty and didn't know if he was coming or going. He would go to the liquor store and buy booze as if buying apples or oranges, very level-headed. Clyde Otis tried to organize a comeback, but Clyde was far too gone on alcohol. He would forget words to songs."

As Clyde's work began to dry up, Curtis realized it was time to do something else as he had to make a living for himself. He stopped working with Clyde in 1970.[47]

"By the time I met him [Clyde], it was later in his career and he had become a hopeless alcoholic," remembered Billy Vera. "We were the house band for this club in New York but just over the border from Greenwich, Connecticut. On weekends we would have either a current hit record act or someone who was a little older but still had a name. Clyde was one of those. I was a big fan. To get ready for his performance I studied up on all his most famous songs that he recorded as a soloist or with the Drifters and Dominoes. I was ready for him. For the rehearsal he was on time and sober. By the time of the show, however, he was pretty drunk, and he didn't do one song that we had rehearsed. He called out all these other songs, and luckily I learned these at home. He didn't have any music that the band could read, but we got through it fine and the audience liked him. Then he got into an argument with the club owner, who was a nice guy, but Clyde was drunk."[48]

For a while, Billy Vera and Clyde had the same manager, a guy named Al Schwartz. One day Schwartz got a call from Bobby Schiffman, who was the owner of the Apollo, which had Clyde on a bill. Clyde had first made his name in Harlem, and he always drew at the Apollo, not necessarily as a headliner, but a good act in a multi-talent show. On this one night, Schwartz received a call from Schiffman, who told him he better get up to the Apollo because Clyde had locked himself in his dressing room and wouldn't come out. Schwartz jumped in a cab and got to the Apollo as quickly as manageable in Manhattan. Finally, he was able to talk Clyde into unlocking the door. When Schwartz walked in, he saw Clyde sitting with blood pouring down from the top of his head. What happened was, in the prior show (often performers would do multiple Apollo shows running day to night) Clyde decided he wanted to do songs from his new record. He said to the audience, "Ladies and gentlemen, what I'm going to do for you now is my latest recording, 'Crying Won't Help You Now' [from 1965] and I dedicate it to all you winos and junkies in the third balcony because crying won't help none of you n-----s up there." The remarks were not appreciated by those in the third balcony, because one of those "winos and junkies," with good accuracy, flung a bottle that hit Clyde in the head and knocked off his toupee. Clyde wouldn't come out for the next show.

Another career apocalypse story is that Clyde was sacked from a Houston club after drinking heavily before a gig, stumbling around on stage, and in his teasing, but now out-of-control, am-I-gay or am-I-not-gay act, began kissing the neck of his piano player. The finale of this performance was Clyde unzipping the fly of his trousers.[49]

Toward the end, it seemed that everyone, especially those who loved Clyde's music and steadfastly went to see him perform all through the later 1960s and early 1970s, came away with a tragic story of an amazing and important performer immolating his career.

One of the most sorrowful tales comes from music historian Marv Goldberg, who wrote that he was at a Clyde show that took place in December 1971. Clyde came on, sang a few songs, took off his tie, sat down on the front of the stage, and (with far too much to drink inside him) told us 'I'm not used to coming on third; I used to be a star.' You had to cry."

Journalist Marcia Vance, who would later become, as Marv Goldberg reported, his "partner," attended an oldies show and was introduced to Clyde as a fan. He responded, "I have no fans."[50]

When Clyde returned to the United States, he did make an effort to stop drinking, going to AA meetings. It was at one of these gatherings where he met his last girlfriend Bertha M. Reid (he was still married to Lena Rackley

McPhatter). Said Deborah McPhatter, "She was also in the program. I remember her as a friendly voice over the phone. There were times my dad called me from her apartment in the Bronx. Or, I would call him and she would answer the phone. She had a son who she wanted me to meet, which didn't sit well with my dad. Her son might have been a drug addict, but I never met him, so I can't say for sure."

In pure Clyde ambivalence to women, even when he was with Bertha, still married to Lena, almost every night he would call Deborah's mother, hoping she would pick up the phone and talk to him. It seemed Clyde couldn't do anything without talking to Lorraine, Deborah's mother. "My mom felt like she was trapped between her child [me], the birth-father of her child [Clyde] and a man [my stepfather] that truly loved her—a man that moved mountains for her," said Deborah.

One day when Clyde wasn't feeling well, Lorraine took him to the doctor, and that's when he learned he had cirrhosis of the liver.

"I asked him one night why he drank so much," said Deborah. "His quick response was 'none of your business,' which he said with that Clyde laugh that I still hear in my head today. So, I replied, 'OK nuisance, I'm hanging up. Bye.' I knew he would call back as soon as he could dial the number. One night he did answer my question, saying he had been drinking since he was a teenager on the road and that all he knew how to do was sing. That was his life, and if he couldn't perform, he had no life."[51]

Singer/songwriter Carol Connors, when she was sixteen and still in high school, was part of a trio called the Teddy Bears. They had a #1 hit in 1958 called "To Know Him Is to Love Him." At the start of the 1960s she had a love affair with Elvis Presley when the sleek, handsome man who set hearts aflutter was still the King of Rock 'n' Roll. The relationship lasted less than a year but she remained friends with him her whole life, last going to visit him within a year of his death. The Elvis she remembered drank nothing stronger than water, was keenly aware of his career and feline in his handsomeness, but when she saw him in 1976, her heart broke because he was bloated, not truly cognizant, and drugged out. She wondered how he could still do his shows, as he was almost incoherent. She recalled, "I could almost see Elvis passing away right in front of me."[52]

Elvis died in August 1977 at the age of forty-two, a couple of years older than Clyde at his death.

The entertainment industry is a tough business. One moment you are emperor of all, and then your reign dissipates. Elvis was once considered the King of Rock 'n' Roll, but he abused prescription drugs and indulged in extreme eating habits, which he had to atone for by immoderate dieting to get into his show costumes. A bad heart combined with drugs caused his death.

Clyde McPhatter, too, was once a king. In the pre–rock 'n' roll days, in the very early 1950s, when R&B was tumbling into the music that would make Elvis famous, Clyde McPhatter was the most important voice in America. His unusual range, especially as a tenor, was mimicked by almost every lead singer of a R&B group in the 1950s, particularly in the music that came to be called doo-wop. And like Elvis, he was devilishly handsome and a heartthrob, but to African American (and some white) teenage girls. Clyde McPhatter was one of the most influential voices in the history of pop music.

Clyde was luckier than most. He basically had three careers: lead singer of the Dominoes, founder and lead singer of the Drifters, and successful solo artist. He was a hitmaker for more than a decade, yet psychologically his descent was relatively quick. Musicologists and those close to him have suggested a number of reasons for this: the decline of his recording career, inability to overcome a fraught relationship with his father, unfaithful wives, or that he was a closeted homosexual. Perhaps it was all of that or even something more. But no one really knows.

Toward the end, Deborah said she was very angry at her father because she sensed that he had given up, just given up on hope. "Sometimes I would answer my phone and it was him. I would immediately hang up. He would call back."

On the night Clyde died, he dialed Deborah. She hung up the phone, but he kept dialing her all night. After Clyde passed, Deborah was left with two terrible emotions, guilt and anger.[53]

As Marv Goldberg concluded, "finally, after years of torturing himself . . . Clyde McPhatter passed away on June 13, 1972, in New York. The world lost one of its brightest talents, one whose contributions are incalculable."[54]

Clyde's death certificate was unintelligible. It listed him as forty-one years of age at death, which was a bit strange since information on the same document said his age at last birthday was thirty-eight. It was also written on the same document that his birth date was November 15, 1933.[55] According to Clyde's military records, he was born on that date in 1932, which would have made him thirty-nine at death.

With Lena, as with his other wives, he mostly did not reside with her. While he was still married to Lena McPhatter at the time of his death, the place of his passing was at Bertha's apartment on 229th Street in the Bronx.

Most people just assume, for example, that Elvis died of a heart attack and that Clyde passed on from his alcoholism. Death is never really so simple, so calculated. The immediate cause of Clyde's death was lobar pneumonia with the underlying causes of fatty liver and chronic ethanolism, which is translatable as alcohol-use disorder.

Two days after Clyde's death, a public memorial service was held in New York City. It was packed with family, friends and many, many fans. Deborah

McPhatter said her most heartfelt memory of that service was of a man who went up to the casket and cried, cried some more, and then screamed, "This should have been me." He damn near jumped in the casket. Deborah never found out for sure who that person was. Someone said it was Bill Pinkney, while another said it was his brother Thomas. There was also an overwhelming number of women present, also crying and trying to kiss the corpse. The viewing had to be stopped and a casket-net was pulled over him. Clyde's sister Gladys sang a gospel tune. Others also sang, but Deborah was so saddened she didn't bother to find out who they were. The only bad part of the ceremony for Deborah was Clyde's wife Lena, who wouldn't leave her alone.

A second memorial service for Clyde was held at the Nesbitt Funeral Home in Englewood, New Jersey, on the same day. Said Deborah, "My nerves were shot and my mother's lawyer, who attended the first ceremony with me, suggested I not attend but go to the cemetery afterward, which is what I did."[56]

Clyde McPhatter was interred at the George Washington Memorial Park in Paramus, New Jersey.

Have Mercy, Baby.

HONORS AND AWARDS

Clyde McPhatter, Rock and Roll Hall of Fame, 1987
As a member of the Drifters, Rock and Roll Hall of Fame, 1988
United States Postal Service issued stamp in Clyde McPhatter's honor, 1993
Clyde McPhatter song "Money Honey," Grammy Hall of Fame, 1999
North Carolina Music Hall of Fame, 2009
National Rhythm and Blues Foundation Hall of Fame, 2023
Rolling Stone ranked Clyde McPhatter at #99 on list of 200 Greatest Singers of All-Time, 2023

SELECTED DISCOGRAPHY

Based on Billboard, Discogs.com, ebay.com, RateYourMusic.com

SINGLES

With The Dominoes (Also Charlie White, Joe Lamont, Bill Brown; James Van Loan and David McNeil replaced White and Brown)

Do Something for Me / Chicken Blues, 1951, Federal 12001
Harbor Lights / No! Says My Heart, 1951, Federal 12010
Sixty Minute Man / I Can't Escape from You, 1951, Federal 12022
Weeping Willow Blues / I Am with You, 1951, Federal 12039
That's What You're Doing to Me / When the Swallows Come Back to Capistrano, 1952, Federal 12059
Have Mercy Baby / Deep Sea Blues, 1952. Federal 12068
I'd Be Satisfied / No Room, 1952, Federal 12105
Yours Forever / I'm Lonely, 1952, Federal 12106
The Bells / Pedal Pushin' Papa, 1953, Federal 12114
These Foolish Things (Remind Me of You) / Don't Leave Me This Way, 1953, Federal 12129

With The Drifters (Also Bill Pinkney, Andrew Thrasher, Gerhart Thrasher, Willie Ferbee, and guitarist Walter Adams; Ferbee left the group; Jimmy Oliver replaced Adams)

Money Honey / The Way I Feel, 1953, Atlantic 1006
Bip Bam / Someday (You'll Want Me to Want You), 1954, Atlantic 1043
White Christmas / The Bells of St. Mary's, 1954, Atlantic 1048
Such A Night / Lucille, 1954, Atlantic 1152
Honey Love / Warm Your Heart, 1954, Atlantic 1209
What'cha Gonna Do / Gone, 1955, Atlantic 1055
Everyone's Laughing / Hot Ziggety, 1955, Atlantic 1070 (attribution just Clyde McPhatter)

SOLO

Money Honey / The Way I Feel, 1953, Atlantic 1006 (attribution Clyde McPhatter and the Drifters)
Such a Night / Lucille, 1954, Atlantic, Atlantic 1019 (attribution Clyde McPhatter and the Drifters)
Honey Love / Warm Your Heart, 1954 Atlantic 1029 (attribution The Drifters featuring Clyde McPhatter)
Love Has Joined Us Together / I Gotta Have You, 1955, Atlantic 1077 (attribution Ruth Brown and Clyde McPhatter)
Seven Days / I'm Not Worthy, 1956, Atlantic 1081
Treasure of Love / When You're Sincere, 1956, Atlantic 1092
Thirty Days / I'm Lonely Tonight, 1956, Atlantic 1106
Without Love (There Is Nothing) / I Make Believe, 1957, Atlantic 1117
Just To Hold My Hand / No Matter What, 1957, Atlantic 1133
Long Lonely Nights / Heartaches, 1957, Atlantic 1149
Rock and Cry / You'll Be There, 1957, Atlantic 1158
Come What May / Let Me Know, 1958, Atlantic 1185
A Lover's Question / I Can't Stand Up Alone, 1958, Atlantic 1199
Lovey Dovey / My Island of Dreams, 1959, Atlantic 2018
Since You've Been Gone / Try Try Baby, 1959, Atlantic 2028
You Went Back on Your Word / There You Go, 1959, Atlantic 2038
I Told Myself a Lie / (I'm Afraid) The Masquerade Is Over, 1959, MGM 12780
Twice As Nice / Where Did I Make My Mistake, 1959, MGM 12816
Let's Try Again / Bless You, 1959, MGM, 12843
Think Me A Kiss / When the Right Time Comes Along, 1960, MGM 12877
This Is Not Goodbye / One Right After Another, 1960, MGM 12949
Just Give Me A Ring / Don't Dog Me, 1960, Atlantic 2049
Deep Sea Ball / Let the Boogie-Woogie Roll, 1960, Atlantic 2060
If I Didn't Love You Like I Do / Go! Yes Go!, 1960, Atlantic 2082
Ta Ta / I Ain't Givin' Up Nothin', 1960, Mercury 71660
I Just Want to Love You / You're for Me, 1960, Mercury 71692
One More Chance / Before I Fall in Love Again (I'll Count to Ten), 1960, Mercury 71740
Tomorrow Is A-Comin' / I'll Love You Til the Cows Come Home, 1961, Mercury 71783
Glory Of Love / Take A Step, 1961, MGM 12988
Whole Heap of Love / You're Movin' Me, 1961, Mercury 71809
I Never Knew / Happiness, 1961, Mercury 71841
Same Time Same Place / Your Second Choice, 1961, Mercury 71868
Lover Please / Let's Forget About the Past, 1962, Mercury 71941
Little Bitty Pretty One / Next to Me, 1962, Mercury 71987
Maybe / I Do Believe, 1962, Mercury 72025
The Best Man Cried / Stop, 1962, Mercury 72051
From One to One / So Close to Being in Love, 1963, Mercury 72166
Deep In the Heart of Harlem / Happy Good Times, 1963, Mercury 72220
In My Tenement / Second Window, Second Floor, 1964, Mercury 72253

Baby Baby / Lucille, 1964, Mercury 72317
Crying Won't Help You Now / I Found My Love, 1965, Mercury 72407
Everybody's Somebody's Fool / I Belong to You, 1965, Amy 941
A Little Bit of Sunshine / Everybody Loves a Good Time, 1966, Amy 950
A Shot of Rhythm and Blues / I'm Not Going to Work Today, 1966, Amy 968
Sweet And Innocent / Lavender Lace, 1967, Amy (Stateside) 975
I Dreamt I Died / Lonely People Can't Afford to Cry, 1967, Amy 993
Only A Fool / Thank You Love, 1968, Deram 202
Baby You Got It / Baby I Could Be So Good at Loving, 1969, Deram 85039
Denver, Tell Me, 1969, B&C 37481
I'll Belong to You / Book of Memories, 1970, Decca 32719
Why Can't We Get Together / The Mixed-Up Cup, 1970, Decca 32753

ALBUMS

Clyde McPhatter With Billy Ward and His Dominoes, 1957, King 559
Love Ballads, 1958, Atlantic 8024
Clyde, 1959, Atlantic 8031
Let's Start Over Again, 1959, MGM 3775
Ta Ta!, 1960, Mercury 60262
Clyde McPhatter, 1959, London 1202
Clyde McPhatter's Greatest Hits, 1960, MGM 3866
Golden Blues Hits, 1961, Mercury 60655
Billy Ward And His Dominoes, 1962 (first 1956). Federal 548
Lover Please, 1962, Mercury 20711
May I Sing for You, 1962, Mercury 16224
Rhythm and Soul: Clyde McPhatter with the Merry Melody Singers, 1962, Mercury 60750
Songs Of the Big City, 1964, Mercury 60902
Live at the Apollo, 1964, Mercury 60915
Welcome Home, 1970, Decca 75231

RESEARCH AND ACKNOWLEDGMENTS

The research behind this book relies on music trade publications, African American newspapers, general-circulation newspapers, magazines, music history books, published biographies, and digital news stories. In addition, I interviewed, verbally and through communication services, numerous individuals who supplied me with relevant, firsthand recollections of the people and events featured in the book.

During the 1980s I interviewed a number of singers who had attained stardom in the 1950s, including Hank Ballard and Frankie Ford. Some of their comments were relevant to this book.

The book probably could not have been written without generous help from Clyde McPhatter's daughter, Deborah McPhatter, who opened up much time for me to discuss Clyde McPhatter's life. I personally visited with Deborah at her home in North Carolina, where she welcomed my wife and me to a vast lunch. Afterward she allowed me to peruse personal items such as letters, photos, and memorabilia that her father had saved. Many times I emailed or messaged her about some small data point or historical circumstance that I needed to double-check. She always responded quickly and in depth. Deborah was not always comfortable with the direction of the book's storyline, but she kept the faith that I would do a thorough job. So, once again, thank you, Deborah.

As mentioned, I interviewed numerous sources for this book. A couple of these interviews were done in the past, but the comments were relevant to this book, so I included them. A big thanks to: Hank Ballard (1980s interview), Tom Bialoglow, Howard Burchette, Tony Burke, Mel Carter, Carol Connors, Bill Curtis, Carlo Ditta, Kenneth Feld, Frankie Ford (1980s interview), Ronald Isley, Terry King, Graham Knight, Beverly Leet, Spencer Leigh, Yusuf Lamont, James Marshall, Deborah McPhatter, Jimmy Merchant, Louise Harris Murray, Isidro Otis, Rudy Protrudi, Margie Singleton, Charlie Thomas, Winfred "Brother" Tolor, Tina Treadwell, Billy Vera, Ian Wallis, and John Wirt.

NOTES

CHAPTER ONE

1. "Popularity Bad for Orioles," *Detroit Tribune*, September 16, 1950, 16.
2. Larry Birnbaum, *Before Elvis: The Prehistory of Rock 'n' Roll* (Scarecrow Press, 2013), 302.
3. "Popularity Bad for Orioles," *Detroit Tribune*, September 16, 1950, 16.
4. Arnold Shaw, *Honkers and Shouters: The Golden Years of Rhythm & Blues* (Collier Books, 1978), 135.
5. "Records Most Played by Disk Jockeys," *Billboard*, December 25, 1948, 92.
6. Betty Miles, "Record Row," *(Washington, DC) Evening Star*, September 26, 1948, D-8.
7. "The Billboard Picks," *Billboard*, September 4, 1948, 33.
8. "The Orioles Wax New Hit Tune," *Chicago World*, November 13, 1948, 3.
9. "Orioles Soar for Second Year in Row," *Detroit Tribune*, October 28, 1950, 18.
10. Shaw, *Honkers and Shouters: The Golden Years of Rhythm & Blues*, 135.
11. Barry Hansen, *The Rolling Stone History of Rock & Roll* (Rolling Stone Press/Random House, 1976), 82.
12. Birnbaum, *Before Elvis: The Prehistory of Rock 'n' Roll*, 303.
13. Hansen, *The Rolling Stone History of Rock & Roll*, 82.
14. *Jet*, August 27, 1953, 62.
15. Liner notes, *Clyde McPhatter Live at the Apollo*.
16. Ruth Brown and Andrew Yule, *Miss Rhythm: The Autobiography of Ruth Brown, Rhythm & Blues Legend* (Donald I. Fine Books, 1996), 133.
17. Shaw, *Honkers And Shouters: The Golden Years of Rhythm & Blues*, 240.
18. John Hartley Fox, *King of the Queen City* (University of Illinois Press, 2009), 6, 7.
19. "Obituaries: Sydney Nathan," *American Israelite* (Cincinnati), March 14, 1968, 17.
20. Fox, *King of the Queen City*.
21. Billy Vera, interview, 2023.
22. Fox, *King of the Queen City*, 88.
23. "King Sets New Tag, 'Federal,'" *Billboard*, November 4, 1950, 16.
24. Nick Tosches, *Unsung Heroes of Rock 'n' Roll* (Harmony Books, 1984), 133.
25. Marv Goldberg, www.uncamarvy.com.
26. Tosches, *Unsung Heroes of Rock 'n' Roll*, 133.
27. Marv Goldberg, www.uncamarvy.com.
28. Tosches, *Unsung Heroes of Rock 'n' Roll*, 133.

29. Shaw, *Honkers and Shouters: The Golden Years of Rhythm and Blues*.
30. Billy Vera, interview, 2023.
31. Fox, *King of the Queen City*, 92.
32. Marv Goldberg, www.uncamarvy.com.
33. Charlie Gillett, *The Sound of the City: The Rise of Rock and Roll* (Outerbridge & Dienstfrey, 1970), 178.
34. Billy Vera, interview, 2023.
35. "Round the Wax Circle," *Cash Box*, January 20, 1951, 9.
36. Shaw, *Honkers and Shouters: The Golden Years of Rhythm and Blues*, 236.
37. "Little Esther Signs Contract with New Federal Label," *Cash Box*, January 20, 1951, 16.
38. Marv Goldberg, www.uncamarvy.com.
39. Birnbaum, *Before Elvis: The Prehistory of Rock 'n' Roll*, 304.
40. "Most Played Jukebox Rhythm & Blues Records," *Billboard*, September 22, 1951, 38.
41. "Rhythm & Blues Notes," *Billboard*, September 22, 1951.
42. "King Plans to Cover All Hillbilly Hits," *Cash Box*, September 29, 1951, 13.
43. Birnbaum, *Before Elvis: The Prehistory of Rock 'n' Roll*, 304.
44. "Palace Theater," *Daily Express*, January 23, 1952, 3.
45. "New Sounds," *Miami Times*, May 31, 1952, 16.
46. Shaw, *Honkers and Shouters: The Golden Years of Rhythm and Blues*, 282–83.
47. "The Final Count," *Cash Box*, December 6, 1952, 6.
48. "Rhythm & Blues Ramblings," *Cash Box*, November 1, 1952, 20.
49. Yusuf Lamont, interview, 2023.
50. *Cash Box*, November 1, 1952, 20.
51. Larry Douglas, "Theatrically Yours," *Arizona Sun*, October 2, 1953, 3.
52. G. Houston Byrd, "Byrdland," *Detroit Tribune*, January 10, 1953, 5.
53. Dave Marsh, *The Heart of Rock & Soul: The 1001 Greatest Singles Ever Made* (New American Library, 1989), 260.
54. "New Records to Watch," *Billboard*, December 20, 1952, 30.
55. "Award O' The Week," *Cash Box*, December 20, 1952, 20.
56. "Billy Ward's Dominoes Steal Show from Stars," *Detroit Tribune*, February 28, 1953, 5.

CHAPTER TWO

1. Howard Burchette, interview, 2023.
2. "Big Voice, Desire to Sing Clyde's Assets," *Carolina Times* (Durham, NC), September 22, 1956, 6.
3. 1940 Census.
4. "Big Voice, Desire to Sing Clyde's Assets," 6.
5. "Hayti District General History," https://www.ibiblio.org.
6. "Biltmore Hotel/Grill/Drugstore," https://www.opendurham.org.
7. Howard Burchette, interview, 2023.
8. Deborah McPhatter, interview, 2023.
9. "Red Robinson interviews Clyde McPhatter (1957)," www.youtube.com.
10. Howard Burchette, interview, 2023.

11. Deborah McPhatter, interview, 2023.
12. Winford "Brother Tolor, interview, 2023.
13. Marv Goldberg, www.uncamarvy.com.
14. Yusef Lamont, interview, 2023.
15. "Clyde McPhatter to Headline Big Show at State Fair Arena April 3," *Carolina Times* (Durham, NC), March 28, 1959, 5.
16. Marv Goldberg, www.uncamarvy.com.
17. Philip Ennis, *The Emergence of Rocknroll in American Popular Music* (Wesleyan University Press, 1992), 75.
18. Bill Pinkney and Maxine Porter, *Drifters 1: Bill Pinkney* (Bill-Max Publishing, 2013), 34–37.
19. Ennis, *The Emergence of Rocknroll in American Popular Music*, 75.
20. Liner notes, *Clyde McPhatter Live at the Apollo, 1965*.
21. Robert Greenfield, *The Last Sultan: The Life and Times of Ahmet Ertegun* (Simon and Schuster, 2011), 40.
22. Greenfield, *The Last Sultan: The Life and Times of Ahmet Ertegun*.
23. "Rating the Records," *St. Paul Recorder* (Minnesota), February 26, 1954, 6.
24. Tom Bialoglow, interview, 2023.
25. Pinkney and Porter, *Drifters 1: Bill Pinkney*, 37.
26. "Red Robinson interviews Clyde McPhatter (1957)," www.youtube.com.

CHAPTER THREE

1. Louise Harris Murray, interview, circa 2015.
2. Richard M. Raichelson, *Beale Street Talks: A Walking Tour Down the Home of the Blues* (Raichelson, 1999).
3. "Amateur Night at the Apollo Fact Sheet," apolloamateurnightfactsheet2021final-2.pdf.
4. Pinkey and Maxine Porter, *Drifters 1: Bill Pinkney*, 34.
5. Deborah McPhatter, interview, 2023.
6. Military registration card, George McPhatter.
7. Winford "Brother" Tolor, interview, 2023.
8. Bethel Bible Institute certificate.
9. Winford "Brother" Tolor, interview, 2023.
10. Winford "Brother" Tolor, interview, 2023.
11. Bill Curtis, interview, 2023.
12. "New York Beat," *Jet*, July 23, 1953, 37.
13. Brown and Yule, *Miss Rhythm: The Autobiography of Ruth Brown*, 133.
14. Deborah McPhatter, interview, 2023.
15. Letter from Clyde McPhatter to Lorraine Lowe, August 1952.
16. Letter from Clyde McPhatter to Lorraine Lowe, February 1953.
17. Telegram from Clyde McPhatter to Lorraine Lowe, January 1953.
18. Telegram from Clyde McPhatter to Lorraine Lowe, April 5, 195?.
19. Deborah McPhatter, interview, 2023.
20. Deborah McPhatter, interview, 2023.

21. Letter from Clyde McPhatter to Lorraine Lowe, January 20, 1968.
22. Bill Curtis, interview, 2023.
23. Deborah McPhatter, interview, 2023.
24. Winford "Brother" Tolor, interview, 2023.

CHAPTER FOUR

1. Yusuf Lamont, interview, 2023.
2. John Bush, "Billy Eckstine Biography," Allmusic, https://allmusic.com.
3. "Mr. B: Bobby Soxers Become Billy Soxers to Boost Baritone Billy Eckstine," *LIFE*, April 24, 1950.
4. Kerrie Mitchell, "LIFE in Pictures: Pop Star Billy Eckstine and the Infamous 1950 Photo that Impacted his Career," June 26, 2019, www.nyhistory.org.
5. Michael Eli Dokosi, "How a Photo of Singer Billy Eckstine Offended the White Community," March 24, 2020, Face2FaceAfrica, https://face2faceafrica.com.
6. Yusuf Lamont, interview, 2023.
7. "No Place Like Home," *Cash Box*, October 3, 1953, 23.
8. Jonny Whiteside, *Cry: The Johnnie Ray Story* (Barricade Books, 1994), 146.
9. "Talking About," *Jet*, June 19, 1952, 41.
10. "Negroes Taught Me to Sing: Famous Cry Crooner Tells What Blues Taught Him," *Ebony*, March 1953.
11. Yusuf Lamont, interview, 2023.
12. Marv Goldberg, www.uncamarvy.com.
13. Marv Goldberg, www.uncamarvy.com.
14. Billy Vera, interview, 2023.
15. Yusuf Lamont, interview, 2023.
16. "New York Beat," *Jet*, June 25, 1953, 63.
17. Yusuf Lamont, interview, 2023.
18. "New York Beat," *Jet*, July 14, 1955, 64.
19. "New York Beat," *Jet*, October 13, 1955, 64.
20. Yusuf Lamont, interview, 2023.
21. "Rhythm & Blues Notes," *Billboard*, November 24, 1951, 122.
22. Marv Goldberg, www.uncamarvy.com.
23. Birnbaum, *Before Elvis: The Prehistory of Rock 'n' Roll*, 310.
24. Charlie Gillett, *Making Tracks: Atlantic Records and the Growth of a Multi-Billion-Dollar Industry* (Dutton, 1974), 58.
25. Marv Goldberg, www.unamarvy.com.
26. "Despondent Singer Found After N.Y. Disappearance," *Jet*, November 11, 1954, 58.
27. Yusuf Lamont, interview, 2023.
28. Marv Goldberg, www.uncamarvy.com.
29. John Hartley Fox, *King of the Queen City* (University of Illinois Press, 2009), 98.
30. Billy Vera, interview, 2023.
31. Marv Goldberg, www.uncamarvy.com.
32. Yusuf Lamont, interview, 2023.

33. "National Best Seller" / "Most Played in Jukeboxes," *Billboard*, February 14, 1953, 42.
34. Clyde McPhatter, letter to Lorraine Lowe, November 19, 1952.
35. Doug Saint Carter, *Jackie Wilson: The Black Elvis* (Heyday Publishing, 1998), 35.
36. Yusuf Lamont, interview, 2023.
37. Deborah McPhatter, interview, 2023.
38. Joe McEwen, *The Rolling Stone Illustrated History of Rock and Roll* (Rolling Stone Press, 1976), 118.
39. Saint Carter, *Jackie Wilson: The Black Elvis*, 28.
40. "New York Beat," *Jet*, July 23, 1953, 37.
41. "Billy Ward's Dominoes to Sing for Ike," *Jet*, August 13, 1953, 60.
42. Sugar Ray-Dominoes Feud May Be Aired in Court," *Jet*, December 10, 1953, 54.
43. "Dominoes Ask Release from Glaser Contract," *Jet*, January 7, 1954, 59.
44. "Billy Ward, Nat Cole to Star at Detroit Fair," *Jackson (Mississippi) Advocate*, August 21, 1954, 4.
45. Yusuf Lamont, interview, 2023.
46. Ruth Brown and Andrew Yule, *Miss Brown: The Autobiography of Ruth Brown, Rhythm and Blues Legend* (Donald I. Fine Books, 1996), 128.
47. Saint Carter, *Jackie Wilson: The Black Elvis*, 35.

CHAPTER FIVE

1. Dorothy Wade and Justine Picardie, *Music Man: Ahmet Ertegun, Atlantic Records, and the Triumph of Rock 'n' Roll* (W.W. Norton, 1990), 30, 33.
2. Gillett, *Making Tracks: Atlantic Records and Growth of a Multi-Billion-Dollar Industry*, 38.
3. Greenfield, *The Last Sultan: The Life and Times of Ahmet Ertegun*, 45.
4. Gillett, *Making Tracks: Atlantic Records and Growth of a Multi-Billion-Dollar Industry*, 45.
5. Greenfield, *The Last Sultan: The Life and Times of Ahmet Ertegun*, 56.
6. Billy Vera, interview, 2023.
7. Gerri Hirshey, *Nowhere to Run: The Story of Soul Music* (Times Books, 1984), 38.
8. Gillett, *Making Tracks: Atlantic Records and Growth of a Multi-Billion-Dollar Industry*, 93.
9. Greenfield, *The Last Sultan: The Life and Times of Ahmet Ertegun*, 132.
10. Billy Vera, interview, 2023.
11. Gillett, *Making Tracks: Atlantic Records and Growth of a Multi-Billion-Dollar Industry*, 93.
12. Jerry Wexler and David Ritz, *Rhythm and Blues: A Life in American Music* (Alfred A. Knopf, 1993), 80.
13. Bill Vera, interview, 2023.
14. "McPhatter Signs with Atlantic," *Billboard*, May 30, 1953, 21.
15. Bob Rolontz, "Rhythm and Blues Notes," *Billboard*, May 30, 1953, 46.
16. Wexler and Ritz, *Rhythm and Blues: A Life in American Music*, 80.
17. Rolontz, "Rhythm and Blues Notes."
18. Larry Douglas, "Theatrically Yours," *Arkansas State Press*, June 12, 1953, 7.
19. Gillett, *Making Tracks: Atlantic Records and Growth of a Multi-Billion-Dollar Industry*, 94.
20. Shaw, *Honkers and Shouters: The Golden Years of Rhythm and Blues*, 382.
21. Wexler and Ritz, *Rhythm and Blues: A Life in American Music*, 89.

22. Pinkney and Porter, *Drifters 1 Bill Pinkney: The Legend of the Original Drifters*, 40.
23. Gillett, *Making Tracks: Atlantic Records and the Growth of a Multi-Billion-Dollar Industry*, 94.
24. Pinkney and Porter, *Drifters 1 Bill Pinkney: The Legend of the Original Drifters*, 40.
25. Gillett, *Making Tracks: Atlantic Records and Growth of a Multi-Billion-Dollar Industry*, 109.
26. Pinkney and Porter, *Drifters 1 Bill Pinkney: The Legend of the Original Drifters*, 42.
27. "McPhatter Claimed by Atlantic and Federal," *Cash Box*, June 13, 1953, 32.
28. "Rhythm N' Blues Ramblings," *Cash Box*, July 4, 1953, 23.
29. Pinkney and Porter, *Drifters 1 Bill Pinkney: The Legend of the Original Drifters*, 40.
30. "McPhatter Forms The Drifters," *Cash Box*, August 29, 1953, 23.
31. Wade and Picardie, *Music Man: Ahmet Ertegun, Atlantic Records, and Triumph of Rock 'n' Roll*, 39.
32. Pinkney and Porter, *Drifters 1 Bill Pinkney: The Legend of the Original Drifters*, 42.
33. Wexler and Ritz, *Rhythm and Blues: A Life in American Music*, 89.
34. "McPhatter Forms The Drifters."
35. Tina Treadwell, interview, 2023.
36. Brown and Yule, *Miss Brown: The Autobiography of Ruth Brown, Rhythm and Blues Legend*, 112.
37. Marv Goldberg, "The Drifters," Marv Goldberg's R&B Notebooks, www.uncamarvy.com.
38. Goldberg, "The Drifters."
39. Spencer Leigh, "Obituary: Jesse Stone," *Independent*, April 4, 1999.
40. Tony Fletcher, "Songwriters: Jesse Stone," Rock and Roll Hall of Fame, Jesse_Stone_2010.pdf.
41. Tosches, *Unsung Heroes of Rock 'n' Roll*, 16.
42. Tosches, *Unsung Heroes of Rock 'n' Roll*, 16.
43. Greenfield, *The Last Sultan: The Life and Times of Ahmet Ertegun*, 91.
44. Shaw, *Honkers and Shouters: The Golden Years of Rhythm and Blues*, 382.
45. Gillett, *Making Tracks: Atlantic Records and Growth of a Multi-Billion-Dollar Industry*, 94.
46. Birnbaum, *Before Elvis: The Prehistory of Rock 'n' Roll*, 308.
47. "Got to Sell Records," *Billboard*, September 12, 1953, 40.
48. "Reviews of this Week's New Records," *Billboard*, September 12, 1953, 22.
49. "New Records to Watch," *Billboard*, September 19, 1953, 40.
50. "Rhythm and Blues Notes," *Billboard*, September 26, 1953, 40.
51. "Inside Harlem," *Cash Box*, 25.
52. "Rhythm and Blues Notes," *Billboard*, 55.
53. Marsh, *The Heart of Rock and Soul: The 1001 Greatest Singles Ever Made*, 265.
54. "Rhythm N' Blues Ramblings," *Cash Box*, December 12, 1953, 31.

CHAPTER SIX

1. "DJ's Would Ban Smut and Racial Barbs on Disks," *Billboard*, February 27, 1954, 22.
2. Larry Douglas, "Theatrically Yours," *Arizona Sun*, October 2, 1953, 3.
3. "DJ's Would Ban Smut and Racial Barbs on Disks."
4. "Negro Radio Comes of Age," *Sponsor*, September 2, 1954, 52.

5. "KGFJ, Hollywood, Cal," *Sponsor*, September 20, 1954, 147.

6. John A. Jackson, *Big Beat Heat: Alan Freed and the Early Years of Rock and Roll* (Schirmer Books, 1991), 73.

7. "The Detroit Tribune Congratulates the Pittsburgh Courier in its Exposure of Smutty Records Fouling Airwaves! But—Your Sex Exploitation Has God's Condemnation," *Detroit Tribune*, November 13, 1954, 1.

8. "Leader Blasts People Who Want Smutty Records," *Jackson (Mississippi) Advocate*, November 20, 1954, 8.

9. L. F. Palmer, "Sexy Records Hit as Harming Nations Juveniles," *St. Paul Recorder*, December 10, 1954, 1.

10. Jackson, *Big Beat Heat: Alan Freed and the Early Years of Rock and Roll*, 72.

11. Ed Ward, *Rock of Ages: The Rolling Stone History of Rock and Roll* (Rolling Stone Press/Summit Books, 1986), 85.

12. Fox, *King of Queen City: The Story of King Records*, 101.

13. Gillett, *Making Tracks: Atlantic Records and the Growth of a Multi-Billion-Dollar Industry*, 94.

14. Fox, *King of Queen City: The Story of King Records*, 102.

15. "Rhythm N' Blues Ramblings," *Cash Box*, November 6, 1954, 25.

16. "Rhythm N' Blues Ramblings," *Cash Box*, October 30, 1954, 23.

17. "Detroit Ban: WXYZ Bars Versions of 'Such Night," *Billboard*, March 20, 1954, 19.

18. Goldberg, "The Drifters."

19. Pinkney and Porter, *Drifters 1 Bill Pinkney: The Legend of the Original Drifters*, 52.

20. Ward, *Rock of Ages: The Rolling Stone History of Rock and Roll*, 90.

21. "Rhythm N' Blues Ramblings," *Cash Box*, January 9, 1954, 17.

22. "Rhythm 'N Blues Reviews," *Cash Box*, January 23, 1954, 22.

23. "New Records to Watch," *Billboard*, January 30, 1954, 34.

24. "Rating the Records," *St. Paul (Minnesota) Recorder*, February 26, 1954, 6.

25. "Dr. Daddy-O Presents Double Attraction Monday, March 1 at Stevens, Gene Ammons & Clyde McPhatter Drifters," *Mississippi Enterprise*, February 27, 1954, 1.

26. "Rhythm N' Blues Ramblings," *Cash Box*, March 6, 1954, 23.

27. "Get the Original," *Cash Box*, March 6, 1954, 16.

28. "Rhythm N' Blues Ramblings," *Cash Box*, March 13, 1954, 66.

29. "The History of Banned Rock 'n' Roll," ClassicBands.com, www.classicbands.com/banned.html.

30. Jackson, *Big Beat Heat: Alan Freed and the Early Years of Rock and Roll*, 73.

31. "The History of Banned Rock 'n' Roll."

32. Ward, *Rock of Ages: The Rolling Stone History of Rock and Roll*, 91.

33. Deborah McPhatter, interview, 2023.

34. Goldberg, "The Drifters."

35. "Review Spotlight On . . . ," *Billboard*, May 29, 1954, 67.

36. Deborah McPhatter, interview, 2023.

37. "Rhythm N' Blues Ramblings," *Cash Box*, June 12, 1954, 25.

38. "Diskeries Drive in R&B Field, as RCA, Decca, Capitol, Merc., Move," *Billboard*, December 11, 1954, 16.

39. Goldberg, "The Drifters."

40. Wexler and Ritz, *Rhythm and the Blues: A Life in American Music*, 90.
41. Goldberg, "The Drifters."
42. Wexler and Ritz, *Rhythm and the Blues: A Life in American Music*, 89.
43. Gillett, *Making Tracks: Atlantic Records and the Growth of a Multi-Billion-Dollar Industry*, 94.
44. "Review Spotlight On . . . ," *Billboard*, November 13, 1954, 99.
45. "Rhythm N' Blues Ramblings," *Cash Box*, December 25, 1954, 35.

CHAPTER SEVEN

1. Lillian Roxon, *Rock Encyclopedia* (Grosset and Dunlap, 1969), 326.
2. Jackson, *Big Beat Heat: Alan Freed and the Early Years of Rock and Roll*, 2–3.
3. Greenfield, *The Last Sultan: The Life and Times of Ahmet Ertegun*, 105.
4. "Freed Signs With WINS," *Broadcasting*, August 23, 1954, 55.
5. Jackson, *Big Beat Heat: Alan Freed and the Early Years of Rock and Roll*, 67.
6. "New 'Top Ten R&B Show' To Do 60 One-Nighters" *Billboard*, November 27, 1954, 14.
7. "Freed Ball Takes 24G At St. Nick," *Billboard*, January 22, 1955, 13.
8. Goldberg, "The Drifters."
9. Pinkney and Porter, *Drifters 1 Bill Pinkney: The Legend of the Original Drifters*, 54.
10. Etta James and David Ritz, *Rage to Survive: The Etta James Story* (Da Capo Press, 1995), 28.
11. Pinkney and Porter, *Drifters 1 Bill Pinkney: The Legend of the Original Drifters*, 55.
12. Ward, *Rock of Ages: The Rolling Stone History of Rock and Roll*, 110.
13. "Rhythm N' Blues Ramblings," *Cash Box*, October 30, 1954, 23.
14. Pinkney and Porter, *Drifters 1 Bill Pinkney: The Legend of the Original Drifters*, 57.
15. Wexler and Ritz, *Rhythm and the Blues*.
16. Brown and Yule, *Miss Rhythm: The Autobiography of Ruth Brown, Rhythm & Blues Legend*, 133.
17. Gillett, *Making Tracks: Atlantic Records and the Growth of a Multi-Billion-Dollar Industry*, 94.
18. Billy Vera, interview, 2023.
19. "Rhythm 'N Blues Reviews," *Cash Box*, February 26, 1954, 32.
20. Birnbaum, *Before Elvis: The Prehistory of Rock 'n' Roll*, 308.
21. "The Popular Scene," *Minneapolis Spokesman*, November 12, 1954, 6.
22. "Rhythm 'N Blues Reviews," *Cash Box*, October 9, 1954, 24.
23. Brown and Yule, *Miss Rhythm: The Autobiography of Ruth Brown, Rhythm and Blues Legend*, 132.
24. This Week's Best Buys," *Billboard*, November 12, 1955, 128.
25. Brown and Yule, *Miss Rhythm: The Autobiography of Ruth Brown, Rhythm and Blues Legend*, 132–35.
26. Larry Douglas, "Theatrically Yours," *Arizona Sun*, February 18, 1955, 3.
27. Brown and Yule, *Miss Rhythm: The Autobiography of Ruth Brown, Rhythm and Blues Legend*, 105, 132.
28. "Ruth Brown, 78, Queen of R&B, Dies," Jon Pareles, *New York Times*, November 18, 2006.
29. Deborah McPhatter, interview, 2023.

CHAPTER EIGHT

1. "Virtual Surrender, 1955: The Year R.&B. Took Over Pop Field," *Billboard*, November 12, 1955, 126.
2. Robert Q. Lewis, "Robert Q. Discourses on Rock 'n' Roll," *Record Whirl*, August 1956, 29.
3. Ed Shelby, "Tommy Smalls, Disc Jockey of the Month: Teenagers by Thousands Rally Around 'Dr. Jive,'" *Record Whirl*, August 1956, 30.
4. "Rhythm N' Blues Ramblings," *Cash Box*, January 7, 1956, 23.
5. "Rhythm N' Blues Ramblings," *Cash Box*, July 28, 1956, 76.
6. "Thanks DJs," *Billboard*, November 12, 1955, 126.
7. Pinkney and Porter, *Drifters 1 Bill Pinkney: The Legend of the Original Drifters*, 85.
8. Steve Bergsman, *Earth Angels: The Short Lives and Controversial Deaths of Three R&B Pioneers* (Texas A&M University Press, 2023), 32.
9. Billy Vera, interview, 2023.
10. Goldberg, "The Drifters."
11. Pinkney and Porter, *Drifters 1 Bill Pinkney: The Legend of the Original Drifters*, 89–90.
12. Pinkney and Porter, *Drifters 1 Bill Pinkney: The Legend of the Original Drifters*, 89–90.
13. "Virtual Surrender, 1955: The Year R.&B. Took Over Pop Field."
14. "Rhythm-Blues Notes," *Billboard*, January 14, 1956, 56.
15. Goldberg, "The Drifters."
16. Gillett, *Making Tracks: Atlantic Records and the Growth of a Multi-Billion-Dollar Industry*, 95.
17. Kenneth Feld, interview, 2023.
18. "Clyde McPhatter Goes Out as a Single; Drifters to Continue As A Group," *Cash Box*, July 23, 1955, 32.
19. Pinkney and Porter, *Drifters 1 Bill Pinkney: The Legend of the Original Drifters*, 66.
20. "Clyde McPhatter Goes Out as a Single; Drifters to Continue As A Group."
21. Deborah McPhatter, interview, 2023.
22. Tina Treadwell, interview, 2023.
23. Bill Curtis, interview, 2023.
24. Tina Treadwell, interview, 2023.
25. "Drifters Drift on to Success," *Jackson (Mississippi) Advocate*, June 7, 1958, 6.
26. "Guitar Slim Signs with Atlantic," *Billboard*, March 17, 1956, 17.
27. Bill Simon, "Rhythm-Blues Notes," *Billboard*, April 14, 1956, 63.
28. Bill Simon, "Rhythm-Blues Notes," *Billboard*, May 26, 1956, 56.
29. Wexler and Ritz, *Rhythm and Blues: A Life in American Music*, 113.
30. Wade and Picardie, *Music Man: Ahmet Ertegun, Atlantic Records, and the Triumph of Rock 'n' Roll*, 48.
31. Ward, *Rock of Ages: The Rolling Stone History of Rock and Roll*, 110.
32. Greenfield, *The Last Sultan: The Life and Times of Ahmet Ertegun*, 114.
33. Wexler and Ritz, *Rhythm and Blues: A Life in American Music*, 113.
34. Greenfield, *The Last Sultan: The Life and Times of Ahmet Ertegun*, 114.
35. Shaw, *Honkers and Shouters: The Golden Years of Rhythm and Blues*, 383.
36. "Review Spotlight On . . . ," *Billboard*, December 17, 1955, 62.
37. "Review Spotlight On . . . ," *Billboard*, April 28, 1956, 60.

38. "This Week's Best Buys," *Billboard*, May 12, 1956, 119.
39. "Rhythm N' Blues Ramblings," *Cash Box*, May 5, 1956, 32.
40. "Award O' The Week, Rhythm 'N Blues Reviews," *Cash Box*, May 5, 1956, 36.
41. "Question 10," *Billboard*, May 12, 1956, 54.
42. "Rhythm N' Blues Ramblings," *Cash Box*, June 16, 1956, 28.
43. "Coming Up Strong," *Billboard*, June 16, 1956, 32.
44. "McPhatter, Presley in Song 'Fight,'" *The Carolinian* (Raleigh, NC), June 30, 1956, 9.
45. "An Unpredictable Year: With More to Spend, Public in '56 Really Turns Fickle," *Billboard*, December 22, 1956, 22.

CHAPTER NINE

1. Shaw, *Honkers and Shouters: The Golden Years of Rhythm and Blues*, 431.
2. Ward, *Rock of Ages: The Rolling Stone History of Rock and Roll*, 127.
3. Merchant v. Lymon, 8282 F. Supp. 1048-Dist. Court, SD New York 1993.
4. Jimmy Merchant, interview (via Facebook messaging), 2023.
5. Kenneth Feld, interview, 2023.
6. Bill Haley Jr. and Peter Benjaminson, *Crazy Man, Crazy* (Backbeat Books, 2019), 95.
7. Jerry Fuentes, "The Biggest Rock n Roll Show of 1956," *A Rock n' Roll Historian*, https://rnrhistorian.blogspot.com.
8. "Rock 'N Roll Show at Dinner Key," *Miami Times*, May 12, 1956, 8.
9. Haley and Benjaminson, *Crazy Man, Crazy*, 95.
10. Fuentes, "The Biggest Rock n Roll Show of 1956."
11. "Income of Persons in the United States: 1955," US Census, www.census.gov.
12. Joan Yates, "That Kra-azy Rock 'N Roll," *Detroit Tribune*, May 19, 1956. 4.
13. Fuentes, "The Biggest Rock n Roll Show of 1956."
14. Billy Vera, interview, 2023.
15. "Review Spotlight on . . . ," *Billboard*, December 1, 1956, 42.
16. "R&B Reviews/Award O' The Week," *Cash Box*, December 8, 1956, 48.
17. "Review Spotlight on . . . ," *Billboard*, December 1, 1956, 42.
18. "R&B Reviews/Award O' The Week," *Cash Box*, December 8, 1956, 48.
19. "This Weeks R&B Best Buys," *Billboard*, December 29, 1956, 33.
20. "This Week's R&B Best Buys," *Billboard*, December 29, 1956, 33.
21. "R&B Ramblings," *Cash Box*, April 27, 1957, 40.
22. "McPhatter's Tune Shop," *Cash Box*, July 20, 1957, 129.
23. "While Clyde McPhatter Sings His Wife Tends Record Store," *Carolinian*, March 1, 1958, 7.
24. "Cash, Albums Stolen from Clyde McPhatter's Shop," *Jet*, May 15, 1958, 62.
25. Wendy Palitz and Michael Robbins, *Brooklyn: A State of Mind* (Workman Publishing, 2000), 160.
26. "Rock 'N Roll Beat," *St. Paul Recorder*, October 11, 1957, 6.
27. "McPhatter New Platter on Tap," *St. Paul Recorder*, November 1, 1957, 6.
28. "R&B Reviews/Award O' The Week," *Cash Box*, September 28, 1957, 48.
29. "R&B Reviews/Award O' The Week," *Cash Box*, July 20, 1957, 84.
30. "The Hottest Artists are on Atlantic," *Cash Box*, July 20, 1957, 61.

CHAPTER TEN

1. "While Clyde McPhatter Sings His Wife Tends Record Store."
2. "McPhatter Sets Howard Record," *Jackson (Mississippi) Advocate*, August 24, 1957, 4.
3. Billy Vera, interview, 2023.
4. "Teen Talk," *Miami Times*, January 26, 1957, 12.
5. Letter Box," *Carolina Times*, November 16, 1957, 14.
6. "The Final Count," *Cash Box*, December 7, 1957, 8.
7. "Show of Stars at Phoenix Coliseum," *Arizona Sun*, September 26, 1957, 5.
8. Fuentes, "The Biggest Rock n Roll Show of 1956."
9. Beverly Lee, interview, 2018.
10. Paul Anka, *My Way* (St. Martin's Press, 2013), 79.
11. Kenneth Feld, interview, 2023.
12. Bill Curtis, interview, 2023.
13. Paul Anka, *My Way*, 53, 54,79.
14. Ken Feld, interview, 2023.
15. "Irvin Feld Retained to Manage Paul Anka," *Cash Box*, February 15, 1958, 29.
16. Anka, *My Way*, 56.
17. Anka, *My Way*, 80.
18. Ken Feld, interview, 2023.
19. "Mrs. Irvin Feld, Vic Selsman Die," *Billboard*, August 4, 1958, 34.
20. "GAC Takeover of Gale Near," *Billboard*, May 5, 1958, 3.
21. "GAC Absorbs Feld's Super Attractions," *Billboard*, June 9, 1958, 43.
22. Wexler and Ritz, *Rhythm and the Blues: A Life in American Music*, 131.
23. June Bundy, "Atlantic's 'Money Man' Is a Woman," *Billboard*, January 13, 1958,41.
24. Dik De Heer, "Brook Benton," https://tims.blackcat.nl.
25. Bill Curtis, interview, 2023.
26. "Review Spotlight on . . . ," *Billboard*, April 7, 1958, 44.
27. "Award o' The Week/R&B Reviews," *Cash Box*, April 19, 1958, 44.
28. Harry Bacas, "Top Teen Tunes: Added Starter Becomes a Hit," *Evening Star (Washington, DC)*, October 19, 1958, 3.
29. "Award o' The Week/R&B Reviews," *Cash Box*, September 20, 1958, 54.
30. "Honor Roll of Hits," *Billboard*, November 10, 1958, 28.
31. Howie Cook, "Road to Hitville Still Wide Open," December 8, 1958, 1.

CHAPTER ELEVEN

1. Preston Lauterbach, *The Chitlin' Circuit and the Road to Rock 'N' Roll* (W.W. Norton, 2011), 12.
2. Bill Curtis, interview, 2023.
3. Fuentes, "The Biggest Rock n Roll Show of 1956."
4. A. L. Singleton, "Togetherness in Show Business," *Evening Star (Washington, DC)*, July 26, 1959, 18.
5. Singleton, "Togetherness in Show Business."

6. "Rock-Roll Unit Cancels Show at Greenville," *Billboard*, June 13, 1960, 51.

7. "Steve Huey, "Jimmy Jones Biography," AllMusic, https://www.allmusic.com.

8. "Rock-Roll Unit Cancels Show at Greenville," *Billboard*, June 13, 1960, 51.

9. "Reflections: Looking Back at Black Atlanta's Social Life Prior to Hip-Hop's Impact," *Atlanta Daily World*, August 3, 2020, https://atlantadailyworld.com.

10. "Supersonic Attractions, Inc.," Georgia Company Directory, https://www.georgiacompanyregistry.com.

11. "People Are," *Jet*, August 6, 1959, 44.

12. "Clyde McPhatter Builds NJ Home," *The Carolinian (Raleigh, NC)*, October 17, 1959, 11.

13. "People Are."

14. "Group Interested in Old Paradise," *Detroit Tribune*, October 14, 1961, 7.

15. "Bits of This," *Arizona Tribune*, April 28, 1961, 7.

16. Marco Young, "They're Talking About," *Minneapolis Spokesman*, August 19, 1960, 13.

17. "Night Club Reviews: Clyde Hot-With Right Songs," *Billboard*, February 23, 1959, 10.

18. "Music as Written/Discourse," *Billboard*, November 16, 1959, 24.

19. "The Final Results," *Cash Box*, December 5, 1959, 22.

20. Brown and Yule, *Miss Rhythm: The Autobiography of Ruth Brown, Rhythm and Blues Legend*, 222.

21. "Spotlight Winners of the Week," *Billboard*, March 9, 1959, 48.

22. "Record Reviews," *Billboard*, May 30, 1959, 40.

23. Mike Barnes, "Composer Ray Ellis Dies at 85," *Hollywood Reporter*, October 31, 2008.

24. "Ellis Top A&R," *Billboard*, February 2, 1959, 50.

25. "McPhatter to MGM," *Cash Box*, March 14, 1959, 45.

26. "Clyde Signs MGM Pact," *Cash Box*, March 21, 1959, 41.

27. "Clyde McPhatter Signs $50,000 MGM Disc Pact, *The Carolinian* (Raleigh, NC), March 21, 1959, 15.

28. "Records," *Billboard*, August 10, 1959, 14.

29. "Distributor News," *Billboard*, March 30, 1959, 11.

30. "& Tomorrow's Tops," *Billboard*, August 10, 1959, 41.

31. "Record Ramblings," *Cash Box*, June 13, 1959, 46.

32. "Album Reviews," *Cash Box*, October 10, 1959, 36.

33. "Fleet: The Baion Sound of the American East Coast" (news clipping from unknown British magazine).

34. Peter Doggett, "Clyde McPhatter," *Record Collector*, February 1988.

35. Peter Keepnews, "Clyde Otis, 83, Executive and Songwriter, Dies," *New York Times*, January 18, 2008.

36. Harry Bacas, "Top Tunes," *Evening Star* (Washington, DC), August 7, 1960, 2.

37. *Ta Ta* (album), liner notes, 1960.

38. Harry Bacas, "Top Tunes," *Evening Star* (Washington, DC), August 7, 1960, 2.

39. "Record Reviews: Pick of the Week," *Cash Box*, July 9, 1960, 10.

40. "Record Ramblings," *Cash Box*, September 10, 1960, 16.

CHAPTER TWELVE

1. Haley and Benjaminson, *Crazy Man, Crazy*, 108–12.
2. Ian Wallis, *American Rock 'N' Roll: The UK Tours 1956–72* (Music Mentor Books, 2003), 19.
3. Haley and Benjaminson, *Crazy Man, Crazy*, 120–21.
4. "A Cavalcade of Rock & Skiffle," *Record Mirror*, December 28, 1957, 18.
5. Barry Miles, *Paul McCartney: Many Years From Now* (Henry Holt, 1997), 19.
6. Wallis, *American Rock 'N' Roll: The UK Tours 1956–72*, 22–30.
7. "Hot Five Coming to Durham, Fri., Greensboro Sat.," *Carolina Times*, August 29, 1959, 7.
8. "Don Nicholl's Disc Date," *Disc*, December 12, 1959, 12.
9. "Bobby Darin For TV," *Disc*, December 26, 1959, 16.
10. "Distributor News," *Billboard*, February 22, 1960, 22.
11. "Music as Written," *Billboard*, March 7, 1960, 24.
12. "British Yen for Disk Names," *Billboard*, March 14, 1960, 11.
13. "Darin, Eddy Leave for British Tour," *Billboard*, March 21, 1960, 16.
14. Wallis, *American Rock 'N' Roll: The UK Tours 1956–72*, 41, 49.
15. Ian Wallis, interview, 2023.
16. Spencer Leigh, interview, 2023.
17. "British Yen for Disk Names," *Billboard*, March 14, 1960, 11.
18. Ian Wallis, interview, 2023.
19. Spencer Leigh, interview, 2023.
20. Brian Smith, interview, 2023.
21. "The Boy Who Followed a Star," Darin, McPhatter, Eddy Concert Tour Booklet, 1960.
22. Wallis, *American Rock 'N' Roll: The UK Tours 1956–72*, 74.
23. Graham Knight, interview, 2023.
24. Bob Howe, "I Remember You, Wack!," Australia's '60s Superstar Frank Ifield Remembers, 1996, https://frankifield.com.
25. Spencer Leigh, interview, 2023.
26. "London Bow Big for Darin, Eddy, McPhatter," *Billboard*, March 28, 1960, 12.
27. "Darin Slams Back at British Rock Fans," *Melody Maker*, April 2, 1960, 1.
28. Ian Wallis, interview, 2023.
29. "This Is Bobby Darin," www.bobbydarin.net/Darin.19060.html.
30. "Darin Off to Home Shores," *Billboard*, April 11, 1960, 6.
31. "Students of Madison County," *Mississippi Enterprise*, April 23, 1960, 6; "Star-Studded Spring Show and Dance at College Park Auditorium in Jackson April 26," *Mississippi Enterprise*, April 9, 1950, 8.

CHAPTER THIRTEEN

1. Peter Guralnick, "A Clearer Vision," *The Guardian*, November 20, 2005, www.theguardian.com.
2. Guralnick, "A Clearer Vision."
3. Bill Curtis, interview, 2023.

4. "Singer Clyde McPhatter Nixes Jim Crow N.C. Date," *Jet*, February 23, 1961, 62.

5. Bill Curtis, interview, 2023.

6. "Militant Artist Ends Atlanta Bias," *The Carolinian*, March 30, 1963, 13.

7. "New York Beat," *Jet*, April 11, 1963, 63.

8. "Militant Artist Ends Atlanta Bias."

9. "Negro Entertainment," *Ebony*, September 1963, 128.

10. Bill Curtis, interview, 2023.

11. Guralnick, "A Clearer Vision."

12. Guralnick, "A Clearer Vision."

13. Brian Leli, "Observing Change: San Cooke and the Civil Rights Movement," February 11, 2010, www.gapersblock.com.

14. "Singing Stars Balk at Dixie Bars," *Arizona Sun*, June 1, 1961, 4.

15. Bill Curtis, interview, 2023.

16. "Durham's Clyde McPhatter In NAACP Convention Spotlight," *Carolina Times*, July 9, 1960, 1.

17. "Line of March," *Jet*, December 15, 1960, 37.

18. Bill Curtis, interview, 2023.

19. "Star Bill Doggett Urges Counter Boycott to Aid Economic Freeze," *The Carolinian*, July 30, 1960, 6.

20. "Lifers Dispel Myth of Laxity," *Ebony*, September 1963, 128.

21. Deborah McPhatter, interview, 2023.

22. Fred Bronson, *The Billboard Book of Number One Hits* (Billboard Publications, 1985), 384.

23. Harry Bacas, "Top Tunes: Clyde Scores with 'Lover Please,'" *Evening Star* (Washington, DC), April 6, 1962, B-7.

24. "Whirling Busily, Shelby Singleton Spreads Gospel of Country Music," *Billboard*, June 25, 1962, 6.

25. Bacas, "Top Tunes: Clyde Scores with 'Lover Please.'"

26. "Whirling Busily, Shelby Singleton Spreads Gospel of Country Music."

27. "Pick of the Week," *Cash Box*, February 10, 1962, 8.

28. "Singles Reviews," *Billboard*, February 10, 1962, 33.

29. "Top 50 in R&B Locations," *Cash Box*, April 7, 1962, 45.

30. Bill Curtis, interview, 2023.

31. New York Beat," *Jet*, April 12, 1962, 64.

32. Bill Curtis, interview, 2023.

33. "Clyde Pleases," *Billboard*, February 17, 1962, 43.

34. "Lover Please," *Cash Box*, February 17, 1962, 9.

35. "Teen Briefs," *Evening Star (Washington, DC)*, February 23, 1962, B-7.

36. "Pick of the Week," *Cash Box*, September 8, 1962, 20.

37. Margie Singleton, interview, 2023.

38. Margie Singleton, interview, 2023.

39. "Whirling Busily, Shelby Singleton Spreads Gospel of Country Music."

40. "Album Reviews," *Cash Box*, December 1, 1962, 22.

41. "Top R&B Records & Artists of 1962," *Cash Box*, December 29, 1962, 54.

CHAPTER FOURTEEN

1. "About the Apollo," Apollo 90, www.apollotheater.org.
2. "Apollo Theater," NYC LGBT Historic Sites Project, www.nylgbtsites.org.
3. Richard Leiby, "Send in the Clowns," *Washington Post*, November 20, 2005.
4. Ronald Isley, interview, 2024.
5. Billy Vera, interview, 2023.
6. Johnny Whiteside, *Cry: The Johnnie Ray Story* (Barricade Books, 1994), 66, 126–28.
7. Audrey Sherborne, interview, 2018.
8. Charles White, *The Life and Times of Little Richard: The Quasar of Rock* (Harmony Books, 1984), 105.
9. Darden Asbury Pyron, *Liberace: An American Boy* (University of Chicago Press, 2000), https://press.uchicago.edu/misc/Chicago/686671.html.
10. Roy Greenslade, "The Meaning of 'fruit': how the Daily Mirror Libeled Liberace," *The Guardian*, May 26, 2009, www.theguardian.com.
11. Scott Thorson, "How Liberace Protected his 'Big Secret' in the Homophobic '50s," www.thewrap.com.
12. Pyron, *Liberace: An American Boy*.
13. Don Nicholl, "Disc Date," *Disc*, December 12, 1959, 12.
14. "Clyde McPhatter," Jackie Wilson Lovers, January 2, 2013, https://jackiewilsonlover.wordpress.com.
15. Billy Vera, interview, 2023.
16. Bill Millar, *The Drifters* (Collier Books, 1971), 91.
17. Tina Treadwell, interview, 2023.
18. "Record Reviews," *Billboard*, October 23, 1949, 74.
19. Sampson, "Larry Darnell: 'I'll Get Along Somehow Part 1 & 2,'" January 2019, www.spontaneouslunacy.net.
20. Shaw, *Honkers and Shouters: The Golden Years of Rhythm and Blues*, 354.
21. "Music as Written," *Billboard*, October 29, 1949, 48.
22. "Philly Areas Spots Make Big Use of Wax Name Draw," *Billboard*, November 5, 1949, 18.
23. John Wirt, notes for "The Irrepressible Bobby Marchan," 64parishes.org/the-irrespressible-Bobby-Marchan.
24. Jason Ankeny, "Bobby Marchan Biography," Allmusic, www.allmusic.com.
25. Carlo Ditta, interview, 2023.
26. Frankie Ford, interview from the mid-1980s.
27. Keith Spera, "Frankie Ford, New Orleans Singer of 'Sea Cruise' Fame, has died," *Times-Picayune*, September 29, 2015.
28. Carlo Ditta, interview, 2023.
29. Terry King, interview, 2024.
30. Beverly Lee, interview, 2016.
31. Billy Vera, interview, 2023.
32. Terry King, interview, 2024.
33. Whiteside, *Cry: The Johnnie Ray Story*, 146.
34. John Wirt, *Huey "Piano" Smith and The Rocking Pneumonia Blues* (Louisiana State University Press, 2014), 62.

35. Carlo Ditta, interview, 2023.
36. "Hot 100," *Cash Box*, May 19, 1951, 14.
37. "Hot 100," *Cash Box*, June 2, 1951, 17.
38. "Best Selling Retal Retail Rhythm & Blues Records," *Cash Box*, August 4, 1951, 27.
39. "Mr. Operator/Dealer Make Sure You Get the Right Record!," *Cash Box*, August 18, 1951, 28.
40. "Billy Wright, 'You Satisfy,'" August 27, 2018, www.spontaneouslunacy.net.
41. Tina Andrews, *Awop Bop Aloo Mop: Little Richard: A Life of Sex, Drugs, Rock and Roll . . . and Religion* (Malibu Press, 2020), 45.
42. White, *The Life and Times of Little Richard: The Quasar of Rock*, 26.
43. James Marshall, interview, 2018.
44. White, *The Life and Times of Little Richard: The Quasar of Rock*, 26.
45. James Marshall, interview, 2018.
46. Rudi Protrudi, interview, 2018.
47. Andrews, *Awop Bop Aloo Mop: Little Richard: A Life of Sex, Drugs, Rock and Roll . . . and Religion*, 45.
48. Brown and Yule, *Miss Rhythm: The Autobiography of Ruth Brown, Rhythm and Blues Legend*, 112.
49. Yusuf Lamont, interview, 2023.
50. "James Cleveland Infected L.A. Youth With HIV," *Jet*, March 2, 1992, 62.
51. Yusuf Lamont, interview, 2023.
52. William "Brother" Tolor, interview, 2023.
53. Bill Curtis, interview, 2023.
54. Bill Millar, notes for magazine article.
55. Graham Knight, interview, 2023.
56. Tony Burke, interview (email), 2023.
57. Graham Knight, interview, 2023.
58. Clyde McPhatter, letter to Lorraine Lowe, August 25, 1968.
59. Clyde McPhatter, letter to Lorraine Lowe, 1968.
60. Brown and Yule, *Miss Rhythm: The Autobiography of Ruth Brown, Rhythm and Blues Legend*, 112.
61. Ian Wallis, interview, 2023.
62. Metropolitan (London) Police memo, January 1, 1970.
63. Deborah McPhatter, interview, 2023.
64. Donald Gatling, interview, 2023.

CHAPTER FIFTEEN

1. David Browne, "How the 45 RPM Single Changed Music Forever," *Rolling Stone*, March 15, 2019.
2. Liner notes, *Clyde McPhatter with Billy Ward and His Dominoes*, King Records, 1957.
3. "Cool Aids for Summer Sales," *Billboard*, 1964.
4. Dik de Heer, "Clyde McPhatter," Tim's This Is My Story, https://tims.blackcat.nl.
5. "Album Reviews," *Billboard*, April 11, 1964, 52.

6. "Atlantic's Drifters Are Piling Up Unique Record—One of Longevity," *Billboard*, December 19, 1964, 26.
7. "Album Reviews," *Billboard*, April 11, 1964, 52.
8. "Signings," *Billboard*, August 7, 1965, 12.
9. "Singles Reviews," *Billboard*, March 20, 1965, 12.
10. "Breakout," *Billboard*, May 1, 1965, 43.
11. David Edwards/Mike Callahan, "The Bell/Amy/Mala Story," Both Sides Now Publications, July 29, 2006, www.bsnpubs.com.
12. "Pick of the Week," *Cash Box*, November 5, 1966, 22.
13. Wallis, *American Rock 'N' Roll: The UK Tours 1965–72*, 195–96, 210–11, 224–25, 241.
14. Wallis, *American Rock 'N' Roll: The UK Tours 1965–72*, 195–96, 210–11, 224–25, 241.
15. *Melody Maker*, May 20, 1967, 16.
16. Clyde McPhatter, letter to Lorraine Lowe, October 14, 1967.
17. Wallis, *American Rock 'N' Roll: The UK Tours 1965–72*, 267.
18. Clyde McPhatter, letter to Lorraine Lowe, October 16, 1967.
19. Clyde McPhatter, letter to Lorraine Lowe, undated.
20. Clyde McPhatter, letter to Lorraine Lowe, January 20, 1968.
21. Wallis, *American Rock 'N' Roll: The UK Tours 1965–72*, 250.
22. "Clubs," *Melody Maker*, February 20, 1968, 23.
23. Clyde McPhatter, letter to Lorraine Lowe, March 8–12, 1968.
24. Wallis, *American Rock 'N' Roll: The UK Tours 1965–72*, 267.
25. "Class Managements Ltd.," advertisement, *Melody Maker*, August 24, 1969, 16.
26. Bill Millar, notes for unpublished magazine article.
27. "Leo Gopthal," British Record Shop Archive, https://www.britishrecordshoparchive.org.
28. Clyde McPhatter, notation in personal ledger.
29. Clyde McPhatter, 1963 Form 1099, "Mercury Record Productions Inc."
30. Clyde McPhatter, Royalties Statement 1968, "Broadcast Music, Inc."
31. Graham Knight, interview, 2023.
32. Wallis, *American Rock 'N' Roll: The UK Tours 1965–72*, 272.
33. Isidro Otis, interview 2023.
34. Bill Millar, notes for unpublished magazine article.
35. Isidro Otis, interview 2023.
36. Ed Ochs, "Soul Source," *Billboard*, page 29, August 8, 1970.
37. Isidro Otis, interview, 2023.
38. Bill Millar, notes for unpublished magazine article.
39. Ed Ochs, "Soul Source, *Billboard*, August 22, 1970, 29.
40. "Welcome Home," *Ebony*, December 1970, 28.
41. "Soul Singles," *Billboard*, August 22, 1970, 29.
42. Bill Millar, notes for unpublished magazine article.
43. Deborah McPhatter, interview, 2023.
44. Newspaper clipping, "The Forty Thieves Club," *Bermudian*, undated, 1963.
45. Mel Carter, interview, 2023.
46. Deborah McPhatter, interview, 2023.
47. Bill Curtis, interview, 2023.
48. Billy Vera, interview, 2023.

49. Bill Millar, notes for unpublished magazine article.
50. Marv Goldberg, "Clyde McPhatter," Marv Goldberg's R&B Notebooks, 2005, 2009, https://www.uncamarvy.com/clydemcphatter/clydemcphattter.html.
51. Deborah McPhatter, interview, 2023.
52. Carol Connors, interview, 2022.
53. Deborah McPhatter, interview, 2023.
54. Goldberg, "Clyde McPhatter."
55. Clyde McPhatter death certificate.
56. Deborah McPhatter, interview, 2003; memorial service flyer.

INDEX

Abernathy, Ralph, 177
Abramson, Herb, 28, 29, 56, 57, 59, 61, 65, 68, 105–7, 144
Abramson, Miriam (Bienstock), 68, 86, 105, 106, 144
Ace, Johnny, 18, 31, 87, 89, 97, 100, 148, 187
Ackerman, Paul, 65, 66
Adams, Faye, 20, 31, 66–68, 91
Adams, Walter, 64
"Adorable," 97–99, 103
"Ain't That a Shame," 95, 97, 100
Alexander, Ernest, 177
"Allegheny Moon," 109
Allen, William B., 56
"All I Have to Do Is Dream," 145, 146
"All Night Long," 171
"All Shook Up," 158
"Almost Grown," 154
Ames Brothers, 40, 76, 120
"Among My Souvenirs," 157
Anderson, Marian, 178
Andrews, Lee (Thompson) and the Hearts, 121, 122
"Angela Jones," 164
"Angels Listened In, The," 158
Anka, Andrew, 142
Anka, Paul, 138–41, 149, 152, 154, 155, 163
"Annie Had a Baby," 66, 73, 74, 91
"Anytime, Any Place, Anywhere," 54
"April in Paris," 72
Armstrong, Louis, 21, 22, 25, 206
"As Long as I'm Moving," 89
"At the Hop," 143
Autry, Gene, 5
Avalon, Frankie, 153, 178

"Baby Come Back," 121
"Baby Count on Me," 144
"Baby Don't Do It," 72
"Baby You Got It," 211
Bacas, Harry, 159
"Back in My Arms Again," 206
"Bad, Bad Whiskey," 54
Bailey, Buddy, 88
Baker, LaVern, 42, 76, 81, 82, 87–89, 95, 97, 103, 105, 112, 114, 116, 118, 119, 122, 139, 143, 144, 149, 151, 171
Baker, Mickey, 61, 97, 207
Baldwin, David, 27
Baldwin, James, 27
Baldwin, Wilmer, 27
Ballad, Hank and the Midnighters, 7, 51, 66, 72–74, 81, 88, 91, 150, 172
Barber, Chris, 167
Barnes, Forestine, 30
Barry, Jeff, 154
Basie, Count, 25, 97, 178
Bass, Ralph, 8–11, 13–18, 21, 51, 59, 73
Bates, L. C., 176
Baughan, David, 91, 99, 102
Baxter, Les, 95
Beatles, 167, 168, 170, 192, 203, 205, 206, 214
"Be-Bop-A-Lula," 66, 109
"Because," 105
"Beep Beep," 147
Bees, 79
Belafonte, Harry, 80, 120, 178
Bell, Benny, 206
"Bells, The," 20, 21, 44, 49, 52, 54
"Bells of Saint Mary's," 80, 82, 121
Belmonts, 99

247

Belvin, Jessie, 48, 86, 150
"Be My Little Girl," 205
Bennett, Tony, 16, 40, 52, 76
Benton Brook (Benjamin Peay), 28, 144–46, 151, 155, 159, 160, 182–84, 206, 212, 213
Berlin, Irving, 81, 82, 114
Berry, Chuck, 79, 97, 119, 138, 139, 141, 143, 145, 154, 165, 178
"Best Man Cried, The," 183
"Beyond the Sea," 171
Bialoglow, Tom, 29
Bickerton, Wayne, 211
Big Mama Thornton, 144
Big Maybelle, 76
Bill Haley and the Comets, 65, 72, 88, 95, 105, 112–14, 119, 161–63, 165–68
Bill Johnson and His Musical Notes, 191
Bill Landford and the Landfordaires, 28
"Bip Bam," 75, 87, 89, 90, 144
Birnbaum, Larry, 3, 7, 16, 17, 45, 66, 89
Black, Bill (Combo), 179
"Black Night," 54
Blackwell, Chris, 211
Blackwell, Otis, 87, 158
Blackwell, Robert (Bumps), 197
"Bless You," 158, 168
"Bloodshot Eyes," 54
Bloom, Allen, 141
"Blueberry Hill," 116
"Blue Monday," 116
"Blues for My Baby," 195
"Blue Suede Shoes," 108
Bobbettes, 122, 139, 145
Bob Miller and the Millermen, 166, 167, 169
Bob Willis and the Texas Playboys, 63
"Bo Diddley," 89, 97
"Boll Weevil Song," 159, 212
"Book of Love," 143
"Book of Memories," 213, 214
Boone, Pat, 92, 95, 97, 117, 162, 163, 165
Bostic, Earl, 17, 54
Boswell, Connee, 67
Boswell Sisters, 27
Bradshaw, Tiny, 54
Braun, David, 191
Braun, Jules, 191

Brenston, Jackie, 16
Brewer, Teresa, 109, 116
Brown, Bill, 12–15, 18, 38, 47, 62
Brown, Charles, 54, 85, 186, 187
Brown, Drew, 34, 93
Brown, James, 31, 108, 148, 204, 206, 214
Brown, Jimmy, 139
Brown, Roy, 7
Brown, Ruth, 8, 16, 31, 34, 35, 53–55, 57, 63, 66–68, 72, 76, 77, 82, 85, 87–94, 96, 97, 100, 122, 139, 151, 153, 186, 198, 200
Brubeck, Dave, 202
"Brubeck Plays Brubeck," 202
Buddy Holly and the Crickets, 139, 165, 166, 168
Burchette, Howard, 25
Burke, Tony, 199
Burnette, Johnny, 160
Butler, Jerry, 149, 151
"Butterfly," 163
Byrd, G. Houston, 20

Cadillacs, 97
Caesar, Shirley, 23
"Call It Stormy Monday," 8
Calloway, Cab, 25
"Calypso," 80
Campbell, Ernestine Harvin, 188
Campbell, Jo-Ann, 165
Cannon, Freddie, 160
Cardinals, 16
"Caribbean," 163
Carmichael, Hoagy, 52, 67
Caronna, Joe, 192
Carson, Martha, 146
Carter, Benny, 63
Carter, Clarence, 214
Carter, Doug Saint, 51
Carter, Mel, 215
Caruso, Dick, 164
"Catch a Falling Star," 207
Cato, Charlie, 150
"C. C. Rider," 117, 122, 143
"Chain Gang," 160, 172
"Chains of Love," 54
Champs, 143, 165

"Chances Are," 156
"Can't Buy Me Love," 205
Chandler, Gene, 214
Chantels, 149
Chaplin, Charlie, 188
Chapman, Grady, 48
Charles, Ray, 57, 65, 66, 67, 89, 97, 108, 122, 144, 153, 198
Charms, 81, 82, 96
Charts, 138
Chase, Lincoln, 76
"Chattanoogie Shoe Shine Boy," 120
"Cheatin' Woman," 192
Checker, Chubby, 88, 160, 163, 180, 181
Checkers, 47
Cheers, 92, 97
Cherry, Don, 97
Chess, Leonard, 25
Chess, Phil, 25
Chevalier, Maurice, 157
"Chickee Wah-Wah," 192
"Chicken Blues," 14
Chi-Lites, 214
"Chloe-E," 17
Chuckles, 97
Church, Eugene, 147
"Church Bells May Ring," 108
Chordettes, 188
Chords, 81, 85
Clanton, Jimmy, 153
Clark, Dick, 140, 141, 148, 150
Clark, Doug, 23
Cleftones, 108
"Clementine," 171
Cleveland, James, 198
Clinton, Larry, 157
"Clock, The," 121
Clooney, Betty, 67
Clooney, Rosemary, 40, 90
Clovers, 16, 45–47, 54, 55, 57, 65, 67, 68, 81, 85, 88, 105, 115, 116, 153, 154, 196, 198
"Clyde," 158
Clyde McPhatter Live at the Apollo, 8
Clyde McPhatter with Billy Ward and His Dominoes, 203
Coasters, 15, 42, 143, 149, 157, 171

Cobb, Danny, 17, 84
Cochran, Eddie, 165, 166
Cohen, Sydney, 185
Cole, Cozy, 147
Cole, Nat King, 16, 39, 52, 107, 112, 113, 212, 213
Coley, Doris, 140
Colts, 97
"Come What May," 145, 146
Como, Perry, 41, 87, 96, 107, 108, 117, 207
Conner, Chris, 116, 122
Connors, Carol, 217
Cook, Howie, 147
Cooke, Charles, 175
Cooke, Sam, 139, 149–53, 160, 172, 173, 175, 176, 181, 184, 200
Cooper, Ralph, 31
Conley, Arthur, 186
Costa, Don, 141
Count Suckle and Sound System, 208
"Crawlin'," 55
Crests, 149, 154, 158, 163
Crew-Cuts, 162
Crosby, Bing, 5, 51, 67
Crows, 6
Crutchfield, Hazel, 30
"Cry," 41, 187
"Crying in the Chapel," 6, 20
"Crying Won't Help You Now," 206, 216
"Cupid," 172
Curtis, Bill, 33, 36, 104, 140, 141, 145, 148, 173, 174, 176, 177, 181, 198, 209, 215
Curtis, King, 180, 184

Damrosch, Walter, 11
"Dancin' Dan," 16
Danny and the Juniors, 143, 165
"Danny Boy," 52
"Dan the Back Door Man," 16
"Dapper Dan the Ladies Man from Dixie Land," 16
Darin, Bobby, 106, 107, 143, 147, 152, 153, 156, 157, 164–71, 205, 208
Darnell, Larry (Leo Edward Darnell), 190, 191, 196
Dave Clark Five, 206
Davis, Billy, 208

Davis, Miles, 9, 203
Davis, Sammy, Jr., 63
"Day-O (The Banana Boat Song)," 120
"Deacon Moves In, The," 15
"Deep in the Heart of Harlem," 204, 205
"Deep Purple," 52, 53
"Deep Sea Ball," 158
De Heer, Dik, 204
Dekker, Desmond, 211
Del Vikings, 138
"Denver," 211
DeRose, Peter, 52
DeShannon, Jackie, 41
"Devil or Angel," 46, 153
Devine, Andy, 61
Diamonds, 139
"Diana," 138, 139, 141, 142, 163
"Diary, The," 155
Diddley, Bo, 89, 92, 97, 112, 117, 140, 149, 163, 171
Dillard, Varetta, 17, 31, 84, 85
Dion, 99, 100, 163
Ditta, Carlo, 192, 194
Dixie Cups, 206
Dixie Hummingbirds, 121
Dobbs, John Wesley, 177
Dobbs, Mattiwilda, 177
Dobie, Andrew, 167
Doggett, Bill, 114, 117, 177
Doggett, Peter, 158
"Do It No More," 21
Domino, Fats, 67, 85, 95, 97, 100, 110, 114, 116, 139, 141, 145
Dominoes (Billy Ward and His Dominoes), 7, 8, 11–14, 16–22, 29, 34, 38–40, 42–49, 51–55, 57–64, 67, 68, 83, 84, 137–39, 149, 187, 192, 194, 195, 208, 215
Don and Dewy, 165
Donegan, Lonnie, 167, 168
Donovan, 207
"Don't Be Cruel," 109
"Don't Dog Me," 75
"Don't Leave Me This Way," 22
"Don't Let Go," 65
"Don't Play That Song," 184, 204
"Don't Take the Love from Me," 54

"Don't You Know I Love You," 46, 54, 153
Dorsey, Jimmy, 65
Dorsey, Lee, 207
"Do Something for Me," 14, 16, 17, 54, 59, 195
"Double Crossing Blues," 15
Douglas, Larry, 19, 20, 60, 70, 92
Dowd, Tom, 60–62, 79, 106, 107
"Dream Baby (How Long Must I Dream)," 180
"Dream Girl," 48, 49
"Dreamin'," 160
"Dream Lover," 171
Dreyer, Dave, 146
Drifters, 20, 25–28, 31, 41, 55, 62–67, 68, 72, 73, 75–90, 94, 97–105, 109, 110, 112, 114, 118, 122, 139, 142, 149, 151, 152, 154, 162, 163, 167–69, 181, 190, 192, 197–99, 204, 205, 208, 210, 215
"Drinkin' Wine Spo-Dee-O-Dee," 56, 57
"Drip Drop," 100
"Drown In My Own Tears," 108
Du Droppers, 81
"Duke of Earl," 214
Duprees, 29

Easy Riders, 120
"Earth Angel," 81, 82, 89, 98
Eckstine, Billy, 16, 39, 40, 46, 65, 198
"Eddie My Love," 108
Eddy, Duane, 164–71, 205, 208
Edwards, Tommy, 143
Eisenhower, Dwight D., 51
Ellington, Mercer, 191
Ellis, Eddie, 150
Ellis, Ray, 156–58
Ellis, Shirley, 76, 205
Emile Ford and the Checkmates, 166–68
"Empty Arms," 115, 122
Ennis, Philip, 28
Epstein, Brian, 170
Ertegun, Ahmet, 28, 29, 45, 46, 49, 50, 55, 56, 58–62, 64, 65, 68, 77, 81, 88, 101, 102, 106, 107, 146, 153–55, 158, 159
Ertegun, Mehmet Munir, 55
Ertegun, Nesuhi, 55, 106, 107
Esquerita (Eskew Reeder), 194, 196, 197
Evans, Ronnie, 193

Evans, Tommy, 100
Everly Brothers, 139, 143, 145, 158, 168
"Every Beat of My Heart," 7
"Everybody's Somebody's Fool," 207
"Everyone's Laughing," 87, 101–3
"Everything Gonna Be All Right," 159

Fabian, 153, 163
"Fabulous," 163
"Fairest, The," 121
Faith, Adam, 164
Falcons, 150
"Feeling Happy," 115
Feingersh, Ed, 113
Feld, Adele, 142
Feld, Irvin, 33, 101, 102, 105, 112, 138–43, 148–50, 152, 156, 186
Feld, Izzy, 141, 149
Feld, Karen, 150
Feld, Kenneth, 101, 112, 140, 142, 150, 186
Ferbee, William, 61
"Ferry Cross the Mersey," 211
"Fever," 108, 109, 158
"Find My Baby," 195
Fisher, Eddie, 4, 107
Fitzgerald, Ella, 6, 31, 67
Five Crowns, 100, 152, 190
Five Keys, 16, 54, 81, 92, 97, 112
5 Royals, 7, 72, 77
Five Satins, 114
"Flamingo," 54
Flamingos, 92, 97
Flemons, Wade, 149
"Flip, Flop and Fly," 88, 89
Flirtations, 210
"Fool, Fool, Fool," 46, 54
"Fool for You, A," 97
"Fools Fall in Love," 100
Foley, Red, 120
Fontaine Sisters, 96
"For All You've Done," 159
Ford, Dee Dee, 151
Ford, Frankie, 192, 193
"Forget Him," 205
"For You My Love," 190, 191
Foundations, 210

Four Buddies, 16, 30
Four Fellows, 97
Four Lads, 20, 156
Four Seasons, 99
Four Tops, 206
Fox, Jon Hartley, 10, 48, 73
Francis, Connie, 155, 157, 163, 164, 205, 207
Frankie Lymon (and the Teenagers), 42, 99, 108, 111–14, 118, 119, 139, 149, 163, 166
Franklin, Aretha, 172, 213, 214
Freddie Bell and the Bellboys, 163
Freed, Alan, 17, 71, 72, 83–85, 92, 96, 97, 112, 118, 145, 148, 165
Freedom Singers, 203
Friedman, Henry, 160
"From Russia with Love," 206
Fuller, Blind Boy, 23
Fuzztones, 197

Gaither, Lloyd "Tommy," 4
Gale, Moe, 67
Gale, Tim, 143
Gant, Cecil, 187
Gardner, Carl, 15
Gardner, Don, 151
Garnes, Sherman, 111
Gatling, Donald, 201
Gay Knights, 145
Gaye, Marvin, 59, 214
Gene and Eunice, 96, 121
"Get a Job," 143
"Get Up, I Feel Like Being a Sex Machine (Parts 1 & 2)," 214
Gibbs, Georgia, 96
Gibson, Althea, 178
Gibson, Don, 160
"Giddy Up a Ding Dong," 163
Gillett, Charlie, 13, 58, 66, 82
"Girl Can't Help It, The," 116
Gladys Knight and the Pips, 7
Glaser, Joe, 22, 51, 52
Glenroy Oakley and The Oracles, 210
"Glory of Love, The," 16, 54
Glover, Henry, 59, 74
Godfrey, Arthur, 13
Goffin, Gerry, 154

"Going to the River," 144
Goldberg, Marv, 11–13, 15, 27, 43, 44, 47, 81, 86, 98, 101, 217, 218
"Golden Blues Hits," 203
Goldner, George, 111
Goodman, Benny, 5, 65
"Good Lovin'," 45, 55, 67, 68
"Goodnight, Sweetheart, Goodnight," 81
"Goodnight Irene," 12
"Good Things," 77
"Good Timin'," 150
"Gone," 60, 64, 88
Gopthal, Lee, 211
Gordon, Dexter, 9
"Gotta Travel On," 155
Gracie, Charlie, 163, 166, 168
Grade, Leslie, 169, 170
Grade, Lew, 169, 170
Grant, Earl, 213
"Great Balls of Fire," 158
"Great Pretender, The," 98, 108
Greene, Al, 65
Greenfield, Howard, 155, 158
Greenfield, Robert, 107
Greenwich, Ellie, 154
"Groovy Situation," 214
Guess Who, 207
"Guitar Boogie," 102
Guitar Slim, 79, 105
Guralnick, Peter, 173, 175

Hall, Darryl, 207
Hall, René Joseph, 13
Hall, Rick, 207
Hall and Oates, 207
Hamilton, Roy, 65, 79, 81, 112, 143, 151
Hamilton, Russ, 117
Hammerstein, Oscar, III, 5
Hampton, Lionel, 119
"Handy Man," 150
"Hanky Panky," 66
"Harbor Lights," 15, 17
Harold Melvin and the Blue Notes, 49
Harptones, 85
Harris, Addie (Micki), 140
Harris, Christopher, 199

Harris, Peppermint, 16, 54
Harris, Thurston, 182
Harris, Wynonie, 10, 54, 148
Harrison, Wilbert, 98
"Have Mercy," 191
"Have Mercy Baby," 7, 18–20, 22, 44, 49, 57–59, 84, 115, 169, 192
"Have Twangy Guitar Will Travel," 168
"Having a Party," 184
Hawkins, Erskine, 67
Hawkins, Screamin' Jay, 20, 94, 165, 187, 196, 197
Hayes, Isaac, 31
Hazelwood, Lee, 167
Heartaches, 122
Heartbeats, 97
"Heartbreaker," 66
"Heartbreak Hotel," 108
Hearts, 30
"Hearts of Stone," 81, 82, 95
"Heavenly Father," 30
Heine, Sonja, 189
"Hello Dolly," 206
Hendricks, Belford, 213
Hendricks, Bobby, 100, 149, 190
Hendrix, Jimi, 31, 209
Henry, Clarence (Frogman), 86
Hershey, Gerri, 58
"Hey Little Girl," 195
Hibbler, Al, 31, 89, 95, 143
Hicks, Zell, 30
Hill, Lauryn, 31
Hoffman, Al, 87
Hoggs, Sydney, 21
"Hold Me, Thrill Me," 215
Holiday, Billie, 31, 63, 186
Hollingsworth, Lacy, 100
Hollis, Bobby Lee, 208
Holmes, Clint, 207
Holmes, Martha, 40
"Honey Hush," 55, 67, 80
"Honey Love," 79–81, 90
"Honky Tonk Parts 1 and 2," 117, 177
Hope, Bob, 51
Hornets, 99
"Hot Diggity (Dog Ziggity Boom)," 87

"Hot Ziggety," 87, 100, 102
"Hound Dog," 20, 109, 144
"House Party-Discotheque," 203
Howes, Arthur, 169, 170
Howlin' Wolf, 77
"(How Much Is) That Doggie in the Window," 72
Hudson, Rock, 189
Huey Piano Smith (and His Clowns), 192, 194
Hughes, Charlie, 100
Hunter, Alberta, 185
Hunter, Ivory Joe, 116, 117, 122, 138, 143–45, 187
Hunter, Tab, 117
"Hurt," 212
"Hustlin' Dan," 16
Hyland, Brian, 160, 207

"I Almost Lost My Mind," 116
"I Am with You," 16, 17
"I Apologize," 39
"I Can Help," 179
"I Can't Escape from You," 17
"I Can't Go on Alone," 152
"I Can't Stand Up Alone," 146, 147
"Idaho," 65
"I'd Be Satisfied," 18, 44
"I Do," 77
"I Do Believe," 182
"I Don't Know," 31
"I Dreamt I Died," 207
"I Found Out," 81
"If You Don't Want Me," 77
"I Got a Woman," 171
"I Got Loaded," 16, 54
"I Got Stung," 147
"I Gotta Get Myself a Woman," 99
"I Gotta Have You," 91
Ike and Tina Turner, 23–25
Iko Iko, 206
"I'll Belong to You," 214
"I'll Get Along Somehow," 190, 191
"(I'm Afraid) The Masquerade Is Over," 157
"I Make Believe," 115
"I'm a Lonely Fool," 116
"I'm Alright," 164
"I'm a Man," 163

"I Met Him on a Sunday," 140
"I'm Gone," 54
"I'm Gonna Get Married," 157
"I Miss You So," 116, 154, 155
"I'm Lonely Tonight," 116
"I'm Not Going to Work Today," 207
"I'm Not Worthy of You," 107
Impellitteri, Vincent, 187
"I'm Sorry," 160
Impalas, 157
"I'm Waiting Just for You," 54
"I'm Walkin'," 116
"I Need a Love Like Yours," 159
Ink Spots, 5–7, 12–14, 27, 28, 43, 46, 67
International Singers of South Carolina, 29
"In the Summer of His Years," 205
"I Only Have Eyes for You," 17, 18, 94
"I Put a Spell on You," 20
Isley, Ronald, 59, 186
Isley Brothers, 186, 213
"Israelites," 211
"I Still Get a Thrill," 157
"It Ain't the Meat," 74
"Itchy Twitchy Feeling," 149
"It Hurts to My Heart," 91
"I Told Myself a Lie," 157
"It Should Have Been Me," 65
"It's Just a Matter of Time," 145, 155, 159
"It's Now or Never," 160
"It's Only Make Believe," 147
"It's Too Soon to Know," 4–6, 31
"Itsy Bitsy Teenie Weenie Yellow Polka Dot Bikini," 160, 207
"I've Got a Woman," 89
"Ivory Tower," 110
"I've Got Sand in My Shoes," 205
"I Want to Hold Your Hand," 205
"I Want to Know," 81
"I Want You to Be My Girl," 112
"I (Who Have Nothing)," 204, 208
"I Will Wait," 30
"I Wonder," 187

Jackson, Bullmoose, 10, 75, 191
Jackson, Chuck, 27, 151
Jackson, John A., 72

Jackson, Willis (Gator Tail), 34, 91–93, 97
Jackson Five, 31, 214
Jagger, Mick, 12
"Jailhouse Rock," 120
"Jamaica Farewell," 80
James, Etta, 51, 89, 95
James, Joni, 157
James, Harry, 157
Jaye Sisters, 144
Jaynetts, 30
Jerusalem Stars, 28
Jesse and Marvin, 49
Jewels, 96
"Jim Dandy," 76, 116
Jo, Damita, 182, 183, 214
John, Little Willie, 7, 51
"Johnny B. Goode," 145, 146
Johnny Ferguson, 164
Johnny Moore's Three Blazers, 187
Johnson, Buddy, 137
Johnson, Bumpy, 150
Johnson, Bunk, 29
Johnson, Fayrene, 63
Johnson, Marv, 150
Johnson, Raymond, 47
Johnnie and Joe, 139
"Joker, The," 154
Jones, Brian, 208
Jones, Jimmy, 150
Jones, Peter, 211
Jones, Quincy, 212
Jones, Tom, 214
Jordan, Louis, 64, 65, 151
"Juanita," 116
"Just a Matter of Time," 212
"Just Give Me a Ring," 158
"Just to Hold My Hand," 117, 118, 169

Kallen, Kitty, 215
Kaufman, Murray (The K), 106
"Keep a Knockin'," 120
"Keeping Up with the Joneses," 183
"Keep Your Hands on Your Heart," 195
Kelly, Machine Gun, 31
Kennon, Robert, 72
Kenny, Bill, 12, 14

Kern, Jerome, 5
"Kiddio," 160
"Kind of Blue," 202
King, B.B., 31, 148, 214
King, Ben E., 25, 26, 88, 104, 152, 154, 167, 184, 190, 204, 205, 208, 209
King, Carol, 154
King, Martin Luther, 174, 177, 178
King, Terry, 193
"King Croesus," 210
Kings, 121, 122
Kingsmen, 205
Kirk, Andy, 191
Kirkland, Nellie, 183
Kirshner, Don, 106
Knight, Graham, 169, 199, 200, 211
Knox, Buddy, 139
"Ko Ko Mo," 96, 121
Krupa, Gene, 156
Krefetz (Kresetz/Krefitz), Lou, 45, 85

Laine, Frankie, 5, 16
Lamont, Joe, 12, 18, 29, 38, 39, 40, 42, 44, 46, 48–50, 198
Lamont, Yusuf, 19, 27, 40, 42–46, 48, 52, 198, 199
Lanza, Mario, 16
Larks, 47
"Last One to Cry," 192
"Last Time, The," 206
Laurie, Annie, 98
Lauterbach, Preston, 148
"Lawdy Miss Clawdy," 18
Lee, Angel (Audrey Sherborne), 187, 188
Lee, Beverly, 140, 193
Lee, Brenda, 160
Lee, Peggy, 108
Leiber, Jerry, 79, 81, 144, 153, 154
Leigh, Spencer, 167, 170
Lennon, John, 214
Les Paul and Mary Ford, 195
"Let Me Go Home, Whiskey," 54, 72
"Let Me Know," 122, 145
"Let Me Shake the Hand," 159
"Let's Start Over Again," 157, 203
"Let's Try Again," 158, 168

"Let the Boogie-Woogie Roll," 64, 158
"Let the Good Times Roll," 109
Lewis, Jerry Lee, 165, 169
Lewis, Ramsey, 206, 214
Lewis, Robert Q., 96
Lewis, Rudy, 104, 190, 204
Liberace, 188, 189, 193
"Lie to Me," 183, 184
"Linger Awhile," 17
"Ling Ting Tong," 81
Little Anthony and the Imperials, 149, 160, 171
"Little Bitty Pretty One," 182, 183
Little Eva, 151
"Little Girl of Mine," 108
Little Milton, 77
"Little Queenie," 154
Little Richard, 50, 97, 108–10, 116, 119, 120, 138, 148, 165, 186–88, 194–97, 200
"Little White Cloud That Cried," 41
Little Willie John, 108
"Lipstick on Your Collar," 157
"Live at the Apollo," 203, 204
Lochlin, Hank, 67
"Loch Lamond," 84
Logan, Harold, 33
"Lonely Nights," 30, 201
"Lonely People Can't Afford to Cry," 207
"Lonesome Town," 147
"Long Lonely Nights," 120–22, 144
"Long Tall Sally," 108
"Louie Louie," 205
"Love Ballads," 144, 158, 203
"Love Comes," 77
"Love Has Joined Us Together," 34, 91, 92, 103
"Love Is Strange," 61, 116, 207
"Love Letters in the Sand," 117
"Love Me Do," 170
"Love Potion No. 9," 46, 153
"Lover Please," 178–81, 183, 184, 203, 204, 206, 208
Lover Please!, 203
"Lover's Question, A," 146, 147, 151–53, 155, 156, 158, 168, 178
"Lovey Dovey," 45, 81, 154, 155, 148
Lowe, Lorraine, 34–37, 49, 50, 80, 94, 200, 208, 209, 217

Lubinsky, Herman, 8–11
Lucas, Buddy, 99
"Lucille," 29, 60, 76, 77
Lynn, Barbara, 151
Lynn, Vera, 47

Mabley, Moms, 203
Mabone, Willie, 31
"Mack the Knife," 152, 157, 170
"Magic Touch," 108
"Mama," 165
"(Mama) He Treats Your Daughter Mean," 55, 68
"Mambo Baby," 82, 90, 91
"Mambo Italiano," 90
Mann, Barry, 154
Mann, Gloria, 97
Manning, Dick, 87
Marchan, Bobby, 191, 192, 194, 196
"Marianne," 120
Markham, Pigmeat, 23
Marks, Rose, 12, 13, 15, 18, 19, 43–45, 62, 186
Marsh, Dave, 21, 68
Marshall, James, 196, 197
Marshall, Maithe, 46
Martha and the Vandellas, 205
Martin, Dean, 143
Martin, Tony, 16, 40
Martino, Al, 76, 107
"Mash Potato Time," 181
Mason, Barbara, 206
Massler, Al, 206
Mathis, Johnny, 156, 186, 202
Matthews, Bill, 183
Matthews, Frank, 150
Maxim, 156
"Maybe," 182, 183
"Maybe You'll Be There," 121
"Maybellene," 97
Mayfield, Curtis, 59
Mayfield, Percy, 16, 187
Mays, Willie, 33
McCartney, Paul, 162
McEwen, Joe, 50
McGhee, Brownie, 9, 57
McGhee, Stick, 54, 56, 57, 191

McGriff, Edna, 30
McGuire Sisters, 95
McKenzie, Ed, 75
McNeil, David, 18, 38, 43, 47, 48
McPhatter, Bertha, 24
McPhatter, Beulah (Reverend), 26, 32, 35, 37
McPhatter, Deborah, 26, 27, 31–37, 49, 50, 69, 79, 80, 93, 104, 178, 201, 208, 215, 217–19
McPhatter, Ethel, 24, 32, 35
McPhatter, George (Reverend), 25, 26, 32, 33, 37
McPhatter, George, Jr., 24
McPhatter, Gladys, 24
McPhatter, Joseph, 24, 33
McPhatter, Lorene, 24
McPhatter, Ronn David (Jackson), 34, 94
McPhatter, Thomas, 24, 219
McPhatter, Thomas (Uncle), 27
McVea, Jack, 8
"Mello-Larks," 215
"Mellow Yellow," 207
Mendelsohn, Fred, 191
"Mend Your Ways," 76
Merchant, Jimmy, 111, 112
"Mercy Mercy," 195
Mermaids, 205
"Merry Christmas Baby," 187
Merry Melody Singers, 182–84, 203
Mesner, Eddie, 54
Mesner, Leo, 54
"Mess Around," 67
Midnighters, 7
"Midnight Special Train," 116
Mickey and Sylvia, 61, 86, 116, 207
Milburn, Amos, 20, 54, 72, 191
Millar, Bill, 199, 210, 211, 213
Miller, Mitch, 156
Miller, Steve, 154
Millinder, Lucky, 19, 20, 31, 54
Mills, Harry, 70
Mills Brothers, 5, 6, 20, 27, 28, 43, 70
Milner, Jimmy, 100
Mintz, Leo, 83
Miracles, 151
Mirt Mirty and the Rhythm Steppers, 179
Mitchell, Guy, 16, 41

Mitchell, Kerrie, 40
Mitchell, Priscilla, 183
"Mixed Up Cup, The," 214
Modugno, Domenico, 143
"Moments to Remember," 20
"Mona Lisa," 39
"Money Honey," 20, 64, 66–69, 73, 76, 80, 83, 114, 115, 162, 169
Monroe, Vaughn, 41
Moody Blues, 209
Moonglows, 82, 95, 114, 115, 138, 145
Moore, Johnny, 91, 98–100, 116, 190, 204, 208
Monotones, 142
Montez, Chris, 151
Morgan, Jaye P., 157
Morgan, Tom, 213
Morris, Joe, 54, 67, 68
Morrison, Marilyn, 187
"Mother's Love, A," 213
Mount Lebanon Singers, 27, 29
"Mr. Heartache," 213
"Mr. Sandman," 188
Murray, Louise Harris, 30, 31, 201
"My Coloring Book," 215
"My Ding-a-Ling," 79
"My Foolish Heart," 39
"My Island of Dreams," 154
"My Song," 18
"My Yiddishe Momme," 52

Nail, John B., 177
Nathan, Syd, 9–11, 13, 14, 16, 17, 21, 47, 51, 59, 62, 74
Negroni, Joe, 111
Nelson, George, 4
Nelson, Ricky, 147, 178
Neville, Aaron, 59
Newman, Jimmy, 157
"Next to Me," 182
Nicholl, Don, 189
Nino Tempo and April Stevens, 52
"Nitty Gritty, The," 76, 205
Nolan, Jimmy, 165
"No Love Like Her Love," 144
"No Matter What," 117
Norwood, Thomas, 23, 25

"No! Says My Heart," 14
Nunn, Bobby, 15

Oates, John, 207
Ochs, Ed, 213
"Oh, Carol," 155
"Oh, What a Dream," 90, 91
"Old Man River," 91, 198
Oliver, Jimmy, 98, 181
"Ol' Man River," 5, 7
"On Broadway," 190, 204, 208
"One Mint Julep," 46, 57, 153, 196, 197
"One Right After Another," 158
"One Scotch, One Bourbon, One Beer," 20, 54, 72
"Only a Fool," 210, 211
"Only the Lonely," 160
"Only You," 95, 98
"Ooby Dooby," 66
"Open the Door, Richard," 8
Orbison, Roy, 66, 160, 180
Original Drifters, 208
Orioles, 3–7, 12, 20, 29, 31, 45
Orlons, 151
Otis, Clyde, 159, 212, 213, 215
Otis, Isidro, 213
Otis, Johnny, 7, 9, 21, 48, 51, 144, 145, 163
"Our Day Will Come," 213, 214
Owens, Shirley, 140

Page, Patti, 109
Palmer, Robert, 18
"Papa Loves Mambo," 87, 90
Parker, Charlie, 9
Parsons, Louella, 187
Patterson, Lover, 153
Paul, Bunny, 75
Paul Weston Orchestra, 98
Paul Williams and His Hucklebuckers, 17, 84
Peake, Mary, 33, 36
"Peddle Pushin' Papa," 44
Pendergrass, Teddy (Theodore), 49
Penguins, 6, 81, 82, 89, 97, 98
Penny, Hank, 89
Perkins, Carl, 108
Perryman, Lee (Piano Red), 117

Perryman, Rufus (Speckled Red), 177
"Peter Gunn," 167
Peterson, Eugene, 208
Phillips, Little Esther, 15
Phillips, Marvin, 48
Pinkney, Bill, 28, 29, 31, 60–62, 75, 81, 86, 87, 90–93, 97–100, 103, 208, 219
"Pitter Patter Boom Boom," 144
Platters, 77, 95, 98, 105, 108, 109, 112, 113, 163, 168
Playboys, 45
"Playground of Your Mind," 207
Playmates, 147
"Please, Please, Please," 108
"Please Don't Freeze," 91
"Please Send Me Someone to Love," 16
"Pledging My Love," 89, 97, 100
"Poison Ivy," 157
Pomus, Doc, 154, 163
"Popsicles and Icicles," 205
"Porgy and Bess," 203
Prado, Perez, 143
Presley, Elvis, 3, 4, 8, 72, 76, 83, 86, 87, 96, 106, 108–10, 120, 138, 139, 143–45, 147, 152, 160, 179, 187, 206, 217
Preston, Billy, 186, 199
"Pretty Eyed Baby," 164
"Pretty Girls Everywhere," 147
Price, Lloyd, 33, 42, 149, 152, 157, 171
"Prisoner of Love," 46
Protrudi, Rudi, 197
"Put Your Head on My Shoulder," 152
Prysock, Arthur, 98

"Queen of the Hop," 147, 170
Ques, 12, 13, 44
"Quicksand," 205

Rabin, David, 165
Rackley, Lena (McPhatter), 33, 36, 37, 216–19
"Rag Mop," 120
"Rags to Riches," 52
"Rainbow," 117
"Rainy Night in Georgia," 145
Ram, Buck, 97, 98
Randolph, A. Philip, 178

Ravens, 5–7, 12, 17, 29, 46, 65, 81
Ray, Johnnie, 4, 41, 75, 76, 79, 186, 188, 193, 194
Reed, Les, 211
Reed, Jimmy, 77, 145
Reed, Jerry, 183
Reed, Johnny, 4
Reese, Della, 143, 151
Reid, Bertha M., 216, 217
"Return to Sender," 87
Rhea, Rube, 177
"Rhythm and Soul," 183, 203
Rich, Charlie, 160
Richards, Keith, 12, 214
Rick 'N' Beckers, 208
Ricks, Jimmy "Ricky," 5, 6
"Riot in Cell Block #9," 79
Ritter, Tex, 67
Robbins, Marty, 115, 202
Robey, Don, 117
Robins, 6, 15, 79
Robinson, Julie, 80
Robinson, Robert (Red), 26, 29
Robinson, Sugar Ray, 21, 22, 51, 52
"Rock and Cry," 119, 120, 144, 167
"Rocket 88," 16, 18, 195
"Rockin' Pneumonia and the Boogie Woogie Flu," 192
"Rock Island Line," 106
"Rods and Ratfinks," 206
Roe, Tommy, 151
Rolling Stones, 168, 206, 208, 214
Rolontz, Bob, 59, 60, 65, 68
Roots, 121
Rose, David, 157
Ross, Diana, 214
"Rossinni Overtures," 203
"Round and Round," 108
Royals, 7, 73
Roxon, Lilian, 83
Ruby and the Romantics, 213
"Ruby Baby," 99
Rydell, Bobby, 205

Sabit, Vahdi, 56, 107
"Saint Theresa of the Roses," 52

"Sally Go Round the Roses," 30
Santiago, Herman, 111
Santo and Johnny, 157
"Saturday Night at the Movies," 205
"Save the Last Dance for Me," 154
Schiffman, Bobby, 216
Schiffman, Jack, 4
Schwartz, Al, 216
Scott, Mabel, 187
Scott, Winfield, 87, 103
"Sea Cruise," 192
Sears, Big Al, 96
"Second Window, Second Floor," 204
Sedaka, Neil, 155, 158
"Seven Days," 101, 107, 109, 112, 113, 156
"Seven Long Days," 54
Seville, David, 143
"Sexy Ways," 73, 74, 81
"Shake, Rattle and Roll," 65, 80, 88
"Shake a Hand," 20, 66–68
Shannon, Del, 207
Shapiro, Joe, 108
Sharp, Alexander, 4
Sharp, Dee Dee, 181
Shaw, Arnold, 6, 12, 23, 66
"Sh-Boom," 81, 85
"She Loves You," 205
Shimkin, Arthur, 206
Shirelles, 140, 193
Shirley and Lee, 109, 110, 112
"Shot of Rhythm and Blues, A," 207
Shuman, Mort, 154, 163
Shuttlesworth, Fred, 177
"Signed, Sealed, Delivered," 214
Silhouettes, 143
Silverman, Max, 27
Simon, Bill, 105
Simon, Paul, 207
Simone, Nina, 186
Sinatra, Frank, 3, 4, 115, 152, 170, 171, 175, 187
Sinatra, Nancy, 297
"Since I Fell for You," 205
"Since I Met You Baby," 116, 117, 143
"Sincerely," 82, 95
"Since You've Been Gone," 153, 155, 158
Singleton, Margie, 182–84

Singleton, Shelby, 179, 182, 183
"Six Nights a Week," 154
"Sixty Minute Man," 7, 14–20, 47, 52, 54, 70, 72, 73, 195
Skip and Flip, 160
"Sleep Walk," 157
"Slow Twistin'," 181
Smalls, Danny, 115
Smalls, Cliff, 200
Smalls, Tommy (Dr. Jive), 92, 96, 97
Smith, Arthur, 102
Smith, Bessie, 186
Smith, Brian, 167, 168
Smith, Lawson, 7
"Sock It to Me, Mattie," 73
"Soft," 54
"So Long," 77, 198
"So Many Ways," 155
"Somebody Touched Me," 90, 91
"Someday (You'll Want Me to Want You)," 89, 90
"Some Kind of Wonderful," 190
"Someone Out There," 210
"Someone to Believe In," 213
"Something Has Changed," 152
"Song from Moulin Rouge, The," 72
"Songs of the Big City," 204, 206
"Son of Rebel Rouser, The," 205
"Sorghum Switch," 65
"Sorry (I Ran All the Way Home)," 157
"Soul Twist," 184
Southern Knights, 28, 29
Spaniels, 81, 139
"Spanish Harlem," 204, 208
Spinners, 214
"Splish Splash," 106, 143, 156, 170, 171
"Stacked Deck," 195
Stallman, Lou, 108
"Stand by Me," 208
"Standing on the Corner," 156
"Star Dust," 52, 53
Starr, Edwin, 214
Starr, Kay, 5
"Steamboat," 99
Steele, Tommy, 163
Stevens, Cat, 209

Stoker, Gordon, 183
Stoller, Mike, 79, 81, 144, 153, 154
Stone, Jesse, 61, 64–66, 68
"Stop," 183
"Stupid Cupid," 155
"Such a Night," 75–80, 89
"Sugar Coated Kisses," 87, 101
"Sugar Town," 207
"Supernatural Thing—Part 1," 204
Supremes, 206
Swallows, 6, 16, 18, 74
Swan, Billy, 179, 180
Swanson, Earl, 93
"Sweet Old Fashioned Girl, A," 109
"Sweet Talk," 66

"Talk Back Trembling Lips," 205
"Talkin' 'Bout You," 144
"Tampa Red," 77
Tarriers, 120
"Ta Ta," 151, 160, 203
Ta Ta!, 159, 203
Taylor, Danny (Run Joe), 98
Taylor, Sam (The Man), 61, 68, 96
"Teach Me Tonight," 82
"Tear Drops," 121
"Teardrops from My Eyes," 16, 54
"Tears Keep Falling Down, The," 66
"Teddy," 164
Teddy Bears, 147
"Teenager In Love, A," 163
Teen Queens, 108, 109
"Tell Me," 211
Tempest, Roy, 208
Temptations, 38, 214
"Tennessee Waltz Blues," 54
Ten Years After, 209
Terry, Johnny, 208
Tharpe, Sister Rosetta, 186
"That's Enough for Me," 144, 145
"That's What You're Doing to Me," 18
"That's Why I Love You So," 154
"There Goes My Baby," 152, 153, 167, 208
"There! I've Said It Again," 205
"There's Something on Your Mind," 192, 196
"There You Go," 155, 164, 189

"These Foolish Things (Remind Me of You)," 52
"Things That I Used to Do, The," 79, 105
"Think Me a Kiss," 164, 167, 169, 171
"Thirty Days," 116
"This Bitter Earth," 212
"This Is Not Goodbye," 158
"This Magic Moment," 154
Thomas, Charlie, 41, 190, 193, 208
Thomas, Rufus, 31
Thompson, Ahmir (Questlove), 121
Thompson, Beachy, 121
Thompson, Donn T., 121
Thompson, Nora (McPhatter), 33–36, 51, 94, 118, 137, 151, 198
Thompson, Ruth, 79
Thornton, Big Mama, 20, 186
Thorson, Scott, 189
Thrasher, Andrew, 61, 98, 100
Thrasher, Gerhart, 61, 98–100, 208
Thrasher Wonders, 27, 61
"Three Thirty Three," 87, 100
Three Tons of Joy, 165
"Ties That Bind, The," 213
Til, Sonny, 3, 4, 6, 7
"(Till) I Kissed You," 158
Till, Emmett, 182
"Till I Waltz Again with You," 72
Tillotson, Johnny, 205
"Time to Cry," 152
"Ting-A-Ling," 57
Tiny Grimes and His Rockin' Highlanders, 17, 84
"To Bell," 79
"To Know Him Is to Love Him," 147, 217
Tolor, Winfred (Brother), 27, 32, 33, 37, 198
Tommy James and the Shondells, 66
"Too Young," 39
"Topsy I," 147
Torme, Mel, 214
Torok, Mitchell, 163
Tosches, Nick, 11, 65
Treadwell, Faye, 198
Treadwell, George, 63, 64, 98–101, 103–5, 152, 153, 190, 198
Treadwell, Tina, 63, 95, 104, 190

"Treasure of Love," 107–9, 117, 153, 156
"Try the Impossible," 121
"Try Try Try," 155
"Tweedle Dee," 81, 82, 87, 89, 103
"Twice as Nice," 157, 158
"Twist, The," 88, 160, 180
"Twistin' the Night Away," 181, 184
Twitty, Conway, 147
Turbans, 92, 97, 112
Turner, Big Joe, 54, 55, 57, 65, 67, 80, 85, 86, 88, 112, 116, 122, 145, 148, 171, 198
Turner, Ike and Tina, 148, 214
Turner, Sonny, 171
"Tutti Frutti," 197

"Unchained Melody," 89, 95
"Under the Boardwalk," 204, 205, 208
"Up on the Roof," 190, 204
Uttal, Larry, 206

Valdalia, Patsy (Irving Ale), 185
Valentines, 97
Vance, Paul, 207
Vandross, Luther, 186
Van Loan, James, 12, 46, 48
Van Loan, Paul, 46
Vaughan, Billy, 143
Vaughan, Sarah, 63, 178, 198, 213
Vee, Bobby, 206
Ventures, 160
Vera, Billy, 10, 13, 14, 44, 58, 59, 88, 98, 114, 186, 187, 190, 193, 215, 216
Village Stompers, 206
Vincent, Gene, 66, 109, 165, 166, 200
Vincent, Johnny, 192
Vinton, Bobby, 205
"Volare (Nel Blu Dipinto Di Blu)," 143

Wade, Adam, 206
"Walk Don't Run," 160
Walker, Ray, 183
Walker, T-Bone, 8
"Walk Like a Man," 99
"Wallflower, The," 89, 95
Wallis, Ian, 165, 167, 169, 171, 199, 200, 209, 210, 212

"War," 214
Ward, Billy, 7, 11–13, 15, 17, 18, 21, 22, 29, 31, 33, 40, 42–53, 58, 62, 68, 86, 114, 118, 140, 186
Ward, Ed, 73, 76, 106, 194, 203
"Warm Your Heart," 75, 80
Warwick, Dionne, 214
Washington, Baby, 150
Washington, Booker T., 24
Washington, Dinah, 6, 19, 21, 82, 212, 213
Waters, Muddy, 25
Watson, Johnny Guitar, 150
"Way I Feel, The," 64, 66, 67
"Wear My Ring Around Your Neck," 145, 146
Webb, Chick, 31, 65, 67
"Wedding Boogie," 21
"Weeping Willow Blues," 14, 16
Weil, Cynthia, 154
Welch, Lenny, 205
"Welcome Home," 213, 214
"(We're Gonna) Rock Around the Clock Tonight," 72, 95, 96, 161, 162
West, Joyce, 30
Wexler, Jerry, 29, 58–63, 65, 66, 68, 73, 79, 81, 84, 85, 87, 88, 106, 107, 143, 146, 153, 155, 158, 159
"Wham! Bam! Thank You Ma'am," 89
"What a Difference a Day Makes," 212
"What'cha Gonna Do," 64, 80, 87–89, 101, 114
"When You're Sincere," 108
"Where Did I Make My Mistake," 157
"What Do You Want," 164
"What Kind of Man Are You," 144
"What's Love to Me," 159
White, Charlie, 12, 18, 27, 29, 38, 45–47
White, Clyde, 29
"White Christmas," 80–82, 87, 163
"White Cliffs of Dover," 47, 121
Whiteman, Paul, 156, 157
Whiting, Margaret, 5
Whitman, Slim, 67
"Who's Worried Now," 159
"Why Can't We Get Together," 214
"Why Do Birds Sing So Gay," 111
"Why Do Fools Fall in Love," 99, 108, 111–13
"Why Was I the One You Chose," 159
"Wild, Wild, Young Men," 55, 72

Williams, Andy, 178
Williams, Cootie, 63
Williams, Jimmy, 146
Williams, Joe, 97
Williams, Mel, 165
Williams, Otis, 110
Willis, Chuck, 76, 116, 117, 122
Willows, 108
Wilson, Jackie, 48–53, 139, 150–54, 184
Wirt, John, 194
"Witch Doctor," 143
"Without Love (There Is Nothing)," 114–17, 156, 168, 169
Wolf, Howlin', 25
Wonder, Stevie, 31, 214
"Work with Me, Annie," 66, 73, 74, 81
World of Oz, 210
Wrens, 97
Wright, Billy, 194–96
Wynn, Henry, 149, 150

"Yakety Yak," 143
"Yes I'm Ready," 206
"You Belong to Me," 29
"You'll Be There," 119, 120
"You'll Never Walk Alone," 79, 80
Young, Faron, 183, 203
"Young Love," 117
"Your Cash Ain't Nothing but Trash," 65
"You're on My Mind," 144
"Your Promise to Be Mine," 99
"You Satisfy," 195
"You Send Me," 150, 172
"You Went Back on Your Word," 155, 164, 189
Yuro, Timi, 212

ABOUT THE AUTHOR

Author Steve Bergsman with Deborah McPhatter, daughter of Clyde McPhatter. Courtesy of the author.

STEVE BERGSMAN has contributed to a wide range of magazines, newspapers, and wire services for more than thirty years, including the *New York Times*, *Wall Street Journal*, *Barron's*, *Toronto's HomeFront*, *Black Enterprise*, *Oldies*, *The Australian*, *Phoenix Magazine*, *Chief Executive*, and Reuters, Inman, Copley, and Creators' Syndicate news services.

His eighteen books fall into four categories: music, travel, memoir, and business.

In regard to music, his books include: *Elvis, Rocky and Me*; *All I Want Is Loving You: Popular Female Singers of the 1950s*; *What A Difference A Day Makes: Women Who Conquered 1950s Music*; *The Wanderers: Killer Teens, Rebel Teens, Gang Teens and the Evolution of the Last Great Greaser Feature*; *Chapel of Love: The Story of New Orleans Girl Group The Dixie Cups* (with Rosa Hawkins); *I Put a Spell On You: The Bizarre Life of Screamin' Jay Hawkins*; *The Friends of Billy Preston*; *The Seduction of Mary Wells*; and *The Death of Johnny Ace*.

Steve Bergsman's travel books are: *Hobnobbing with Ghosts: A Literature and Lyric Junkie Travels the World*; and *Hobnobbing with Ghosts II: A Lyric and Literature Junkie Travels the World*.

His sole memoir is *Growing Up Levittown: In a Time of Conformity, Controversy and Cultural Crisis*.

Finally, Steve Bergsman's five business books are *Maverick Real Estate Investing: The Art of Buying and Selling Properties like TRUMP, ZELL, SIMON and the World's Greatest Land Owners*; *Maverick Real Estate Financing: The Art of Raising Capital and Owning Properties Like Ross, Sanders and Carey*; *After the Fall: Opportunities and Strategies for Real Estate Investing in the Coming Decade*; *Passport to Exotic Real Estate: Buying U.S. and Foreign Property in Breathtaking, Beautiful, Faraway Lands*; and *Transforming Dirt into Gold: Land Investments: Finding Opportunity Where Others Fail to See It* (with Ronald McRae).

www.ingramcontent.com/pod-product-compliance
Lightning Source LLC
Chambersburg PA
CBHW030105170426
43198CB00009B/492